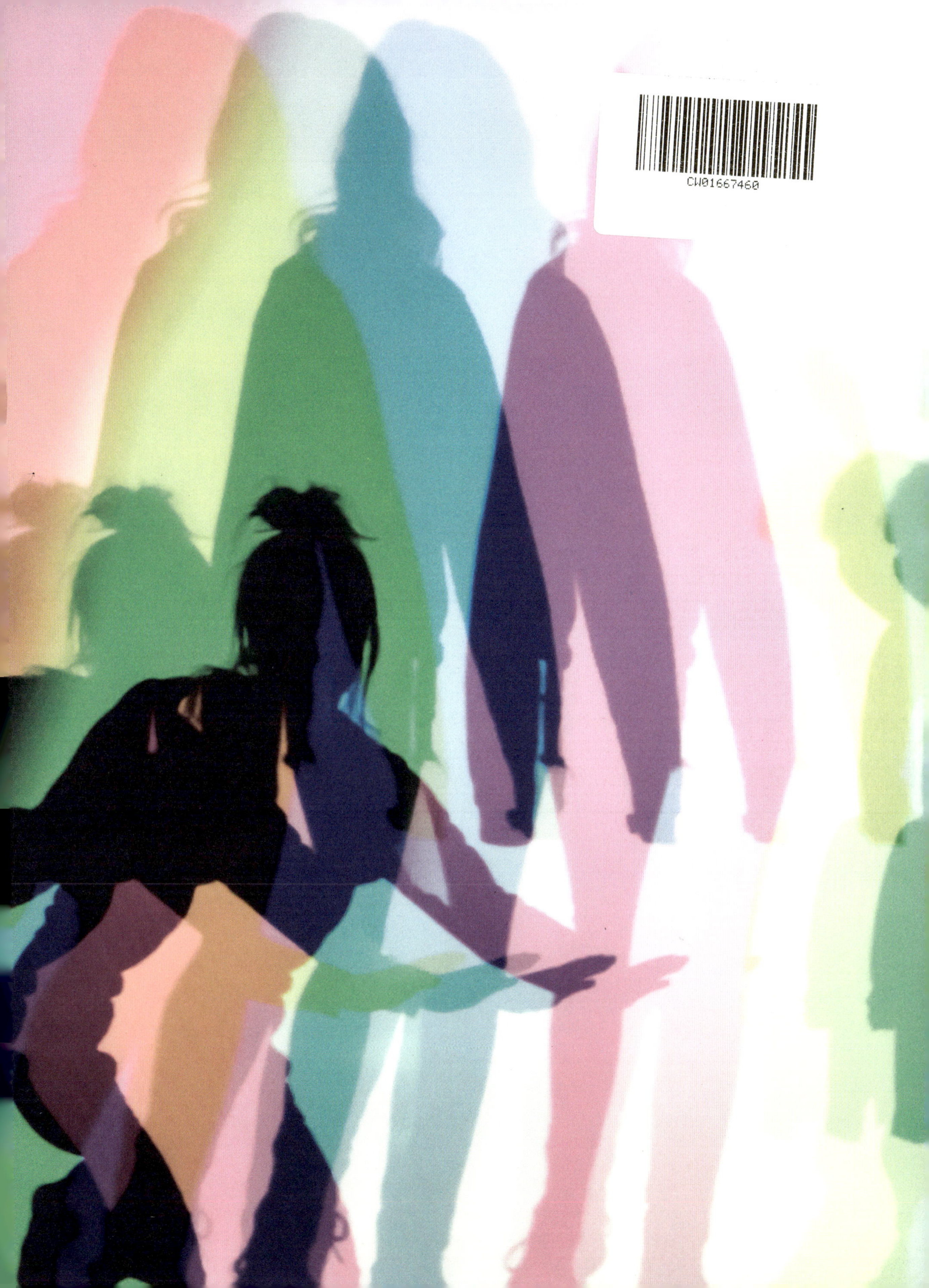

CW01667460

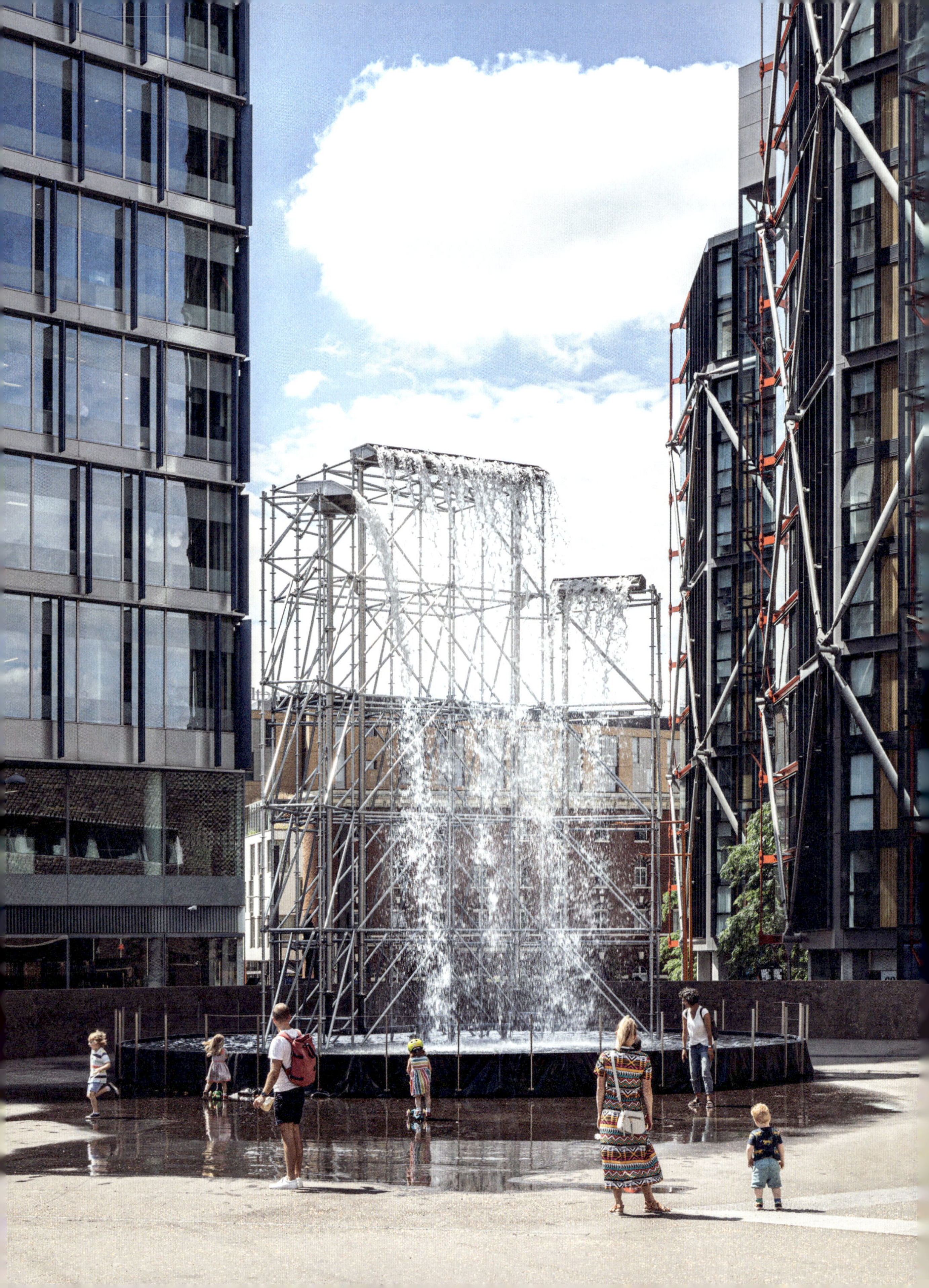

OLAFUR ELIASSON IN REAL LIFE

EDITED BY MARK GODFREY

TATE

First published 2019 by order of the Tate Trustees
by Tate Publishing, a division of Tate Enterprises Ltd,
Millbank, London SW1P 4RG
www.tate.org.uk/publishing

on the occasion of the exhibition
OLAFUR ELIASSON: IN REAL LIFE

Tate Modern, London
11 July 2019 – 6 January 2020

Guggenheim Museum Bilbao
14 February – 21 June 2020

Supported by

AKO Foundation

With additional support from the
Olafur Eliasson Exhibition Supporters Circle:
New Carlsberg Foundation
Beckett-Fonden
Danish Arts Foundation

Tate Patrons and Tate Members

With special thanks to the New Carlsberg Foundation
for their support of the development, research and
publication of the *Olafur Eliasson: In real life* catalogue

NY
CARLSBERG
FONDET
NEW CARLSBERG FOUNDATION

Reprinted with new installation photography 2019

© Tate Enterprises Ltd 2019
Conversation texts © Studio Olafur Eliasson 2019
All artworks by Olafur Eliasson © Olafur Eliasson 2019

All rights reserved. No part of this book may be reprinted or reproduced or utilised in any form or by any electronic, mechanical or other means, now known or hereafter invented, including photocopying and recording, or in any information storage or retrieval system, without permission in writing from the publishers or a licence from the Copyright Licensing Agency Ltd, www.cla.co.uk

A catalogue record for this book is available
from the British Library

ISBN 978 1 84976 632 6

Distributed in the United States and Canada
by ABRAMS, New York
Library of Congress Control Number applied for

Project Editor: Nicola Bion
Production Controller: Bill Jones
Picture Researcher: Emma O'Neill
Designer: Michael Jensen, Copenhagen

Editorial team Studio Olafur Eliasson:
Anna Engberg-Pedersen, Geoffrey Garrison,
Biljana Joksimović-Große, Kristina Köper,
Kathryn Politis, Miranda Robbins, Vajra Spook

Conversation with Josefine Klougart
translated by Misha Hoekstra
Conversations with René Redzepi and Andreas Roepstorff
translated by Dan Marmorstein

Colour reproduction by Graphicom
Printed and bound in Italy by Graphicom

Cover and pp.1, 240:
Your uncertain shadow (colour) 2010 (details)
p.2: *Waterfall* 2019

MIX
Paper from
responsible sources
FSC® C013123

CONTENTS

In 2003 Olafur Eliasson became the youngest artist to date to realise the Unilever Commission for the vast Turbine Hall which forms the central spine of Tate Modern's post-industrial spaces. Only in his mid-thirties, Eliasson once and for all changed the parameters for what a Commission in this monumental setting could be, understanding that the Turbine Hall was as much a new kind of public forum as it was an architectural volume. Eliasson brought to the project his experimental research with mirrors, light, and fog, honed over the first decade of his practice, but more importantly, he brought to Tate his deep thinking about the institution and viewers, and about what we do when we see art together. So it was that with *The weather project*, the Turbine Hall was transformed into an unforgettable social space, experienced by over two million visitors in six months. People gazed through the fog towards 'the Sun'; they looked up to find their distant reflection; they joined hands; they lay down to form shapes and words reflected in the mirror high above. The Turbine Hall commission was undoubtedly an important platform for Olafur Eliasson at a key point in his career, but it was also a turning point in Tate Modern's history, as we learned from the artist how best to use our new spaces, and what kind of a twenty-first century museum we could become.

This transformative moment was the beginning of a long-lasting relationship with this artist. Two works were added to the collection, one of which, *Your double-lighthouse projection*, was soon shown in the largest gallery in the building. In 2012, the year of the London Olympics, Eliasson approached Tate about his new project, Little Sun, a solar-powered hand-held torch that was being created as a social business, and sold across the world, and whose use was especially pertinent in off-grid areas where people otherwise rely on gas and oil for night-time light. Tate was excited to help Eliasson launch the project, and seven Saturday evenings, our visitors were able to walk through the surrealist galleries in the dark, lighting up our Dalís and Ernsts with Little Suns. Two years later, Eliasson also showed a series of new paintings in the Clore galleries at Tate Britain, each canvas a distillation of the colour shadings in the eighteenth-century paintings by J.M.W. Turner who, like Eliasson, was acutely sensitive to atmosphere and light.

FOREWORD

FRANCES MORRIS
DIRECTOR, TATE MODERN

Olafur Eliasson has been with us at key moments of our history and so it is a great pleasure to welcome him back to Tate Modern three years after the new and expanded museum opened to the public. The open spaces of the Blavatnik Building host a survey of almost thirty years of his art, *Olafur Eliasson: In real life*, which, true to the spirit of his work, does not remain confined to the white cube gallery spaces but spills out onto the concourse, the staircase, the Terrace Bar and the South Landscape. We are exceptionally grateful to him for dedicating so much time to this exciting project. It is an exhibition that brings together sculptures, installations, paintings and photographs, and that demonstrates his interests and research into natural phenomena, complex geometries, motion, reflection, colour and light. But it is also a chance for viewers to discover the full range of Eliasson and his studio's activities and ambitions. An area of the exhibition will explore his projects addressing global warming, sustainable energy, and migration, and how such projects are conceived in his studio through the processes of research, collaborative questioning, and imaginative thinking. Eliasson also runs a kitchen in his studio, and visitors will be able to sample the kind of dishes served there, and learn about the artist's passionate concerns with questions of sustainable and organic food production.

We are very grateful to the curators, Mark Godfrey, Senior Curator, International Art, and Emma Lewis, Assistant Curator, International Art, for their commitment to this project, and for conceiving a wide-ranging exhibition unlike any other survey of Eliasson's work to date.

In February 2020 *Olafur Eliasson: In real life* will travel to Guggenheim Museum, Bilbao. We would like to express our deepest gratitude to Juan Ignacio Vidarte, Deputy Director and Chief Officer for Global Systems, Solomon R. Guggenheim Foundation, Daniel Vega, Deputy Director, and Lucia Aguirre, Curator, for their partnership and collegiality.

At every stage in the exhibition planning the curators have worked closely with the Studio Olafur Eliasson team: Caroline Eggel, Anna Engberg-Pedersen, Patricia Bondesson Kavanagh, Vanja Zanko, Daniel Mock and Dayoung Shin, to each of whom we owe deepest thanks for the imagination, dedication and collaborative spirit that they have brought to this ambitious project. In Tate's Curatorial department, Helen Sainsbury, Head of Exhibitions and Programme Management, Rachel Kent, Senior Programme Manager and Neil Casey, Business and Operations Manager have provided invaluable senior support. Special thanks are due to Achim Borchardt-Hume, Director of Exhibitions and Programmes, Tate Modern, for his encouragement and foresight.
The display of the many complex installations in this exhibition is a result of the tireless work of Phil Monk, Design and Production Manager, Richard Install, Art Installation Manager, and Greg Lofthouse, Exhibition Registrar, who managed loans with great resourcefulness and care. The team has been ably assisted by Emilie Ursulet, former Exhibitions Assistant, and curatorial interns Margot Mottaz and Wendy Fang.

Many of the artworks in this exhibition have come to us from Studio Olafur Eliasson and we are grateful to them for preparing these often technically complex installations for loan. We are also indebted to the individuals and institutions who were willing to temporarily part with works from their collection, or who generously agreed to their reproduction: Boros Collection, Berlin; Centre Pompidou, Musée national d'art moderne, Paris; Hamburger Kunsthalle, Kunstmuseum Basel; Städtische Galerie im Lenbachhaus, und Kunstbau München (KiCo Collection); Moderna Museet, Stockholm; Solomon R. Guggenheim Museum, New York; Thyssen-Bornemisza Art Contemporary Collection, Vienna; The Museum of Contemporary Art, Los Angeles; The Museum of Modern Art, New York; Queensland Art Gallery | Gallery of Modern Art; and Eleanor and Francis Shen, Toronto. We are very grateful to the artist's galleries neugerriemschneider, Berlin and Tanya Bonakdar, New York and Los Angeles for their assistance in facilitating loans and for their invaluable advice and support.

The exhibition could not have been realised without the remarkable efforts of many departments across Tate. Special thanks are due to Sandra Sykorova, Curator, Public Programmes and Hamish Anderson, CEO, Tate Catering. Together with Liat Rosenthal, Production Coordinator, Uniqlo Tate Lates, Isabella Nimmo, Assistant Curator, Public Programmes, and Chris Dines, Executive Chef, they have enriched this exhibition with an inspired public programme and food offering.

Eliasson's practice involves many different media and its successful installation is thanks to the expertise of many. Special appreciation goes to Owen Hodgkinson and the Art Handling team, Dan Crompton, Audio Visual Services Manager, and Pete Triggs, Audio Visual Coordinator, who worked closely with technicians from Studio Olafur Eliasson including Anders Hellsten Nissen, Jöran Imholze and Christian Uchtmann. The preservation of the artwork is thanks to the expertise of Betty Sacher, Preventative Conservator and colleagues across the Conservation department. Appreciation is due to Donald Hyslop, Head of Regeneration and Community Partnerships, Barry Palmer, Head of Safety and Security, and Sandra McLean, Senior Visitor Manager who, together with our many colleagues in Visitor Experience, Operations and Estates, enabled us to present the exhibition to our visitors across Tate Modern's landscapes as well as our galleries. Outside of Tate, Jennifer Crook, Producer, deserves thanks for her work with us on *Ice Watch* at Tate Modern. Communicating the ambitions of an exhibition such as *Olafur Eliasson: In real life* to a broad audience is a significant undertaking. This was executed with dedication and flair by Chris Condron, Head of Marketing; Elli Cartwright, Senior Marketing Manager; Stephanie Biddle, Marketing Manager; Rudi Minto de Wijs, Marketing Officer; Saskia Mercuri, Tate Kids Producer; Rachael Young, Senior Press and Communications Manager; Joanna Sandler, Press and Communications Officer; and Camilla Kragelund at Studio Olafur Eliasson. Also at the Studio, Christina Werner worked on the SOE Kitchen and Terrace Bar collaboration, and Sophie Erlund on public programming. The work of Kirsteen McSwein, Curator, Interpretation, and Soraya Chumroo, Senior Designer contributed greatly to our audiences's understanding and enjoyment of this exhibition. Colleagues in the Development department deserve huge thanks for their tireless efforts in securing support for this show.

At Tate Publishing we are very grateful to Nicola Bion, Project Editor, for her wisdom and collegial support while overseeing all aspects of this insightful catalogue. Its stunning design is thanks to Michael Jensen. We would also like to thank Jane Ace, Editorial Manager; Bill Jones, Production Manager; Emma O'Neill, Picture Researcher; and especially Miranda Robbins and Kristina Köper, and the entire editorial team at Studio Olafur Eliasson.

In view of the artist's wide interests and collaborations, and the various components of the show, the curators conceived this book with him, inviting him to choose a number of individuals to meet to discuss their work and his. We are very grateful to all the contributors: Sultan Sooud Al-Qassemi; Alejandro Aravena; Fred Brathwaite (Fab 5 Freddy); Cao Fei; Marcus Engman; Marie-Agnès Gillot; Jónsi; Josefine Klougart; Mariana Mazzucato; René Redzepi; Mary Robinson; Andreas Roepstorff; Tania Singer; Barry Smith; Zubaida Tahiri; Brook Teklehaimanot; Elke Weber; and Anna Wirz-Justice.

The exhibition is generously supported by the AKO Foundation and its founder Nicolai Tangen; we owe them huge thanks. We are most grateful to the Olafur Eliasson Supporters Circle: New Carlsberg Foundation, Beckett-Fonden and Danish Arts Foundation. We would also like to thank Tate Patrons and Tate Members for supporting the exhibition; and New Carlsberg Foundation for their support of the development, research and publication of the *Olafur Eliasson: In real life* catalogue. The exhibition has been made possible by the provision of insurance through the UK Government Indemnity Scheme. We would like to thank HM Government for providing Government Indemnity and the Department for Digital, Culture, Media and Sport and Arts Council England for arranging this indemnity.

Finally, our deepest thanks go again to Olafur Eliasson himself for accepting our invitation to return to Tate Modern to make this thoughtful and ambitious survey.
It has been our great pleasure to work with him and his team.

BUSY

Since conversations began three years ago about his 2019 exhibition at Tate Modern, Olafur Eliasson has been extremely busy. He has worked with us to develop the concept and list of works for the exhibition. He has helped to plan out the position of around twenty installations on the second floor of the Blavatnik Building involving water, strobes, mirrors, natural gas and artificial fog. A new *Waterfall* for Tate's outside space has been designed. The Terrace Bar is being temporarily taken over by the Studio Olafur Eliasson Kitchen, serving a range of dishes inspired by the daily lunches at his Berlin studio as well as offering talks on food, among other topics. He has undertaken a series of conversations for this book. The 2019 Tate show is, after all, a return to the museum where *The weather project* made the artist internationally famous in 2003, and the stakes are high.

Other things have kept him busy too. Eliasson's recent projects have included a collaboration with Wayne McGregor and Jamie XX on a stage adaptation of Jonathan Safran Foer's *Tree of Codes*; a private commission for a building in Vejle, Denmark, its interior incorporating various artworks and furniture; a talk at the World Economic Forum in Davos; an exhibition of newly conceived site-specific installations at the Château de Versailles; the realisation of the *Green light* workshop in Vienna and then at the Venice Biennale; regular visits to Addis Ababa to develop a park dedicated to the late Ethiopian Prime Minister Meles Zenawi; an exhibition of watercolours and other drawing projects in the Pinakothek der Moderne in Munich; regular meetings for his Little Sun project, which sells solar-powered lamps in off-grid areas of the world; the production of his first virtual reality work, *Rainbow*; a project to 'revitalize the values of the UN';[1] costume, set and lighting design for the Berlin Staatsoper's staging of Rameau's baroque opera *Hippolyte et Aricie*; the development of his online TV channel; a pop-up restaurant in Reykjavik; a talk on 'Art in the Digital Age' at the Verbier Art Summit; a light installation in a former Masonic

OLAFUR ELIASSON: A NEW MODEL OF ARTIST

MARK GODFREY

Temple in Los Angeles; major institutional exhibitions in Seoul, Beijing and Shanghai; the staging in London of *Ice Watch* and talks with its sponsor Michael Bloomberg at a climate change summit; several new publications, including a major survey, *Experience*; and the creation of new works for smaller exhibitions mounted at his galleries in Berlin, New York, Los Angeles and Madrid. All this while overseeing (and being supported by) a studio of 120 in Berlin. No wonder Netflix have made a documentary.

Many other important artists today make new works in their studios, show them at exhibitions, and deliver the occasional lecture in art schools and museums. Clearly Eliasson's activities and collaborations go far beyond that: he has created opportunities that few artists even seek. Indeed, it is evident from these activities that he has created an entirely new and original model of being an artist. How do we make sense of his expansive practice in its widest sense? Rather than just surveying his sculptures and installations, we need to consider Eliasson's project in general, asking how this range of activities emerged, what critical issues he has faced and what challenges persist, and what his model for the artist and for art means as we approach the third decade of the century.

ELIASSON EMERGES

Let's first go back to the beginning. After his studies at the Royal Danish Academy of Fine Arts in Copenhagen, Olafur Eliasson emerged onto the European art scene in the

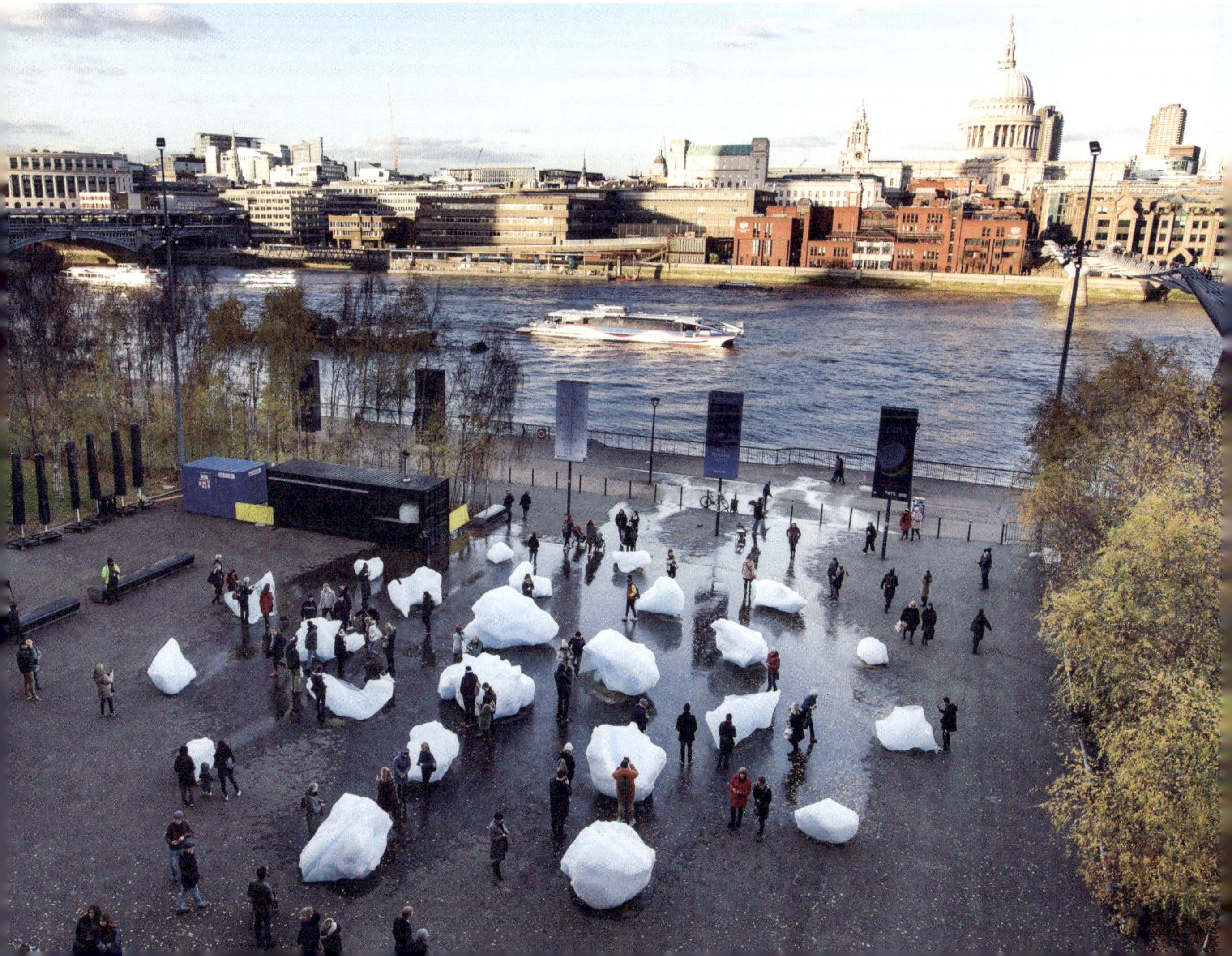

ICE WATCH 2014
TATE MODERN,
LONDON, 2018

mid-1990s with a series of captivating installations. Realised with minimal expense, these used basic technology to create temporary illusions and compelling spatial situations. While various artists in the previous decade had been preoccupied with representation, finding ways to deconstruct media imagery or to forge new representations of various identity groups, Eliasson was part of a generation of artists creating situations and new realities. Peers included Pierre Huyghe, Carsten Höller and Dominique Gonzalez-Foerster; Eliasson showed with them on many occasions.

These early works announced interests that have continued to occupy Eliasson ever since. One group of works involved light projections, reflections and distortions. For *Window projection* 1990 (p.38), a floor-standing lamp is set up in the middle of a space and fitted with a gobo, casting an image of a window frame onto a wall. Until you notice the lamp, you assume that the image on the wall comes from light entering through an actual window in the room. *Wannabe* 1991 (p.41) involved a single spotlight pointed directly towards the floor, letting the visitor decide whether to stand in its glow or to watch others become the spectacle. The installation *Eine Beschreibung einer Reflexion, oder aber eine angenehme Übung zu deren Eigenschaften* (*A description of a reflection or, a pleasant exercise on its qualities*) 1995 (pp.63–5) employed four components. A ceiling-mounted spotlight pointed towards a circular mirror in the corner of a room; this was angled towards another mirror with an uneven surface on a rotating device. The reflection was then bounced onto a large circular projection screen in the centre of the room where the bulb's light appeared as a changing amorphous glow like an interstellar cloud, somehow much stranger than the

GREEN RIVER 1998
BREMEN

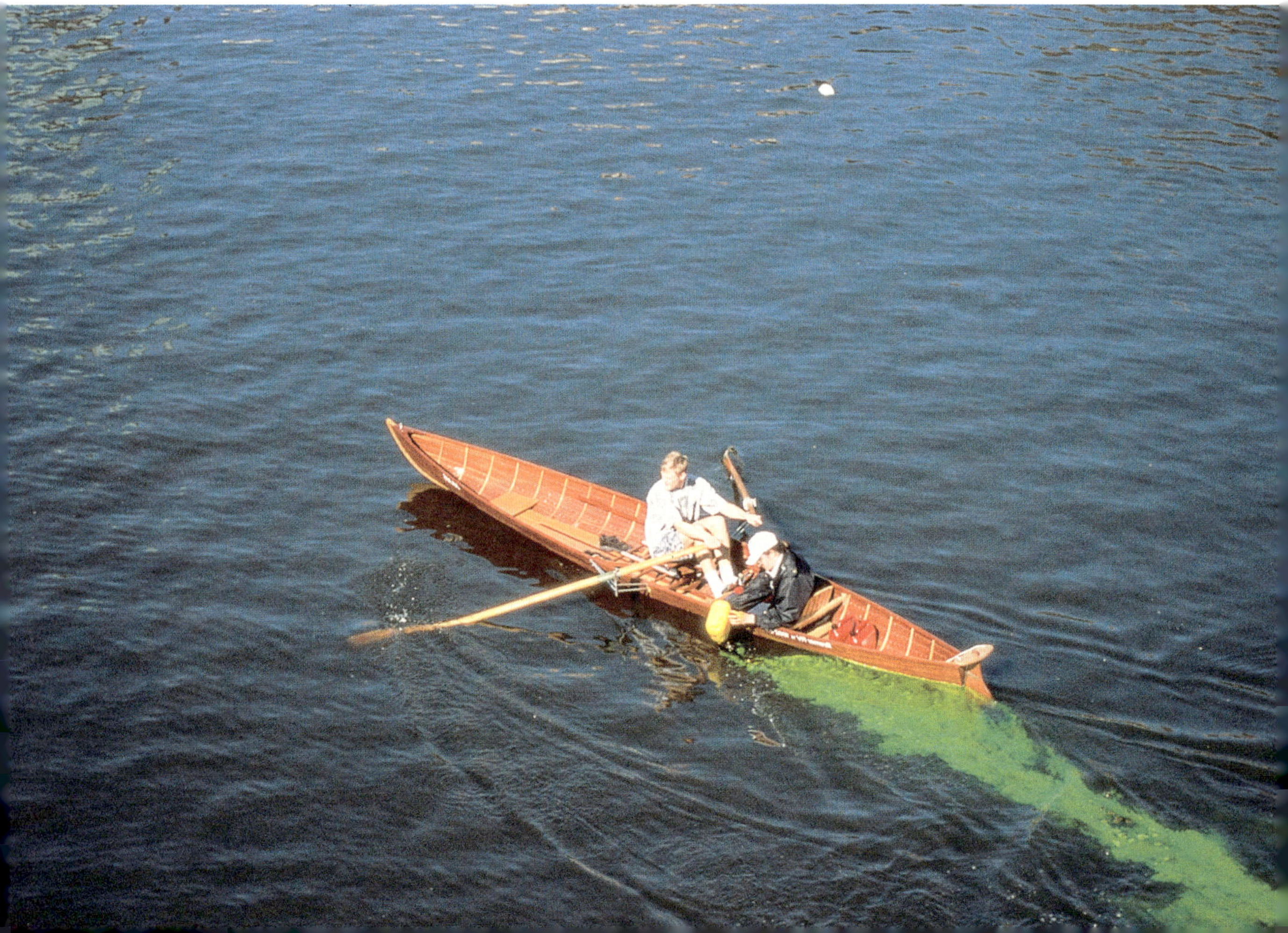

simple set-up would indicate. Two years later, for his first exhibition in California, Eliasson cut a hole into the roof of his gallery so that a shaft of bright sunlight fell onto the ground. He called the work *Your sun machine* 1997, since the movement of the beam in the space described the mechanics of the solar system, the earth's daily rotation. That this work at first seemed to be another illusion created with projected electric light was itself the illusion; in fact, no technology had been used.

In 1993 Eliasson debuted another piece involving projected light. It shone through a hazy curtain of droplets sprinkling out of tiny holes in a ceiling-mounted hosepipe, so that when you encountered the simple set-up at a particular angle, the effect of a rainbow was produced. Perhaps because the experience so greatly exceeded the prosaic kit on show, Eliasson named the work *Beauty* (pp.46–9). It was the first of a group of works recreating meteorological and natural phenomena indoors with various bits of mediation and machinery: Eliasson went on to find ways of replicating gusts of wind, waves, rain, fog, whirlpools, sandstorms and sunsets. In his first *Waterfall* in 1998 he recreated these dramatic landscape features through the basic deployment of scaffolding, pipes and pumps. He also made clandestine interventions in cities to bring the force of nature into urban space: in Johannesburg he used a pump to empty a reservoir, creating a temporary river rushing through the streets (*Erosion* 1997); the following year in Bremen, he released a non-toxic green dye into the Weser river, temporarily displacing its postcard-friendly identity and making more visible its ever-changing currents and flows (*Green river* 1998).

In these years too, in a kind of reverse movement, Eliasson brought parts of the landscape into gallery spaces, transforming the architecture and the experience of the space. He covered the entire wall of a booth at the 1994 Cologne Art Fair with reindeer moss, so that in the antiseptic environment of a convention centre viewers had to confront a living organism – one that softened the space but also gave it an odour quite out of place in an art fair. Decidedly uncommercial, the work was never sold. *Moss wall* (pp.54–7) would be regularly included in his shows thereafter. A few years later, he filled the floor of the Centre Pompidou in Paris with lava (*Lava floor* 2002).

The experience of space was transformed in other ways with light, sound, heat, colour and mirrors. For *Infinity* 1991, his first work based on a horizon line, Eliasson projected a blue line at his eye level, so that you marked your scale and your presence in the space in relation to the artist's. A ring of short blue natural gas flames met you as you discovered *No nights in summer, no days in winter* 1994 (pp.58–9), whose title alluded to the Arctic seasons. In 1997's *Room for one colour* (pp.74–5) Eliasson used yellow monofrequency lamps for the first time; the bulbs turned the space yellow. This was soon followed by *Room for all colours* 1999, the first of many environments involving changing coloured spaces. You stood in front of a screen whose intense and changing hue filled the room, but to enter this space you had to pass the mechanics behind it: a grid of bulbs with foils of three colours over them, the colours shifting depending on which bulbs were illuminated. Another important early architectural intervention was staged at the Museum of Modern Art, New York in Eliasson's first appearance there for his *Projects* show in 2001. For *Seeing yourself sensing* (p.15) he replaced the windows onto the sculpture garden with sheets made up of alternating and equally wide strips of transparent and mirrored glass, so that your experience of looking out was interrupted by your reflection; likewise, you could not concentrate on your own reflection without also being aware of the space beyond the mirror.

Where did all these installations of the 1990s and early 2000s come from? One reading, suggested by Eliasson himself, has been through his biography, and in particular his experiences of Iceland, where he spent a considerable part of his youth. Wandering the landscape he became attuned to incredible meteorological phenomena and landscape features – rainbows, steam billowing over hot pools in freezing weather, caves, glaciers, volcanoes. The terrain not only provided an endless array of things to see as you walked through it: it was also a place to feel a sharp sense of embodiment, especially when the temperature dropped, when you smelled a blast of sulphur from a hot pool, or when you hiked from moss banks onto lava fields or up steep moraine. Eliasson also learned how to use the landscape to measure space and time. For him a waterfall was not just a pretty thing to view: you could judge how far you were from it based on what sound you heard or how fast the water appeared to fall. Eliasson's experience and use of Iceland as a testing ground for perception and measurement was recorded in the photographic work he considers of crucial importance to his artistic practice: instead of isolating one particularly dramatic scene, he made grids of images, enabling comparison and study. Iceland was also essential for his installations, as he found ways to translate some of his experiences and enquiries into the space of the gallery. In his youth, Eliasson was also a keen breakdancer, and this too sharpened his sense of his own physicality and his consciousness of space: How many steps between me and the edge of the stage? How fast can I move across it? How can I use lighting to alter the way my movement appears? Again, these questions would work their way into his projects.

Another way of locating Eliasson's early work is through art history. Recalling the work he made in the 1990s, he has spoken about the impact on him of Lucy Lippard's *Six Years: The Dematerialisation of the Art Object 1966–72*, which he discovered in the late 1980s. At a time when the art world was dominated by commerce, the non-commercial artworks Lippard recorded were particularly resonant for Eliasson, strengthening his early conviction that one could make a career without selling objects.[2] Eliasson has also noted the importance of the Californian 'Light and Space' artists such as Robert Irwin, James Turrell, Larry Bell, Doug Wheeler and Maria Nordman (though Nordman has never accepted this term to describe her practice). When one considers Irwin's use of coloured lights and scrims, Turrell's early corner installations of projected coloured light transforming one's sense of architectural space, Bell's mirrored boxes, and the simple way Nordman changed the experience of buildings by uncovering skylights and covering apertures with coloured filters, it is easy to see why Eliasson's work has been associated with this group. In the 1990s Eliasson also became interested in American postminimalism and land art, and the installations of artists like Mel Bochner, Gordon Matta-Clark and Dan Graham; the early fog sculptures of the Japanese artist Fujiko Nakaya; Italian arte povera; and the installations of coloured chambers realised by the Venezuelan artist Carlos Cruz-Diez and the Brazilian Hélio Oiticica.

In some early publications Eliasson discussed his work with artists of this generation. In a conversation published in *Artforum*, Daniel Buren told him that he had done 'exactly the same piece' in 1971 as Eliasson made in 2001, and asked him whether he had known the work of the Argentine Nicolás García Uriburu when he made *Green river*, since Uriburu had dyed rivers green in 1968.[3] Buren was concerned that when repetitions like these happen, the memory of an earlier generation's contribution is lost. But accusations of repetition fail to register the way an artist of one generation reworks an inherited vocabulary under new conditions. In the 1990s many other artists as well as Eliasson were rethinking the language of 1960s and 1970s sculpture: Roni Horn, Felix Gonzales-Torres and Cady Noland among them. Those artists often repurposed an inherited vocabulary to address issues of identity, sexuality or power. There are several important pieces by Eliasson with no formal relationship to the work of earlier artists (for instance *Beauty* or *Moss wall*), but in respect to those of his works which *do* relate to earlier artworks, the question is how Eliasson reworked his inherited vocabulary – and to what end?

To begin an answer one might compare Bruce Nauman's *Yellow room (triangular)* 1973 with Eliasson's yellow *Room for one colour*. Nauman constructed a plywood room in the gallery which one could walk into and see yellow light while experiencing a sense of confinement exacerbated by the angled architecture. Eliasson, who has never been interested in such confinement, uses a very different yellow light that renders everything monochrome so that people within *Room for one colour* look at each other in a different and heightened way. In my own experience, it is surprising and strange to see that yellow light drains all other colours from people's skin and clothes, turning everything either yellow or black. Another comparison would contrast Hans Haacke's *Blue sail* 1964–5 with Eliasson's *Ventilator* 1997. While both artists are interested in the systematic motions of a regular desk fan, Haacke's is placed below a blue sheet, keeping it waving aloft, so that one sees the result of the fan's motion as an image; Eliasson's fan swings in the space of the gallery, so that you feel its motion. When I saw it in a show in New York, people chased it, jumping up as if to catch it. His work with gas flames, *No nights in summer, no days in winter*, is a small

SEEING YOURSELF SENSING 2001
THE MUSEUM OF MODERN ART, NEW YORK

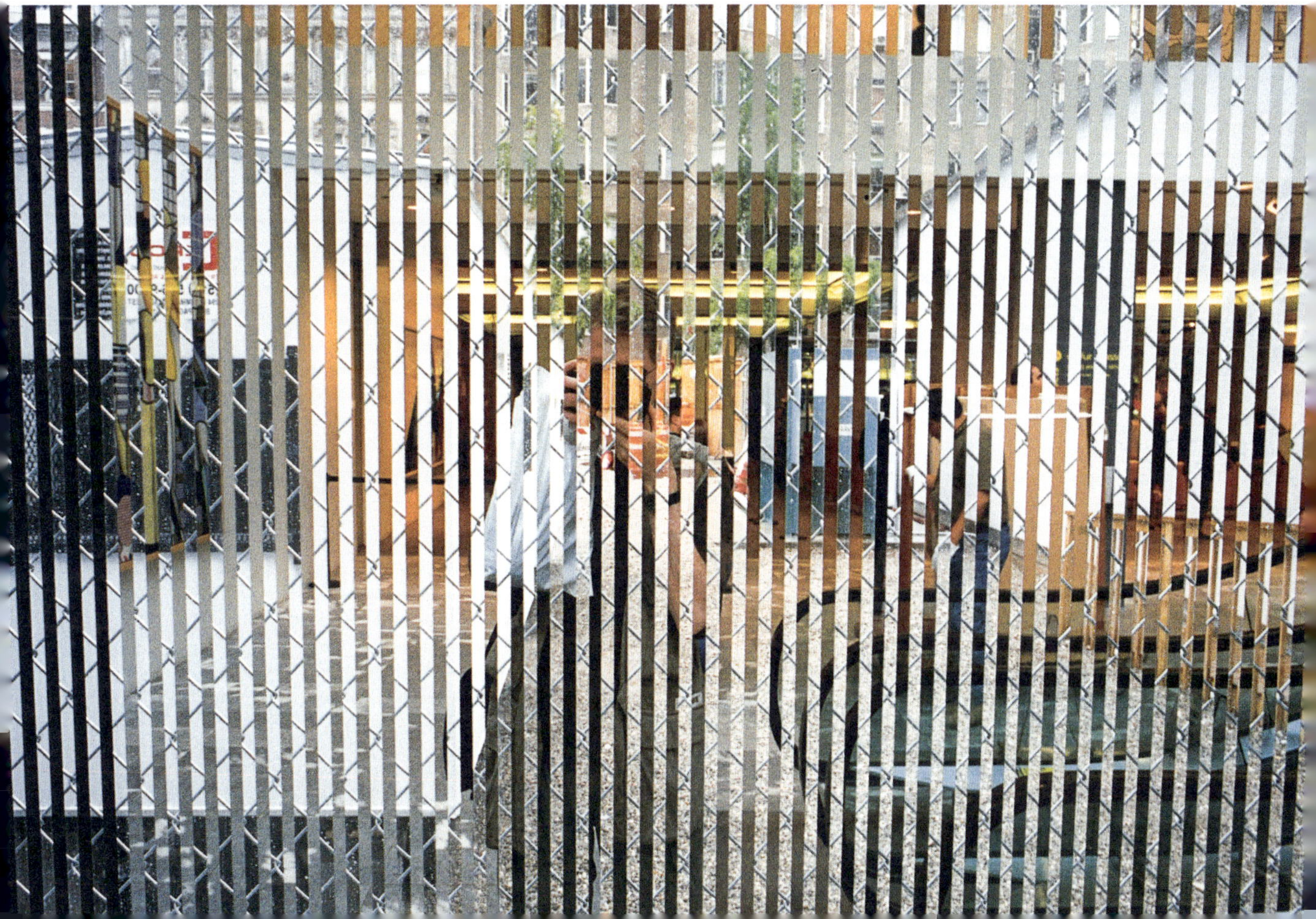

ring of fire that is keyed to the size of your face as you stand in front of it; calling to mind an eclipse, or the way light peaks on the horizon in the Icelandic winter, it feels delicate and warming. For an installation in 1969, by contrast, Jannis Kounellis placed gas canisters on the floor of the gallery, with tubes running up to fixtures and nozzles placed at head height from which long gas flames shot out into the space. Viewers could go in but it was deliberately intimidating and unwelcoming. Think also about the difference between Walter de Maria's 1977 *Earth Room*, for which the floor of an entire apartment in New York was covered in earth, and Eliasson's 2002 *Lava floor*, where he placed lava over the ground of a Paris museum. De Maria created an image of waste, rendering a piece of highly rentable real estate unusable, and viewers only saw it from the threshold. Eliasson transposed an Icelandic landscape to Paris, evoking the aftermath of a calamitous volcanic eruption, and encouraged his audience to step through the field, a tricky task of balance and poise.

These examples show how, in comparison to his predecessors, Eliasson developed a greater interest in audience, in the idea of welcome, and in movement. He also cannily read changes in societal and technological conditions that changed the way audiences responded to art between the 1960s and 1990s. As daily work is increasingly spent in front of computer screens, and as physical activities are displaced by digital programmes, so there is a greater desire for bodily experience of the kind provided by immersive installations. And as social life is more and more mediated through technology, the opportunity to come together in a space to enjoy an unusual experience with other people becomes rarer and more appealing. Noting all these different conditions, Eliasson could use a vocabulary to access a much larger audience than was ever available to the artists of the 1960s and 1970s. He registered another shift since the 1960s: the increasing penetration of commerce into daily life. In response to rampant capitalism, he felt it all the more urgent to reclaim wonder and beauty from commerce and, against the multicoloured techno-

THE MEDIATED MOTION 2001 KUNSTHAUS BREGENZ

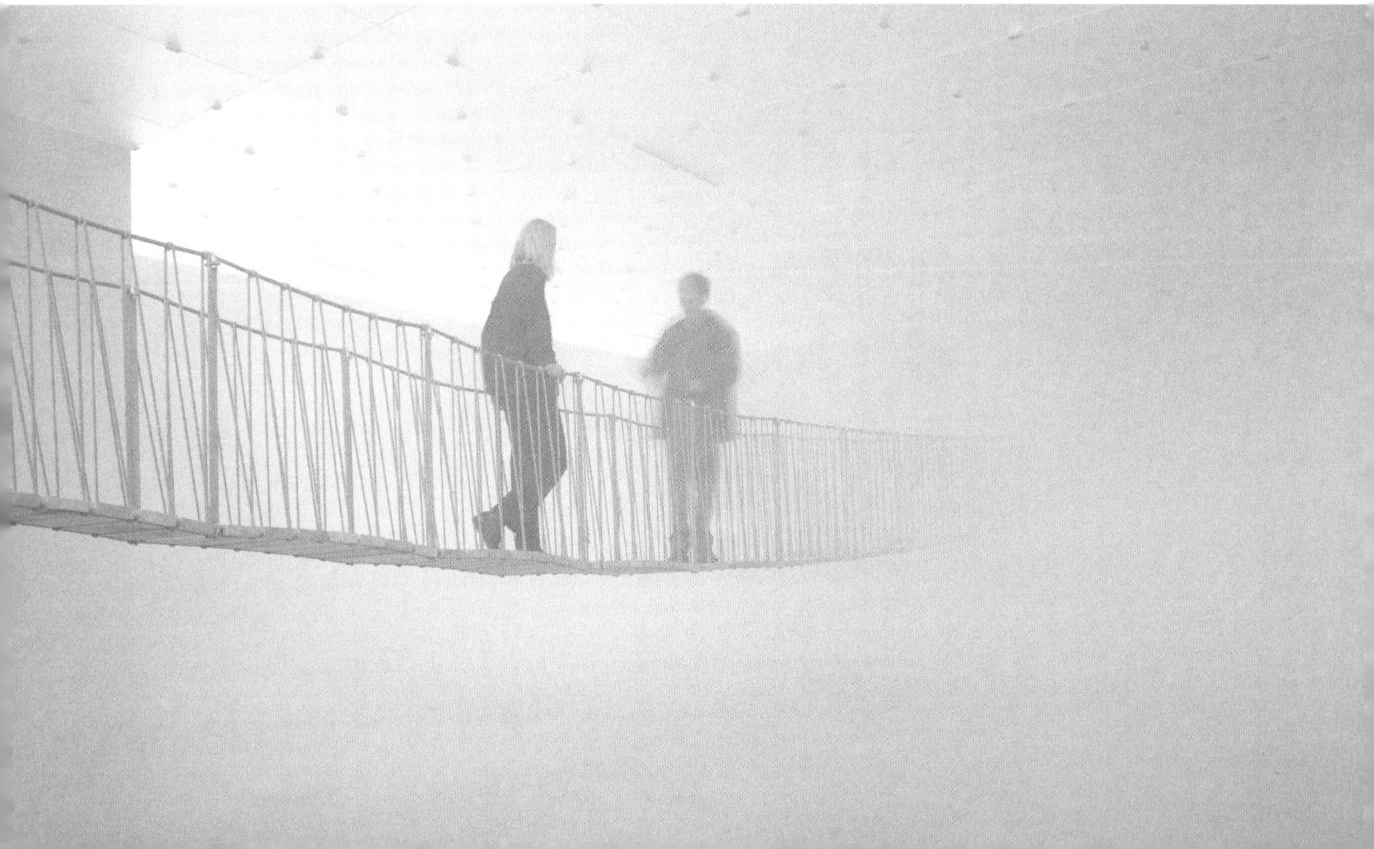

spectacles we find in urban shopping centres, to make a rainbow with little more than a punctured hosepipe and a spotlight.

NEW OBJECTS AND NEW DEBATES

Two new tendencies emerged in Eliasson's practice before the century was out. Starting with the 1997 show *The curious garden* at the Kunsthalle in Basel, he began to bring together different objects and installations to form environments where the total experience was conceived as a journey through different sequential spaces.[4] Leaving the *Room for one colour* you moved through a blue passage into a space divided by a hawthorn hedge and then to a final room where a boulder sat on the floor beneath *Ventilator* (pp.82–3). Four years later at Kunsthaus Bregenz, collaborating with the landscape architect Günther Vogt on the exhibition *The mediated motion*, Eliasson created perhaps his most magical exhibition, a different environment on each floor of the museum. On the first floor, a thin wooden pathway crossed an artificial pond covered in duckweed; steps led up to a floor where you could walk over a gently sloping surface of packed earth; up another flight was a room filled with fog whose colour shifted in changing daylight. A wooden suspension bridge allowed you to traverse the space. On the ground floor, mushrooms grew from wooden branches propped against the wall like a postminimalist sculpture.

The other shift in the work was the production of objects, which had tended to be absent in the first few years of Eliasson's output. Many of these were the result of a long collaboration with Einar Thorsteinn, an Icelandic architect and specialist in geometry. In 1996 Eliasson made his first sculptures structured with tessellation: two domes originally installed in Hvidovre, Denmark emerged from the ground as if mostly submerged; their frameworks were composed from tessellated hexagons, with a single pentagon at the apex. Kids could use the stainless steel structure as a climbing frame, while adults could join

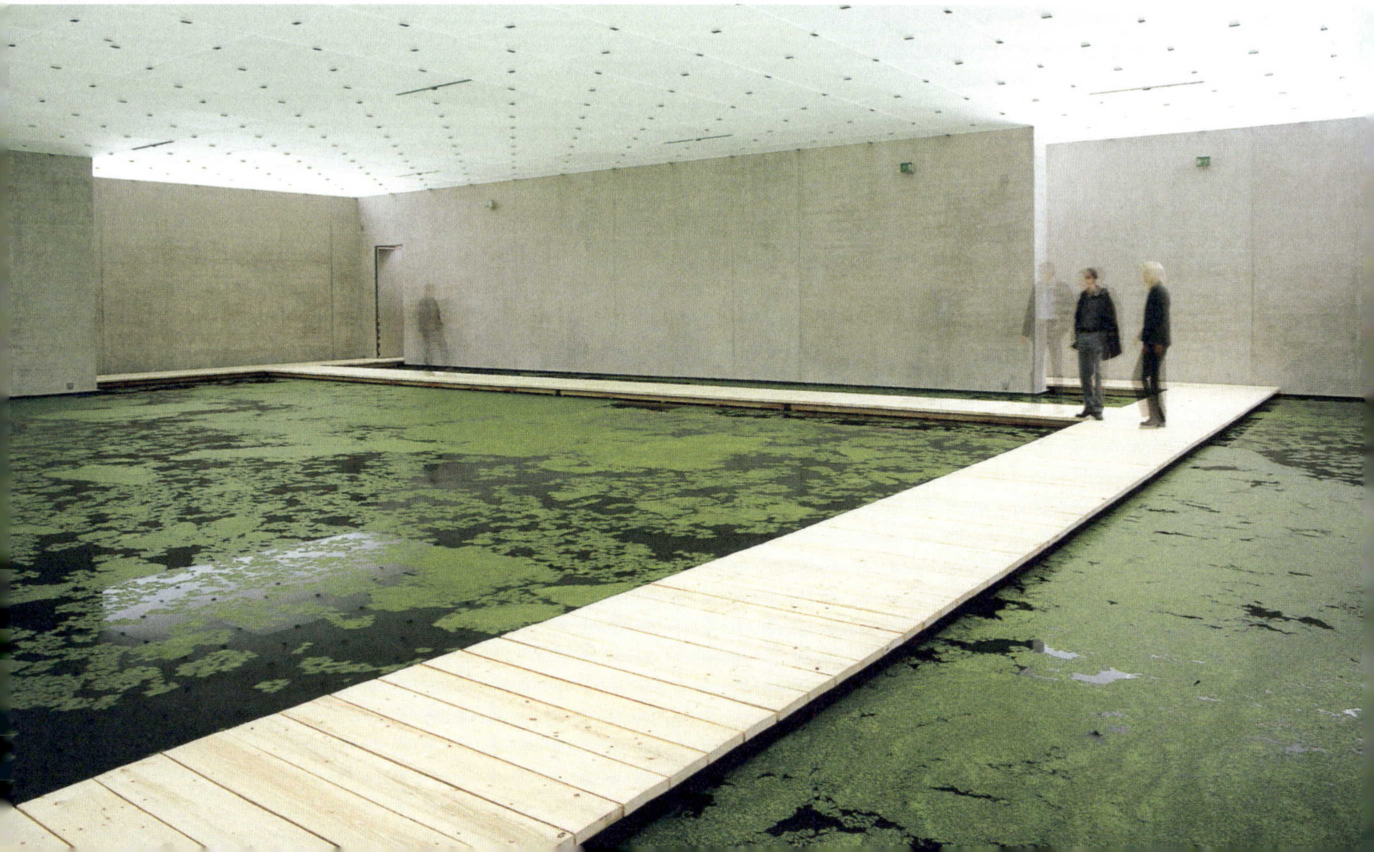

Eliasson on a journey exploring complex lines and shapes and their interrelationships. The next step along this journey was his first work using a lattice based on five-fold symmetry, the *5-dimensionel pavillon* of 1998: Eliasson liked the lattice because it created a 'combination of harmony and confusion and defies viewers' expectations'.[5] He also began to use reflective materials to create kaleidoscopic objects. *Your compound view* 1998, first shown at Kjarvalsstaðir in Iceland, was a tapering tunnel – you could look through to a friend on the far side, both your reflections bouncing over its mirrored sides. In the much more ambitious *Your spiral view* 2002 (pp.103–5), not only could you walk right through, but the internal walls were made from regularly folded mirrored surfaces. There followed several major penetrable kaleidoscopic sculptures such as *La situazione antispettiva* 2003, the centrepiece of his Danish Pavilion at the 2003 Venice Biennale.

Where Eliasson's first works had indicated a debt to the art of the 1960s and 1970s, these works reached back further, but not to the regular geometries that characterised modernist architecture. Partly Eliasson was looking to Buckminster Fuller, but more to the complex and irregular forms of expressionist architecture – to figures such as Bruno Taut and Paul Scheerbart. He was also beginning to hone his critique of classical architecture and of Renaissance ideas of perspective. A classical space (or indeed modernist space) centres the viewer, allowing them to feel a sense of authority over the space they occupy. Eliasson – whether with complex reflective surfaces, by exchanging rectangular and right-angled architecture with curved and folded structures or by filling an environment with artificial fog – created spaces where you were never quite certain of your coordinates. In this uncertainty there was not just the possibility of a more playful response to your situation, but

5-DIMENSIONEL PAVILLON 1998 STRANDPARKEN, HOLBÆK

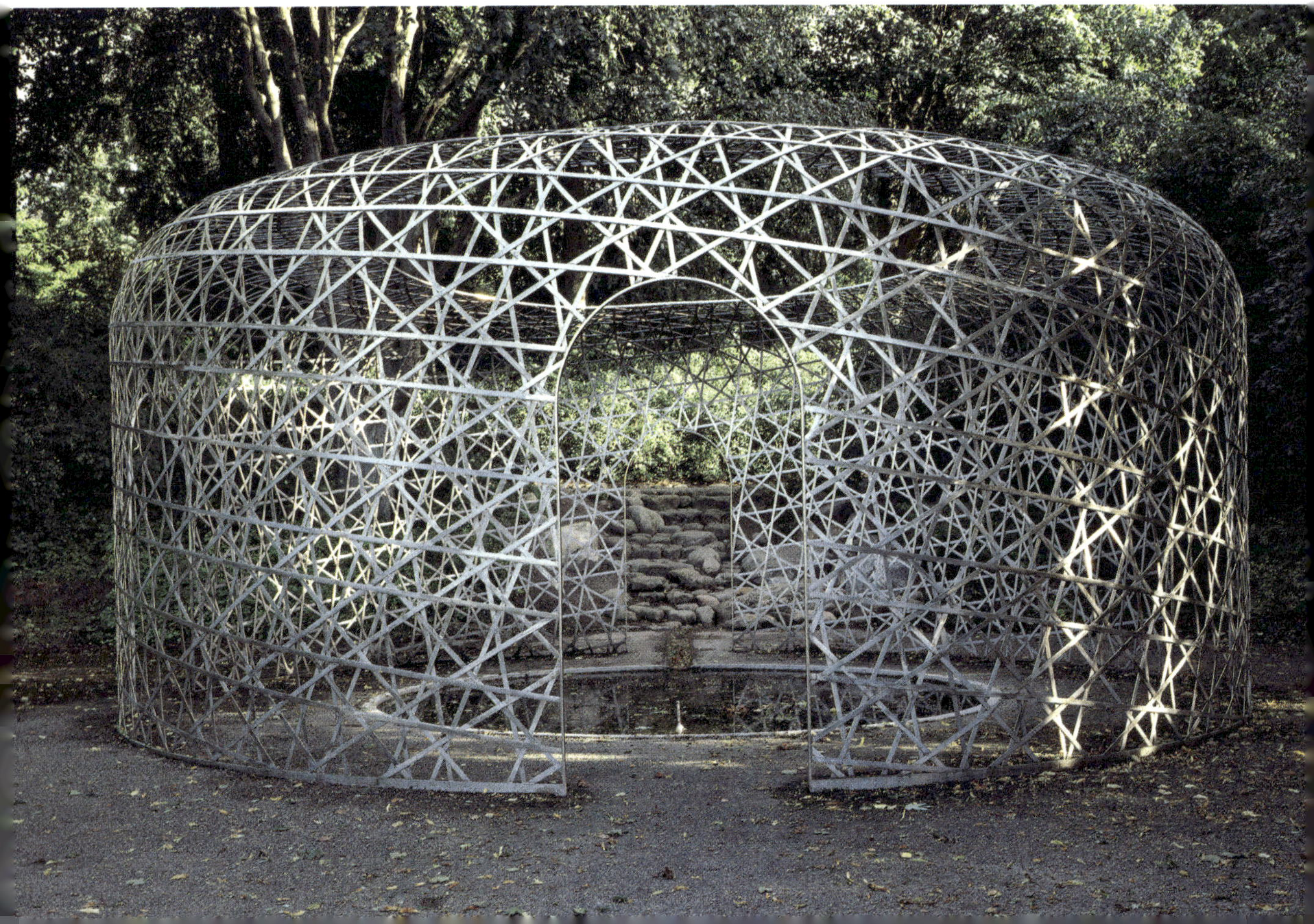

the opportunity to enter into a less familiar relationship with those around you as they also tried to navigate these curious spaces.

In 2003 Eliasson created *The weather project* (p.21) for the Unilever Commission, an installation in the Turbine Hall at Tate Modern that brought together several physical elements of his work to date and, most importantly, gave him the chance to work with his ideas about audiences on a new scale. Eliasson mirrored the ceiling of the hall so that – after some searching – you could see yourself (along with your friends) a huge distance away in the doubled height of the space. At one end of the building, monofrequency lights behind a screen were diffused into a semi-circle which, reflected in the mirror, became a full circle: a glowing sun. Fog was pumped into the space to give it density and depth, and to soften the industrial architecture. People lay down beneath the glow, basking in the unusual weather; some protested the Iraq War. Eliasson perfectly recognised the need to transform the cold, intimidating, post-industrial space of the Turbine Hall into a more mysterious and playful environment. Paradoxically, while doubling its apparent height he also made it feel more intimate. Quite soon the work got a nickname that stuck: 'The Sun'. It became one of the most visited and most reproduced artworks of the first decade of the century.

By this point, alongside the production of all these works, Eliasson was publishing statements and giving frequent interviews and talks. In these texts, four key theoretical principles recur that he saw as underlying almost everything he was doing, especially *The weather project*. The first of these is summed up in the phrase 'seeing yourself sensing'.[6] Eliasson wanted to make works where you would become aware of the processes of perception, aware of your body as it made sense of the environment, conscious of the space you occupied and how you were navigating it, attuned to your experience unfolding over time. This increased self-reflection could in turn lead to a more reflective attitude towards the world outside the artwork.

A second principle linked to the first: the viewer was a co-producer of the work. Some might have felt that Eliasson was trying to impose a supposedly universal language of colour, shape, surface, or light on his viewers. However, in line with psychological and scientific studies into how experience is transformed into meaning, the artist argued that you brought your body to the work, your eyesight, your own sense of smell and so on, but also your own cultural associations. Water or sunlight or fog would trigger personal memories – and so the work's meanings were made in the merging of the forms he built and the associations viewers brought to them. This is why, from 1996, Eliasson began to use 'Your' in so many of his titles, offering the work to his viewer.

But these works were never conceived for 'you' alone. Eliasson's third core principle states that in the process of seeing yourself sensing, of bringing your associations to what you experience, you also become more alert to those around you who are undergoing a similar experience. Strangely coloured light that drains colour from your clothes, reflective surfaces or decreased visibility through fog might all heighten your awareness of people around you – but so might cold or warmth, a blast of air, a flashing strobe or even a rainbow that others say they can see but that you, from your position, cannot. In these conditions, what Eliasson later called 'we-ness' emerges: a sense of togetherness not tied to any credo or specific agenda, but which has progressive potential precisely because its function is not prescribed.

Finally, 'feelings are facts'.[7] As much as Eliasson was insistent about revealing the relatively simple technology behind his artworks' construction, he also knew that they would be experienced in less analytical ways. He knew that they would trigger powerful feelings in their viewers. Many artists whose work he admired, as well as art historians and critics, were wary about any talk of feeling, especially in the context of artworks that were to be encountered by massive audiences; they were suspicious of the way feelings could be manipulated to serve political and corporate agendas, and mindful of the worst outcomes of such manipulations in the twentieth century. But Eliasson did not want to shy away from a language of feeling. He believed that feelings were as real as bulbs, mirrors and scrims. They could be harnessed in the cause of social, economic and environmental attentiveness and responsibility. Feelings could lead to actions – and indeed this was the very reason to make art.

These four principles summarise much of Eliasson's thinking between *The weather project* and his first major museum survey, *Take your time*, which opened at San Francisco Museum of Modern Art in 2007. It was during these years that a critical debate emerged around Eliasson's work, and indeed about his position within contemporary art. In some accounts, it was suggested that his work simply celebrated existing conditions of contemporary life, or even that it was complicit in consumer culture and the entertainment industry: he was identified as the key culprit in the 'spectacularisation of contemporary art'. For the art historian and critic Hal Foster, Eliasson's work was indicative of what he called 'the catastrophe of Minimalism': a turn away from minimalism's concerns with scale and phenomenology towards phenomena and mere affect.[8] Eliasson's work, he contended, overawes us with sensory overload fostering emotional rather than critical responses; it was too easily apprehended as otherworldly, even spiritual; Eliasson manufactured the 'technological sublime'.[9] And because he made his work relatively inexpensively, and was prepared to travel around the world to install his pieces, Eliasson was exactly the kind of artist that museums could call on in order to fill their newly inflated spaces and generate huge crowds too.[10]

The curator of *Take your time*, Madeleine Grynsztejn, stood on the other side of this debate. She emphasised the work's 'conspicuous exposure of its own fabrication', its 'resistance to all-out illusionism', the 'full disclosure' each piece gave about its own production.[11] Eliasson had developed an 'arsenal of strategies for encouraging individual awareness, reflection, and ultimately a greater consciousness of the workings of large economic and political frameworks';[12] his exhibitions, she said, 'return viewers to themselves as less docile members of society'.[13] For Grynsztejn, Eliasson was the inheritor of institutional critique and the radical political practices begun by artists such as Hans Haacke some decades before.

In retrospect, both these positions are arguable. When Grynsztejn evoked institutional critique as a framework for Eliasson's art, she explained that for the first generation of artists associated with this term, such as Michael Asher and Hans Haacke, 'the museum became an object of artistic analysis, investigation, and unveiling'.[14] She might have had in mind projects where 1970s artists identified connections between museum board members, oppressive businesses and reactionary political parties. She argued that a subsequent generation of artists, including Andrea Fraser, Fred Wilson and Eliasson, continued the practice of institutional critique by 'embolden[ing the museum] as a place from which to articulate a speculative and critical approach'.[15] At the time she was writing, Eliasson

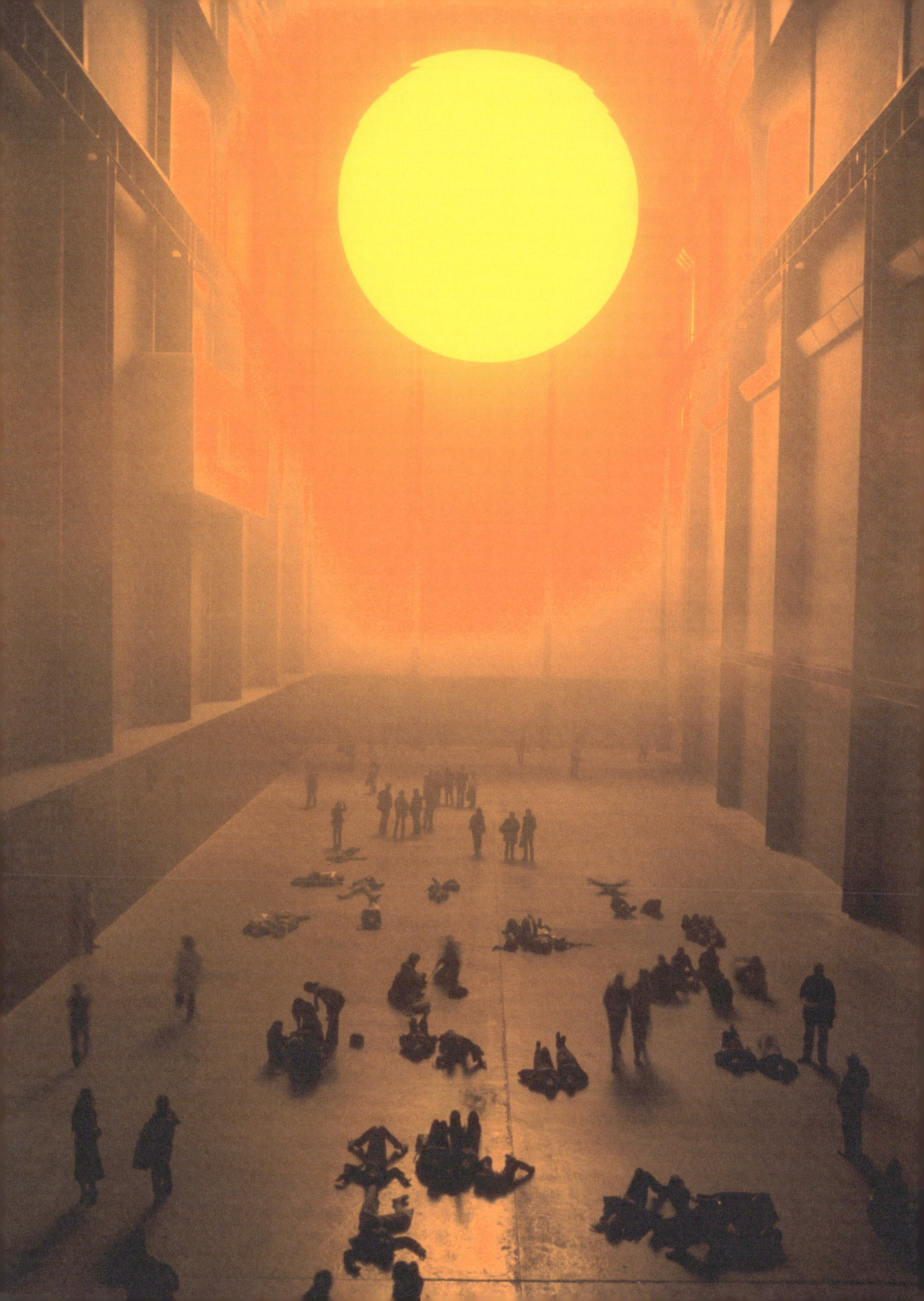

tended to unveil the means by which his illusions were produced: for instance, visitors to the Turbine Hall could see behind the scrim that turned the lights into a 'sun'. But unlike Fraser or Wilson, Eliasson did not specify the targets of any critique, be it the funding structures for contemporary art, the kind of didactic panels found in museum guides, or the museum's colonialist origins. Eliasson's works could spawn a 'speculative approach' to how we exist in the world in more general ways, but by placing his work in the line of followers of 1970s institutional critique, Grynsztejn's reading of Eliasson's practice feels rather forced.

Hal Foster had good reason to be concerned with the spectacular turn in art in the early 2000s and the deployment by many of Eliasson's contemporaries of multiple screens, oversize projected digital images and so on. But actually, he had little to say about the range of Eliasson's work, focusing on *The weather project* as if it were representative of everything Eliasson had done. Nor did Foster consider whether an installation initially experienced as immersive, spectacular and playful can later be reflected on in different ways. For instance, people leaving *The weather project* might think back on an atmosphere of unexpected generosity, of sociability. They might recall a time when their focus wasn't so much on themselves as their experience among others. Maybe this experience served in some ways to brand the museum where they'd had it, but it could also give them a hint of a way of being in the world that was a break from the rule of entertainment and consumption.

A NEW MODEL OF ART PRACTICE

By the time of his 2007 mid-career survey, Eliasson was beginning to feel the limitations of the art world and its model of what an art practice could be. He had turned forty and become a parent, and had already ticked most boxes signifying a successful art career – invitations to every major biennial, representing his country in Venice, countless museum shows, the travelling retrospective and catalogue. The model of the artist as celebrity established by Andy Warhol and extended by Jeff Koons, Damien Hirst and Takashi Murakami was irrelevant to Eliasson, as it was too tied to the marketing of saleable objects. Like those other artists of his generation who were not content with a career defined only by the continuing affirmation of colleagues, curators, critics and collectors – figures such as Steve McQueen, Theaster Gates and Wolfgang Tillmans – Eliasson set his horizons further. As he said: 'an artist can be many things – an entrepreneur, policy-maker, activist, researcher, a gardener of sorts'.[16]

As he developed a new model of what an artist can do, and how art can impact society, Eliasson also built the new internal infrastructure necessary to achieve these ambitions. In 2008 he moved his studio to a four-floor converted brewery in Berlin where people came to work within five teams – designers and architects under Sebastian Behmann; exhibition planners with Caroline Eggel; Anna Engberg-Pedersen's research and communications wing; Myriam Thomas's design and production department; and Anja Gerstmann's finance team. There is also the Studio Olafur Eliasson Kitchen which prepares lunch for all the teams, served 'family style' at long wooden tables. It supports local farmers growing healthy organic vegetarian produce, and arranges an irregular programme of talks about food-related issues.

Eliasson also refined his external network. He had for a long time sought out productive dialogues with architects, geometricians, lighting experts, chefs, choreographers, and others with whom he could research and collaborate on new projects. Now he began to forge strong relationships with the powerful politicians and businesspeople whose backing facilitated his projects in one way or another. This set Eliasson apart from many other artists, some of whom want little to do with such people, others who believe that they will only ever be concerned with their own agendas, and still others who insist that artists have to confront those maintaining the hegemony of capitalism. While recognising that the support of these figures could benefit potential future projects, Eliasson was also genuinely interested in their work and in how they were attempting to create change. He was confident that if such conversations could be fostered, artists could stop their voices being marginalised, and indeed politicians and businesspeople could learn from artists.[17] This confidence has led to productive dialogues with the German Social Democratic Party and with the UN among other political organisations, many of whom have contacted Eliasson and worked with him, sometimes at his studio and sometimes at their headquarters.

With these refinements, Eliasson was able to respond to more and more invitations from different entities – not just for room-sized installations for galleries and biennials, but large projects for museums, companies, brands and cities. Already in 2003, commissioned by the high-end shopping mall Fünf Höfe in Munich, he had installed his first hanging *Sphere*, made from a complex lattice of stainless steel bands, based on fivefold symmetry, that filtered the light and cast a web of shadows onto the spaces below. In 2005 he made *Dufttunnel (Scent Tunnel)* – a tunnel made from hundreds of pots of scented plants – for

SPHERE 2003
FÜNF HÖFE,
VISCARDIHOF,
MUNICH, 2011

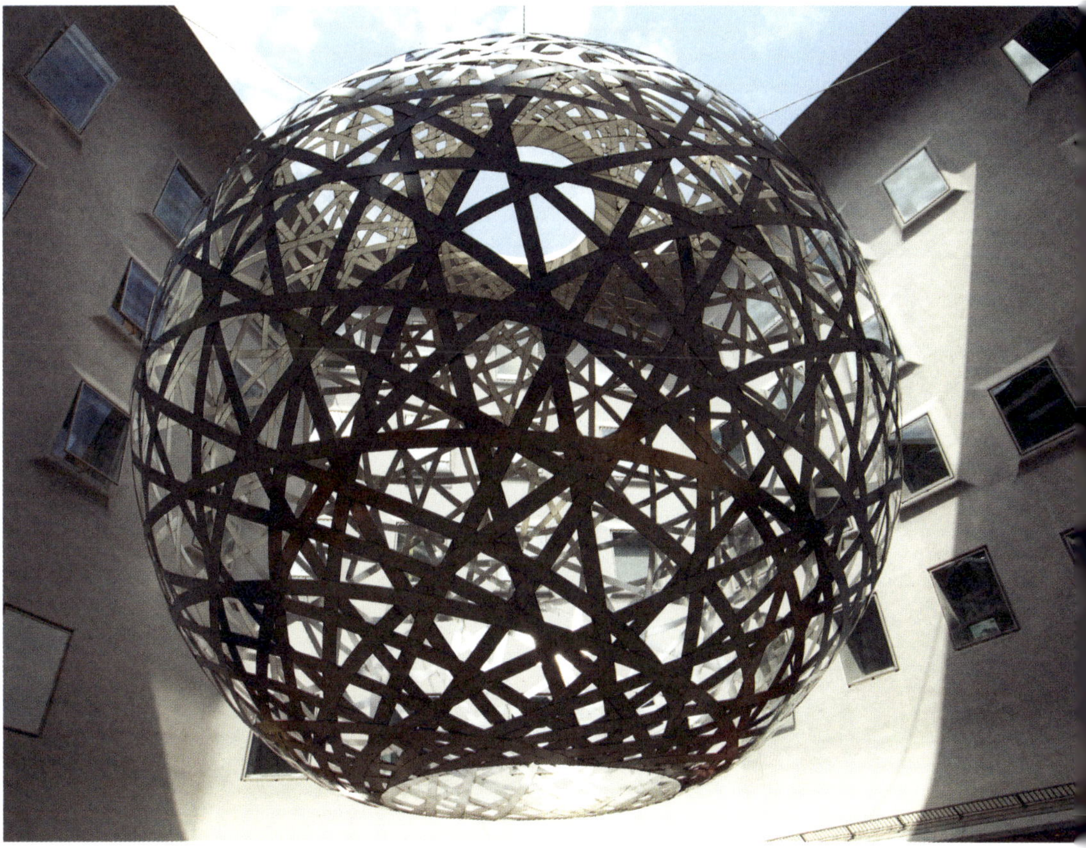

the Autostadt at the Volkswagen headquarters in Wolfsburg, and in 2006 he created a special lamp, *Eye see you*, for the windows of 360 Louis Vuitton shops across the world. This also gave him the opportunity to spread awareness of a foundation he had set up called 121Ethiopia.org, and to raise funds for it through the sale of the lamps after the Louis Vuitton project ended. He also began work with the ARoS Aarhus Kunstmuseum to erect a giant structure, *Your rainbow panorama*, on its roof (pp.26–7). Around this time, he started work on the façade of the Harpa Concert Hall in Reykjavik, while in 2007 he partnered with the architect Kjetil Thorsen to build the Serpentine Gallery Pavilion in Hyde Park. In 2008 he completed his commission for New York's Public Art Fund – four waterfalls pumping water up from, and sending it tumbling down into, the East River.

In 2009 Eliasson gave his first TED Talk. He would go on to make such presentations regularly, speaking on a circuit that rarely invites artists to participate, including the World Economic Forum in Davos and the 2016 'Power and Care' summit in Brussels where he was in dialogue with the Dalai Lama. He also used his website and TV channel to distribute his ideas. Stepping onto these new platforms, he was leaving behind an art world which sometimes functions as an echo chamber, where critics talk to other critics and are not necessarily worried about the wider reception or potential of art. In these situations, and keeping in mind the more general audience that he was building, Eliasson's discourse shifted somewhat. He began to talk more generally about the value of art and the importance of the cultural sector, adopting the kind of rhetoric that we usually find in the speeches of museum directors and ministers of culture. 'Art, the creative muscle, is a trust machine ... Nowadays, art has great potential for changing the world and improving people's lives, partly because it can nurture a degree of trust. It's important, because as

FACADE FOR HARPA REYKJAVIK CONCERT HALL AND CONFERENCE CENTRE 2005–2011 REYKJAVIK

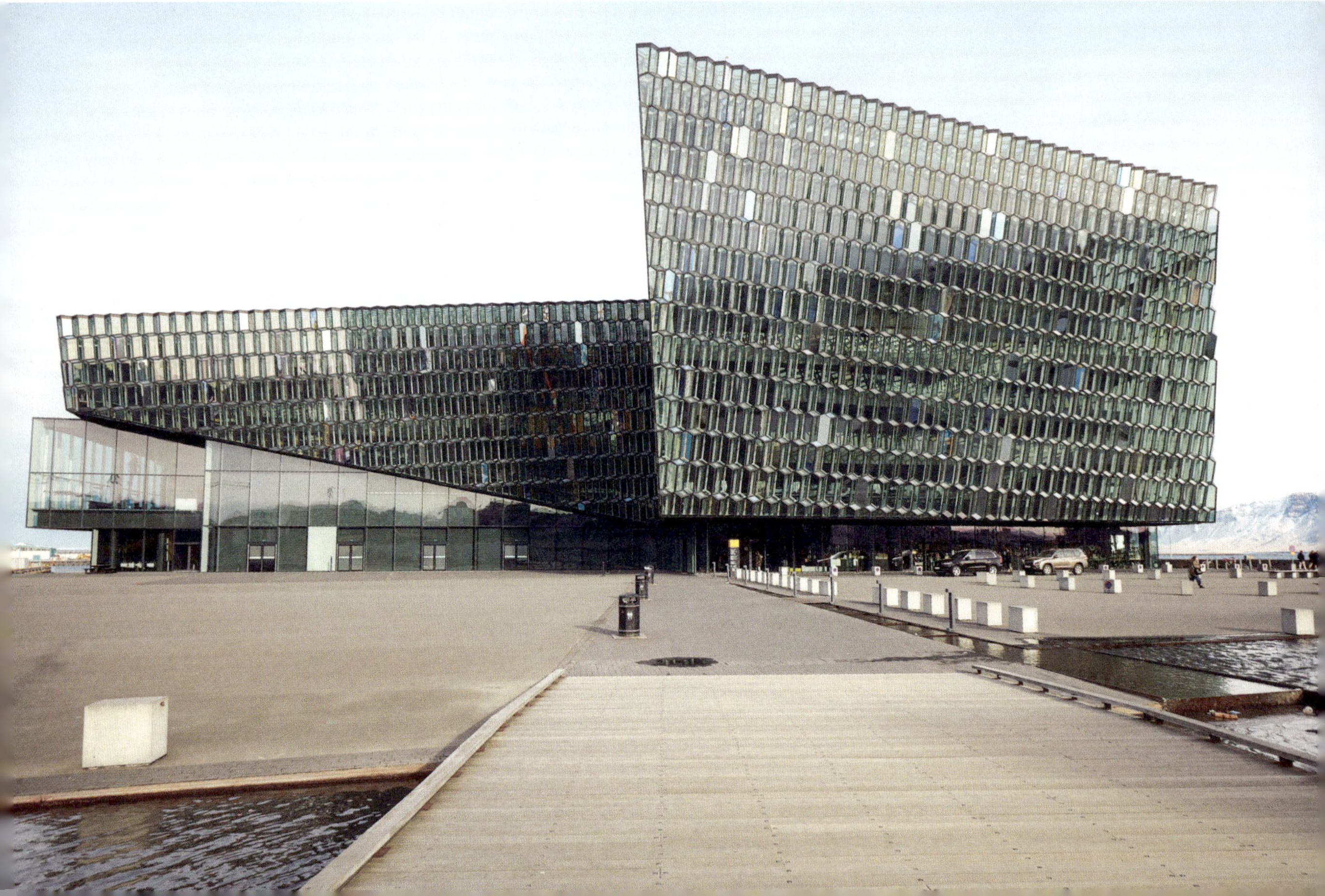

politics, business and finance are losing people's trust, artists are retaining it. Culture has the highest public trust levels of any economic sector. And it can bring about not only the potential for feeling, but also for acting.'[18] It is striking that Eliasson should speak of culture in general, rather than specific art works, or a particular discipline like sculpture or painting. Few other artists talk this way, and perhaps this language indicates his origins as much as his beliefs. Eliasson's contemporaries who work from identity positions that have been historically marginalised or oppressed tend to see a very different role for their work, while his colleagues who come from countries whose recent histories are blemished by totalitarianism are still affected by a history where total 'trust' in the 'cultural sphere' was shattered. Eliasson is a child of the late 1960s from Scandinavia, and his confidence that art builds trust and inspires progressive action comes out of this specific historical and geographical formation.

Around this time, the question arose whether there were contradictions in accepting invitations from Louis Vuitton as well as the Public Art Fund. 'The idea of artists creating art for shops can be a trap and even confuse or weaken their art', Hans Ulrich Obrist told Eliasson, before reassuring him what a 'radical statement' he had made in the Paris HQ of the fashion house.[19] Eliasson defended his projects, claiming that even when he situated a work in a commercial space, he somehow took people out of the realm of consumerism[20] or provided 'a certain type of subversion'.[21] He was referring to a work situated in a Louis Vuitton shop where an elevator was darkened in such a way that it disorientated consumers and disrupted their shopping trip. Of course this work was only accessible to people who went into the store in the first place, so perhaps a better example of this subversion is his series of projects using Lego bricks, the first of which was realised in Aarhus, near the

THE CUBIC STRUCTURAL EVOLUTION PROJECT 2004 QUEENSLAND ART GALLERY | GALLERY OF MODERN ART 2011

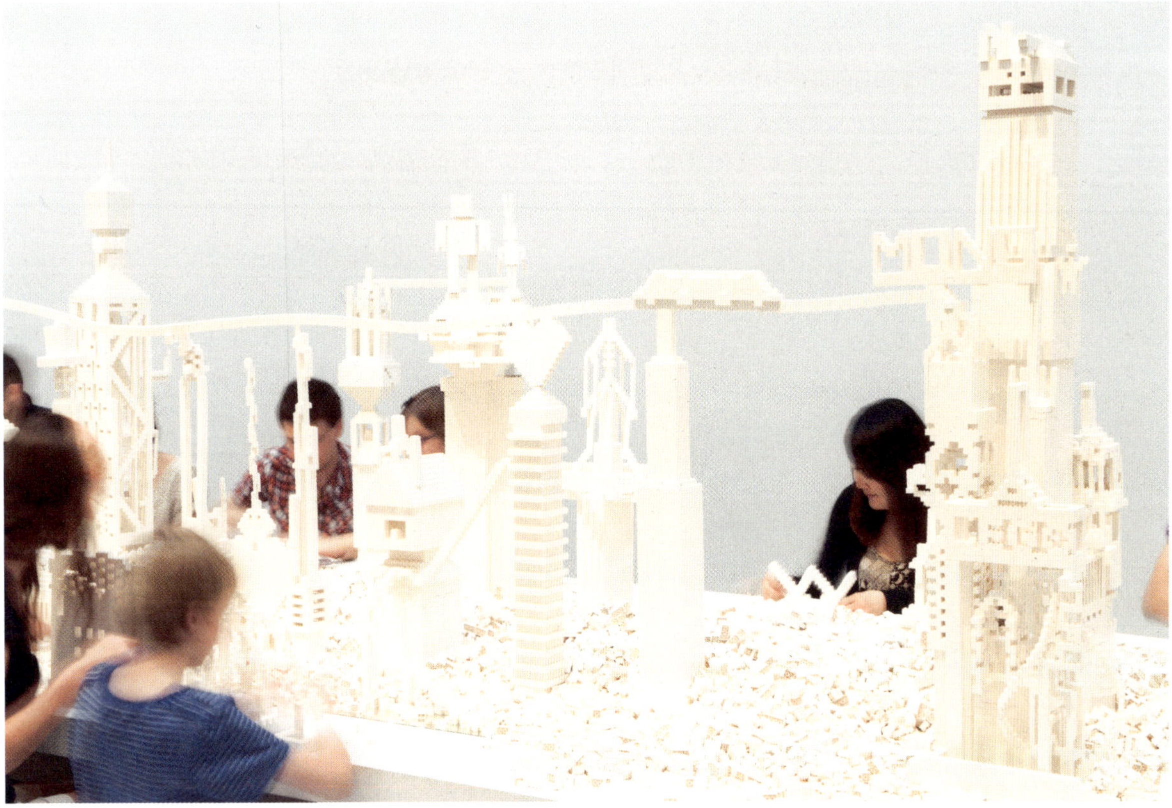

toy giant's base. At a time when Lego was strengthening its partnerships with entertainment brands (notably *Star Wars*), Eliasson launched a work involving tonnes of white bricks that his audiences could build into undetermined structures, collaborating to create temporary cities that could be taken apart and reassembled again and again. The *Cubic structural evolution project* 2004 (p.25) and its later development *The collectivity project* 2005 were brilliant ways of subtly recalling Lego's less brand-based beginnings and bringing strangers together to imagine creative futures.

The question of Eliasson's relationship to Lego or Louis Vuitton opens another concerning the emergence and discourse of mega-companies that became prominent in the 2000s, such as Google, Facebook and Amazon. In the digital economy, these companies structure our daily interaction with other brands selling us products, services and experiences. Crucial to their function and mission is the idea of sharing and evaluation. We constantly endure these companies asking us to evaluate the products we use and the experiences we consume. Many feel they do it to collect our data and monetise our feedback rather than respond helpfully to it, but whatever the reasons behind this, it is fair to say that we have become used to 'sharing' and 'rating' our experiences. With this change one might well ask how Eliasson's own notion of self-evaluation stands up. One of the keys to his conviction about the potential of art was the notion of self-reflexivity. 'I feel it is more important than ever to work with the self-evaluative quality of experience that art offers. I believe that

YOUR RAINBOW PANORAMA 2006–2011 AROS AARHUS KUNSTMUSEUM, AARHUS

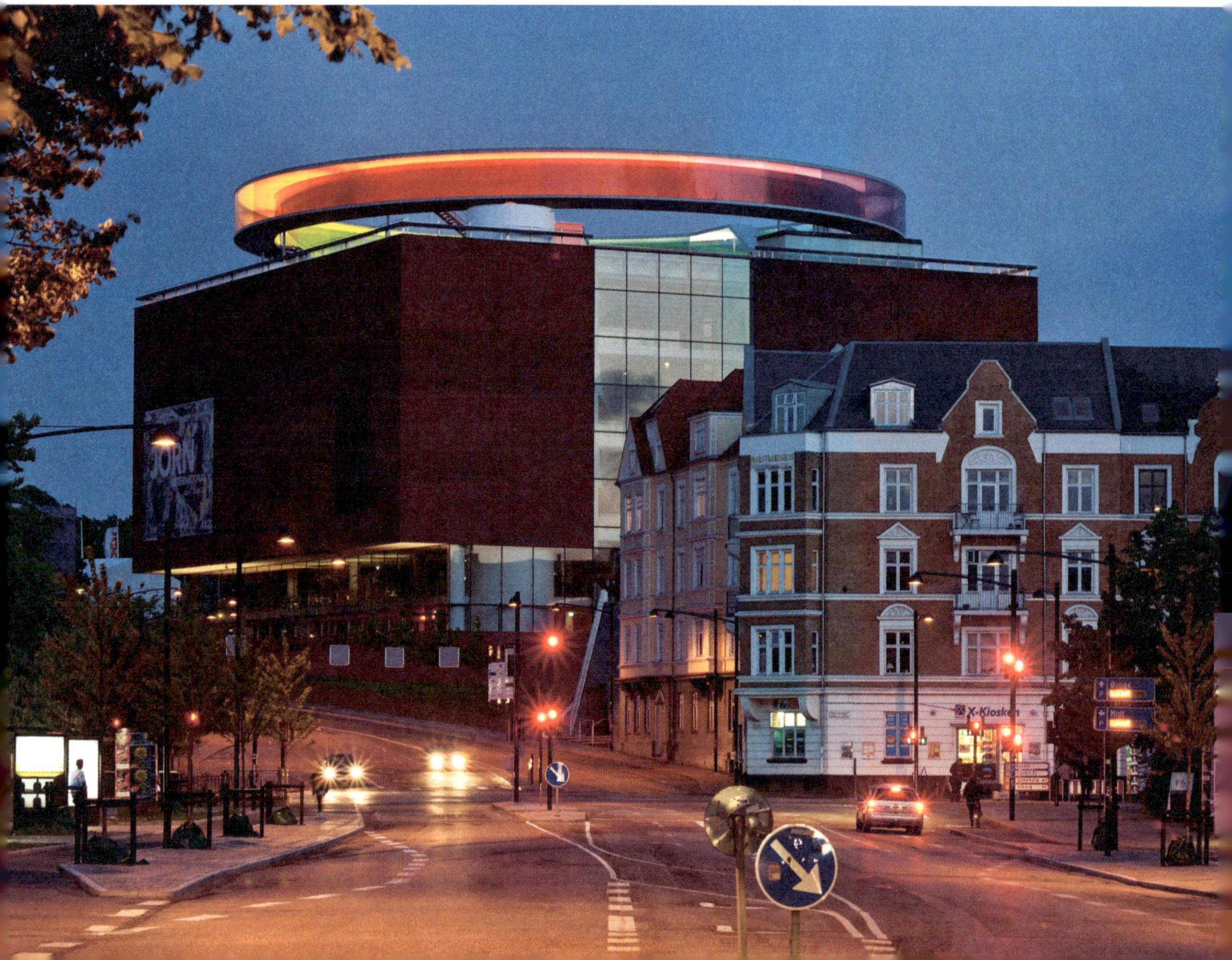

self-evaluation gives us the opportunity to reflect on the relativity of the world in which we live, to reimagine it, and to reposition ourselves in society.'[22] Eliasson had this belief long before new companies asked us to evaluate our experiences, but once this kind of discourse became so prominent in daily life, could it still hold critical potential within art?

Of course, the self-questioning that Eliasson's best works provoke is much more nuanced than these online surveys. In his installations, self-questioning is prompted by an interlinking of embodied and social experiences, in specific locations shaped by architectural, economic and cultural conditions. Take, for instance, *Your rainbow panorama*. Eighteenth-century panoramas led visitors up to a platform where they were encircled by a painting transporting them to a completely different place; the illusion was complete because they couldn't see the painting's top or bottom edge. On first seeing the ring of *Your rainbow panorama* from ground level on the streets of Aarhus, you would expect the piece to allow you, once inside, to feel like you are walking in the sky within a rainbow whose colour gradually shifts along the spectrum. And, indeed, sometimes the colour does change almost seamlessly as you walk around the inner circumference, passing from one panel to the next. But at other junctions – due to the limitations of the commercially available transparent coloured sheets, sandwiched between glass in different combinations, from which the work is made – the gradations are jolty, like the physical manifestation of a screen glitch. All the while, you look down upon the industrial town where life is going on

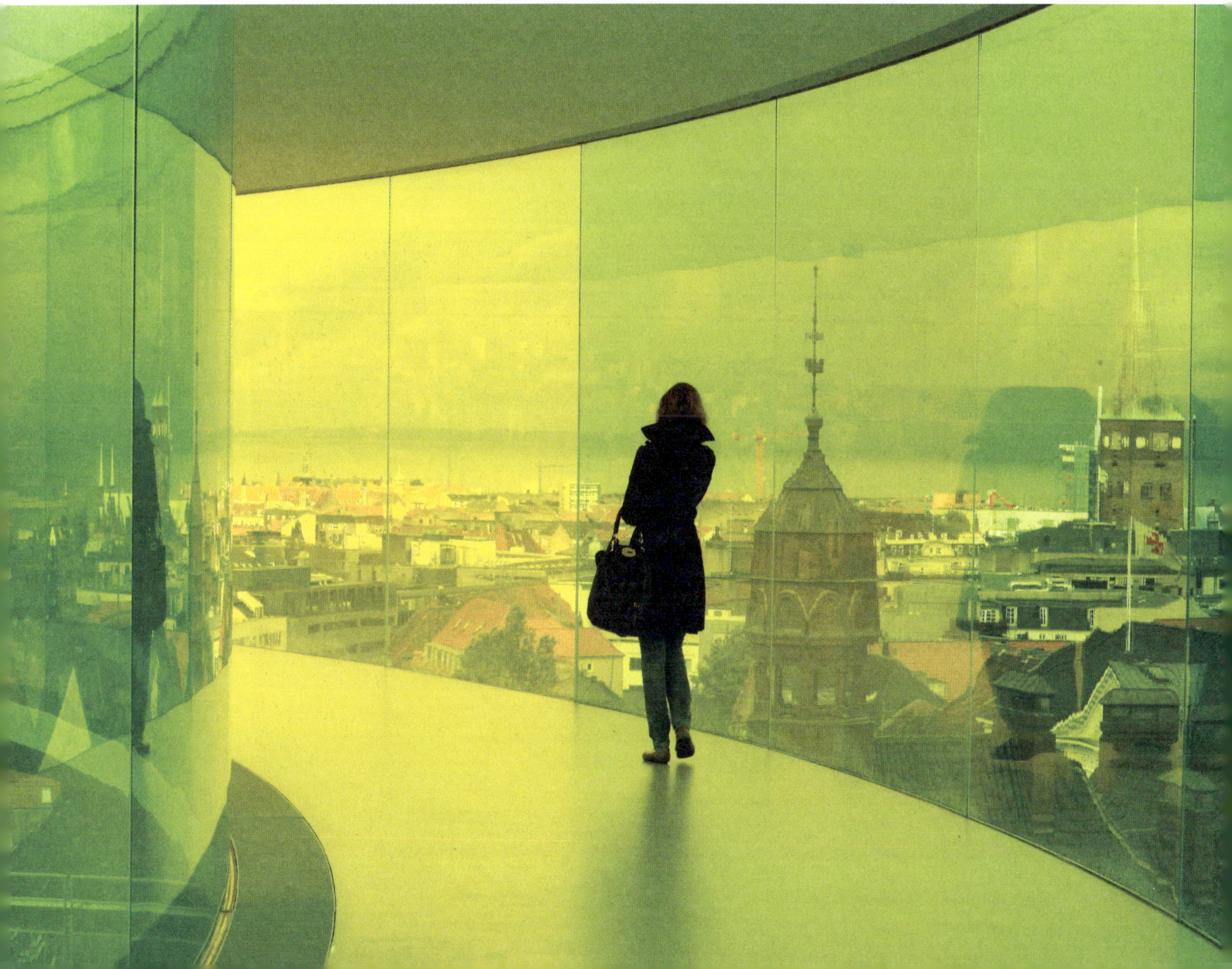

and to which you will soon return. You can't see the colours without being reminded of the ordinary, the everyday. Comparing what you imagined (seamless colour transitions, escape to the sky) with what you're actually experiencing, you might start to think about *why* it is that you desired this escape so much. Everyone will answer this in different ways, and since you can see other people in the panorama coming towards you or walking in the same direction, you might well start to wonder what they are thinking. This was Eliasson's 'self-evaluation' at work.

THE ARTIST AND THE WORLD

The title of Eliasson's blog for the 2016 World Economic Forum was 'Why art has the power to change the world'. The blog was written while Eliasson was working on several projects that spanned art and activism. These were not about national politics, nor the abuses of mega-companies, but addressed global crises: issues of energy poverty, climate change and migration. From 2012 three main projects developed, each one extending a strand of Eliasson's existing practice, but requiring new kinds of collaboration and skills: working with NGOs, lawyers, local politicians, and activist groups amongst others. Each was given a powerful two-word title: Little Sun, *Ice Watch*, and *Green light*. He effectively combined symbols (a green light for migrants; a watch ticking away) with eye-catching objects and scenarios. This concision helped publicise and extend the reach of each of these projects.

It was also during this period that Eliasson set up an art school in his studio, in collaboration with Berlin University of the Arts (UdK), which he called Institut für Raumexperimente (2009–14). Among the many distinguished visiting speakers with whom he engaged was Chantal Mouffe, who, sitting next to Eliasson in Berlin, asked 'How can artistic practices contribute to the creation of agonistic public space?'[23] Mouffe's idea was that for a more progressive society to emerge, what is needed are spaces for dissensus rather than

LITTLE SUN 2012 CHILDREN STUDYING IN ETHIOPIA

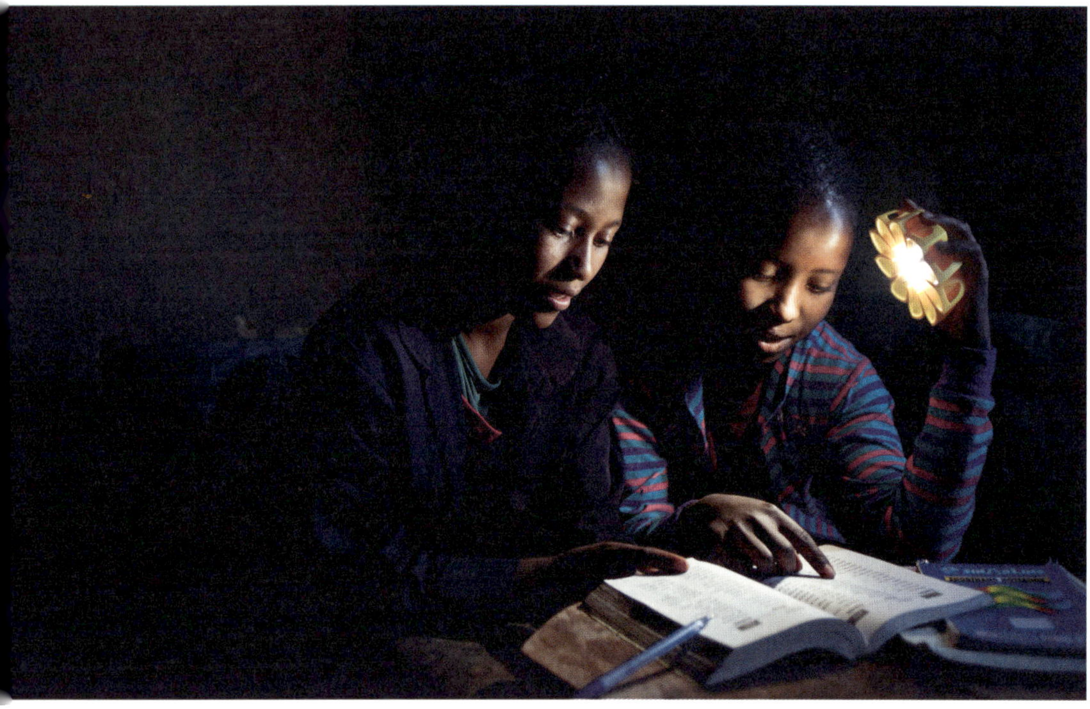

consensus. Eliasson was affected by this exchange and, using Mouffe's language, later stated: 'I'm very curious to what extent some artistic agendas foster the inclusion of disagreement or antagonism or the disagreeing person.'[24] In another context, he insisted that 'Viewing art is one of those rare moments where we can all come together from disparate backgrounds and share an experience – and we can also disagree and it's OK!'[25]

Eliasson's often-stated claim that art is most useful when it leads to productive disagreement is a good lens through which to view works like Little Sun, *Ice Watch* and *Green light*. I would argue that to assess them properly one has not only to think about the impact for those directly involved in them: a child using a Little Sun torch, for instance. One also needs to consider the works' broader reception – by, say, the person researching the entire Little Sun project and considering it as one among many social businesses addressing sustainability and clean energy. As we will see, Eliasson's projects generated intense debate in print and on social media, and this very debate seems to be a successful realisation of the ambitions that he and Mouffe articulated.

Little Sun was launched in 2012, its name signalling that it was the child not just of 'The Sun' at Tate Modern, but of all Eliasson's work with illumination going right back to 1990. Working with solar engineer Frederik Ottesen, he designed a solar-powered hand-held lamp that could be sold and used all around the world. The lamp's design was 'inspired by the Ethiopian meskel flower, a national symbol of positivity and beauty'.[26] In off-grid areas, most rural parts of Ethiopia for instance, it could have particularly important functions – making owners safer when walking outside after dark, enabling children to do homework, or simply illuminating a game or a family meal. A business model was conceived whereby Little Sun was sold in America and Europe for around three times its price in off-grid areas, the profits from the former subsidising the latter. Because it was being sold everywhere, it did not conform to a long-questioned charitable model of free handouts. Sales targets were set; Eliasson promoted Little Sun wherever he went, often wearing a lamp around his neck; media campaigns were launched, and events too, as when Eliasson worked with Tate to send visitors through the darkened spaces of the permanent collection galleries with Little Suns. Over half a million units have now been distributed to off-grid areas.

Eliasson first worked with ice in 1998 when he made a pavilion topped by a sprinkler that dripped only on freezing days, the resulting long icicles forming a kind of curtain, and when he showed his work *The very large ice step* in Paris. In 2006, in *Your waste of time*, he collected huge lumps of ice from the Vatnajökull glacier in Iceland, and set up a refrigeration environment in his Berlin gallery so they would remain stable as sculptural objects during the show. Spending time in Iceland from childhood onwards had made Eliasson particularly aware of how these glaciers were changing. He began a conversation with the Greenlandic geologist Minik Rosing about the impact of global warming on Greenland's glaciers. All this led to *Ice Watch*. The work was first realised in Copenhagen in 2014 to mark the publication of the UN's climate change report, and next in Paris in December 2015 to coincide with the UN Climate Conference COP21. For both installations, twelve blocks of ice that had fallen off the glaciers were harvested in the seas off Greenland, shipped in fishing containers to the city and installed in a prominent location in a circle – one block for each hour on a watch. As the blocks melted over some days, the clock arrangement sharpened the idea that time was running out to avert climate disasters. *Ice*

Watch came to London in the last days of 2018, supported by Bloomberg Philanthropies, and in connection to this show, twenty-four blocks of ice were arranged in a 'grove' outside Tate Modern.

Green light – An artistic workshop came about after Eliasson spent time in Vienna in 2015 preparing his show *Baroque Baroque* at The Winter Palace of Prince Eugene of Savoy. That summer, as he worked on the show for this opulent venue, thousands of migrants were arriving in central Europe having fled crises in Syria and Afghanistan, as well as from North Africa. With many Europeans anxious about the influx, and a resurgent right wing that was overtly hostile, Eliasson wanted to signal a green light to migration. Francesca von Habsburg, whose collection of Eliasson's works was central to *Baroque Baroque*, shared his concerns, and offered her foundation TBA21's space in the Augarten park for him to set up a workshop, produced by TBA21, in spring of 2016 where migrants would be welcomed.[27] They could come together to build lights made from balsa wood, recycled plastic connectors and green LEDs. The shape – determined by the connectors – derived from Eliasson's and Einar Thorsteinn's long research into geometry, and the lights were modular, so could be joined together in clusters. Under Austrian law the asylum seekers could not be paid, and participated as volunteers; however, they were offered meals, language lessons and other courses, and funds raised by the sale of the lights went to the Red Cross and Caritas, an organisation offering migrants free legal advice. People from Afghanistan, Syria, Nigeria, Tajikistan, Somalia and Iraq worked together, and the workshop was open to the public, so that Austrians could meet newcomers and even build the lights together. Short films were made and published online; individual refugees were able to tell their stories. The workshop closed after three months, but was restaged the following summer at the Venice Biennale, in the largest space in the Central Pavilion, as part of Christine Macel's show *Viva Arte Viva*. This time, most of the migrants had crossed into Europe from Africa. As they assembled the green lights, the Biennale opened and the international art world descended.

As I have already indicated, each of these three projects provoked as much enthusiasm and support as scepticism and criticism, but precisely this debate must be seen as part of their success. To start with Little Sun*:* many commentators have connected the use of sustainable solar power to the feeling of empowerment, recognising that Little Sun would give people more time and more independence; people would save money otherwise spent on petroleum lamps; there were health benefits from eliminating the use of kerosene. But when the first press releases referred to spirituality, some questioned whether Eliasson was imposing a European idea of the metaphysical power of light on the anticipated users of the lamp, no matter their different traditions. Others asked why he was producing the units in China rather than working with local designers and materials, and why he was not putting his efforts into creating infrastructural change instead of importing objects that were hard to recycle and repair, or indeed using his influence to support local projects such as Sanga Moses's Eco-fuel Africa.[28] The Little Sun website addressed many of these questions,[29] and in time, the language around the project shifted: references to spirituality dropped away, and its website foregrounded local collaborations. It continues to inspire vibrant discussions.

Some questioned the carbon footprint of *Ice Watch*, and all the other resources needed to haul ice from Greenland to European capitals (for its Paris and London iterations, Eliasson acknowledged the criticism and worked with Julie's Bicycle to publish the carbon footprint of *Ice Watch* and to offset it). Others were dubious about Eliasson's claim that giving people a sensory close-up encounter with ice that has only melted because of climate change would lastingly alter their behaviour in relation to energy use after they had posted their selfies amongst the mini-bergs; perhaps news stories and pictures of stranded polar bears were more effective in raising and changing consciousness. Eliasson had wanted to make tangible a crisis that for many was abstract and distant. But perhaps more importantly, having recognised that climate change was usually communicated through a discourse of impending catastrophe inspiring fear, he had wondered how instead to create an enjoyable experience that would trigger more positive emotions associated with the *gains* of caring for the environment. Outside Tate Modern, I saw people walking around the blocks, touching them or even pressing ears against their surfaces to hear cracks and tiny air bubbles popping. Thousands of people appeared to enjoy and be moved by the physical impact of the blocks. Some blocks were almost transparent, others opaque; many were a spectacular glowing blue. With St Paul's Cathedral in the background, *Ice Watch* was an extraordinary sight. After three weeks it was gone. The palpable enjoyment of the installation must have for some viewers heightened a concern with what is being lost today as a result of climate change.

GREEN LIGHT – AN ARTISTIC WORKSHOP 2016 VENICE BIENNALE 2017

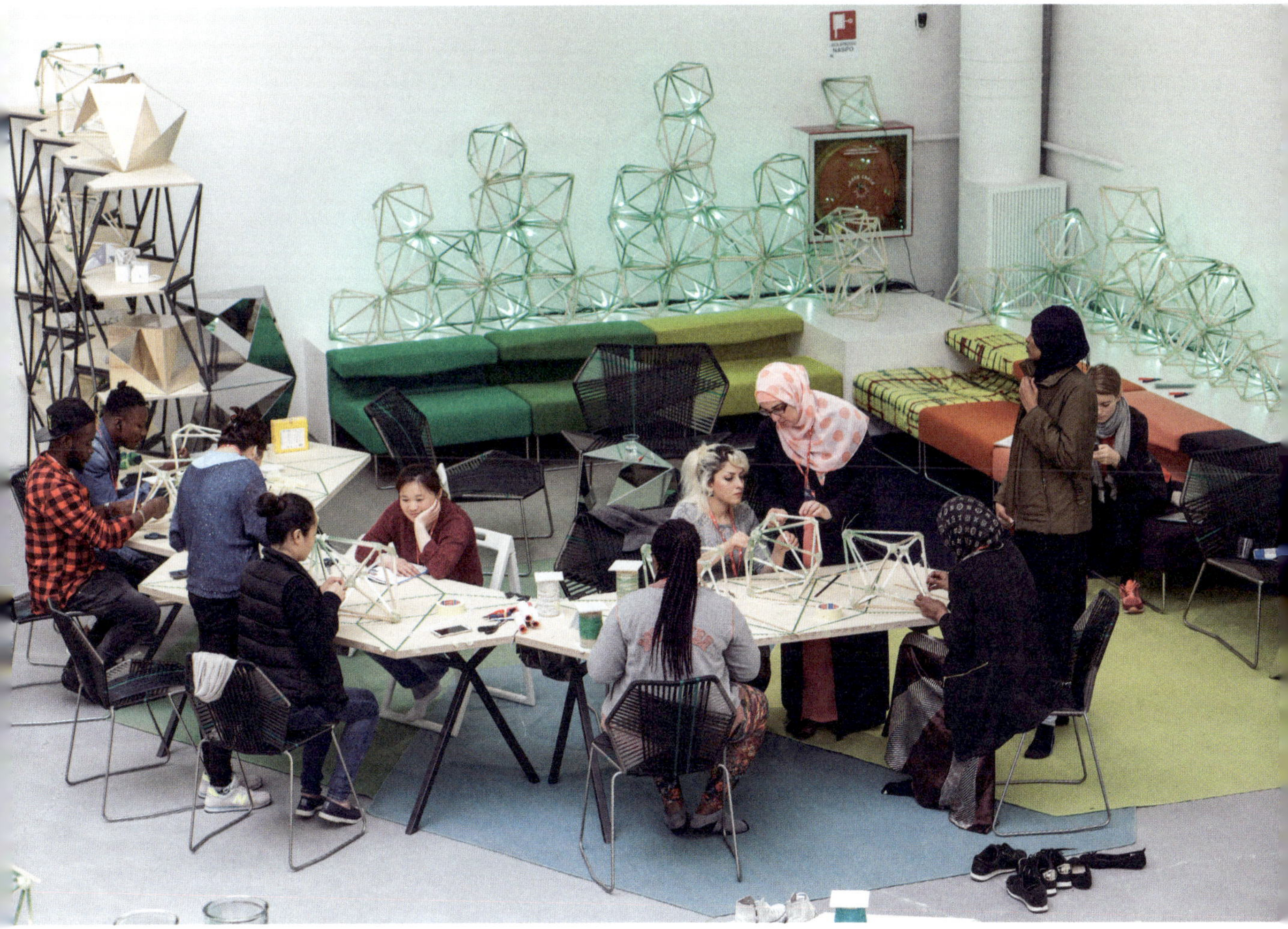

When *Green light* was launched in Vienna, many local residents came specifically to visit the workshop, to meet newcomers to their city and hear their stories. The work met with great praise. However, when it was restaged in Venice, the situation triggered more questions. Eliasson was trying to confront the Biennale audience with the realities of the world outside, but in the bustle of the opening it seemed to many that the migrants were on view as exhibits in what one critic called a 'human zoo'.[30] In Venice, few visitors arriving from abroad expected to walk into a room full of people building lights, and the conditions for conversation were not ideal. As a visitor I found it hard to understand why each migrant had been assigned the same task in the construction of the lamps, regardless of their individual skills, and what agency they had, if any, in the functioning of the project as a whole. (As later explained to me, each person in the workshop chose where they wanted to be stationed based on their skills and interests, and for how long – but this was not legible for most viewers.) Nor was it clear whether those running the workshop would continue to support these migrant workers once the Biennale closed. The *Art Newspaper*'s former editor Cristina Ruiz wrote, 'Everything about putting refugees on display as exhibits in an art show feels wrong to me',[31] but her colleague Javier Pes took time to speak to some migrants and learned from one that if he was not being hosted in the workshop, he would be 'hanging out at a railway station drinking or possibly selling drugs'. Pes concluded that this was 'a project designed and evolving to meet migrants' real needs and encourage conversations'.[32]

In general, art critics like those attending the opening events in Venice are more comfortable with artists addressing questions of inequality, climate change and migration on the level of documentary (for instance Ursula Biemann's epic film *Sahara Chronicle* 2006–9), allegory (Francis Alÿs's action and video installation *Don't Cross the Bridge Before You Get to the River* 2008, in which two lines of children on either side of the Straits of Gibraltar walk into the sea separating Africa and Europe carrying small boats fashioned from old

LUNCH AT THE KITCHEN OF STUDIO OLAFUR ELIASSON, BERLIN

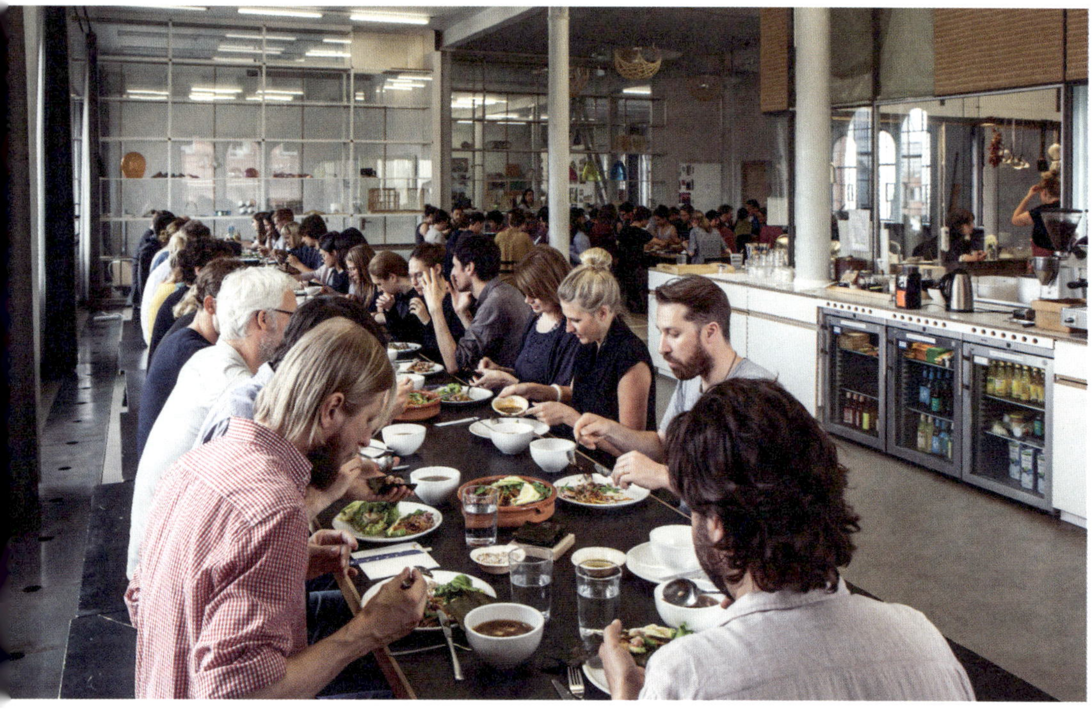

shoes) or with works that expose painful questions and contradictions, like Renzo Martens's film *Enjoy Poverty* 2008, in which the artist travels to the Congo to meet local photographers who make wedding pictures, and trains them to take and sell images of local poverty instead, thereby undercutting the work of foreign photojournalists (the subtext of the work is a critique of western approaches to representing and empowering Africans).[33]

It is not surprising, then, that there has been ambivalence towards Eliasson's projects; by comparison with these examples, they seem too earnest, embarrassingly direct, and even naïvely optimistic about art's capacity to change the world. In turn, Eliasson would likely be sceptical about the value of art that responds to world problems by ruminating on the impossibility of change, or fashioning critical representations of society's contradictory approaches to crises: he believes what is needed is action, and projects that raise awareness by communicating crises in imaginative ways. But he also believes in the importance of disagreement, and what I find so compelling about his projects is that beyond immediate action, each one has provoked the kind of disagreement he talked about with Chantal Mouffe. The disagreement is not so much about the main issues (is climate change a real danger? Should migrants be welcomed?) as the way they are being tackled. The debates about whether to invite migrants to make lights within the Venice Biennale are not so distant from the response to Martens's work. Precisely by provoking people to ask questions, Eliasson has prompted viewers to reconsider their own views and approaches to the causes he tackles, and this is a profoundly important contribution.

REALITY PROJECTOR 2018
MARCIANO ART FOUNDATION, LOS ANGELES

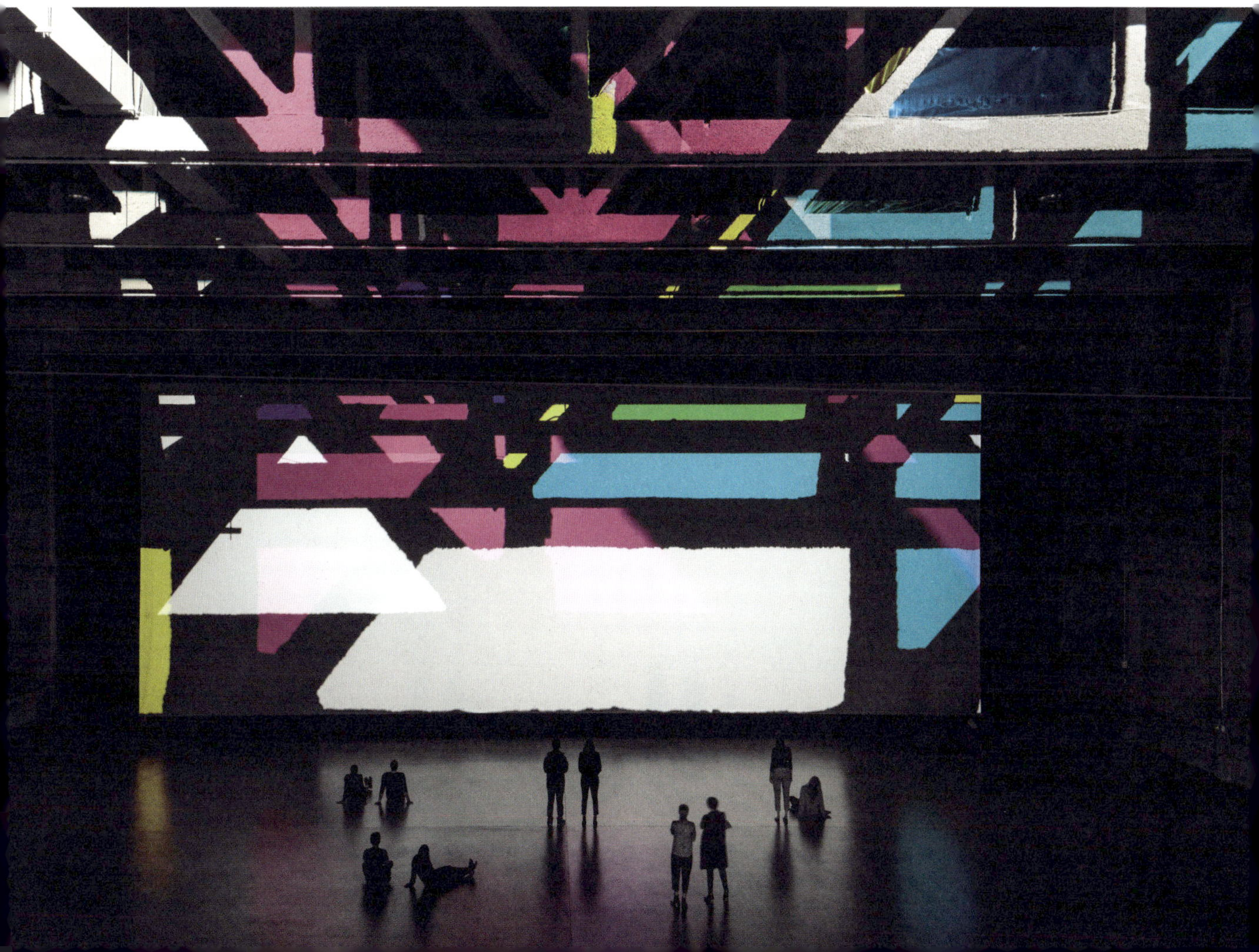

INTO THE FUTURE

Walking into Eliasson's studio in Berlin, one is struck by the range of activities and materials. People are using complex computer programmes to develop and visualise new exhibitions. Architects in a separate company, Studio Other Spaces, are working under Eliasson and Sebastian Behmann to conceive and design major architectural projects around the world. Others develop the website and online TV channel. In different workshops colleagues work with driftwood, paint, wool, bricks, sheets of coloured glass, lenses, lightbulbs, inks and glacial meltwater. Some pieces – such as the collections of glass globes with mirrored backs – look out of place because they are slightly impersonal, possibly because they are made with parts manufactured outside the studio and only assembled there. But if these works seem destined only for the market, you would find the same kind of thing in many other artists' studios, and in Eliasson's they are certainly balanced by modestly made intimate capsules of his thinking such as his *Compasses* (pp.204–5), which bring together driftwood, metal and objects found on Icelandic beaches. For the most part, production is very artisanal, even when it comes to assembling large works like the spheres made from folded metal, wire and small mirrored panels.

Away from the studio, Eliasson's recent large installations rely on a quality he has honed since his first works: a stark yet pleasurable contrast between the clarity of construction and the unpredictability of the experience. A good example is *Reality projector* (p.33), made in Los Angeles in 2018. Visiting the Marciano Foundation – a former Masonic temple – Eliasson was struck by the exposed beams in the ceiling and the irregular triangular and quadrilateral gaps between them. He installed coloured transparent filters in some of the gaps and set up lights on tracks to move behind the beams, pointing through the filters

SOLAR COMPRESSION 2016 CHÂTEAU DE VERSAILLES

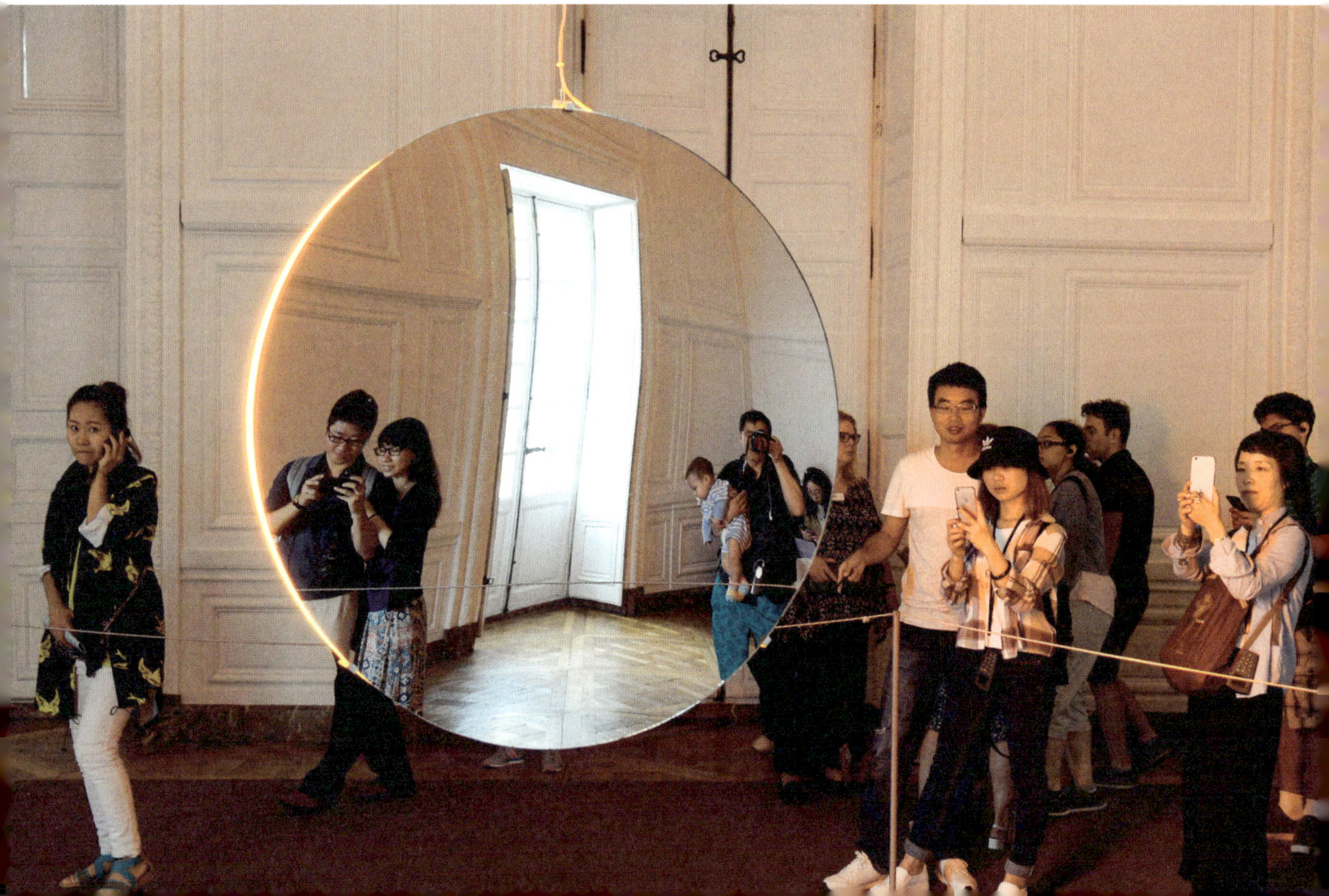

onto the massive back wall of the space to create an epic abstract film generated by the architecture. Narrative made way for the gradual movement of shadows and the slow overlapping of unpixellated colours.[34] By all accounts, many people watched for hours. That *Reality projector* was created right next to Hollywood is one aspect of its critical charge, but the work also suggests a kind of promise: that habits of experiencing space and time can be changed with minimal means.[35] Other recent works with complex polyhedrons carry a different kind of promise. *Your sound galaxy* 2012, shown at the Red Brick Art Museum in Beijing in 2018, for instance, is made up of twenty-seven hanging polyhedrons whose faces are the black backs of mirrors turned inwards. Each unit is a different combination of simple shapes – a cube combined with an octahedron, for instance – and the combinations get more complex as you go around the circle. Halogen lights in each unit shine through the gaps to create exquisite shadow play, but the geometrical progression is still legible. If Hollywood is a lens through which to consider *Reality projector*, one way to think about *Your sound galaxy* is to contrast its maths with the scarily powerful algorithms used by tech companies to track consumer behaviour. There is a kind of democracy to Eliasson's visible and physical maths, since anyone can understand and enjoy the increasing complexity of combination and form.

While Eliasson uses his oldest tools (coloured light, geometry) to create powerful new pieces in new conditions, the practice nonetheless faces steep challenges. Increasingly, his projects are staged in private institutions. They provide welcome opportunities (and indeed funds) to realise ambitious projects, which by now often are outside the remit of public funding. However, will they always be open to the more critical components of Eliasson's practice? And how easy is it to reconcile the artist's utopian rhetoric, the shrinking of

YOUR SOUND GALAXY 2012 RED BRICK ART MUSEUM, BEIJING

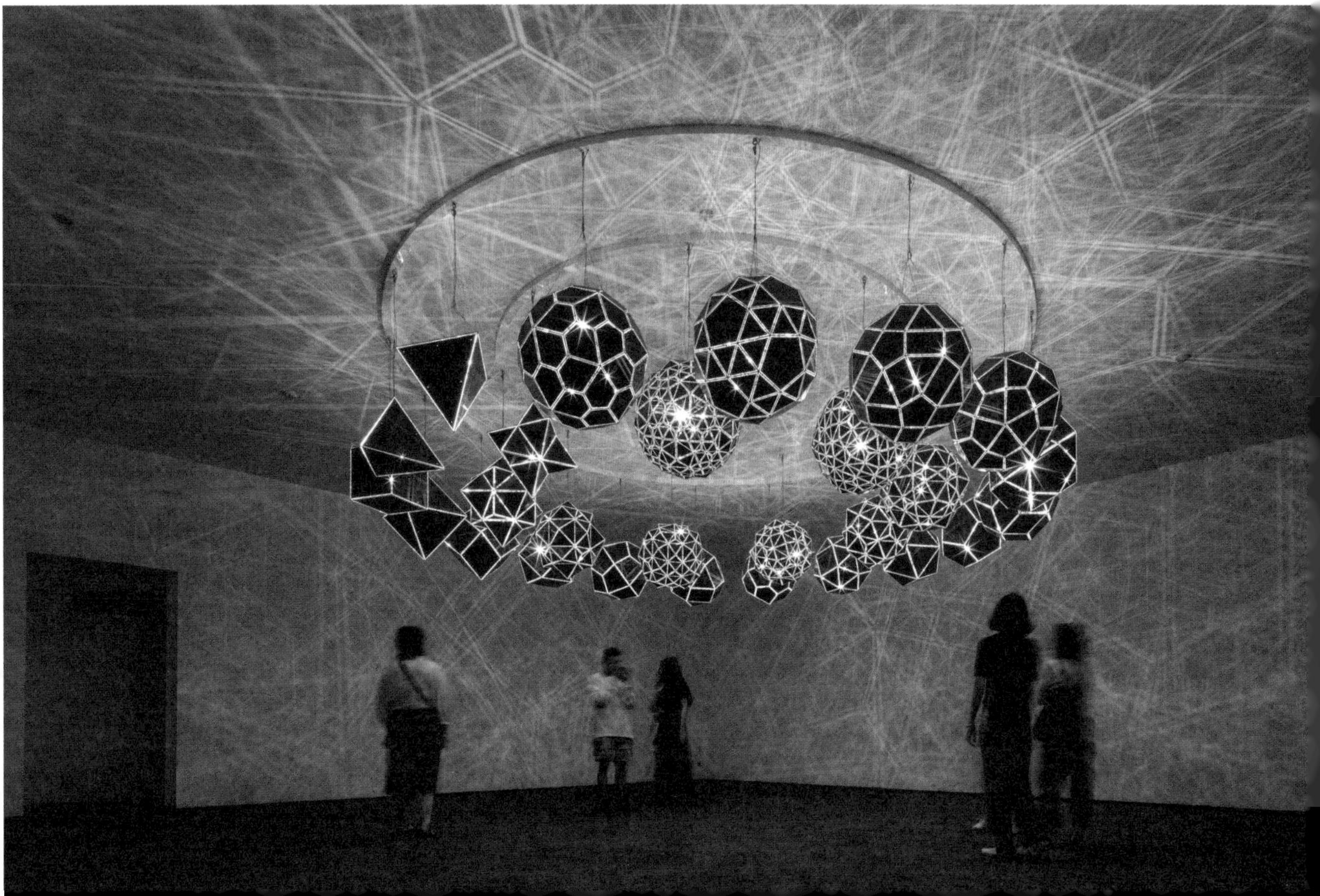

the public sphere, and the growing dominance of private interests? Other invitations have come from sites of mass tourism, such as the Château de Versailles, where around 20,000 people a day saw his work in the summer of 2016. Eliasson is one of the rare artists who is interested in communicating with audiences on this scale, but are the conditions at such sites ideal to ensure his ideas are legible and to allow viewers to fully appreciate his goals? When I visited Versailles, crowds stood around each of the installations, arms outstretched with smartphones. Viewers consumed each work with a click, or turned their backs to the art so it could provide a backdrop to their selfies. *Solar compression* (p.34) is made from two circular mirrors, each slightly convex, with a monofrequency light sandwiched in between. Suspended in the centre of the room, it rotates slowly, and alters as you move around it. But this motion, and the interplay of the surrounding architecture and its strange changing reflections, is reduced to flatness in a phone-photo. The smartphone might provide one of the greatest challenges to Eliasson at this moment, at least in regard to his installation work. Since he started exhibiting in 1990, it has changed how we perceive our environment, and so it necessarily changes what 'seeing yourself sensing' means. It has withered our attention spans too, posing a serious challenge to his invitation to 'Take your time'. Screens also change the experience of being in a space with other people, because we're with others in our social network at the same time, sharing, liking, tagging. What is 'we-ness' now?

These conditions show why theatre opportunities have been so important to Eliasson of late. I watched *Tree of Codes* at Sadler's Wells in 2016, sitting still with my phone off. Eliasson's vast mirrored discs rotated ever so slowly in front of the dancers, the lights changing from blue to pink in such a way that at times I did not know if they were coming from the space behind the discs or bouncing off them. The work was captivating, and the conditions to appreciate the interplay of his set and the choreography were perfect. But what happens back in the gallery, when we move around with our phones back on, sharing Eliasson's work on social media platforms? For sure, the studio has used social media very effectively in spreading knowledge of projects like *Ice Watch* and in outlining the conditions motivating it. But when it comes to his gallery art, the new conditions of perception, attention and social life brought about by phones create a new challenge: how to ensure that the embodied-experience-with-phone encounter remains critical and probing, so that instead of just snapping and sharing, visitors become interestingly self-reflexive about their phone use. Technology has altered subjectivity, and it will be interesting to see how, in this context, Eliasson reconfigures old ambitions or indeed develops new ones. (Of course, the question of phone use is certainly not one for Eliasson alone; it affects any artist interested in how their work is viewed. But it seems particularly relevant to Eliasson because his work has always been about how we perceive.)

You can find questions like these all through the spaces of Eliasson's Berlin studio. Among the models, between the desks, and on the way from workshops to the Kitchen, walls have turned into pin-boards covered with notes, quotes, pictures and articles. Papers cluster around sheets of typed questions, which might originate in a discussion launched by Eliasson or a conversation that a team is having without him. A cluster might emerge as people work and think together about an ongoing project; it might be sparked by the visit of an external speaker (there is an irregular programme of such talks). However the clusters begin, anyone can add to them, and there is no hierarchy in the way the

questions are asked. As well as a place of production, the studio is a place for questioning and self-questioning, an environment that Eliasson has carefully created and refined.
From this rather utopian hub, Eliasson and his teams think through the issues facing his work. Some questions pertain to the basic components of his sculptures, installations and buildings. How do different coloured lights affect attitudes and behaviours? How does one sensory input impact another? How do bodies move through spaces when architectural contours are curved or strangely angled rather than rectilinear? Other questions concern the locations in which his works will be presented. How can museums listen to their audiences? How can public spaces be maintained in increasingly privatised cities? But the most crucial questions, it seems, have much wider concerns. What is trust? How do we listen to people's needs? What is the difference between compassion and empathy? How does emotion lead to action? When might overload lead to passivity? How is hope to be created in conditions that seem to destroy it?
These are the matters Eliasson is considering today. Of course, most do not have simple solutions, but in 2019 we can say for sure that they are important and urgent questions to be asking. Sometimes one wonders whether Eliasson will find time away from all his projects to think through them, but we can be certain that success has not made him complacent, confident that he is as inquisitive as ever, and sure that he has established a network of people with whom to discuss these questions. That is clear from the conversations with scientists, economists, architects, dancers, musicians, artists, chefs, politicians, psychologists and activists that follow. We don't know what the next chapter of Eliasson's work will bring, but it will be informed by all the ideas discussed in this book.

TREE OF CODES 2015
MANCHESTER
INTERNATIONAL
FESTIVAL,
OPERA HOUSE,
MANCHESTER

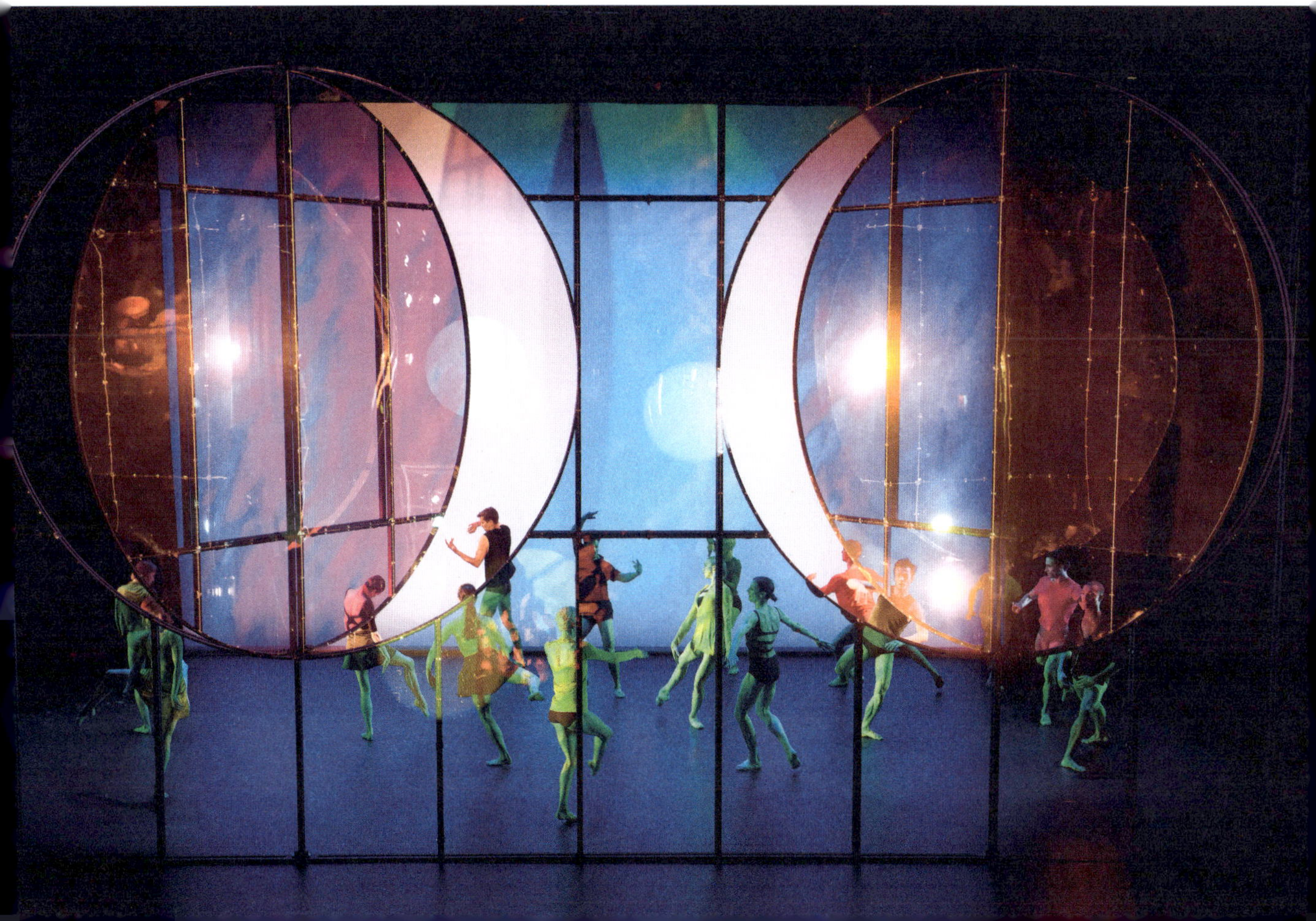

WINDOW PROJECTION 1990
> I GREW UP IN SOLITUDE AND SILENCE 1991

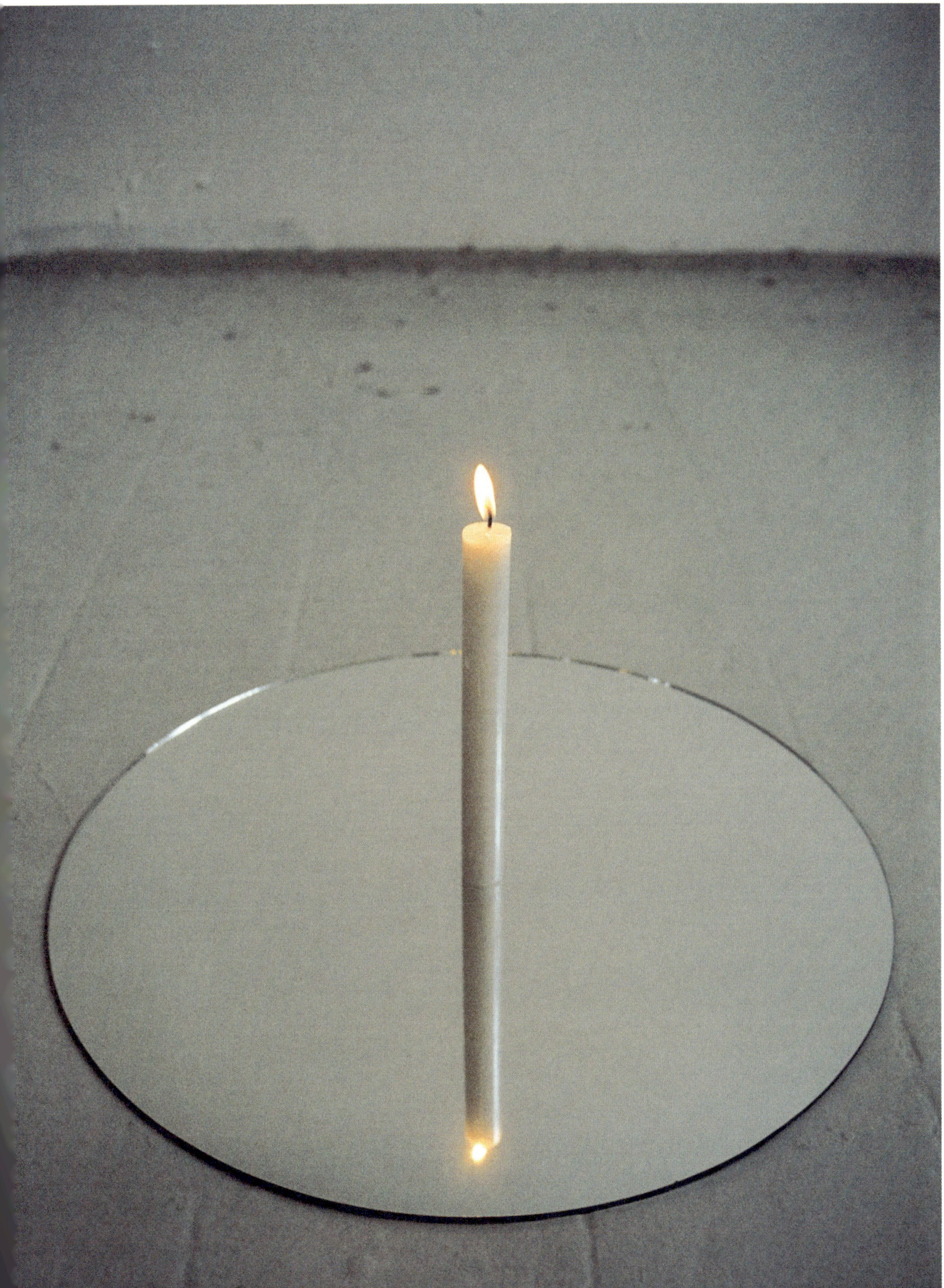

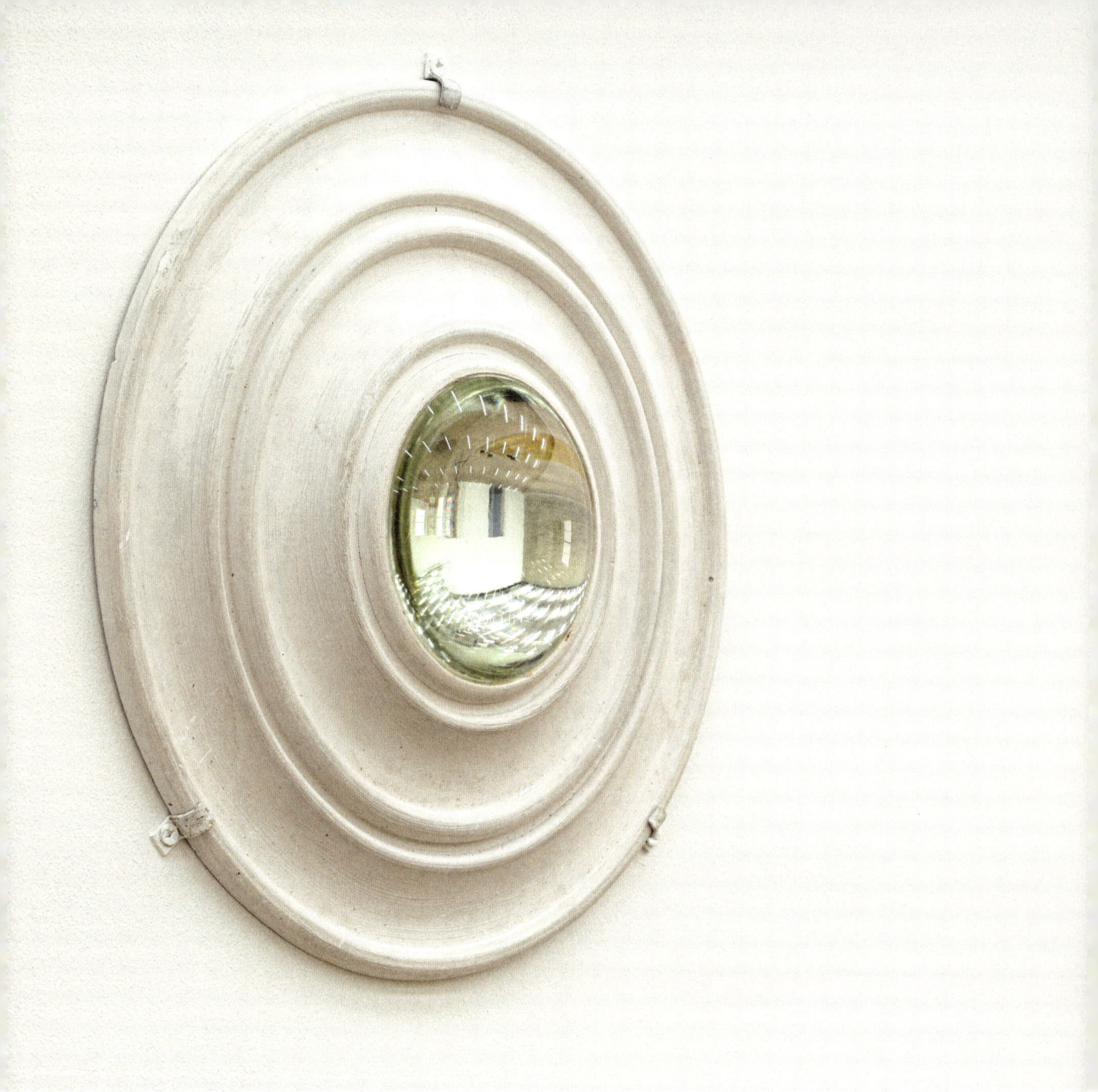

UNTITLED 1993

> WANNABE 1991
THE SEEING SPACE 2015

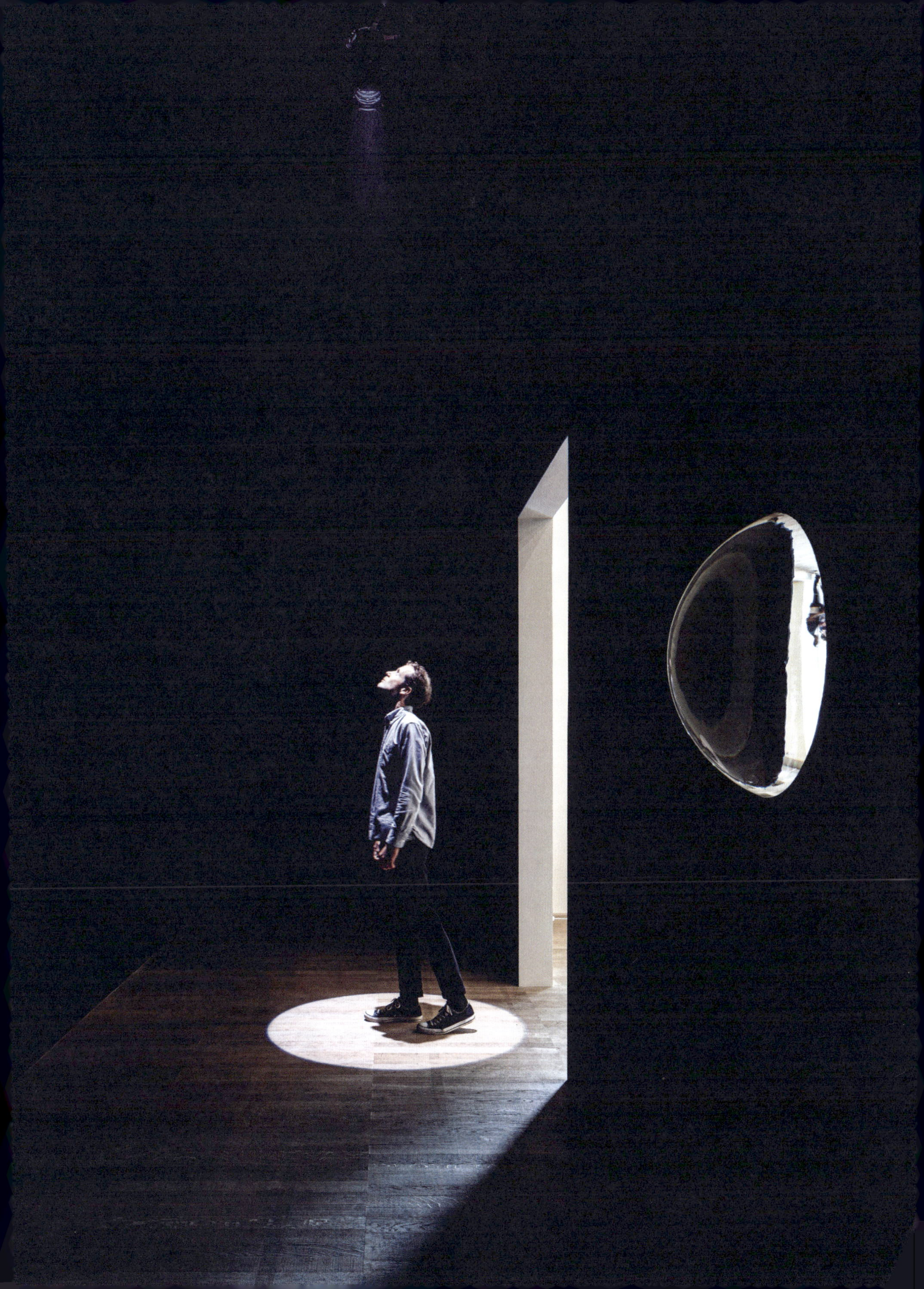

Olafur Eliasson: As you know, I work a lot with light in my artworks – with daylight, LED light and monofrequency light, and with how light is diffused, reflected and refracted. More recently I've also started working with sustainable light through my Little Sun solar lamp project. I've become increasingly interested in the seamlessness of what is normally divided into aesthetics and beauty, on one side, and medicine and biology on the other. One of the themes I'm pursuing in these interviews is that the boundary between nature and culture is constructed, it's not a given. The experience of light, for example, combines a set of biological elements with a set of cultural, interpretive elements. Would you start by quickly describing your field? Its name alone – chronobiology – is so intriguing.

Anna Wirz-Justice: Chronobiology is the science of biological time, of our daily rhythms – we call them circadian rhythms – and the seasonal rhythms that govern our behaviour and physiology. In the course of evolution, the changing pattern of day and night across the seasons has been a powerful signal. All living organisms have internalised these external, geophysical rhythms as a biological clock. From the smallest bacteria, fungi and plants to flies and fish and mammals, living things all have a remarkably similar set of 'clock genes' that generate an internal cycle of about twenty-four hours. The discovery of how clock genes tick and the ubiquity of circadian rhythms was recognised with a Nobel Prize, awarded to chronobiologists in 2017.

DAYLIGHT

ANNA WIRZ-JUSTICE is Professor Emerita at the Centre for Chronobiology at the University of Basel's Psychiatric Hospital and has conducted pioneering research into light therapy and the chronobiology of depressive illness. Eliasson met Wirz-Justice in 2016 at the Daylight Award ceremony at the Ny Carlsberg Glyptotek, Copenhagen. That same year, Wirz-Justice invited Eliasson to become a founding member of the Daylight Academy. The academy connects scientists, architects and other professionals, and promotes interdisciplinary and transdisciplinary thinking about daylight.

Right. I've become really interested in the effects light has on our health and on our everyday lives. How does this work?

The biological clock that drives our daily rhythms receives light input from the outside world via the eye and the optic nerves. We all know about the normal photoreceptors for vision in the retina – the rods, which allow us to see in the dark, and the cones, which allow us to see colours, shape, lines and movement during the day – but about fifteen years ago a novel type of photoreceptor was discovered in the eye, in a subset of the retinal ganglion cells, that contains a specific photo-pigment called melanopsin that is sensitive to light at blue wavelengths. What's really interesting is that there's a separate optic track leading from these cells directly to the biological clock – using light to provide non-visual information to the brain. Light has a surprisingly large number of effects that have nothing to do with our visual system – most importantly, acting as a synchronising agent to the circadian clock. Oddly enough, the circadian cycle diverges from twenty-four hours. In mice it's about twenty-three hours, and in humans it's longer than twenty-four hours. People often wonder why that is, and one putative explanation comes from oscillatory theory in physics – the biological clock can better synchronise to the external twenty-four-hour day if it has a slightly different periodicity.

That's really interesting. It even has existential dimension: we are always a little bit off, never quite synchronised, and that kind of keeps us going, keeps us on our toes.

You know, Olafur, I love your brain! So the clock requires this daily light signal to stay in sync. Every cell in the body contains clock genes that tick at their natural rhythm and need to be synchronised both with each other and with the outside world. You can imagine what a task that is and how easily it can go awry – as anyone knows who has experienced de-synchronisation of their sleep and appetite and other rhythms from jetlag or from working night shifts.

The synchronising effect of light is one thing, but light also has direct mood-enhancing effects, and can modify vigilance, cognition and performance. We're continually broadening our understanding of the importance of light in so many aspects of our daily life. The effect of light on our mental and physical health is enormous and wide-ranging; it includes sleep, mood and somatic well-being.

Doesn't cold light activate a more outgoing and alert mode, while warm light does the opposite?

Yes. Cold light contains a lot of blue – the wavelength that hits the biological clock – so it does make us more alert and awake. Warm light, light with more orange and red, is much more calming. That's a difference that we have to think about when we want to apply these basic principles to select lighting for different times of day or different situations or different people.

I actually applied this in Fjordenhus, the building I designed with my studio in Vejle in Denmark. The lighting at the centre of the offices is warmer than usual office lighting. We wanted to create a sort of 'campfire area' for working together. The light on the periphery of the circular offices, on the other hand, has more blue tones; here people go to sit by themselves. These zones between outside and campfire centre offer conditions for a feeling of alertness.

Biologically, we need a little push in the early morning to synchronise our clocks – the signal of dawn. For daily life, this means we need to spend half an hour outside in the early morning or have a lamp that simulates dawn beside our beds. So go to work by foot or bicycle and get your half an hour outdoors every morning, no matter what the weather! That will reset your clock. But also make sure that your night-time environment is dark. People forget about that. We talk about light all the time, but darkness is also important.

Do you think people have become more aware of light conditions? Do you see movement towards greater consciousness of light?

I do. The whole story began thirty years ago, when we used light therapy to treat seasonal depression. This treatment – the first non-drug treatment in psychiatry to be scientifically investigated – is based on what we know about day length being crucial to the seasonal rhythms of hibernation and reproduction in other mammals. The idea was to see whether people would get better if we simulated a summer day in the middle of winter. And it actually worked! Light therapy is now the established treatment of choice for winter depression, particularly prevalent in countries with long winters.

So people are aware of this clinical application, but they tend to overlook the implications for everyday life. Very few people realise the importance of having light of the right intensity at the right time of day. Light therapy studies have broadened to address all kinds of depression and sleep disturbances, and light is also being used to enhance well-being, vigilance and performance during the day in, for example, schools and offices.

You told me about how your research led to a rethinking of the illumination of neonatal floors in hospitals. When nurses had the lights on all the time, early-born children couldn't sync their biological clocks, which hindered their healing.

The light-dark cycle for early-borns, and indeed for all newborns, is an area where there's quite established research. Put the cradles near to windows to give them a dawn-dusk signal! Research also shows the importance of creating day-night signals in intensive care units, where you can't have a light-dark cycle because light is always needed. In these circumstances, where a cycle of light and dark is impossible, the trick is to have a cycle of white light and amber light, because amber blocks the blue wavelength that triggers our clock. The nurses and doctors can see what they're doing, but for the circadian clock it's 'night', which improves sleep and recovery. This is also an application suitable for retirement homes and for Alzheimer's patients: to make the night lights amber, not white or blue.

Yeah, I've set the phones of my kids to go amber at six or seven o'clock at night, to disrupt the obsessive relationship they have with their phones, which keep them awake at night.

That's good! When you ask how we can apply this knowledge to improve our well-being, ask a few simple questions about your lifestyle. Do you sit at the computer all day? Do you work in the evening, or use your iPad or phone late at night? Most computer screens are blue, which directly affects the circadian system and keeps you alert, pushing back your readiness for sleep and leading to insomnia. So set the screen to become amber at night. If it's dark when you get up to go to work, you want to have good lighting and perhaps even a lightbox for the morning wake-up effect. And go outside on your lunch break, even in Reykjavik in midwinter – get that half-hour of real daylight!

How much interest have you seen in this from architects or urban planners over the last ten or twenty years, as this science has become more accessible?
Chronobiology is only slowly infiltrating architectural practice, but the discovery of the non-visual, blue-sensitive photoreceptors has already transformed the lighting industry. There are now lamps with different colour temperatures for different functions. There are LEDs programmed to mimic outdoor daylight via dynamic changes in colour tone across the day. And the organisations that determine official international lighting standards have begun to incorporate effects on circadian rhythms into their guidelines, which until now were focused exclusively on visual comfort. So the importance of the non-visual aspects of light has really been recognised.
There are so many potential applications of this knowledge – not just functional applications but also implications for our definition of aesthetics and our understanding of human and animal well-being. There are implications for the idea of a good life. Do you think people are starting to use light in a more sophisticated way? One reason I'm interested in making people conscious of light – in making our relationship to light more explicit – is because our relationship with the climate is essentially about light. I'm thinking about how our relationship with light could introduce a more direct relationship with challenges like climate change.
The importance of our 'biological' connection with light certainly needs to be more widely recognised. You're a member of the recently formed Daylight Academy – a broad group of eco-scientists, botanists, chronobiologists, urbanists, physicists and artists who are interested in this question. We don't have the answers yet, but more interdisciplinary research will certainly lead to developments in architecture and urban planning that incorporate concern for the climate and provide a natural way of living.
It's my experience that when you start to understand the impact light has on you, you also start to realise the impact that you can have on the light in your surroundings and, through that, on the world. My focus is not just on understanding your field of knowledge, it's also about what my understanding of this does to my understanding of the world. This connects to our discussions about embarking on a collective artistic agenda together and potentially making a work of art.
Yes! I would love to transfer this knowledge about daily biological rhythms into an installation or an intervention where it could be physically and emotionally experienced. In terms of circadian rhythms, we're talking about light signals in nature. The really important signal is twilight – dawn and dusk; I think that's what we want people to experience.
August 2018

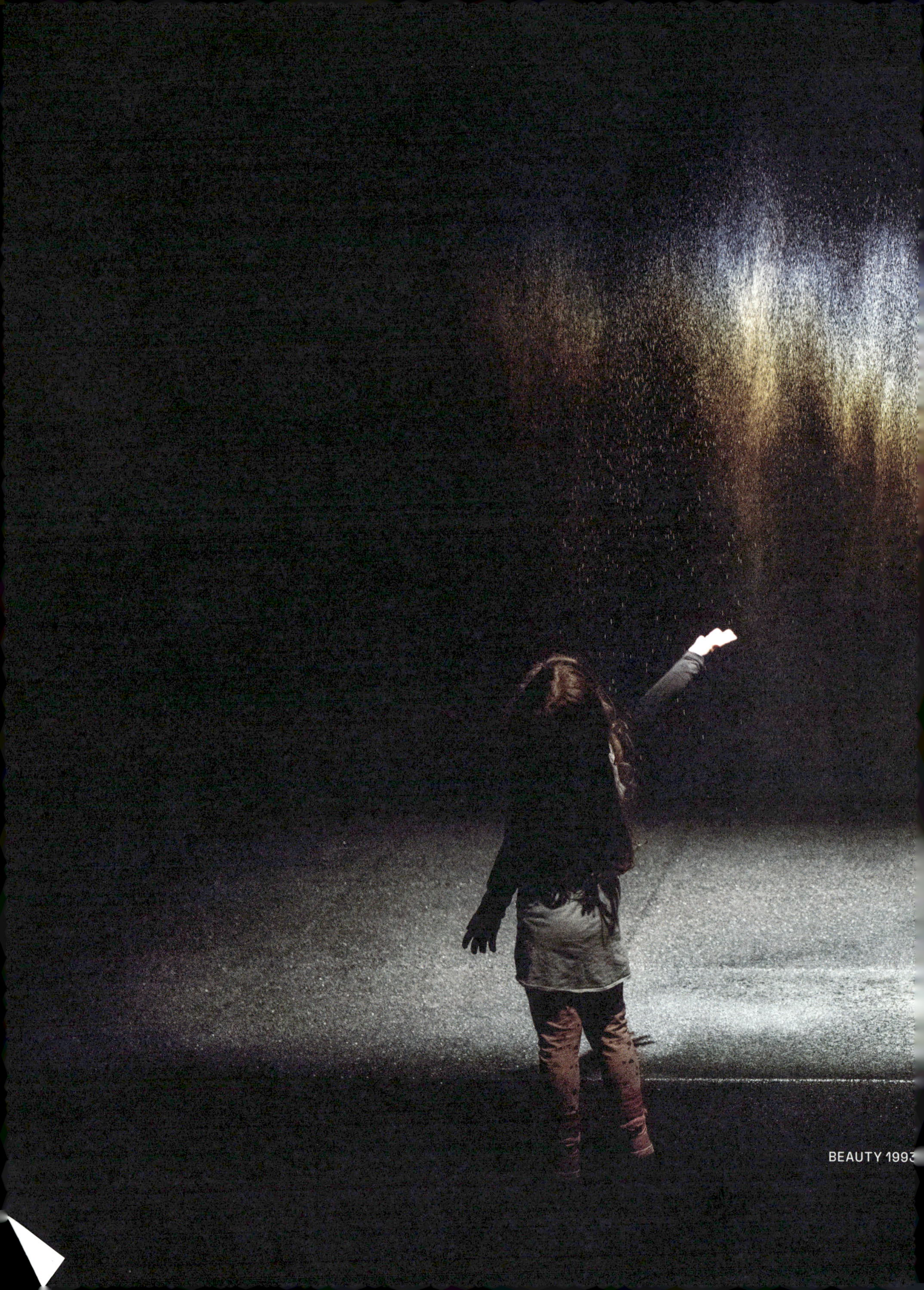

BEAUTY 1993

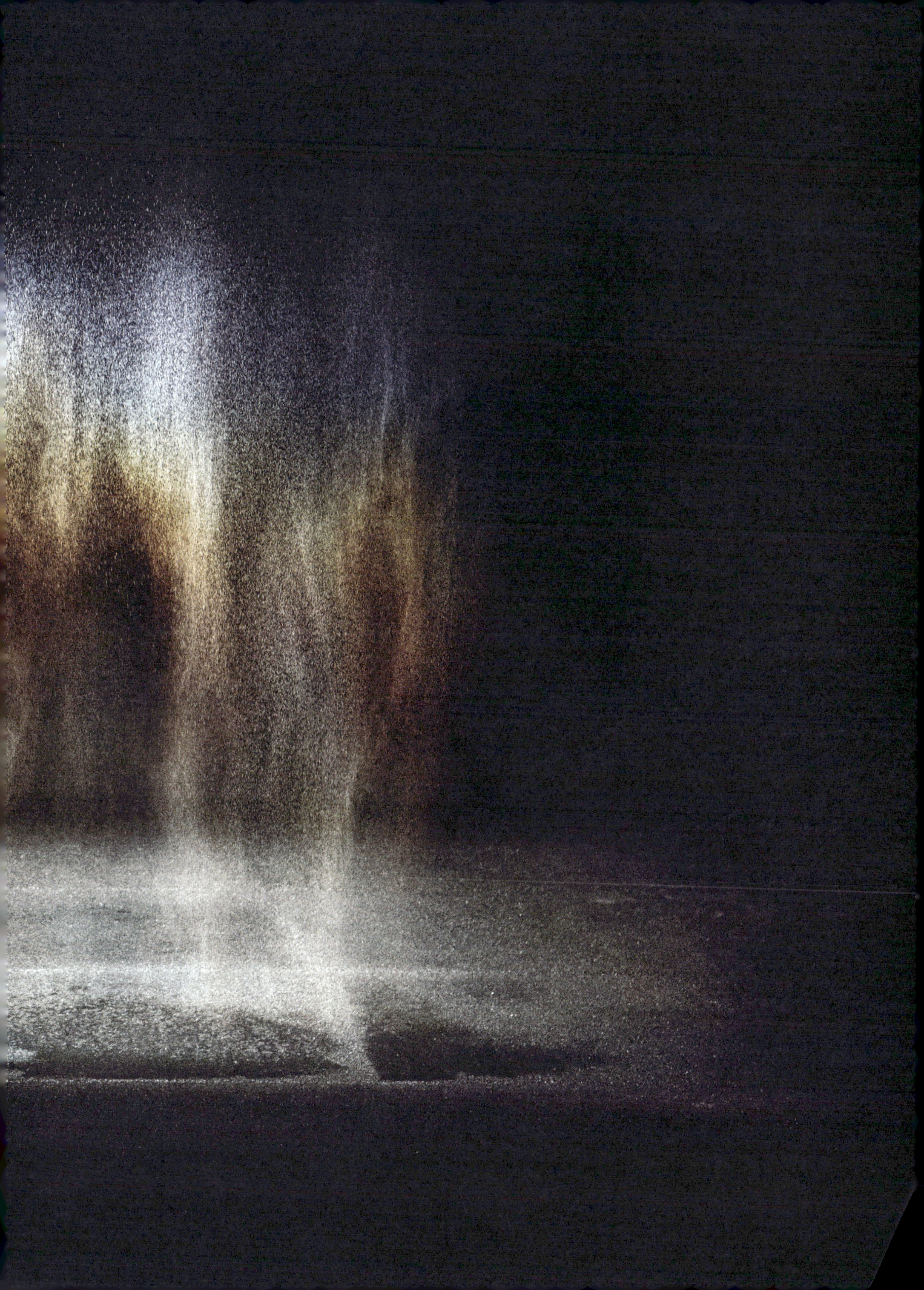

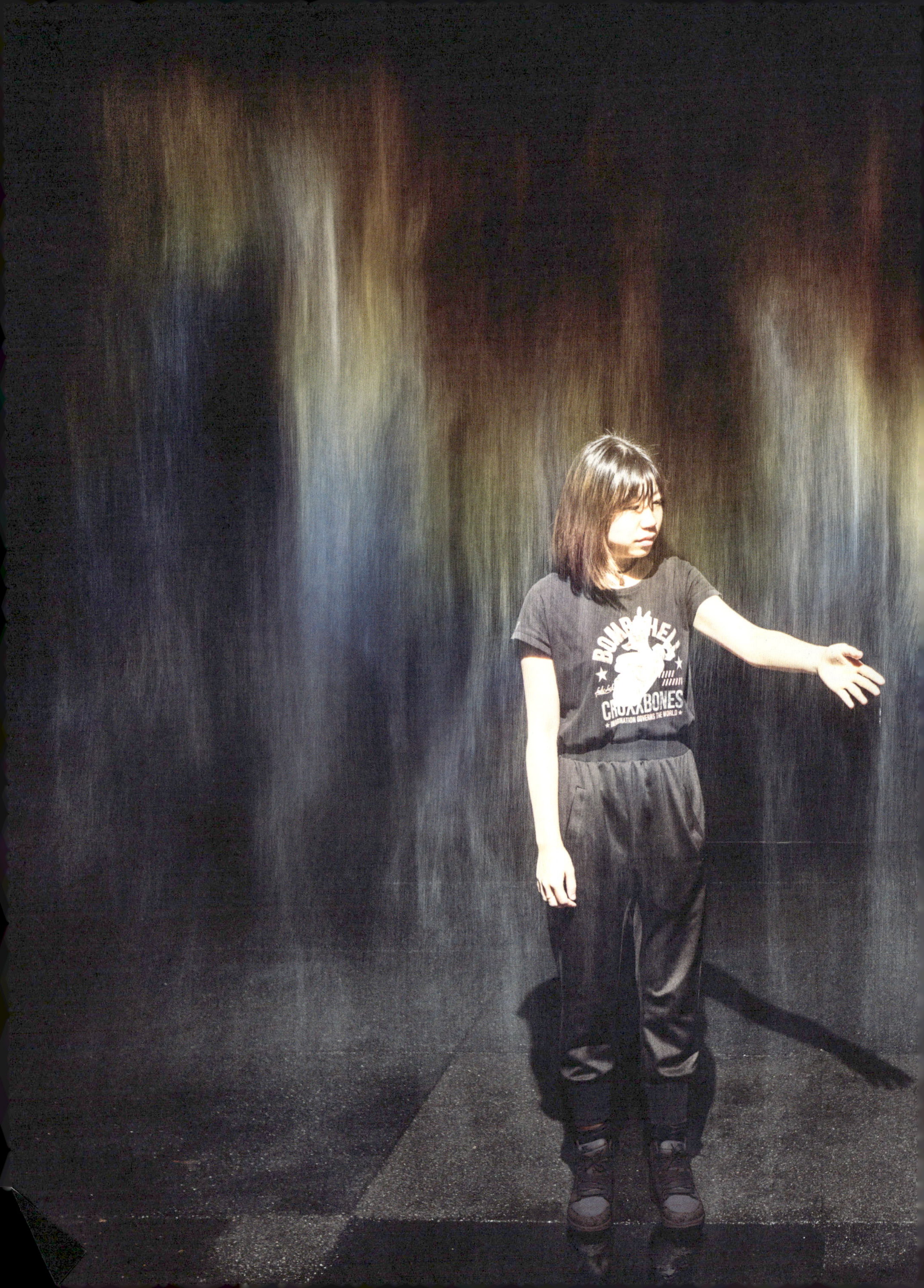
CROXXBONES
IMAGINATION GOVERNS THE WORLD

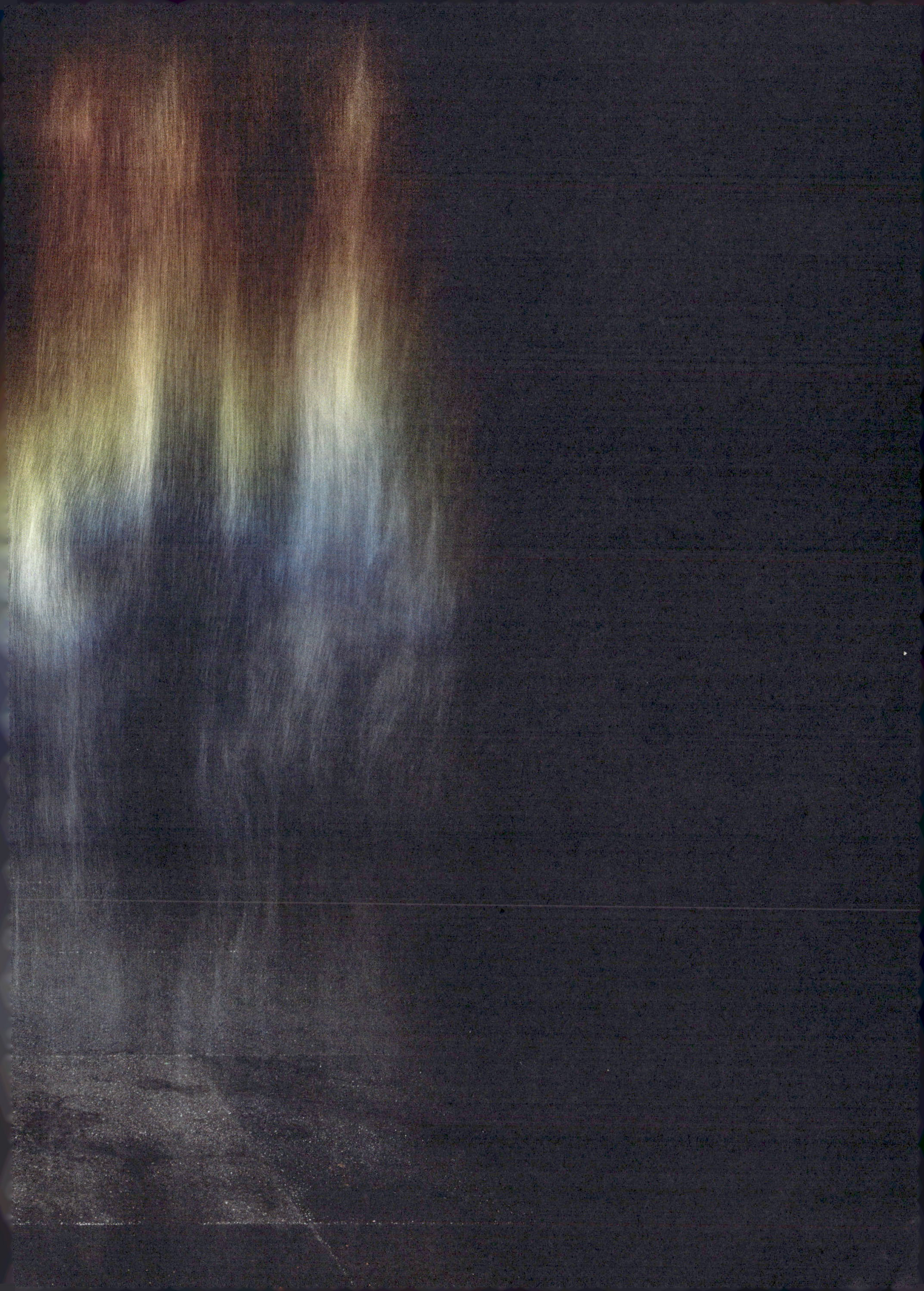

Olafur Eliasson: I know you're very busy, René, so apologies for pushing you even harder.

René Redzepi: No problem. This year has been crazy. We're actually planting cabbage right now: five hundred heads of biodynamic cabbage, which will supposedly be enough to last us through the winter. Right now, an uncultivated bit of land here in front of the restaurant is being transformed into a cabbage patch.

Are you and your team buying the cabbage as plants or as seeds?

As plants. We ordered them in advance from Svanholm [a community 60 km from Copenhagen that has long pioneered organic farming in Denmark]. Some of the cabbages are already half a metre tall – like some of the Brussels sprouts and the kale.

But how do you protect the cabbage in winter?

They don't die because they've been bred for our climate. That's what's so beautiful about cabbage. You can walk outside with a hammer and a chisel when it's twenty degrees below zero and chop off a piece of kale or cabbage. You can set it on the kitchen counter, let it thaw and it's ready to be boiled. The same goes for Brussels sprouts. They keep beautifully. It's crazy. Plus, they're going to be beautiful in the first frost, under sparking crystals of ice.

Congratulations on reinventing Noma, by the way [the restaurant re-opened in February 2018 in a new location]. I had a chance to sample the menu during your first two seasons. What will you focus on in the third?

This autumn, we're heading out to the forest. As of now, we've ordered five thousand reindeer brains from a Sami tribe up in northern Norway that we've visited a few times. We've also ordered reindeer tongue, sweetbreads and marrow. And we've been fermenting squirrels – a thousand of them.

Squirrels? You mean the ordinary squirrel, with the tail?

Yes, real squirrels. Fermenting squirrel results in a potent brine that tastes insanely good. There are also pheasants and wild duck. Just today, a thousand wild duck were delivered. It's going to take fifty people an entire week to pluck them down to the last

TASTE TO THE LIMIT

RENÉ REDZEPI is a Danish chef and the co-owner of Noma, the celebrated Copenhagen restaurant. Redzepi first visited Eliasson's Berlin studio in 2007, when he prepared an experimental lunch for the symposium 'Life in Space'. He founded the non-profit MAD (Danish for 'food'), which, among other things, organises the annual MAD symposium and VILD MAD, an educational programme on food for young people, with a focus on foraging. Redzepi also established a fermentation laboratory, and recently re-opened Noma at a new location in Copenhagen, turning his focus to the region's three distinct seasons – the restaurant's menu changes to match the ingredients that are at their peak at any given time of year.

feather. Every muscular part of the duck will be carved into individual morsels and prepared for a serving that will extend over six duck courses. You'll be able to taste different parts of this particular example of game. Then there are the mushrooms! We've already pickled and preserved eight hundred of them. They've simply exploded over the past three weeks [of September]. We've also dried and cured fourteen thousand plums, which we'll have with us all the way through next spring.

David Zilber heads your fermentation lab, right?

Yes.

I think he's really brilliant. I've been to Korea a few times, so I have been introduced to fermentation – more through coercion than by choice, I admit. But David took it to a whole new level for me. Of course by the time this interview appears in print, everything we've been speaking about will have been eaten. Zooming out to a longer view, I hear you describing how you and your team collaborate intensively with those who supply and deliver the goods – how you work with an enormous team and balance incredible logistics, including how to source, handle and store. Certainly it's not just a question of standing there and making food – or eating it. There is a tremendous preliminary effort, with a lot of ethical and aesthetic decisions involved. I would really like to delve into our senses. I feel you're searching for the boundary of our sensory faculties – trying to reach something out there on the other side, not just something I've never tasted before but something that I cannot even place. How do you approach the flavours that lie beyond the familiar?

We actually talk about this a lot. Often, while we're creating something, we think to ourselves, 'Now, we've hit upon something that's brand new.' Then we let it settle a bit, and when we taste it again we think, 'Hey, wait, it's all too early for this.' We've got a team of ten people who've been experimenting intensively for ten to fifteen years. They've travelled all over the world, tasting everything, diving down into everything. They're completely fearless. Clearly, our take on good flavour and on what we find dull differs radically from the opinions of the 'I-eat-pretty-much-the-same-thing-every-day' people – people who have maybe been eating ten or fifteen or twenty different things throughout their whole lives. So we are always trying to take things right up to the limit, but then we often turn down the volume. In a few instances you really can try to drive it all the way out there, but otherwise, you've got to take people by the hand a little bit. It won't work if they push aside their plates and say, 'This, I just can't understand – not this.' And there are also many who feel provoked.

You might say that it's 'out there' when the sensory faculties are actually being put to a test, when you're not entirely sure of whether the experience of tasting something is happening in the mouth, for example, or in the tip of the nose or all the way up in the nasal cavity. Where, you might ask, is the faculty of taste situated? I know that you and your team take quite an extreme approach to all this, and I find that extra fascinating.

For us, the very best we can achieve is for people to really forget about time and just grasp that they are right here, right now. They're eating this food; this is how this particular moment tastes – this is how it is. I see this as one of the most powerful achievements. And for it to happen, you really have to have your sense faculties in tip-top shape. Something has to click. It may be a single dish, where you suddenly zoom in, and you somehow sprout roots.

It's like experiencing a work of art. You feel a connectedness to where you are but also a sense of connectedness to where you came from and maybe all the way forward to where you're headed. It's a sensation of *presence*. You could call it a kind of sense of place, but it's something we often happen to forget.

Let's consider for a moment the 'here' part of the 'here and now' equation. You and your crew have this fantastic architectonic solution, based on an utterly exceptional interior design philosophy. Visiting your restaurant is a 360-degree experience. Do you think that a side project or a side kitchen might emerge with some kind of even more intense space?

We've thought of putting a small table inside our test kitchen so that, once a month, all the experiments could be presented full throttle. That would give us a small group of people on whom we could really test out all the things.

Our fall menu will include a piece of toffee made with duck fat instead of butter. It's a dessert in the form of duck feet, which we just think is funny. But when we served it the other day to four people who were trying out the coming menu, they were completely shocked and could barely bring themselves to eat it. Right then and there we thought, 'Okay, we're damn well going to need to have some kind of forum for getting people to taste so they really can say what they think.' We also have another dish with wild duck where we poke a hole in the cranium, with the result that the brain actually swells out as it is being cooked and it's eaten with a very small spoon. That also shocked our tasters.

I can imagine that! Have you thought about using the rituals surrounding the food to maybe prepare people a bit more for what's in store? Talking about this brings to mind that, on my most recent visit to your restaurant, the menu was one hundred per cent vegetarian. For this reason, it's extra trippy to hear you speaking about these adventures with meat ...

It's also a bit trippy for us! After working just with vegetables, herbs and plants for five months, it's truly a dramatic experience to suddenly find yourself chopping off animal heads. Blood flows onto the chopping board, where only three weeks ago there were chlorophyll stains. Now I'm seeing thousands of ducks – thousands of dead animals – being hung up. You'd better believe that it's quite different from having thousands of artichokes in the kitchen.

But don't you think that we're moving towards vegetarianism?

Yes, I do believe that. Absolutely. It's going to take time. People are going to have to learn to make food all over again and really taste things. But there's no doubt about it: the plant kingdom is a treasure chest without equal. There's simply so much diversity and so much flavour, and so many textures that we don't yet fully understand. When most people have twenty different kinds of leaves in front of them, they just see a large salad, right? They cannot imagine that five different dishes could be made from these leaves. If we eat more greens, we'll be making ourselves healthier, and, by all accounts, this is also going to make our planet happier. But we won't be dropping meat completely at the restaurant.

You've always been extremely interested in ecology and have come into contact, through this, with climate issues. You've spoken about the need for a healthy and synergistic relation between the act of making food and protecting the climate.

Of course, this is the future for all of us. If we fail to cultivate a healthy relationship with what we're making, then we're making a tremendous mistake. Ecological concerns are going to be the driving force of the future. They will determine how we choose our clothing, how we choose what to eat, everything.

Are you thinking about conveying this utterly fundamental knowledge and expertise on how food relates to ecology to a larger group of people? Because your restaurant is also a little elitist – it's radical, it takes people to the edge of their senses, it's almost impossible to get a table there.

Sure, we're thinking about this a lot. Last year we created and launched a foraging food app called *Vild Mad* [Wild Food – 'mad' is Danish for food], and we had twenty thousand people attending Vild Mad workshops last year, including schoolchildren. It is a part of our DNA to get out into nature. This is how everything started for us: getting in touch with the seasons, getting in touch with what kind of food is growing and getting in touch with how things taste. This has been such a powerful influence, not only on our creativity but also on the way we've organised and furnished the restaurant – on our whole philosophy of life. Moreover, simply by virtue of getting out into nature, you also feel the urge to take better care of it. This comes as a completely natural impulse. Learning to understand it makes us feel connected to it.

It is shocking to see how far people are from the reality of nature. It would be so good to get people to open their doors, take a breath and notice that the temperature has fallen, and, instead of just getting annoyed or morose about the onset of autumn, they could say, 'Ah, now the such-and-such mushrooms will be on their way up,' or 'Hey, who knows how the plums will be this year?' One of the most powerful things we can accomplish as a restaurant right now is to push people out into nature.

That holistic view inspires me. We have both a responsibility to dive down into our specialisations and to anchor ourselves in society on a broader scale.

There's one more thing that I wanted to ask you about: namely, about the number of women who are chefs. As you know, my sister Victoria [Eliasdóttir] is a chef, and I credit her with having made me more aware of the issues women still face in the culinary world. What are your thoughts on this?

The restaurant world has historically been male-dominated – and by a rather boastful group of men at that. The atmosphere has been very extreme and domineering for a long time. It's scary to come along as the only woman and join a team of sixteen or so men. But this is in the process of changing. There's a social movement going on all over the world, and I believe Noma must be cutting edge on this front. Today, we think in a completely different way about how we recruit. We carefully examine the mood among the chefs in the kitchen. As you know, we are aiming to set up an academy for 'food leaders' where we will try to radically change our whole culinary sector from within. The MAD academy will be a permanent space dedicated to pursuing the ideas and aspirations born out of our annual MAD symposia. We want to consider and disseminate all these sensitive, humanistic and holistic values. But at the same time, one also has to be creative and daring, and has to be able to understand and work within a capitalist world. The MAD academy's vision is to play a part in changing the culinary sector by suggesting new forms of leadership.

I'm very excited to be following along. I may have a couple of ideas in connection with this. But ... René, you've got to finish planting your cabbages. Thanks a lot for your time.

Don't mention it.

September 2018

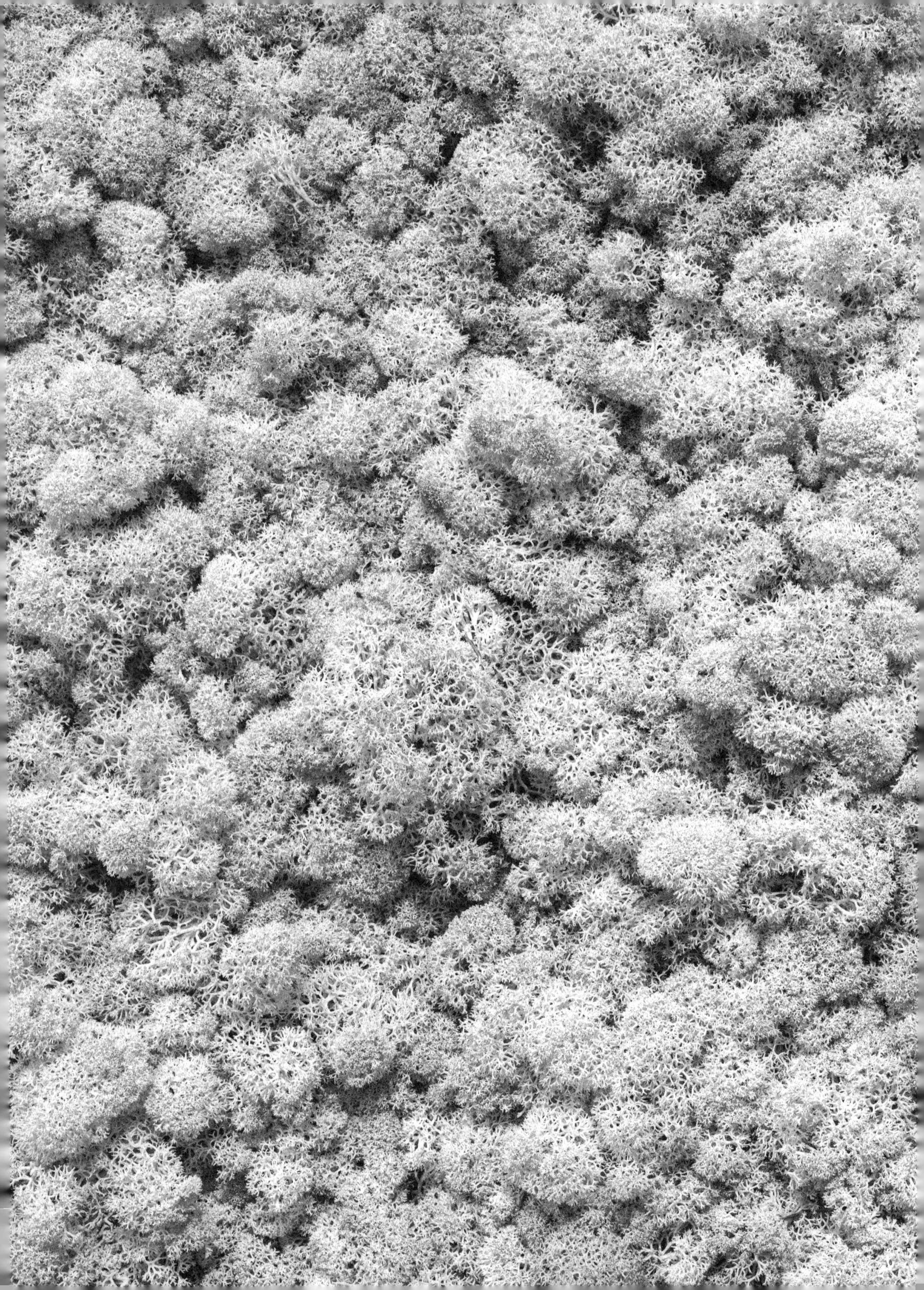

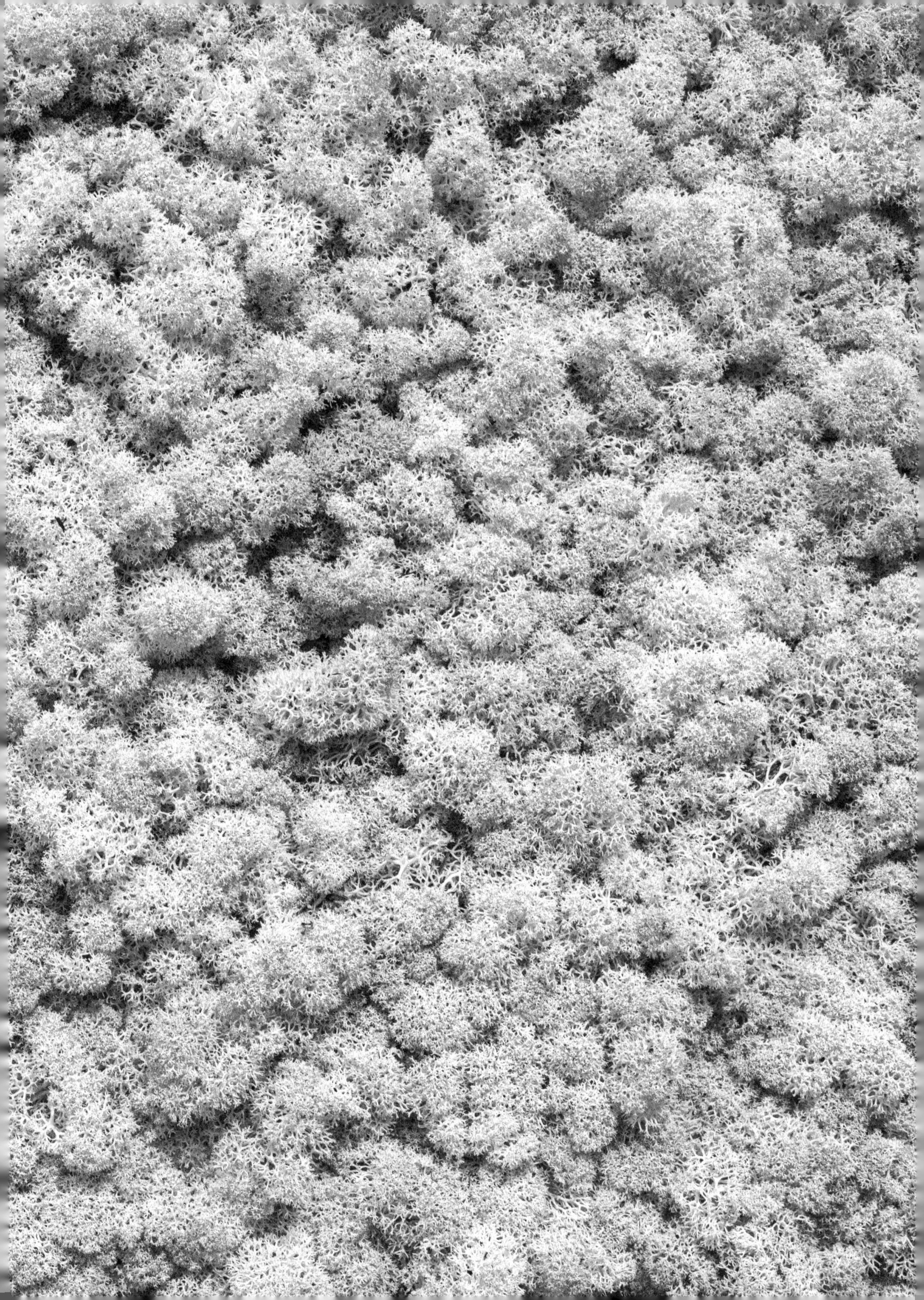

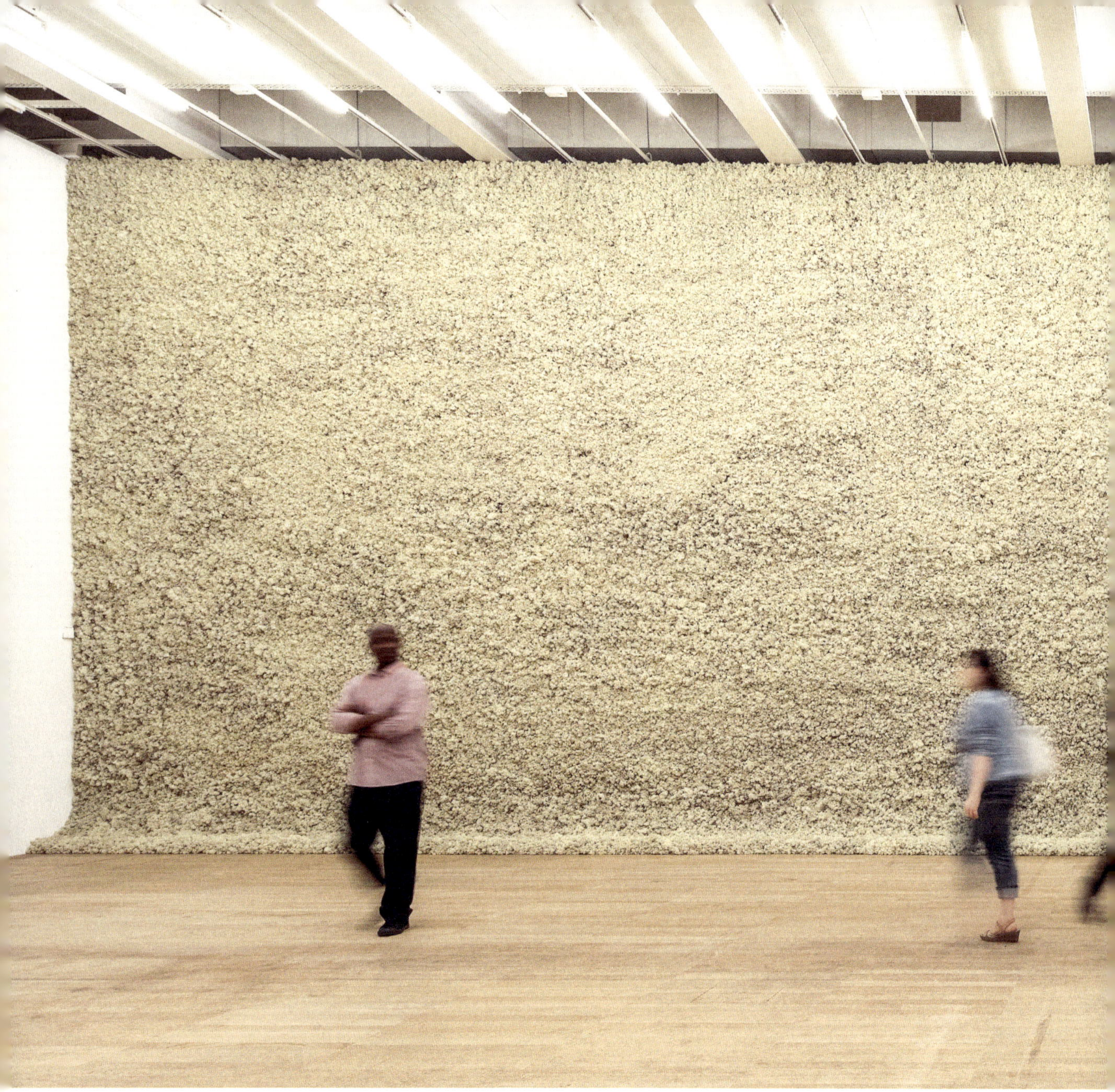

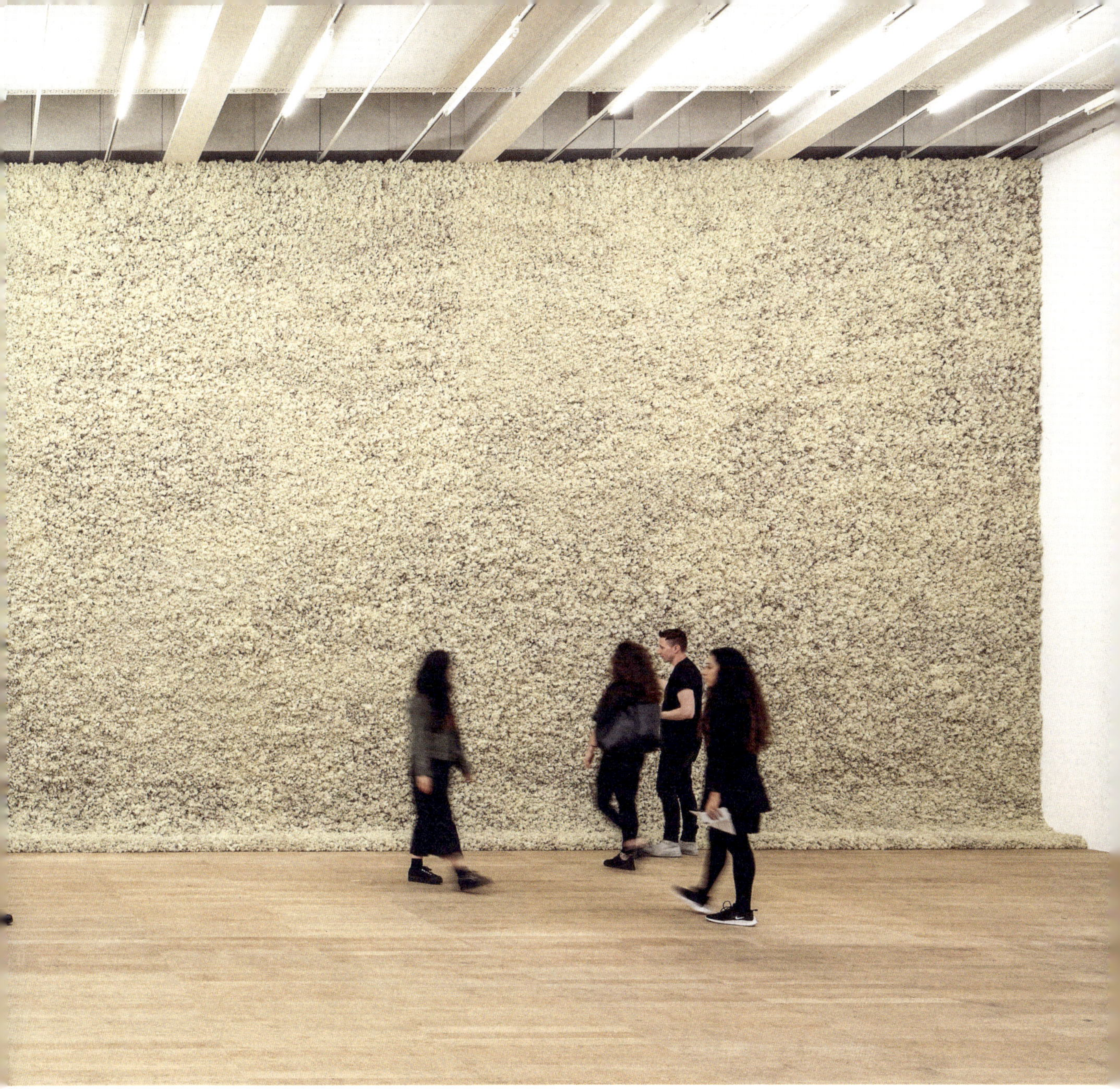

MOSS WALL 1994

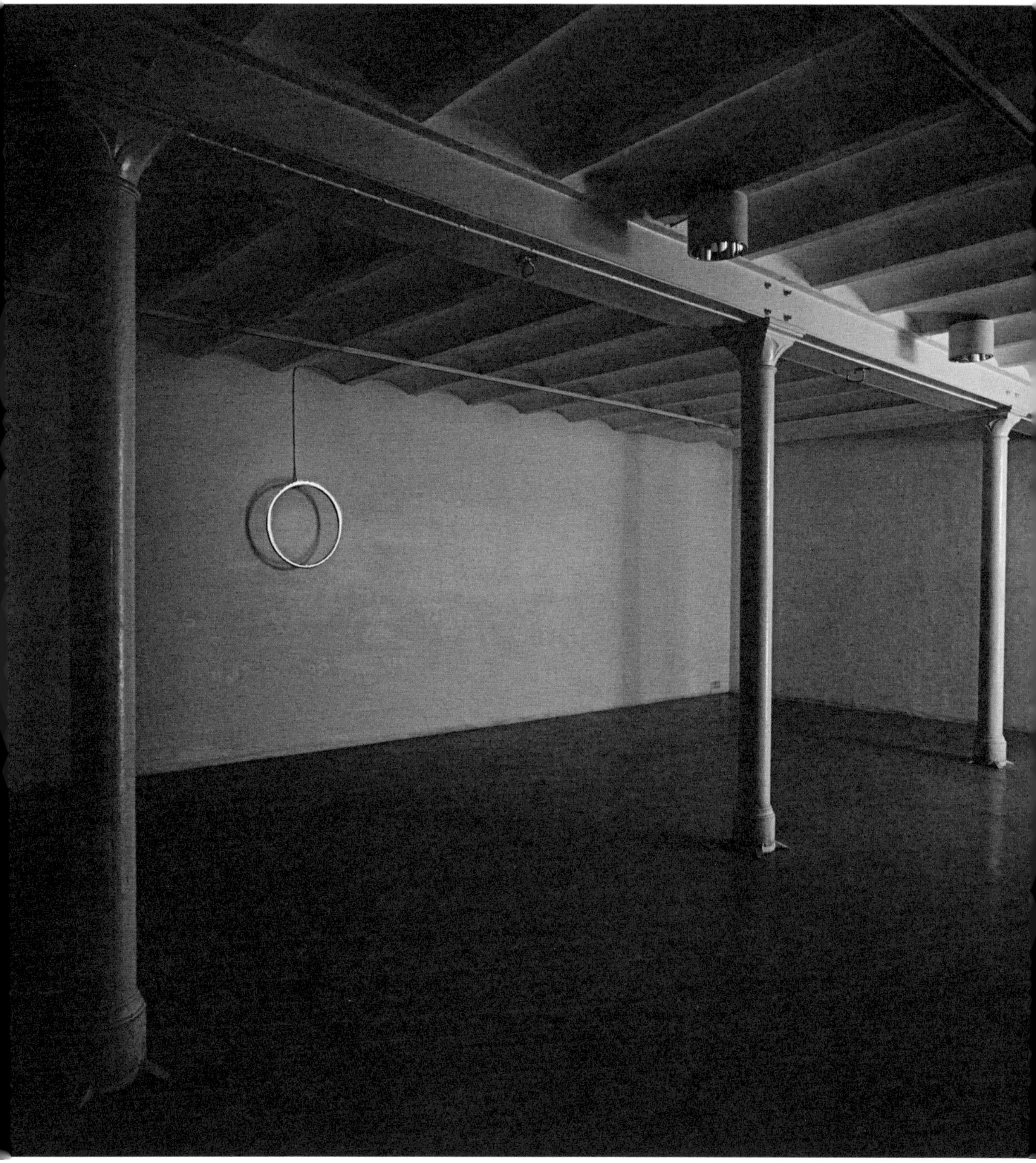

NO NIGHTS IN SUMMER, NO DAYS IN WINTER 1994

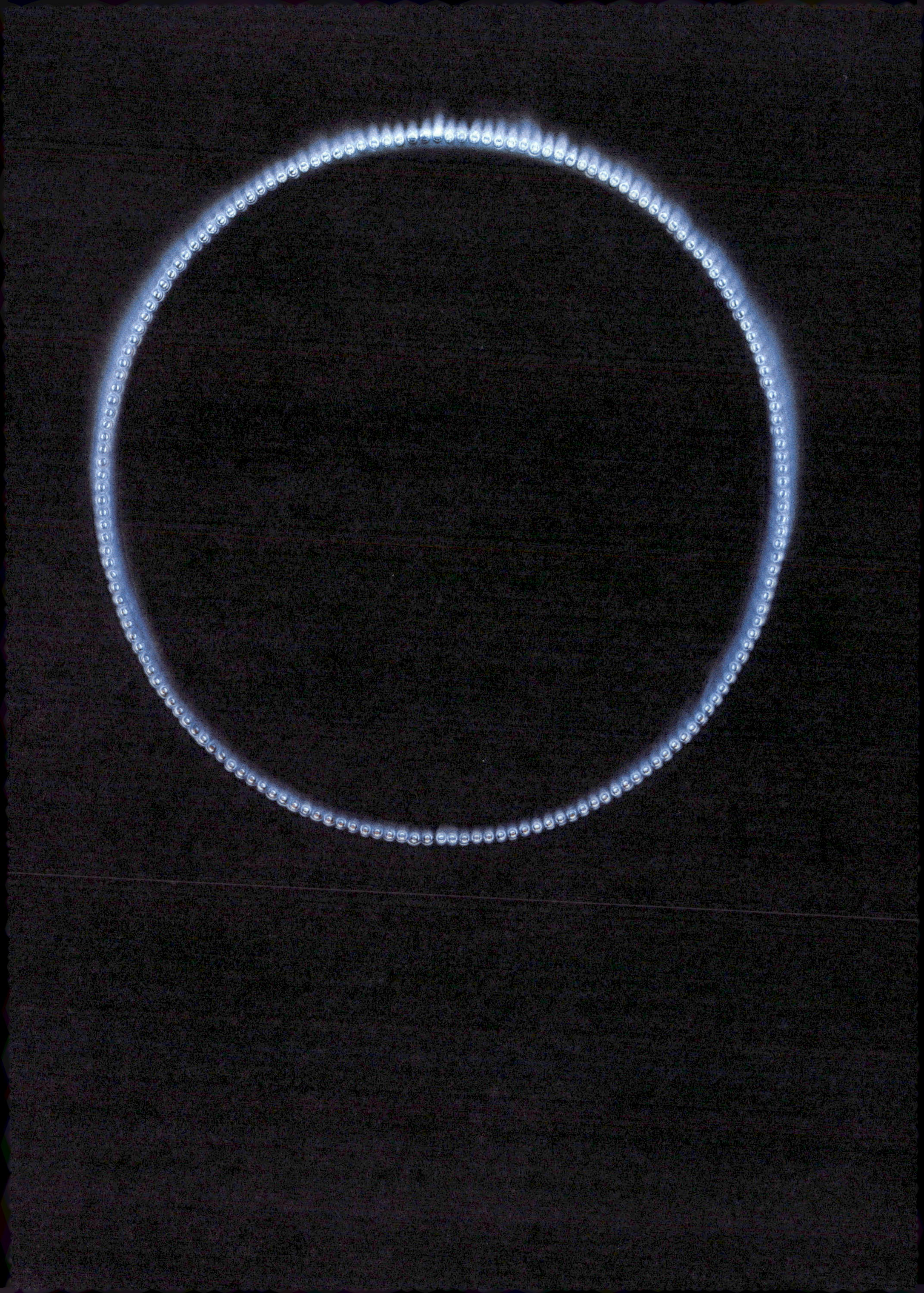

Olafur Eliasson: Jónsi, I like the idea that you can look at perfumes as a kind of shell or an armour, or almost like an architecture around your body. Tell me, how did you get involved in fragrances, in perfumes and odours?

Jónsi (Jón Thór Birgisson): I've been obsessed with smells now for many years. I really like it: you start buying essential oils and just experimenting with mixtures, and creating different blends, and then you slowly realise there's a whole world of aroma molecules and all kinds of different things out there that you had no clue existed. Then you gradually start to expand. It's interesting. The perfume world is very secretive. I really want to learn, but it's very hard to get knowledge. You can't learn from books about perfumery, you have to learn with somebody, with a master.

And when people involved in fragrances talk about smell, is it like a dimension or is it like a suit – or something else? What's the shape of smell for professional people in that world?

It's like music, it's invisible. I like working with something that is invisible – you can't see it, but it still moves you in some invisible way. It isn't possible to explain how music moves you or why it moves you, and it's similar with smells. Maybe not so intense, but it can definitely trigger some really powerful emotions.

In the professional world of smell, is there a time-based element, as with music? There's the first note and then the next and the last ...

It's similar to music: there are base smells, mid-range, or 'heart' smells and top notes. In the same way you train your ear when you're singing, you can train your nose to be more sensitive to scent and to different scents. The more you practise, the better you will become at life. It's like cooking – like everything.

What's the geography of placing the smell on your body? Is there a topography of the body for smells – you know, some on the hand, some on the face, some on the back?

THE SHAPE OF SMELL

JÓNSI (JÓN THÓR BIRGISSON) is a musician and vocalist in the Icelandic post-rock band Sigur Rós. He is known for his distinct falsetto and for playing a wide range of instruments, from the piano to the banjo, but perhaps most recognisably for playing his guitar, 'The Bird', with a bow. Jónsi has pursued a number of side projects over the years, including recording three albums of electronic music with his solo project Frakkur, and Jónsi & Alex, an art collaboration with Alex Somers. For several years now, Jónsi has experimented with creating and capturing smells. In 2018, he collaborated with Eliasson on the musical score to *Reality projector*, Eliasson's site-specific light installation at the Marciano Art Foundation in Los Angeles.

Yes, it's all different. Some people spray it on their clothes – it's kind of pure on the clothes. But on the skin it's always different, on every single skin. It depends on your skin, on the composition of the oils on your skin, things like that. Different perfumes are different on different people.

Smell is, for me, almost a spatial thing – you detect the intimate distance from another person based on the quality or the intensity of their smell, but it also makes the space between us explicit. I remember we met in Iceland at a party this winter. When I walked up to you I could tell already from pretty far away that you were wearing a particular scent. You were occupying a much bigger space than usual. You had a house, so to speak, around you. And I realised when I walked up to you, I just entered your atmosphere, your architecture – your aura. Then it was more like you were hosting my visit in your scent, and immediately you became like the person who was receiving my visit. I probably stank a bit and then – you were so kind – you said you had just made this perfume that you had with you in your hand, and you asked me, 'Do you mind me just giving you a few drops? It's a lovely intense scent.' And I, being humble and not wanting to reject you, immediately said yes. You gave me drops on both sides of my neck, and I said to myself, 'I guess I'm going to smell like you now.' And I thought, 'I am not a guest in your house – I'm actually making the house with you.' It was as if we were building it together, until I noticed that my smell was really not the same as yours. And not only did I notice that but I also noticed that my smell was unbelievably strong! [Laughs.] It made me very aware of my nose. But it was a very beautiful smell. Do you recall it?

No.

It was kind of leathery ... with more smoke than leather. And it was kind of sharp, because it was very deep. If it were a colour it would definitely be a dark colour. If it were a space, it would be more like a void than a volume. Later, when I got back to my hotel, I realised how I filled up this anonymous hotel space and personalised it with my smell – which obviously at that point was still not completely mine, because it was very much your smell. And I thought, 'Oh my god, that's so powerful.' And then I went to bed, because it had been a long day and a long night also. Then I woke up in the morning, and it was still as strong! The smell stayed with me for a few days. It must have been of great quality, and it gave me this trace of our meeting.

Yeah, a particular memory.

This lovely memory, like an echo. I enjoyed it a lot. I couldn't really categorise it as a perfume, but it just introduced a number of spatial, scent-based associations. In terms of dimension, does smell have a colour, do you think? Does it correspond to colour or sound or space? Do you have a secondary language for it?

No. No ...

How do you talk about it if you don't have any way of describing it?

It's hard. Doing perfumes is a very private pursuit. You're just engulfed in different smells and scents. I think it's a very lonely profession at heart. But the scent I made, the one you smelled, was perhaps the pure blend. Usually you dilute it in alcohol so it's maybe only at ten or twenty per cent strength. This was probably just pure blend, so that's why it was so intense. I usually don't wear perfumes – I think they are mostly horrible. They're too this and too that – too flowery or too sweet.

Do you wear your own scents?

Yes I do, but that's the only thing I wear. The egocentric man! I just wear my own stuff [laughs]. I have a small house in Stokkseyri, so I have also been doing the burning. We were talking about the smoky and leathery ... burned stuff. So I've been doing my own oils, like a birch tar oil – it's basically a completely black oil. You take the bark off the trees, put it in a compact bottler on one side, make up a big fire round it, and then the bark burns without flames and all the oil goes from the bark into the oil. I have another can that collects it at the bottom. It's the most intense burnt smell you've ever smelled in your life. It's really good. I use it sometimes in perfume to get that really burnt smell.

Interesting. I think we tend to underappreciate things that are non-quantifiable, such as atmospheres and ethereal qualities, even though if we feel stressed out or if we feel happy, it's often because of an atmosphere. Our mood and our sense of presence, of feeling welcomed, of hosting others in a generous way, are really very much questions of atmosphere. It's a combination of visual, acoustic and basic things like temperature, materials and even smells. I think it's fair to say that smell is the one aspect that is not considered. Construction just finished on the Fjordenhus, in Vejle, Denmark. In designing that building, we worked a lot with the quality of light and sound, because it's a working environment, and also with the air quality and with temperature and climate control – the heat and the humidity as well. The one thing I did not work on was smell. Smell is not a major thing in architecture. Why is that?

I think it has been forgotten – because if people don't think about things, they forget about them.

As an architectural dimension? Do you think you could make a show with smells?

Only smells?

Well, maybe not only ...

Yeah, but I would like to do that, that's kind of my thing. I really want to mix sound, sculpture and smell. I think I just want to trick your senses, because art – you talk about art – it can be kind of boring and not moving. I think while you're on this earth it's maybe nice to try to move people, in any way – a bad or good way. So yes, I think if you add more senses, you begin to trigger more senses, that's good.

I could not agree more. But when people are stressed or fearful, I guess they also smell differently.

Like sour sweat.

I mean, we have a range or palette of odours, and when we are in love or erotically aroused, obviously we have certain other smells.

Yes, definitely.

Do you think a perfume always has to be a positive amplifier?

I don't know. I really like burnt stuff, but a lot of people don't like it. It's too heavy for them, not pleasant ... It reminds me of campfires, that kind of stuff. It's something to do with roots and instinct and elements that trigger something you connect with automatically. But people are very different.

I think smell has been ruined a little bit. Like if you smell shampoos and you smell, say, rose perfumes and you hate them, but when you smell a real rose in a garden, it's incredible. This stuff has in a way been violated.

June 2018

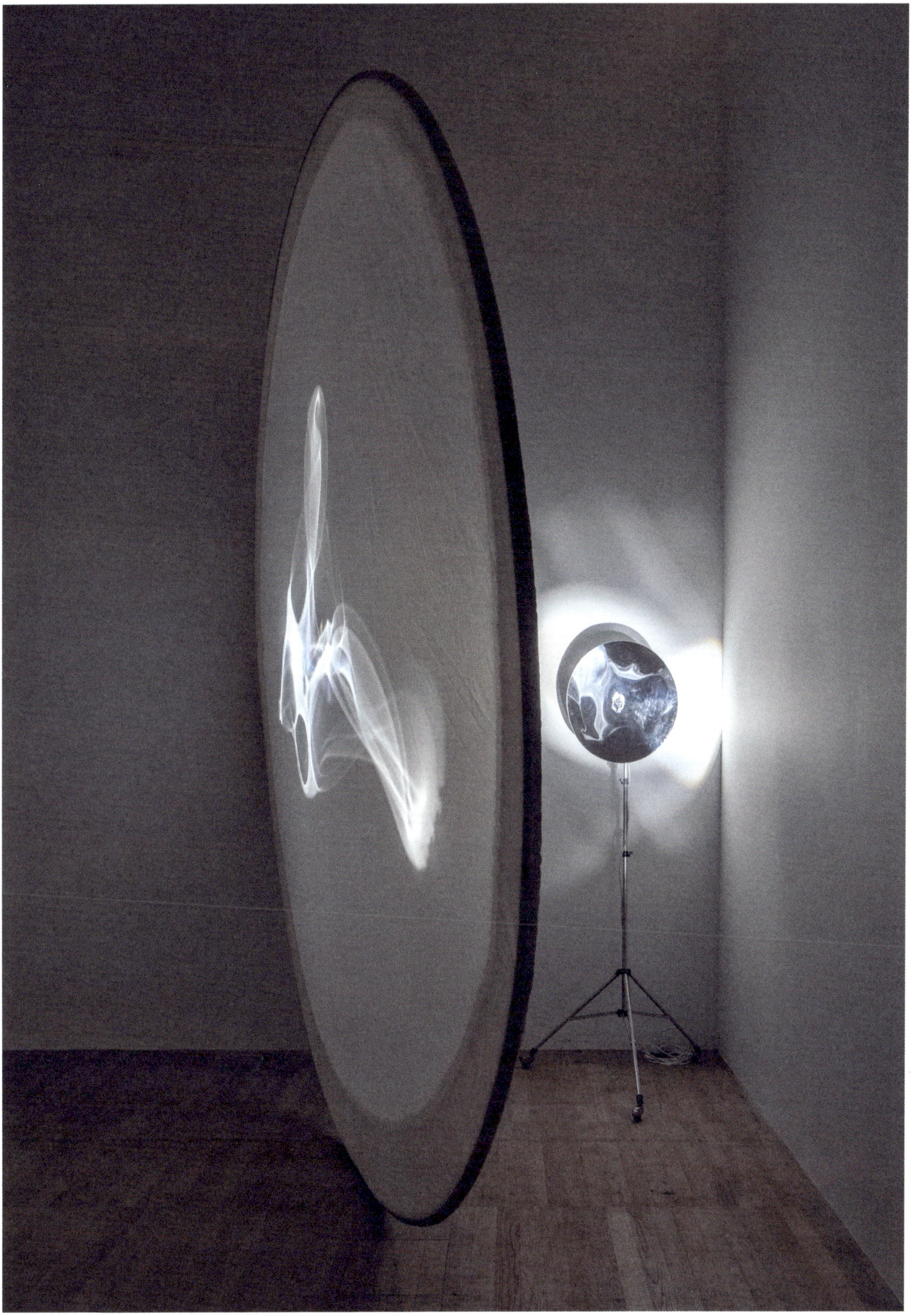

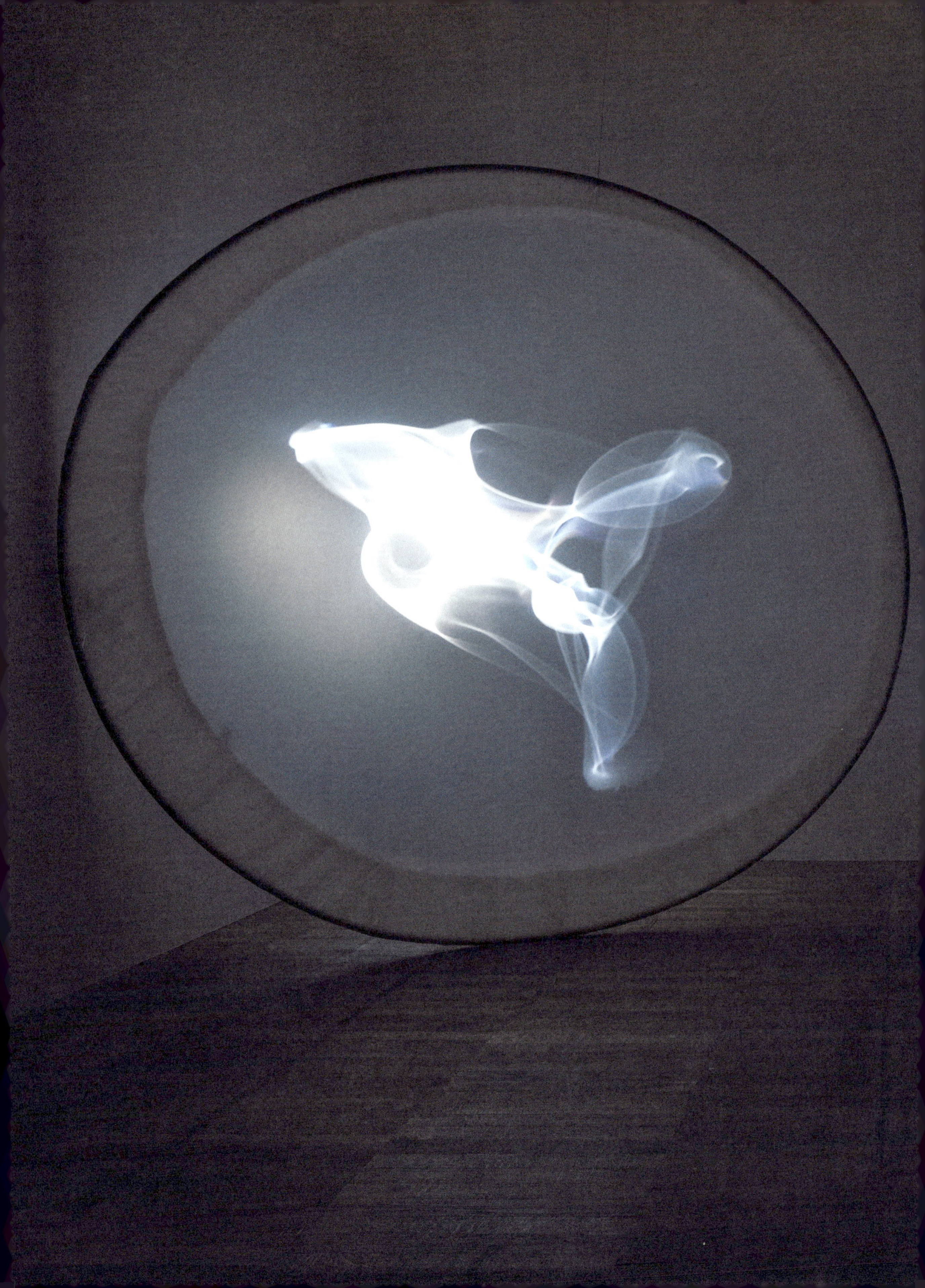

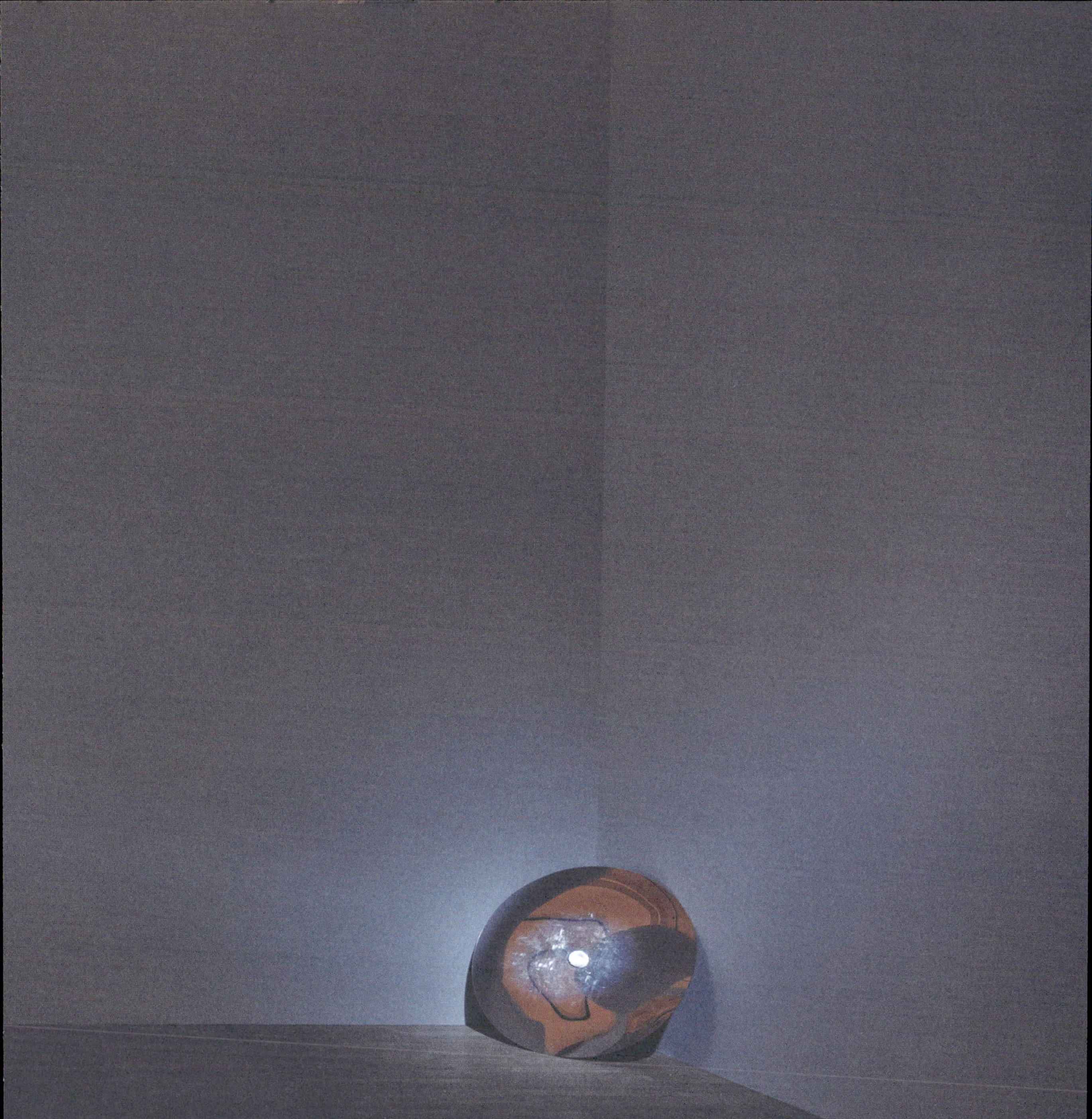

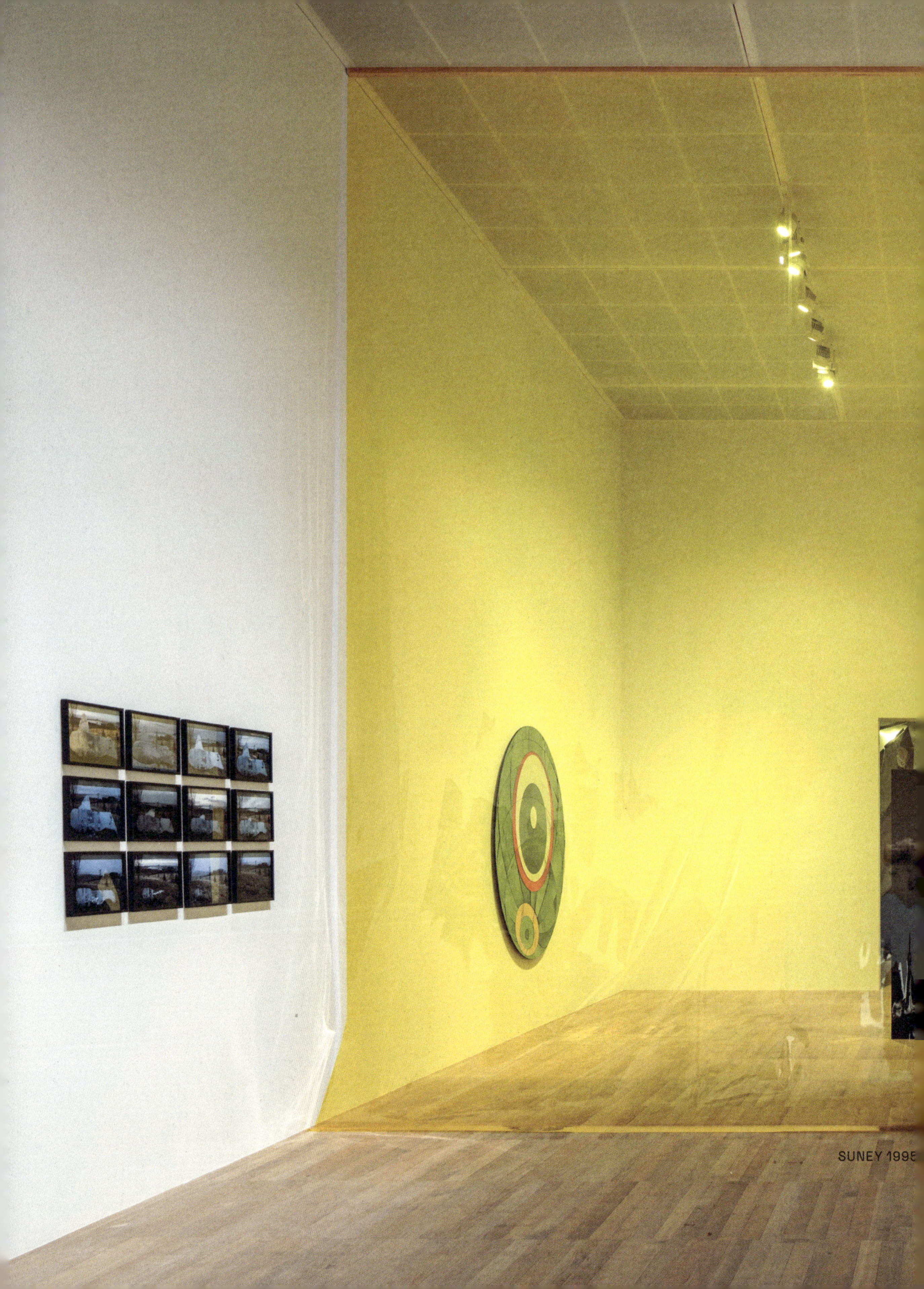

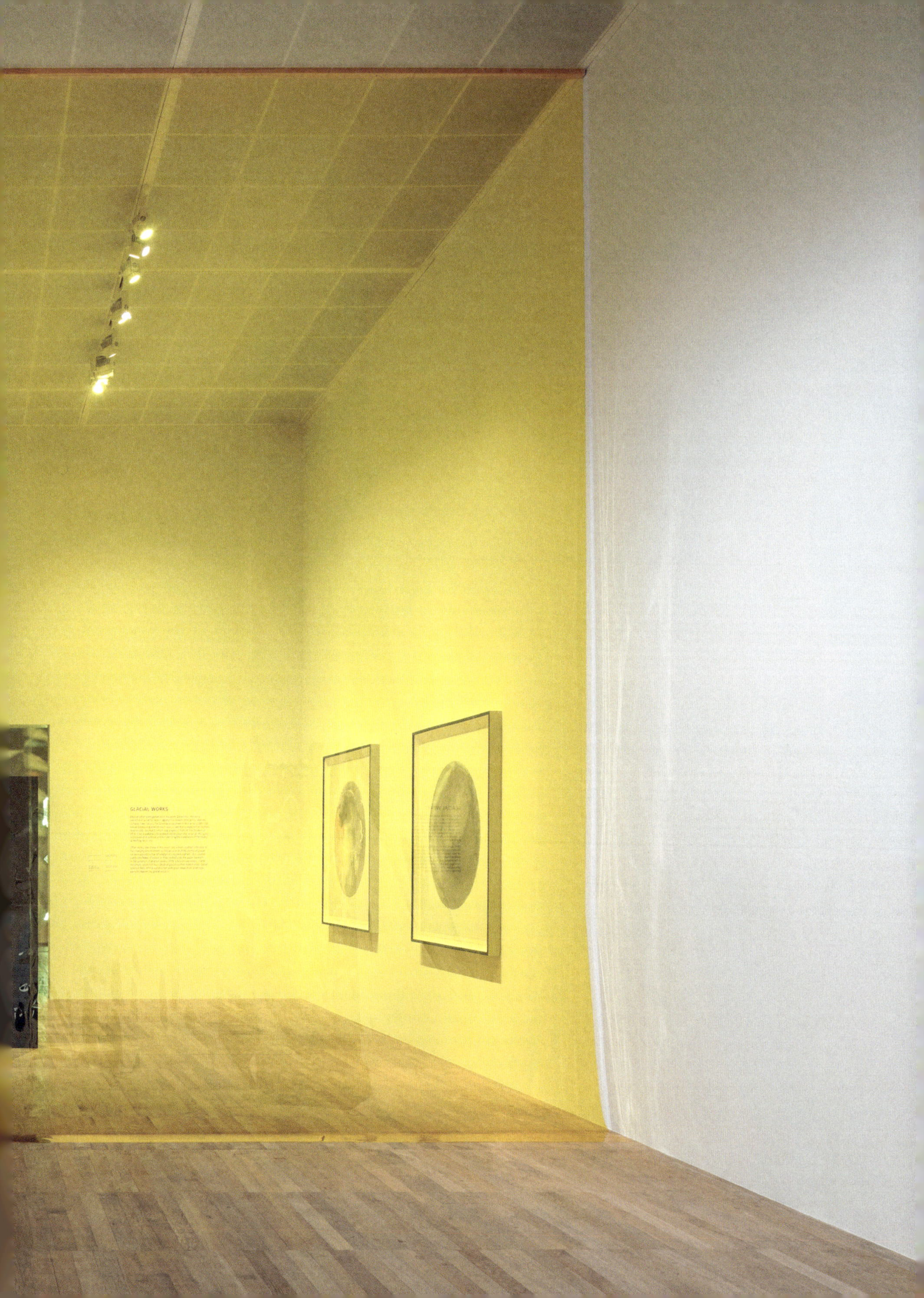
GLACIAL WORKS

Olafur Eliasson: As a teenager, I was not just interested in street culture but obsessed by it, and your movie *Wild Style* [1982–3] had a major impact on me when I saw it. There has been a tendency to criminalise the presence of Black kids on the streets in order to prevent the idea of a community defined by street culture and collective activity on the street. How did you experience this in the early era of street culture?

Fred Brathwaite, aka Fab 5 Freddy: When I was a young teenager back in the 1970s in New York City, very few had anything positive to say about the graffiti art we were making, the breakdancing or the rap music. Poor white kids in New York were also doing graffiti and similar things, but because of racism, it was the Blacks and Latinos who were criminalised constantly in the local press. No one saw anything positive in what they were doing. That's where the idea for *Wild Style* came from. I wanted people to see that we were artists, that we were expressing ourselves in new ways – that there was an important creative movement happening.

The film successfully documented not just a very creative culture with a strong sense of artistic content, but also its resilience, its conviction. It's clear to everyone now that art history was being made. Where did this incredible resilience and self-confidence come from?

I saw a documentary recently called *Shake the Dust* [2014]. It looks at breakdancing in a lot of different places, like war-torn areas of the Middle East, Africa, and in really poor places in South America. These kids are so poor that they don't even have cardboard or a piece of old linoleum to breakdance on. The dust billows up when they do their moves. These kids literally have nothing – in some cities all the buildings in their area are bombed out. Still you can feel the energy that they get from doing all these breakdance moves. You can feel the energy and pride. Seeing the film I could recall the original ideas and feelings of the kids that created this stuff in New York City at that particular time in the 1970s. When I see these kids – who have much less than what even the poorest New York kids had back then – I realise that the roots of this are very deep.

The basic idea for doing graffiti and hip-hop music back then was a desire to make people know that we exist – 'I'm here! I'm somebody!' – and to claim space: 'See that building over there, which looks like shit? I'm going to go and paint something brilliant and colourful on it.' It wasn't about trying to be rich or famous – it was just to be known in your community

WILD STYLE

FAB 5 FREDDY (FRED BRATHWAITE) is a hip-hop pioneer who began working in late 1970s New York. He was instrumental in bringing together young practitioners of street culture from Brooklyn and the Bronx with the downtown art and punk scenes. As a young painter and promoter of graffiti, breakdancing and rap, he was a driving force behind Charlie Ahearn's 1982–3 cult film *Wild Style*, a major point of reference for Eliasson in his pre-art school years as a breakdancer in Scandinavia.

and to raise the self-esteem of poor people. It was so simple and basic and pure that I think, like a tree, the roots went down very deep – this was before the hit records, film and TV shows, before street artists began showing in galleries and museums. And it's amazing to see that it still continues in that real, raw, honest way. It's more than I could have ever asked for, more than forty years later. I had no idea this scene would be so strong for so long, or that it would spread around the globe.

Yeah, street culture still addresses people who are not heard, people who are considered to be on the periphery. And, yes, doing graffiti, doing block parties, doing dance in the streets, is a way to claim not just identity but also space. You know, I grew up in the countryside in Denmark, and on one of my trips to Copenhagen – I think I was probably thirteen or fourteen – I saw some slightly older kids standing in a shop window and moving like robots. It was my first contact with electric boogie. From that day on I couldn't even take a glass of milk out of the fridge without doing it as if I was a robot. It was the biggest epiphany!

Before cable TV, before the internet, whoever had a VHS tape with some street dance on it was sitting on gold. After about a year I had come to understand that this was something bigger. I familiarised myself with graffiti, which had not yet made its way to Denmark, and became more aware of the whole idea of breakdancing and electric boogie. So there I was, a white kid in rural Denmark, watching the wave coming from where you were. And you were pushing that wave ahead. This was 1983, '84, when most of my friends were listening to British pop, and I was tuning in to late-night radio stations to hear Kurtis Blow and Herbie Hancock. I would sit there with my tape recorder, pressing record for anything remotely connected to hip-hop.

By the time *Wild Style* came out, my crew and I had developed some dancing skills. We were by no means established, but we had recognition within that very Scandinavian street-culture scene. Being a dancer and a part of this movement was a very influential part of my youth. Even though we were so far from the Bronx and Harlem, there was something about the resilience of street culture that gave me an opportunity to claim identity, claim my body. It was the start of what later became so important to me – my relation with public space.

I love to hear stories like this! I could never have dreamt that so many different people in so many places would connect with this.

At the time, I also loved drawing. My father was an artist and my mother supported the idea of being an artist a lot, so when I got into the dance scene, it was natural for me to start doing graffiti. Because I was the only kid who could actually draw some semblance of, say, a cow, I quickly defined a small space for myself in what would later evolve into the graffiti scene. You were working as an artist at the time, right? As a painter.

Yeah, I originally wanted to be an architect, then a visual artist. I wanted to paint and have my work shown in galleries and museums, but I could see no clear way to making that happen. I didn't see many people that looked like me doing anything in the art world. But, like other graffiti artists, I figured out a way to get my name all over the city and paint pictures anywhere I felt I wanted to. In a very rebellious, renegade way, I figured I would be able to find a way into the art world – in that same way Malcolm X famously said, 'by any means necessary'.

And, again, my motivation for the ideas that became the film *Wild Style* was to make us look better and change people's perception of us. I wanted to show that we were artists, not just thugs, gangsters and criminals. I wanted to create the idea that this new culture was all linked. Although not everybody doing graffiti was into hip-hop music, and not everybody into hip-hop was into graffiti or breakdancing, I had this idea to use cinema to create these connections and make our movement look strong and cohesive. I was sure if I could create a story that linked everything, it would make a strong impression to counter the negative narrative. Lee Quiñones, the legendary graffiti artist and my co-conspirator [who played a major role in the film], shared this idea of breaking into the art world and we were determined to make them take a look at our new culture and treat us with respect.

I met the filmmaker Charlie Ahearn in 1980 at the *Times Square Show*, which was sort of our equivalent of the 1913 [groundbreaking modern art exhibition] *Armory Show*. Charlie's twin brother John was a sculptor and was exhibiting at the show. Charlie had already made an underground, low-budget, urban kung-fu movie called *The Deadly Art of Survival* [1979]. I pitched him my idea of making a movie about this music and this graffiti painting and breakdancing. So, at the *Times Square Show*, he said, 'Let's work together – come to my office tomorrow.' The problem was that when we went around to the people who fund independent films, we couldn't get any money.

Why?

For one thing, because people didn't believe it. We went in with pictures, cassette tapes, stories, but there had been no media about this, no articles. We said, 'This is a new important culture developing in New York City – help us make a movie.' Nobody wanted to give us any money. In fact, the first people to give us money were in Europe. The German TV channel ZDF gave us about twenty-five or thirty thousand dollars – starting money – in exchange for the rights to air the movie on TV. Then Channel 4 in London gave us a similar amount. And with that, we went back to some of the people we'd first met in America and said, 'Look, the people in Europe are ready to help.'

And that's how *Wild Style* got made. And it aired on German TV before it was even in movie theatres in the US! The kids recorded it, because you guys had VCRs before we did – maybe that's how your friends first saw it – so it began to hit the streets, and the video recordings began to circulate around Europe. I remember hearing about kids doing the moves, the exact same moves the Rock Steady Crew do in the movie. That was when I realised it was spreading beyond my expectations.

This is so great. It almost raises the hair on my arm to hear you say this. Because I remember hearing about this movie and taking a train to Copenhagen to see it. I had my crew with me, and the cinema was packed with all the graffiti artists and breakdancers and electric boogie dancers and DJs and everybody. And it was completely white, completely and utterly white! The moment the film starts, everybody jumps up and stands in the cinema. It was unbelievable. And as the film goes on, everybody is dancing and standing on the chairs. And at that scene where Crazy Legs does his footwork at a party, halfway through the movie, we all start literally running around in the cinema – the cinema people are yelling at us – and we're doing footwork and swipes and turtles up on the stage in front of the screen. It was like we were trying to jump into the movie.

And even though it sounds so funny today, I did walk around in my Michael Jackson lookalike suit – the knee pads, the big shoulders – and I did have my piece of cardboard to dance on. We would just put out our ghetto blaster in the pedestrian zone in downtown Copenhagen and do our moves. And if petty cash ran low, we had a hat.
Classic!
A few years later, after I stopped being so involved with dancing, I applied to art school. That was where I learned that historically many artists had worked on the street – performance artists, Marcel Marceau, the Situationists – and I suddenly realised what I had learned from being a street dancer. Later, as I became involved with art and space and architecture, I would think about how it felt to actually *own* a space – what it felt like to claim it and say, 'This space reflects my emotional agenda.' I realise now that it was rooted in this idea of street culture and public space. And that is why I still have the *Wild Style* record today, and still listen to it.
You know, I didn't know a lot about your work until the *New York City Waterfalls* [2008], which I would notice at night driving home across the East River to my house in Harlem. I guess you claimed that space thoroughly and totally! Especially at night. There would be some lights on it, and it was just so exciting to drive past. I would almost crash trying to be sure I got a good look at it. It's so great to hear that hip-hop urban culture and street dance were sparks for that. Yours is one of the most unique stories I have heard about how this movement influenced someone. I could not have dreamt this up!
Of course hip-hop went on to become mainstream, and a huge business. You have successfully managed to balance the creative potential with commercialisation, which can work against it. But to go back to that early time: as I got a little older, [music-oriented television channel] MTV suddenly arrived. You started hosting your show *Yo! MTV Raps*, and suddenly people had access. Only then did it strike me, quite late in the process, actually, that improvisation is a major part of it as well. Improvisation is in every part of how we claim space, and improvisation is super important to my work today. How did that start off for you?
I come from a jazz background. My father was very close to the bebop scene and to the drummer Max Roach, and as a kid I heard him and his friends talking a lot about jazz culture. Thelonious Monk was my favourite musician. I found his number in my father's phonebook one day and just called him up for a conversation. I was probably about nine or ten years old. His wife, Nelly Monk, talked to me for about twenty minutes! Jazz, she said to me, is like a conversation: you state your case at the beginning of the song, and then you give examples – you explain and support your argument. Each musician does that differently, and that's improvisation. Once I got that, I was ready to apply it to other things.
For me – and, I think, for African-Americans, for people who have very little – the actual core of improvisation is the idea that you have to find some way to make it happen. You don't have as much as you need in any category – food, clothes, resources – so how can you improvise and make what you do have more *you*, more original, more flavourful? How do you make it different? That was the beneficial outcome.
And it's like creating a dialogue. In jazz you allow the listener the fantasy of becoming a co-composer.

Or even a co-conspirator! Your description of hip-hop culture in Denmark reminds me of hearing Max Roach and his friends talking about how they felt more accepted in Europe, without the bullshit they experienced in America. That's why so many jazz musicians become expatriates. Many were well-read and intellectual and felt better treated abroad than in America. Not that racism didn't exist in Europe, but Europe acknowledged them as the creatives they were. When we found that first money to make *Wild Style* in Europe, the situation was a bit like what jazz artists had experienced.

I don't think it's just a lucky punch that Germany gave public money for the film. Having come out of the war, Germany really was looking for ways to support subcultures and respect identity. These days, cuts are being made everywhere, but especially in America, to public support for grassroots and diversified cultural activity. And all the big museums in America are to a large extent white: the boards are mostly white; the funding is mostly white; the shows are mostly white; art history writing is still very white. There is still a long way to go toward equal presentation of other types of experience, whether Latino or Black or Asian.

I'm so happy to hear you say it, Olafur. You know, discussions like this were the genesis of my friendship with Jean-Michel Basquiat. 'How can we get in when we know there's no improvisation going on at the galleries, on the boards, with the curators of these institutions?' Jean-Michel and I would strategise on our assault on pop culture and we had what we called our Museum Club. We would often go to the Metropolitan Museum of Art together and just talk about paintings and have lunch and make sketches like we were art students. We had both spent a lot of time in museums as kids, so when we met we could discuss artists from Jasper Johns to Caravaggio. We were excited that we were both young and Black and could talk about all these painters, because we couldn't talk about them with too many other people. Not many of our contemporaries knew these guys. We were going to find a way to get in to these institutions – working with music, working with film, working with art. And that is what Jean-Michel did and what I continue to do.

I am so glad we could chat, Fab. It's just of great personal importance to me to be able to share this part of my life. To a large extent that period of my life – that prologue – has not figured very much in my art, and so I'm glad finally to have nailed it. And with the man himself. With Fab fucking Five ... oh, man, I'm so excited!

September 2018

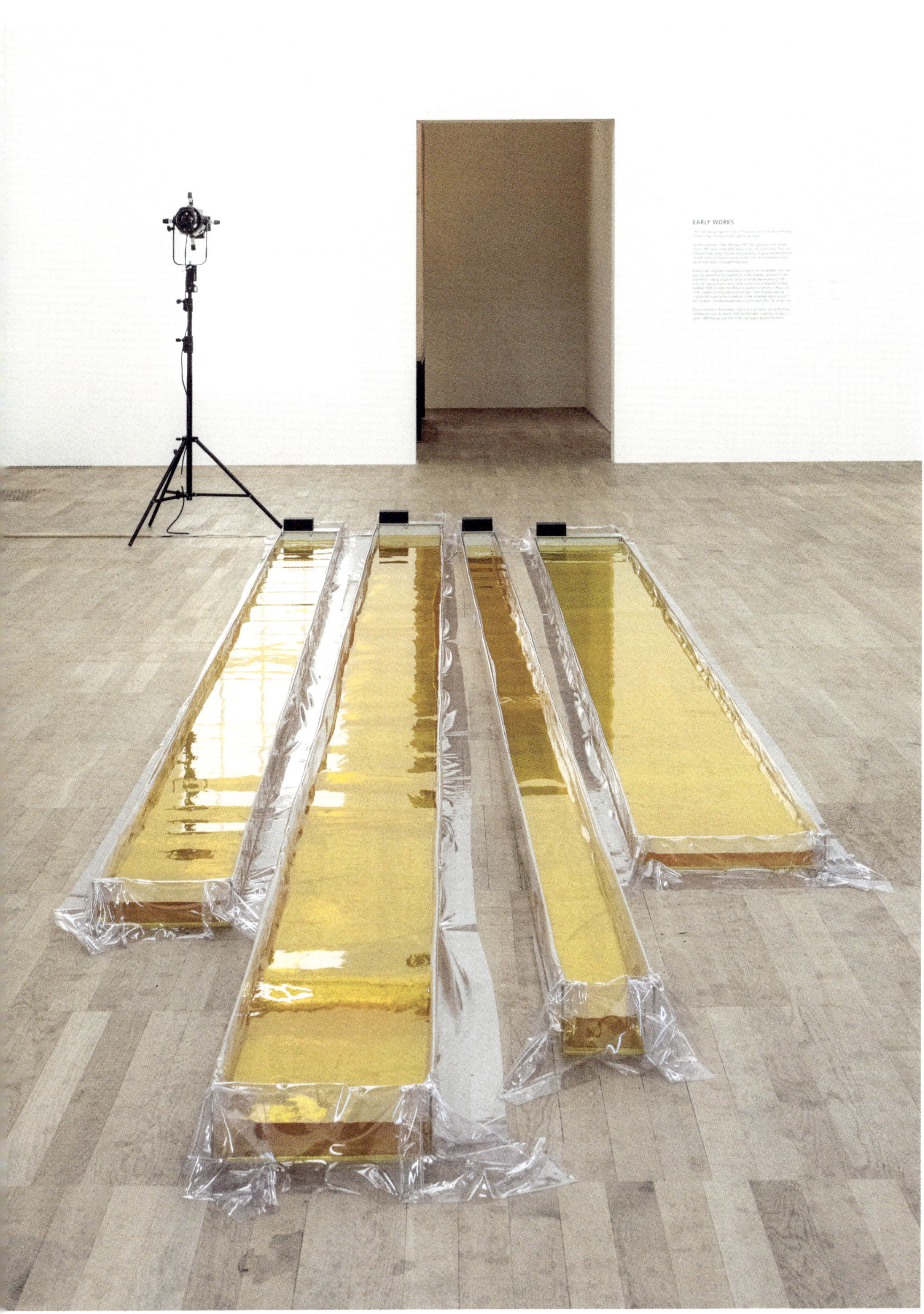
EARLY WORKS

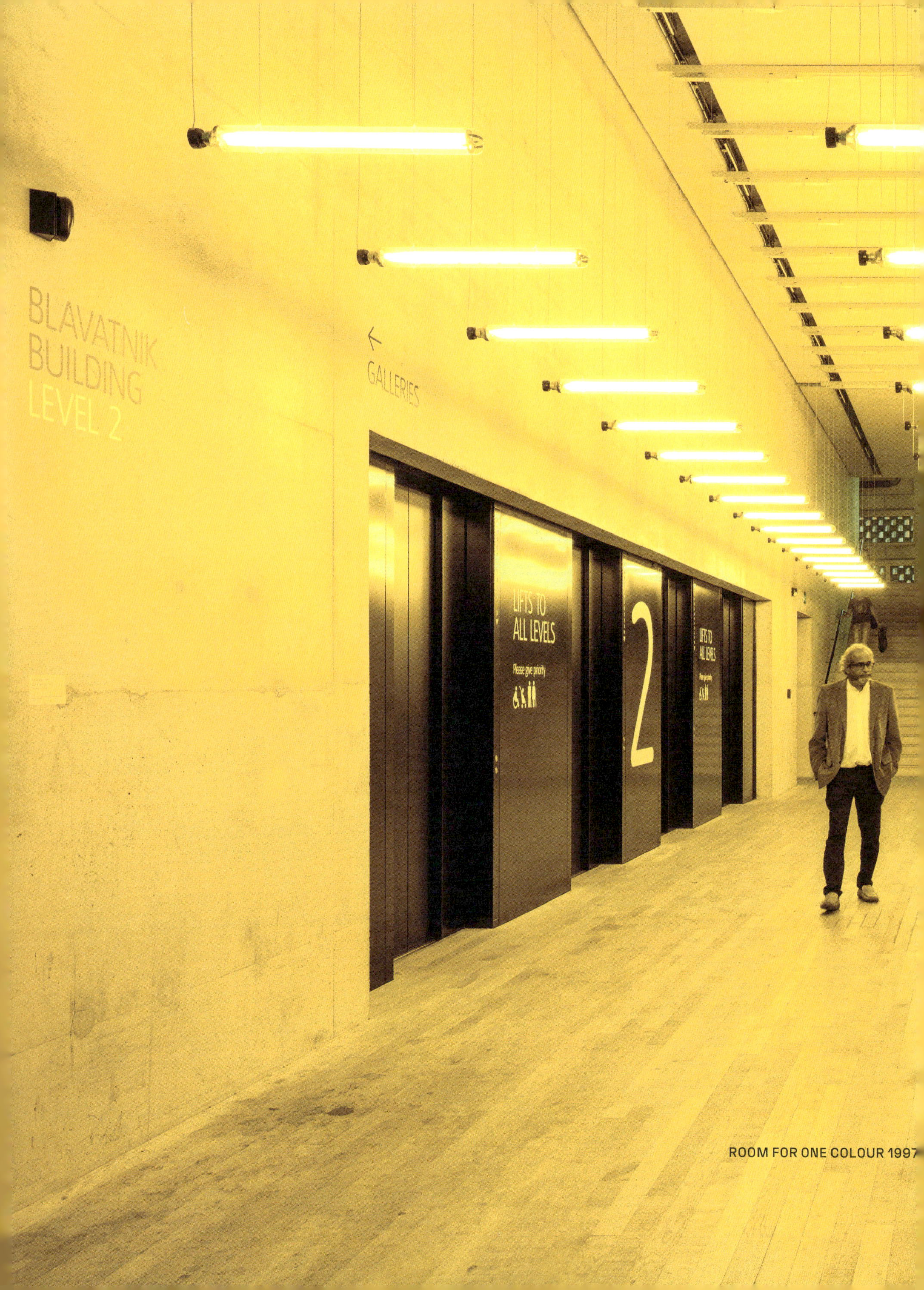

ROOM FOR ONE COLOUR 1997

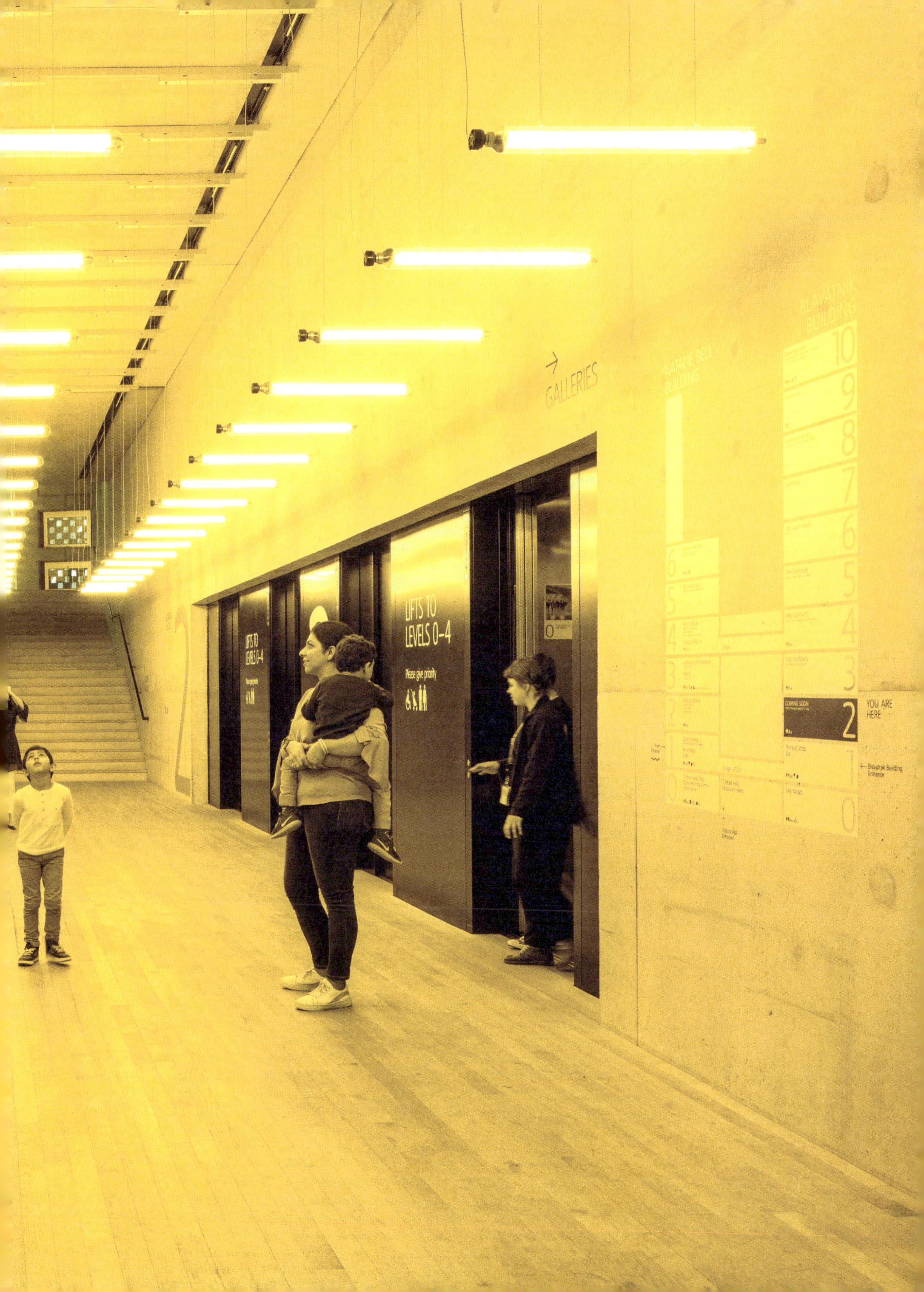

GALLERIES
LIFTS TO LEVELS 0–4
Please give priority
NATALIE BELL BUILDING
BLAVATNIK BUILDING
COMING SOON
YOU ARE HERE

Olafur Eliasson: Marie-Agnès, as a dancer you are obviously incredibly conscious about the presence of your body; you have a hyper-connection to it. You always know exactly where every part of your body is, whereas, right now, for example, my brain knows only roughly where my hand is: it's somewhere over here holding a phone. Do you think that's equally true for both classical and modern dancers?

Marie-Agnès Gillot: Oh, yes. But I think the consciousness I have of my body is also probably because I spent a lot of my youth as a handicapped person. From the time I was eleven until I was seventeen years old, I had to wear a back brace – like Frida Kahlo – to treat my scoliosis. I could only take that corset off for a few hours a day. The rest of the time, I was paralysed, immobile. During my precious moments of freedom, I felt like I was *holding* my body. I felt everything, because the rest of the time I was blocked by that corset. So I think that my really extreme sensitivity to my body was not because of my training in dance but because of my handicap.

I didn't know that. How incredible. My own understanding of the body comes from my intense interest in architecture and space, especially public space, and from my teenage years as a street dancer. And when I say you are so conscious of your body, it's not just because you can express yourself with your body so incredibly well – it's more than that. When you think about space, you think *though* your body.

When we collaborated on Wayne McGregor's *Tree of Codes* [2015], I remember that it was the first time in my life that the set was like another dance partner, because it was so mobile and complex. It was my first experience with your art in *my* space, and I was very impressed. It felt like the set was moving like a dancer. I don't know if you felt that.

BODY

MARIE-AGNÈS GILLOT is a dancer and choreographer who has worked with many of the most renowned choreographers in classical ballet and contemporary dance, including William Forsythe, Rudolf Nureyev, Wayne McGregor and Pina Bausch. In 2004 Gillot became an 'étoile', or principal dancer, of the Paris Opera Ballet, remaining there until her retirement in 2018. Gillot has worked collaboratively outside the world of classical ballet with other dancers and artists on numerous projects. Eliasson and Gillot first met when she starred in McGregor's *Tree of Codes*, for which Eliasson created the stage design.

Actually, I never thought of it that way. But for me it was a beginning. In 2007, I had done the sets for Hans Werner Henze's *Phaedra* at the Staatsoper Berlin, but that had been a more conventional stage design, and rather static. This autumn, while working on my second opera there – Jean-Philippe Rameau's baroque *Hippolyte et Aricie* with conductor Simon Rattle – I realised that our collaboration with *Tree of Codes* had been a chance to really think about the relationships between the body and space and the dancers' consciousness of their bodies. I am inspired by the way your body's movements and the movement of time and space are so interconnected. In a way, you're not dancing on stage but dancing *with* the stage. I like this sort of blending. I am still exploring how to blur those boundaries.

I think the body is the most intelligent material, even more intelligent than the head. It's not 'I think, therefore I dance' – it's more like 'I dance, and then I think.' The way I investigate space is through physicality, not mentally.

I like this a lot. We normally say we are surrounded by dimensions – you know, the three dimensions and the dimension of time – but those dimensions are relative to our physical engagement. I'm not saying that by using our bodies we can change the dimensions completely, but we can negotiate the extent to which these dimensions control us. And we can challenge them and liberate ourselves. Do you agree that this does not necessarily require a professionally trained body? It can be anybody who dances, as long as they acknowledge that there is a body.

Of course, yes!

I know you've worked quite a lot with non-professionals.

Yes! Everyone can dance. I love it when people feel that. For me, dancing was the first art. Music came soon after, but the first art was dance. The memory of the body is universal. Sometimes language is a barrier and we cannot understand each other. But sensation – the feeling of touch – is the same for all of us, and dance respects this. We all have this sense of space, of air, of the weight of the air on the body, of reacting to sound. We all have the same capacity to feel; it's just a matter of sensitivity.

I'm very curious about how you bring our attention to the physical body that way. Because I think sometimes it's difficult to leave your head.

Often it's through touch that I get people to feel. I try to do dance with people who are deaf or who are blind. I find they often have a higher level of consciousness about their senses and respond with more sensitivity than when all five senses are intact.

And you've also worked with people in prison?

Yes. The discipline and the routine of prisons can be very damaging to the natural body, you know? I've asked prisoners to tell me about the gestures that they have to repeat every day: the daily searches by the guards; the constant checks and controls; the limited physical exercise. Every day when they leave their cells, this check involves the same gestures. Obviously it's not at all like dance, but it is a discipline, part of a tradition of gesture, a movement that you repeat the same way every time. And I wanted to see what it does to their bodies.

Prisons mix architecture, power, physical constraints, physical repetition ... A jail is supposed to be a 'corrective facility', but obviously it's also an abusive facility. This constant physical repetition obviously brings with it a physical memory, like a trauma in the body.

It damages the body's freedom. Which interests me a lot because, in music and in dance, it is discipline and repetition and routine that in the end make us free. We repeat – we practise and practise and practise – until it becomes natural. I wanted to see what effect this kind of movement has on people in prison. They are doing these repeated gestures every day and it is the opposite of freedom. But I did see that people in jail are incredibly aware of their bodies. Their dreams may be dead, but their bodies are still so alive. So they are all very aware of their physicality.

Did you choreograph any work around your research in prisons?

Yes. I did a piece for the Nuit Blanche [all-night arts] festival in Paris to Maurice Ravel's *Bolero* – a piece of music that is all about repetition. For the festival, I danced it five times over the whole night. I also performed it in jail – in the prison gymnasium, because, of course, there are no theatres in jail. *Bolero* for me is the most important music in the world because it's the most listened-to work of classical music – millions of people hear it every day. It's now in the public domain. That's also why I chose to perform it for people in jail.

Of course I'm curious about those moments where you reach out beyond your comfort zone, outside your space, into modern dance, into the public and into the notion of the regular body – the bodies that we all have. And when I watch you dance, I am also dancing inside myself. You know, when I look at dance, I can almost feel the physical experience of the dancing itself

Yes, it's true, actually. You can read everything on the body. Even in a non-professional dancer, you can read so much on the body that you cannot see on the face or in the mind. Working with people in jail, I wanted to study what those repetitive movements did to them. The body remembers the trauma, keeps the scars, but it's like in nature; if you lose something, it comes back, it grows again. The body is the same material – the body can feel pain or loss, but nature will come back.

Yes, I'm very interested in this idea. It connects to what I call the presence of absence. You recently came to an exhibition I did in in Switzerland [*Objects defined by activity*, Espace Muraille, Geneva, 2018], and did an extraordinary performance with Luc Bruyère inside the show. Luc is missing a limb – his left arm. Your performance was amazing. You often stood behind him with your left arm placed in the position of his left arm – and you were not looking at each other – and your arm was his arm, completely.

Yes, I gave him my arm.

Our bodies are much more connected than we think. Are you still working with Luc?

I've been continuing my research with him. We are starting a new piece in which I ask Luc to put on his fake arm, and I put on my corset. So we start out both wearing our orthopaedic medical devices, in this handicapped condition. Later we take them off. We begin just with two, I would say, broken bodies [laughs].

That's super interesting. I like this idea of orthopaedic devices contributing to a certain body architecture and that this is then transformed when you work your way through the choreography. My fascination with dancers is about the quality of a relationship. That's also why I'm so interested in breakdance. Of course, breakdance has its own cultural history, but still, when I watch it I also feel very connected to space. Breakdance is like a language through which I can understand the space around the dancers. In the same way, your ability to move allows me to understand the space around you. So you are a kind of conduit for me to see everything else. I'm always trying to find out how I can use that when I think about space. These days I watch hip-hop mostly on Instagram.

Oh, really? Me too!

I follow a young woman from South Korea, Keumsae Pae [@keumsae_pae]. I started watching her because my friend Slim Boogie [Anthony Armstrong – @slimboogie777] follows her, and he has a great network of young, talented dancers. What I like is that her robotic movements blend with Asian urban culture. Seeing her on Insta gives me access to that informal street culture. To me it's a very interesting mix of dance identity, space and architecture.

Well, as you know, Marie-Agnès, I would love to do some experiments with you. We could work on eliminating the boundary between the brain and the body, the body and space, the body and time – space and time. Let's call it 'dimensionality blurring'. Because, clearly, architecture can be dancing too, and the body is also architecture, so there is a great deal to explore there. We'll need some time to set it up. It's more like research – let's experiment and see what we can do together.

I'd love to!

November 2018

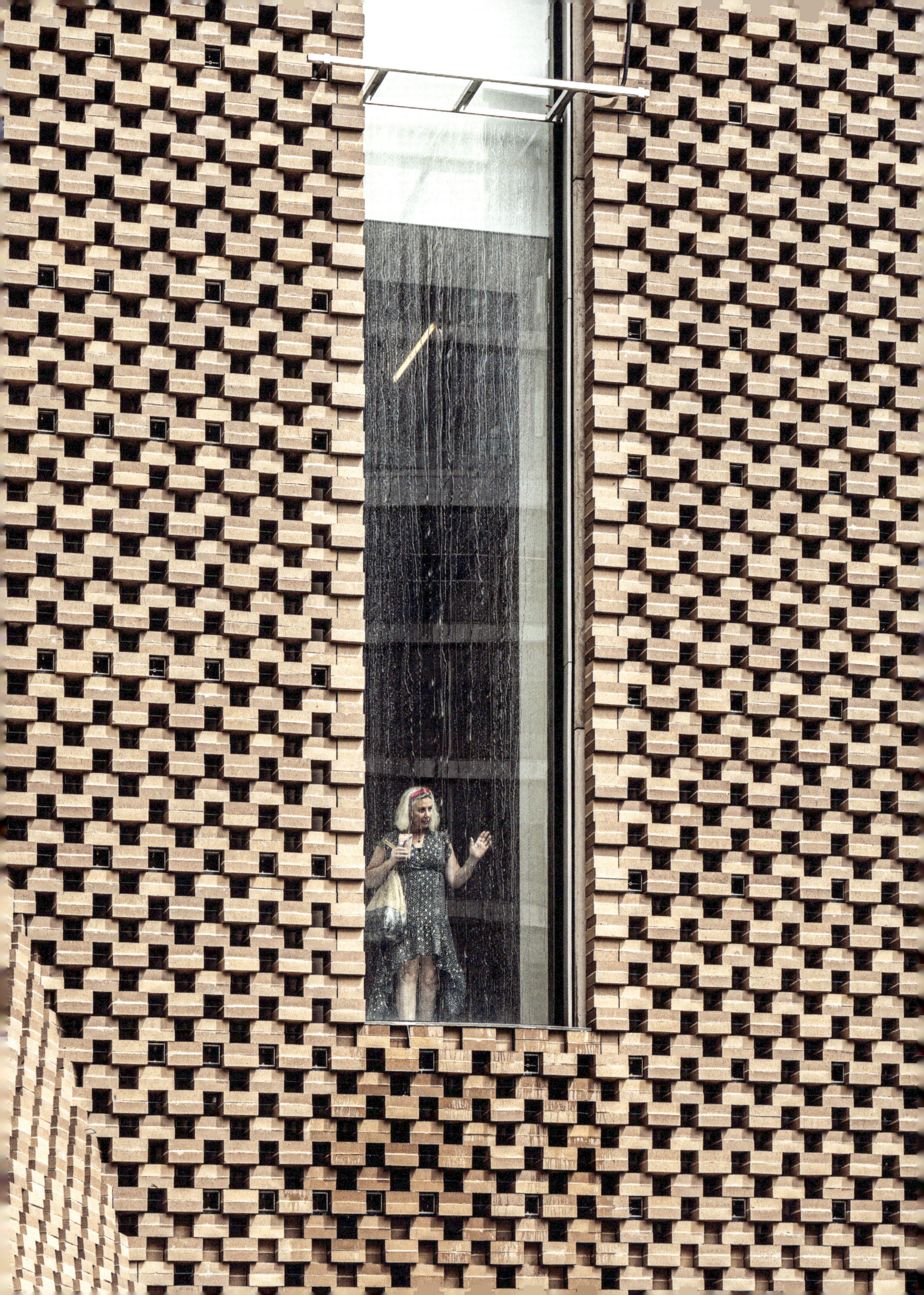

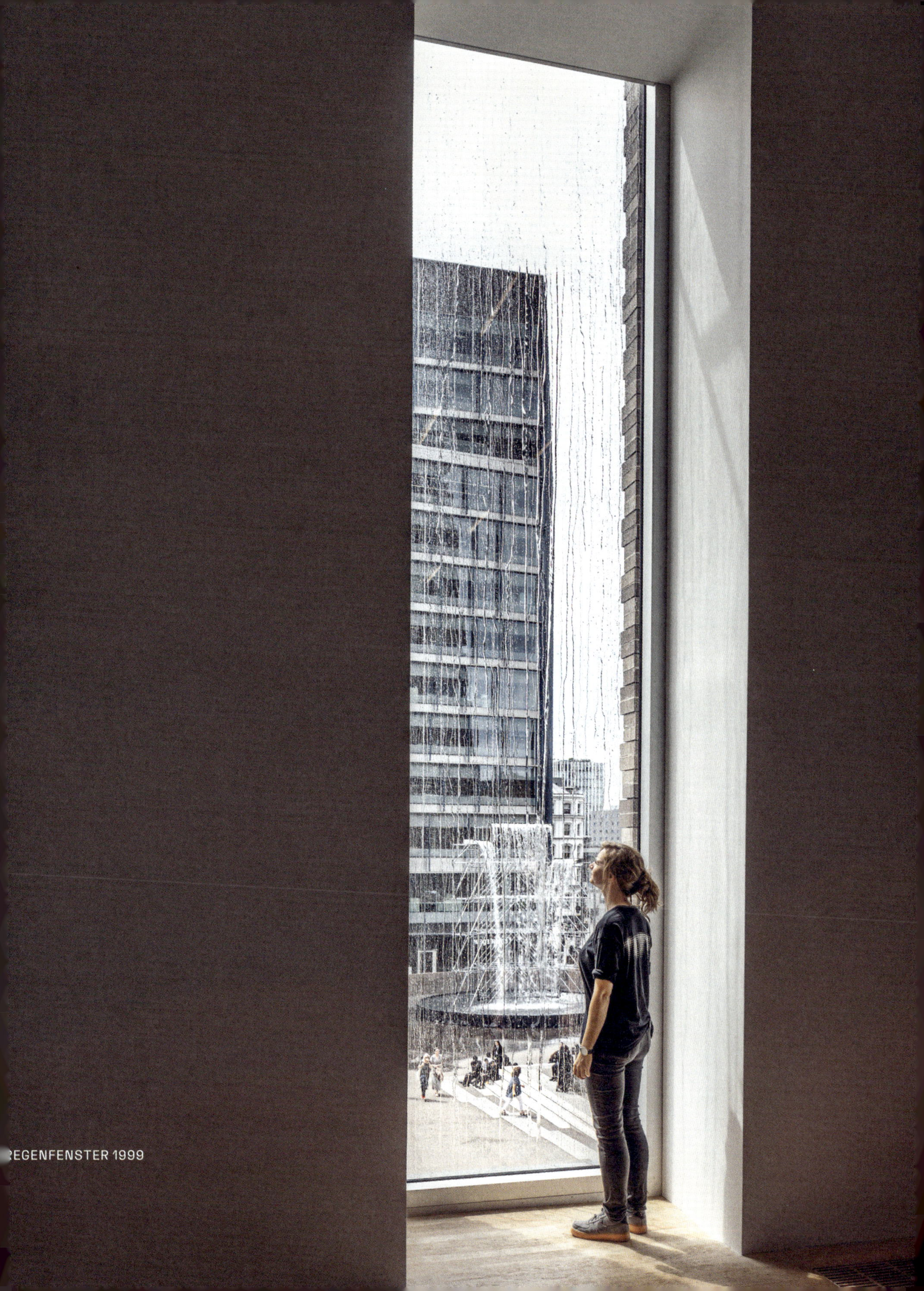

REGENFENSTER 1999

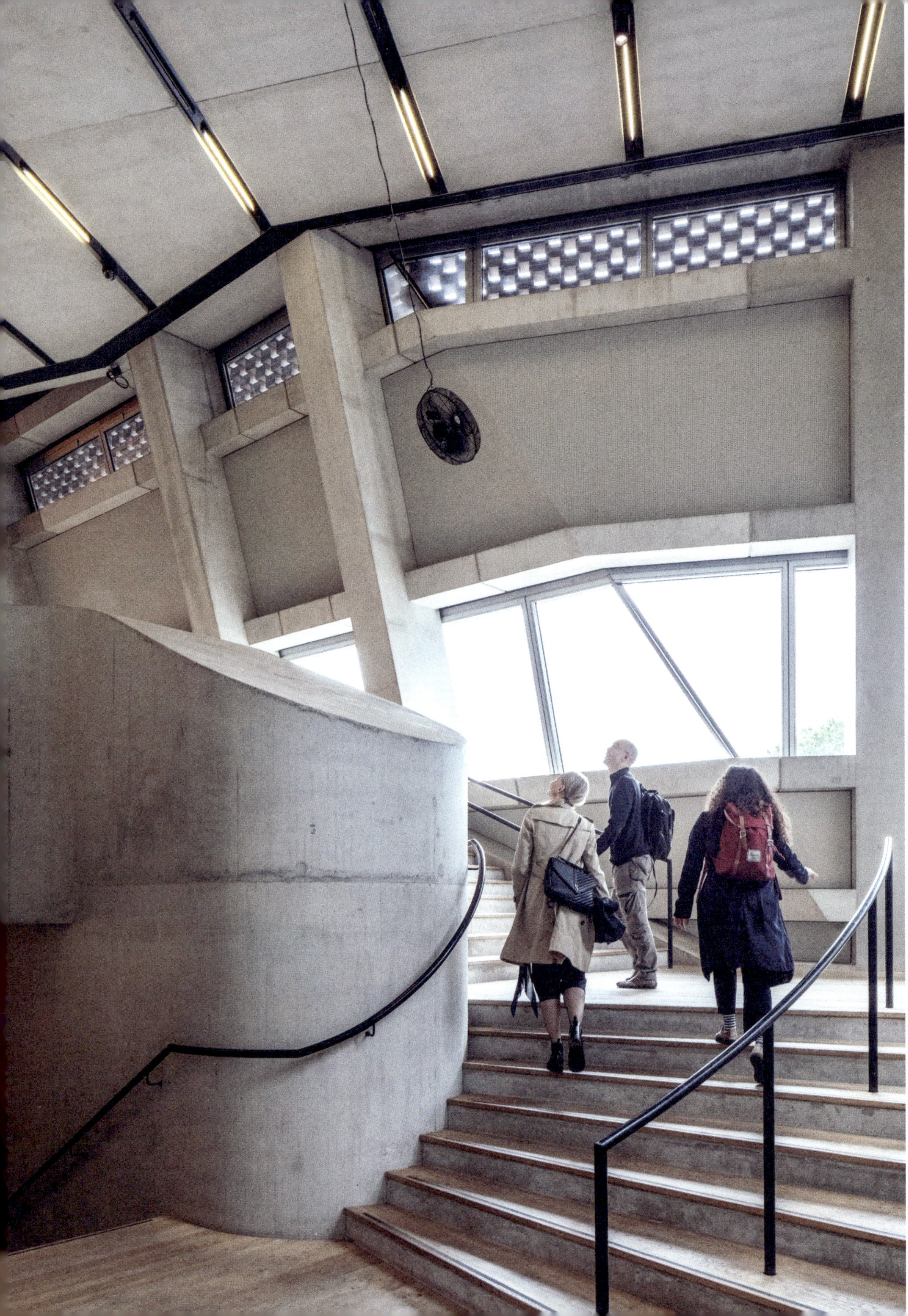

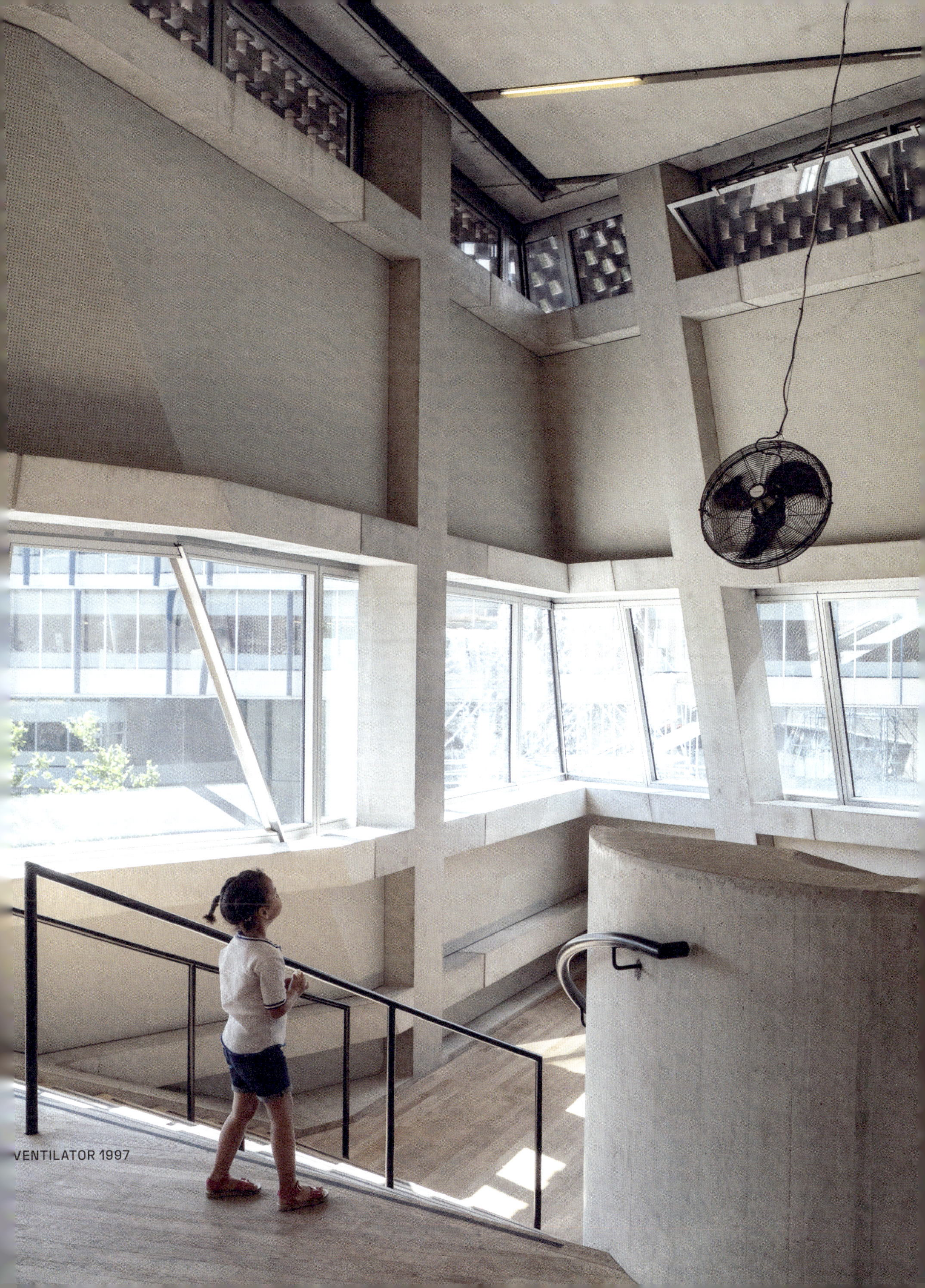

VENTILATOR 1997

<u>Olafur Eliasson:</u> Barry, I am intrigued by the seamless way you draw science, particularly psychology and neuroscience, into your work as a philosopher. How did you become so comfortable in these different areas?

<u>Barry C. Smith:</u> I'm interested in perception and experience but became frustrated with the approach of traditional philosophy. When philosophers talk about perception they often just talk about vision, focusing on a theory of how we see the world around us. I wanted to talk about taste and smell and touch and so on. I was interested in wine and wine tasting, and I thought, 'Well, if I want to know how taste works, I'd better go and talk to my colleagues in psychology and neuroscience.' They told me tasting is always a multisensory experience; it involves taste, touch and smell. It's also influenced by how we see things, by the sounds we hear. This made me really want to get a proper understanding of all the phenomena that affect and shape experience.

Think about tasting. It happens so quickly. You put something in your mouth, you eat it, you chew, you swallow and it's gone. It's ephemeral, and yet a huge amount of brain-work is going on. Many senses are involved.

To do certain things as an artist, Olafur, you have to know about the materials, and you have to know about the process. I feel the same as a philosopher. If I'm going to talk about an experience – if I'm going to understand what it's like for us to eat and to taste things – I need to know the science. I need to understand what makes those experiences possible and shapes them. But though I'm working with scientists and doing experiments with them, I never want to lose sight of what really interests me: getting at the nature of our experiences and why they're so significant and powerful for us.

ANTI-NUMBNESS

BARRY C. SMITH is a philosopher who explores the senses – particularly taste and smell – in collaboration with neuroscientists and psychologists. He directs the Institute of Philosophy at the University of London's School of Advanced Study, where he is also the founding director of the Centre for the Study of the Senses (CenSes). In 2017, he presented a series on multisensory experience for BBC Radio 4, *The Uncommon Senses*. Eliasson invited Smith to Berlin in 2018 to participate in the day-long workshop 'Experimenting, Experiencing, Reflecting: Art and Science at Work in the Public Realm', conceived and hosted with anthropologist Andreas Roepstorff (see pp.154–8).

Last June I was lucky enough to take part in a few of your experiments with wine and food, together with a group of scholars, experimental scientists, and a team from my studio. You worked on a few dishes with my sister, Victoria Eliasdóttir, who is a trained chef, and the studio's kitchen team.

Yes, it was such a delight. I think we agree that the best way to start a workshop is with a dinner. So I thought, let's use that dinner as an opportunity to get people to experience something together. You had invited people to eat with earplugs. I suggested they try certain foods, like blue cheese and seaweed, while wearing a nose clip, to show how smell contributes to what we call taste. We also played sounds to show how this, too, influences how we perceive tastes. It's exciting to try to give people something between an experience and an experiment, something that involves both science and philosophy, instead of just recording participants' behaviour and getting the data from them. We wanted them to experience something themselves – to think about what's going on in them.

People were eating crunchy crisp bread with earplugs in. That makes an enormous noise inside your head – an explosion. We forget that sound also contributes to taste. It can have a destructive impact on what we're eating and drinking. For example, being on an aeroplane with eighty-nine decibels of white noise in your ears has a detrimental effect on your ability to taste salt and sour. Being in a noisy restaurant will interfere with what you're eating, too. You only need to put your fingers in your ears and block out the sound to realise the intensity of the flavours in your mouth.

For the dinner, our experiment also involved another sonic element of eating. We asked whether sound can change flavour. We had people drink a white wine – a Riesling with crisp acidity and some sweetness in it. After their initial tasting, we had them taste it again to the sound of a violin making a very high-pitched noise. When people tried the wine again, they said the wine was more sour. Then we played them some nice, soft, tinkling piano music, and when they tried the wine again they said, 'Oh, now it tastes sweet.' We were trying to show them that lots of factors in your sensory world and the context in which you're eating and drinking affect your response. The wine already had some sweetness and sourness. First we had them attend to the sour note by using that high-pitched violin. Then we had them pay attention to the sweetness by that different correspondence.

I enjoyed that experiment, Barry. Frankly, I was quite surprised that the different sounds changed my perception of the wine. I also heard people using different verbal toolboxes to describe their experiences. Now I am wondering if one can do this in reverse. Can we play a piece of music and then create food, or a meal, to correspond with that musical concept?

It is fascinating how quickly people get it. Once the brain has grasped the idea of what those correspondences are, you can turn it around, creating sounds and asking people what corresponding flavours they imagine. All of this may seem very novel, but humans have intuitively known this for a long time. There were marvellous banquets in quattrocento Italy, for example in the city of Ferrara. Dishes would be brought in, and musicians were primed to start playing as soon as the spoon or the fork went to the mouth. It was understood that music could combine with and influence food. Today we know more about why it works and why it doesn't because we've done the science.

Yes. In traditional art history, there's been a focus on objectivity with regard to our relationship with our surroundings. There was little attention to or understanding of the fact that our senses are relative to our degree of engagement with the subject matter. That, in turn, means that our senses can be trained.

I actually want there to be both some objectivity *and* some subjectivity. I'm interested in both. I want to distinguish between flavours and flavour perception, just as we distinguish between sounds and sound perception, or between colours and colour perception. Flavours, as made by chefs and nature, are there objectively, but we can influence our subjective perceptions of flavour. We can enhance them by paying attention to one part or another.

You mentioned our fellow workshop participants drawing on different 'verbal toolboxes' to describe their experiences. That connects to the notion of specialist vocabulary. I worry that when we talk about wine, or even cuisine, people say, 'Oh, I don't have the language to describe this. Only experts know how to talk about flavours or wine aromas or even perfumes.' I always encourage people to try to describe their impressions by moving to another sense. When eating a lemon, you might say that lemons are 'sharp'. Now, 'sharp' relates to touch, not taste, but it's very natural for that metaphor to come to mind. Similarly, people smelling mint might say it strikes a high note and describe beef as having a low note. You're often able to unlock in people ways in which they might use touch or sound, or they might use another sense to describe their experience.

Take wine. People are scared to describe wine. There's snobbery surrounding it. I never want to go to another one of those meetings where an expert stands at the front swirling a glass and saying, 'This is a tight-knit claret, showing just a bit of green tannin.' And everybody in the room feels left out, thinking 'I've no idea what he's talking about. I'll never get that.' I want to democratise wine, to make sure people can get some of these tastes. For example, you can invite people to smell a red wine and just ask them, 'Red fruit or black fruit?' And people can instantly say, 'black fruit'. 'Okay, is it blackberries, or black cherry, or something else?' And they start to do it. They feel confidence – rightly so – because they now know how to interrogate.

So now you're exploring *your experience* as well as the wine. You're investigating how you react to it. Exploring it is rich and gives you a chance to concentrate on your own experience and what you're noticing, both about the wine and about yourself as you interact with it.

It's similar with art, actually. There is this counter-productive force, a 'governing body of right and wrong', and at first people may feel they aren't welcome to express what they think. The art world, museums, have failed to accommodate the need to verbalise one's own interpretation. So I appreciate that you stress the importance of allowing people to give structure, language, colour, sensibility to ephemeral sensations. Wouldn't you say those are ways of further embodying the experience?

Yes! And language anchors experience. We're talking about things that are ephemeral, very transient – a passing odour, a fading sound. But if we have found a way to anchor these with words, we can hold them in memory. We can return to them. Neuroscience has found evidence that even using the words for particular smells – like cinnamon or vanilla or strawberry – activates the same parts of the olfactory cortex we use when we're actually smelling those things. Again, when we talk about 'mental imagery', people think first and foremost of visual imagery. They may not often have olfactory imagery, but they can acquire it by using their senses, paying attention to smells and the distinctions between them.

Returning to the question of why the art world has failed – and I think the wine world has failed in the same way, and maybe gastronomy, too – we often see a contrast between experts, who use language that excludes others, and a populism that is reduced merely to liking or disliking. People come to an artwork – or to a wine – and just give it thumbs up or thumbs down. I call it the 'Roman Emperor response'. But we've got to get beyond liking. If you're facing something beautifully crafted and complex in front of you, you need to find the means of unlocking that complexity or you won't be able to appreciate it and discriminate. I think our senses – and the crosstalk between the senses – can help people unblock the complexity and find what is interesting in those experiences. People will have better experiences, make better judgments and really know their own preferences. By knowing better why they like something, they'll be able to engage with it more.

And that leads to the question of subjective enquiry and criticality. The really interesting thing is that once you have critical tools for examining your surroundings, you are also more likely to work to change your surroundings. I think it's crucial for people to see themselves as being participants in the world – producers, rather than simply passive consumers. So what do you do to bring your ideas to a broader audience? How can we democratise your agenda?

I love doing public events. We can do things in the lab and investigate effects, but we also want to know if they'll scale up and work outside the lab. Can we do this with children, for example? I don't think we should just be teaching people at school to memorise lots of facts, or just to do arithmetic and a bit of science. We should teach something immersive so they can discover something about themselves. That's transformative. You're noticing what happens, you're beginning to understand why it happens, and that gives you the tools to go out and explore further.

I would count you as key member of the 'counter-numbness' team, as somebody who encourages us to own our senses.

Yes, I do think people are quite isolated from each other today. So yes, there is a numbness. You're right to say that I'm working to counter numbness. I want to intervene. Absolutely! I want people to feel and smell and taste. I want them to notice sensation, and notice how it can go missing. The sense of touch is really important.

The cultural sector, in my definition, encourages people to claim – and own – their individual sensations of the world. At a local level, this makes them participants in steering Spaceship Earth, rather than being passengers. That's why, in the broader scheme of counter-numbness activity, I think democratisation of access to art and culture is so important.

I think there's an analogy between what the church used to do and what commerce does now. The church used to claim that sight and sound were the 'higher senses', suited to lifting your eyes from the earth to the heavens and receiving the Word of God. Whereas the 'lower senses' – the bodily senses of taste, touch and smell – were corrupt, they were all about sensations in you. Now, interestingly, our culture is largely in a corporate space that privileges the digital world, and the digital world is audiovisual. Touch is less involved. We do not have taste and smell. We don't have feelings of embodiment. So there is something here, again, that privileges sight and sound as the 'higher' senses. If you're connected, plugged in, part of the digital economy, sight and sound are what matters.

When someone is in front of the computer screen all day, it's like a knight dying inside his armour, to paraphrase John le Carré. There's a bit of us that's going numb and there's a bit of us that is left out. But there is a glimmer of hope, because even as we're glued to our screens, looking at films, we cannot look at images without in some way embodying them, without having a visceral response – without having a feeling of anticipated movement.

We have to reach out and capture that. The sort of art interventions you do, Olafur, and the sort of sensory experiences that my colleagues and I create at festivals, really do bring people away from their screens. They meet one another, put things in their mouths, smell things with their noses and actually feel like whole human beings. I want to give people experiences that they can share with others. We have to wake people up and invite them to feel the embodiment. And I want to use neuroscience, too, to include the public, to inform them and enable them to pay attention to their experiences. And I actually think they'll make better political choices if they'll realise that they can connect with people.

At the moment I think one of the great political dangers is that people see a simple choice between populism and elitism. There are those with the authority to tell us what to think – whether or not they actually have the knowledge they seem to have – and when people recoil from that, they rush towards populism, towards a 'democracy of taste', in which anybody's opinion is as good as anyone else's. But it's a false choice. Elitism suggests there are only some people who have knowledge, and populism seems the only alternative. I want to reject that and say, 'You can know these things, too, you just don't know them yet. Let's find ways in which you can explore things beyond your first impressions and your first reactions, and this will make your experiences much richer, more enjoyable, and not limit you to immediate likes and dislikes. This will give you a better understanding of yourself and of others.' That's what we want.

And it's only fair to say that the polarisation of populism happens through a pull from both sides. It is not just one group failing the other. You're very right about the importance of decentralising the ownership of knowledge, and I love the idea of occupying your own senses. Everybody has senses. We just need to reclaim them – because they have been turned into commodities.

Exactly. They've been muted. Commodified and numbed. We share even more than I thought we did, Olafur! Now we've got to get the word out there.

September 2018

THE GLACIER SERIES 1999
/ DETAIL

> THE GLACIER
SERIES 1999

>> THE RIVER-RAFT
SERIES 2000

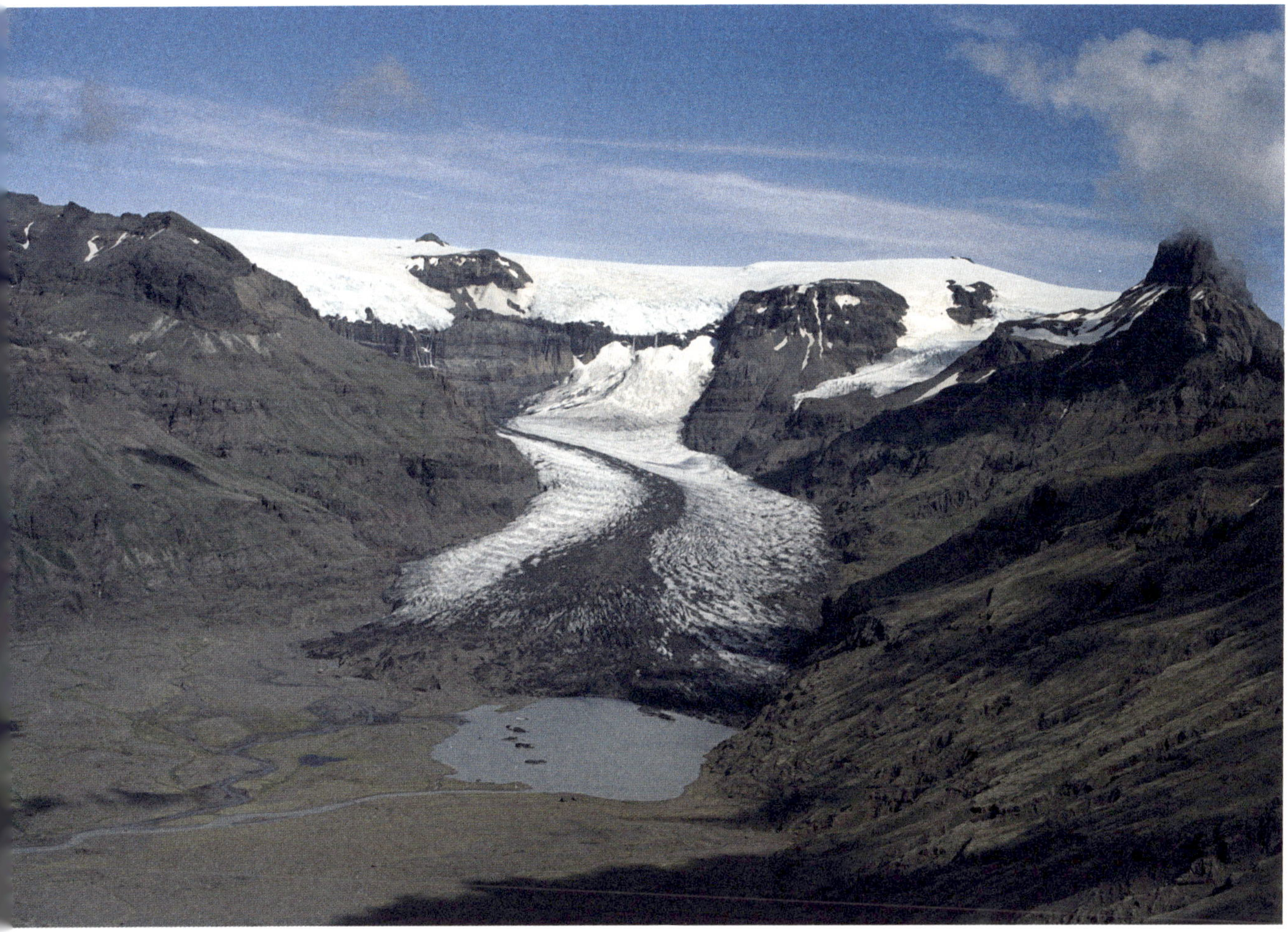

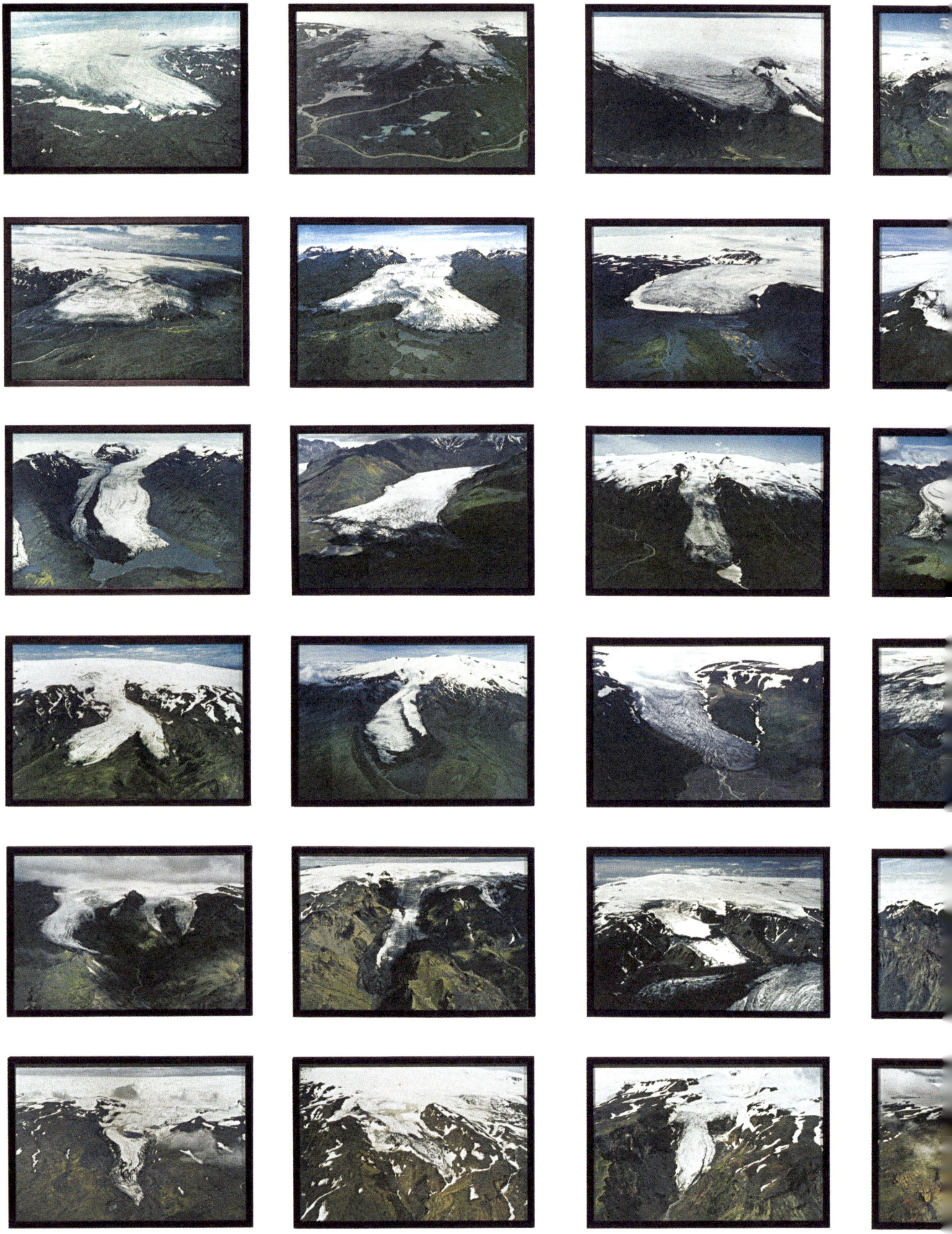

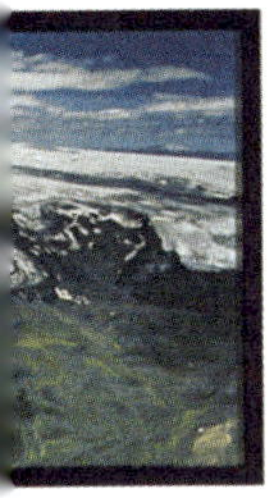
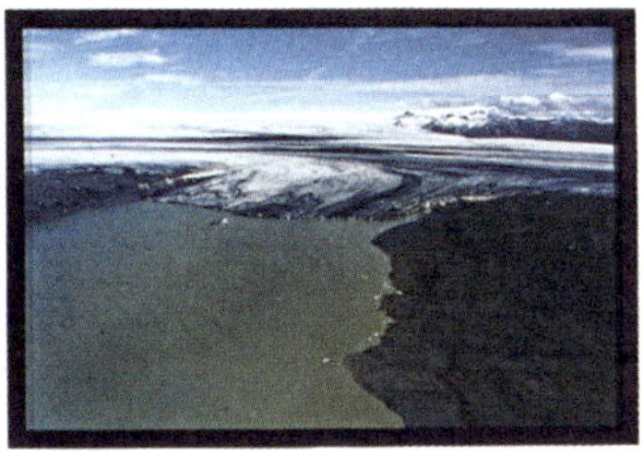
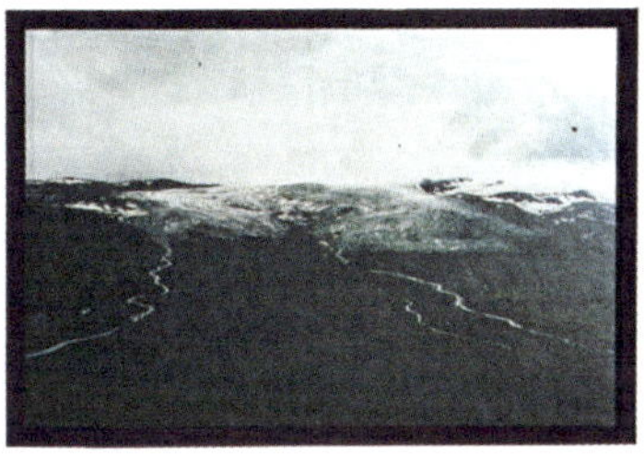
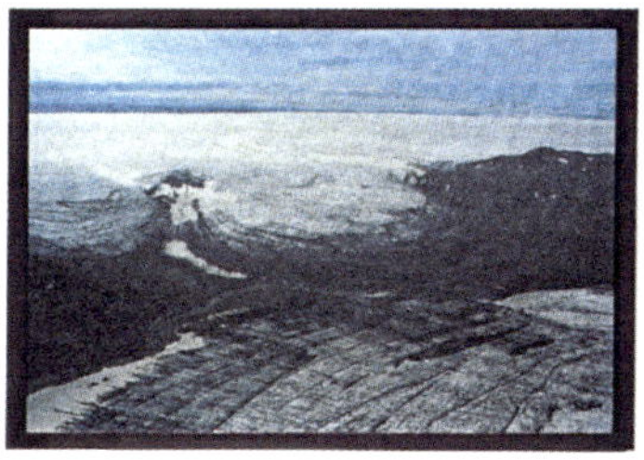
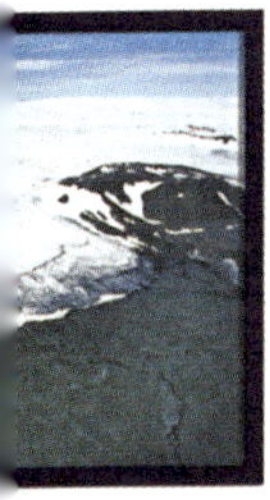
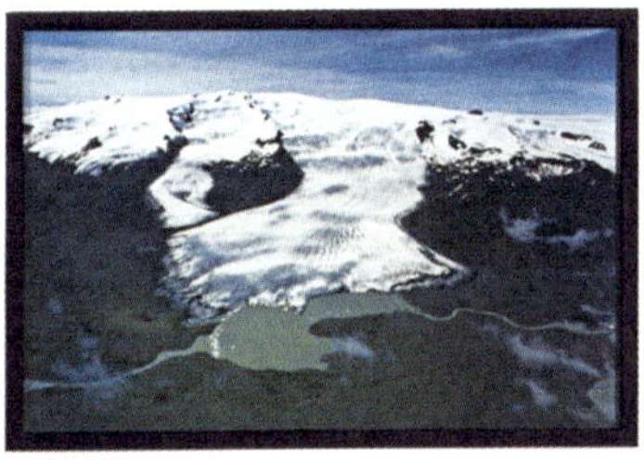
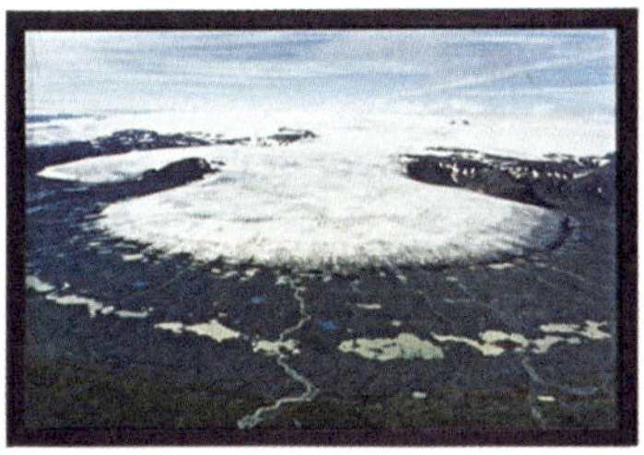
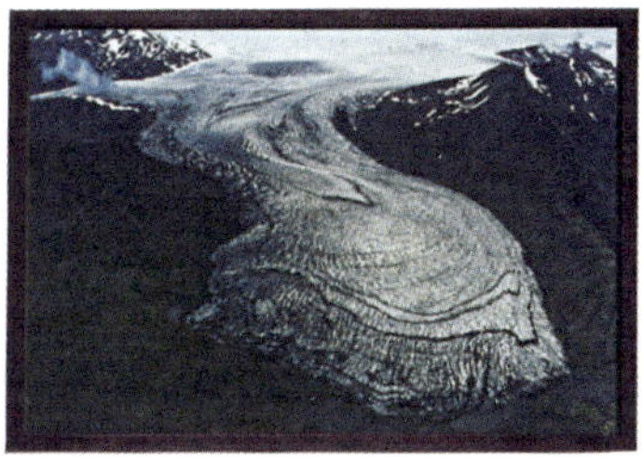
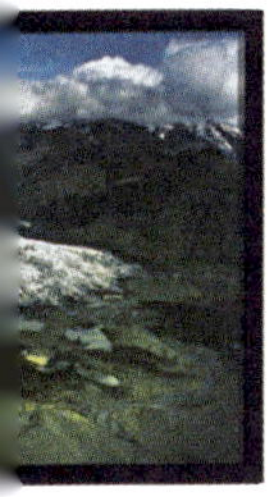
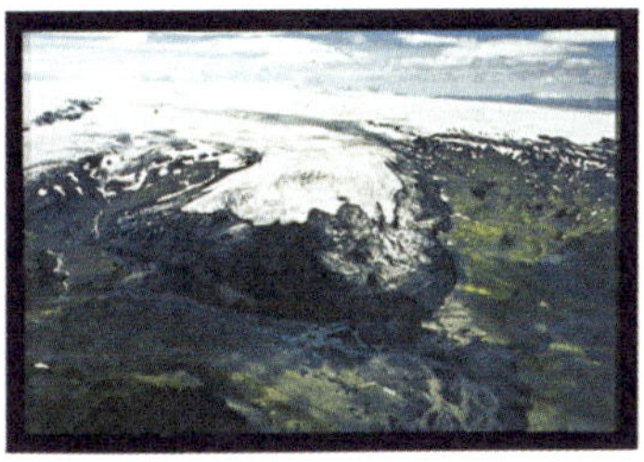
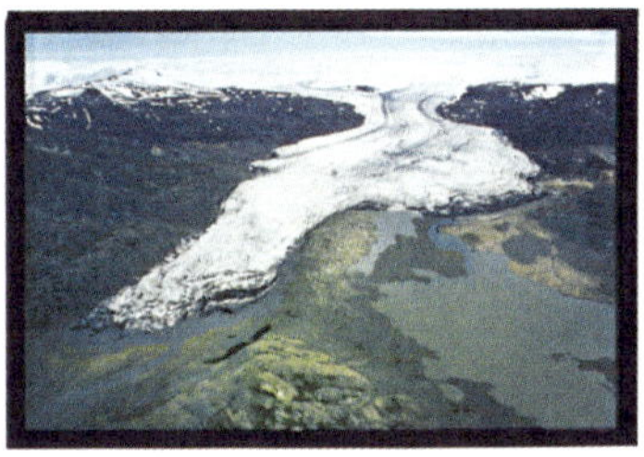
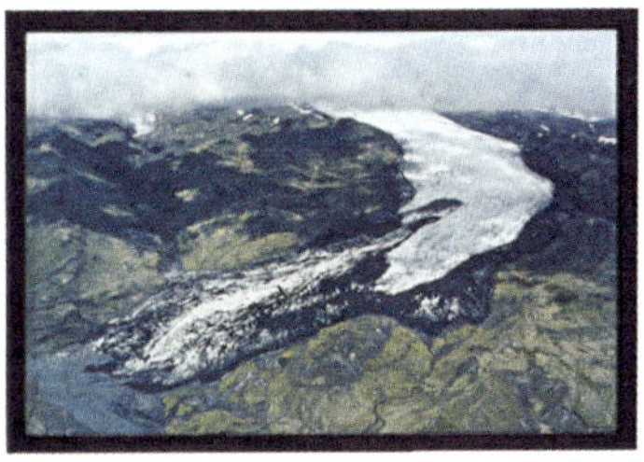
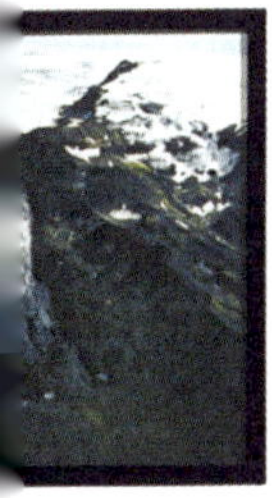
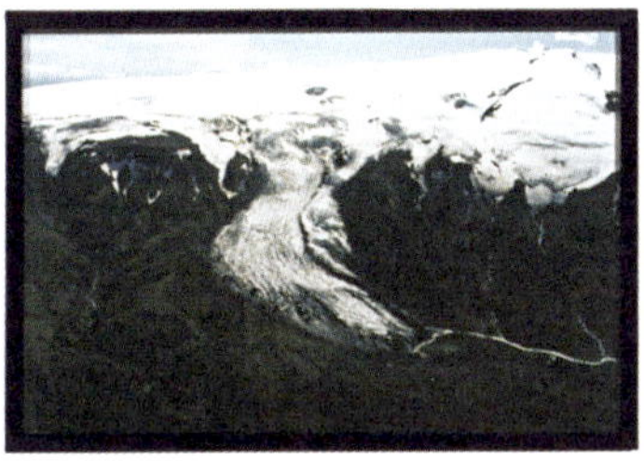
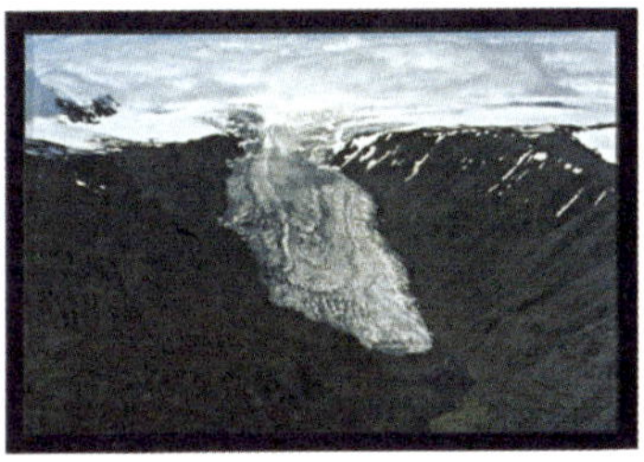
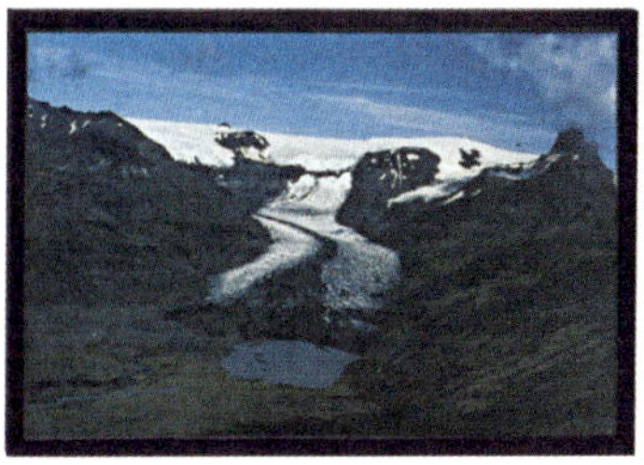
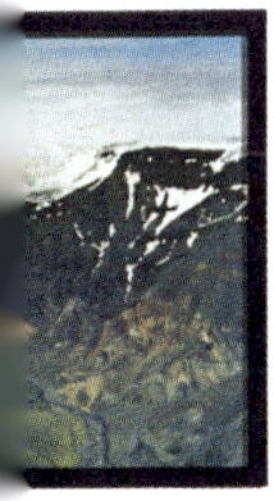
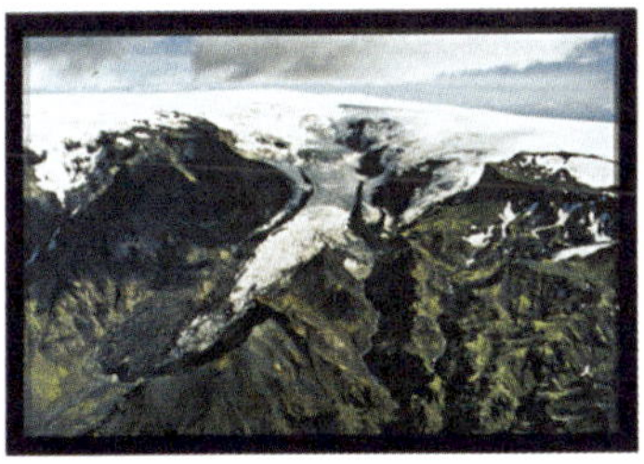
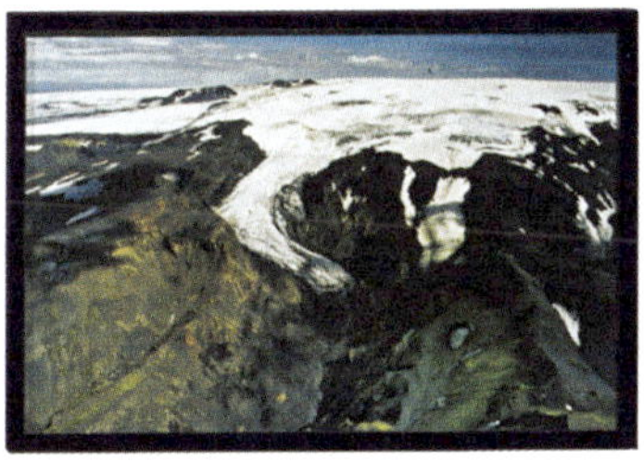
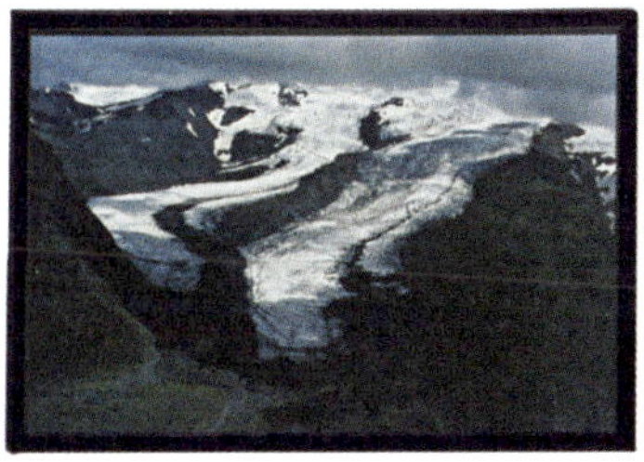
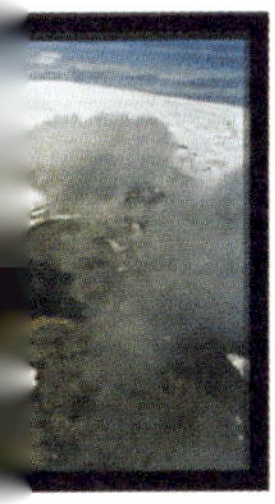
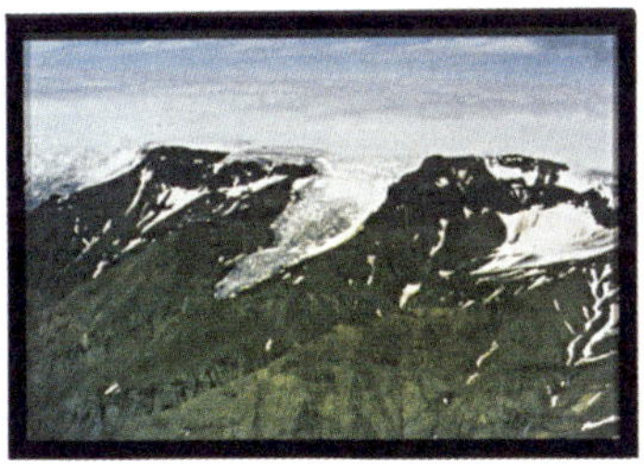
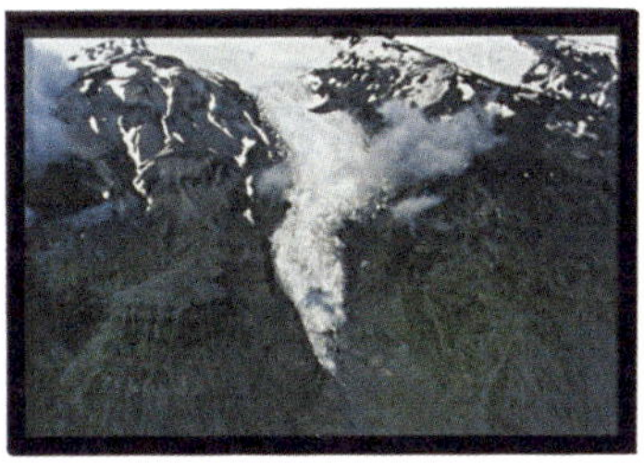
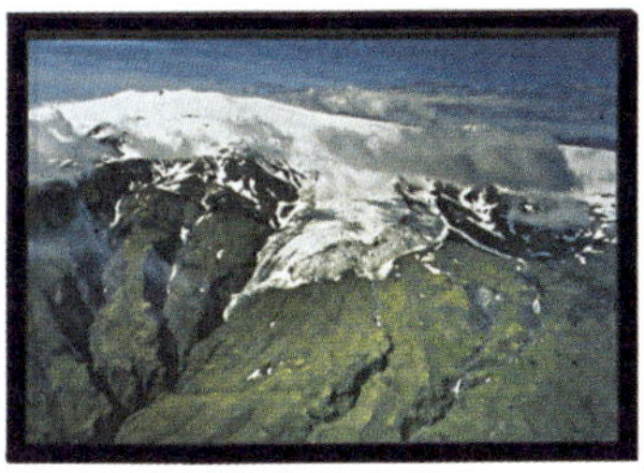

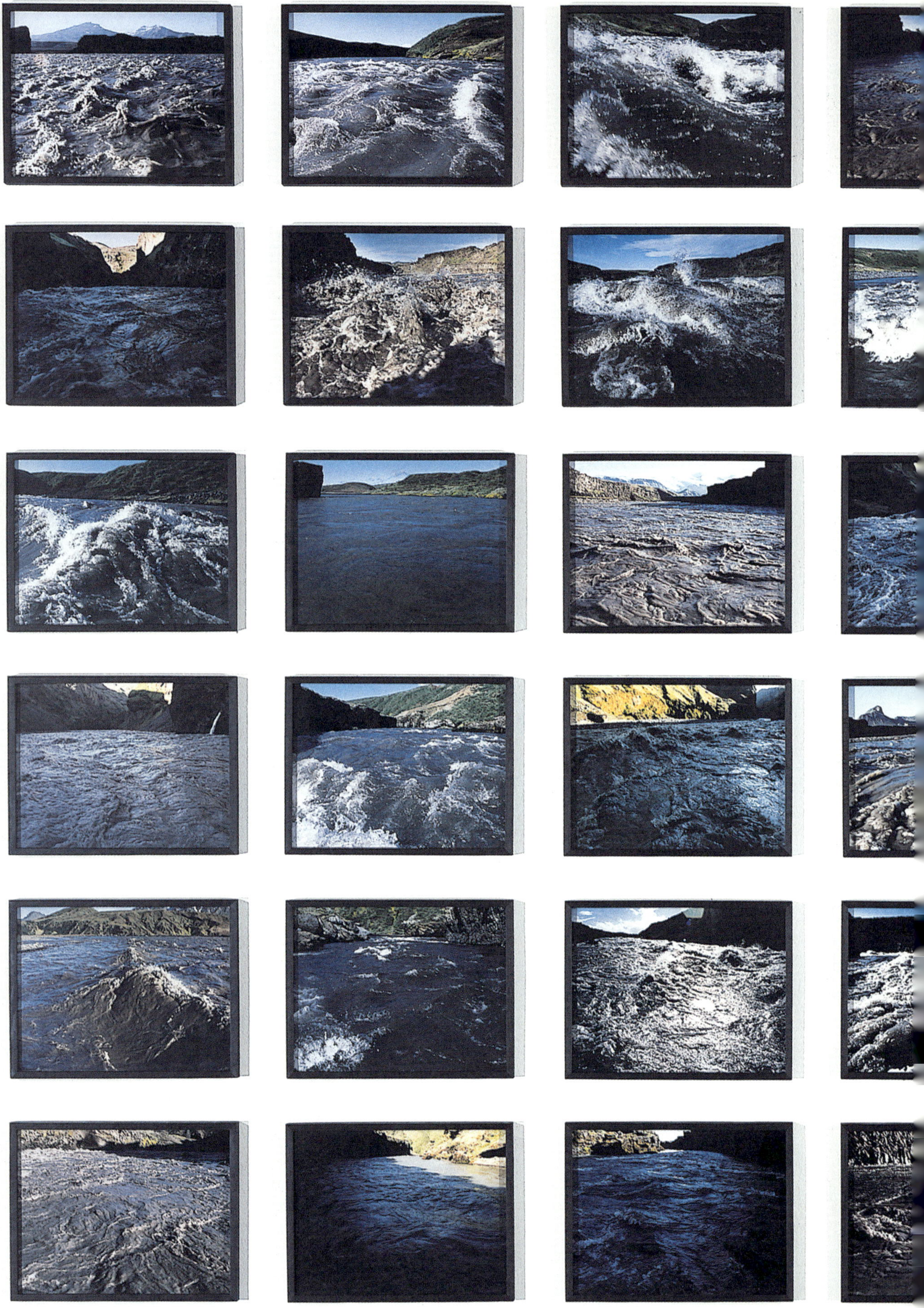

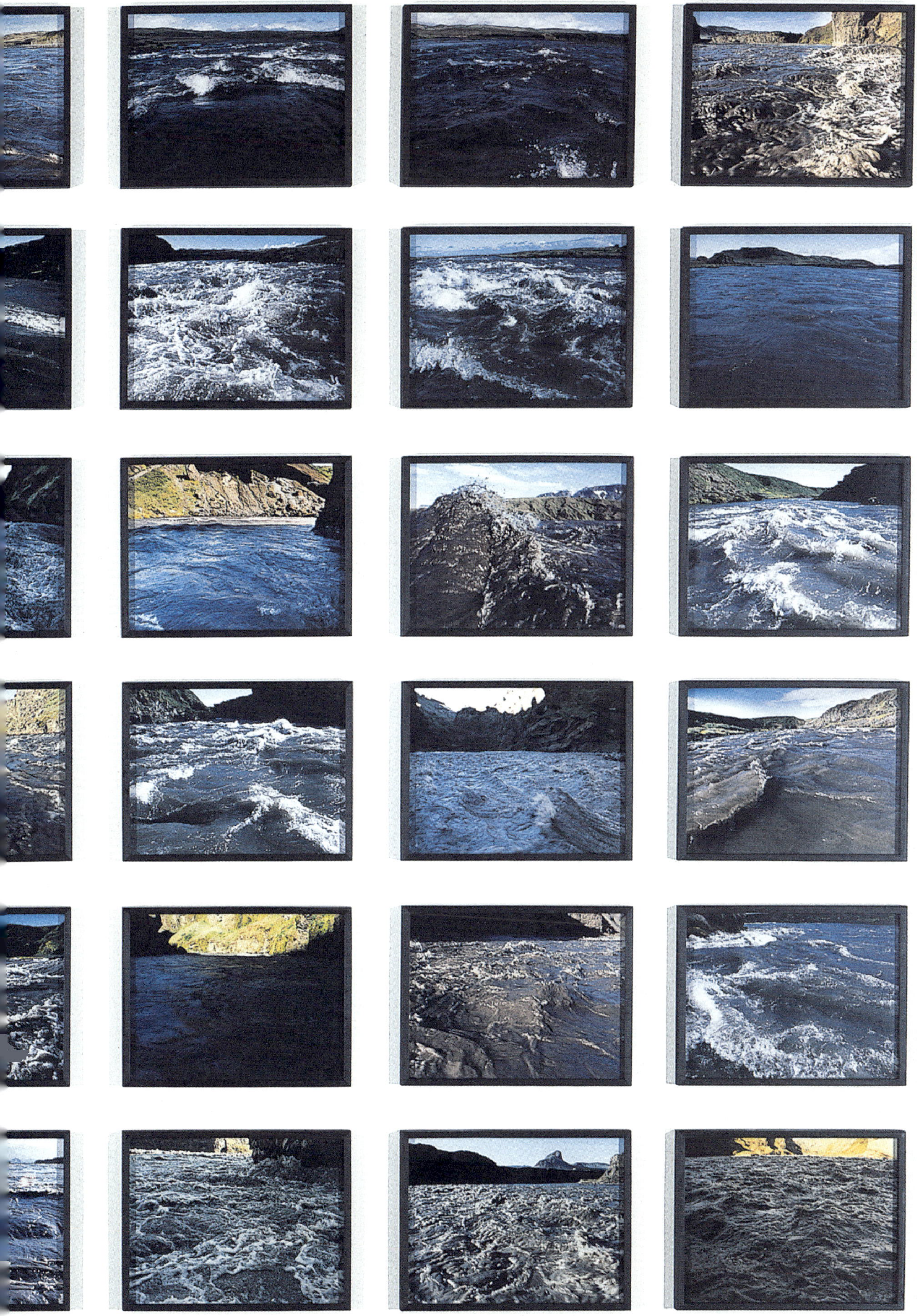

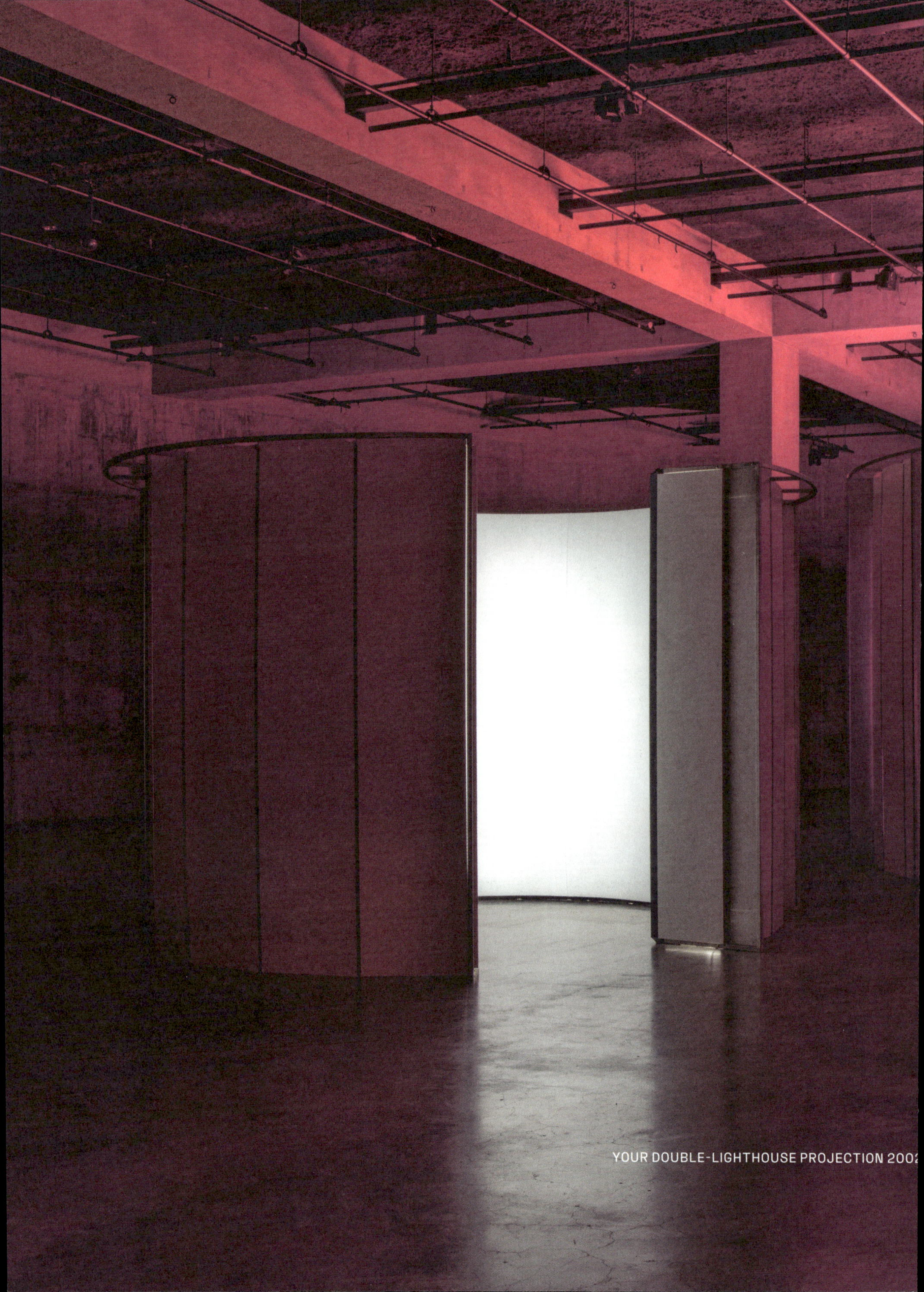

YOUR DOUBLE-LIGHTHOUSE PROJECTION 200

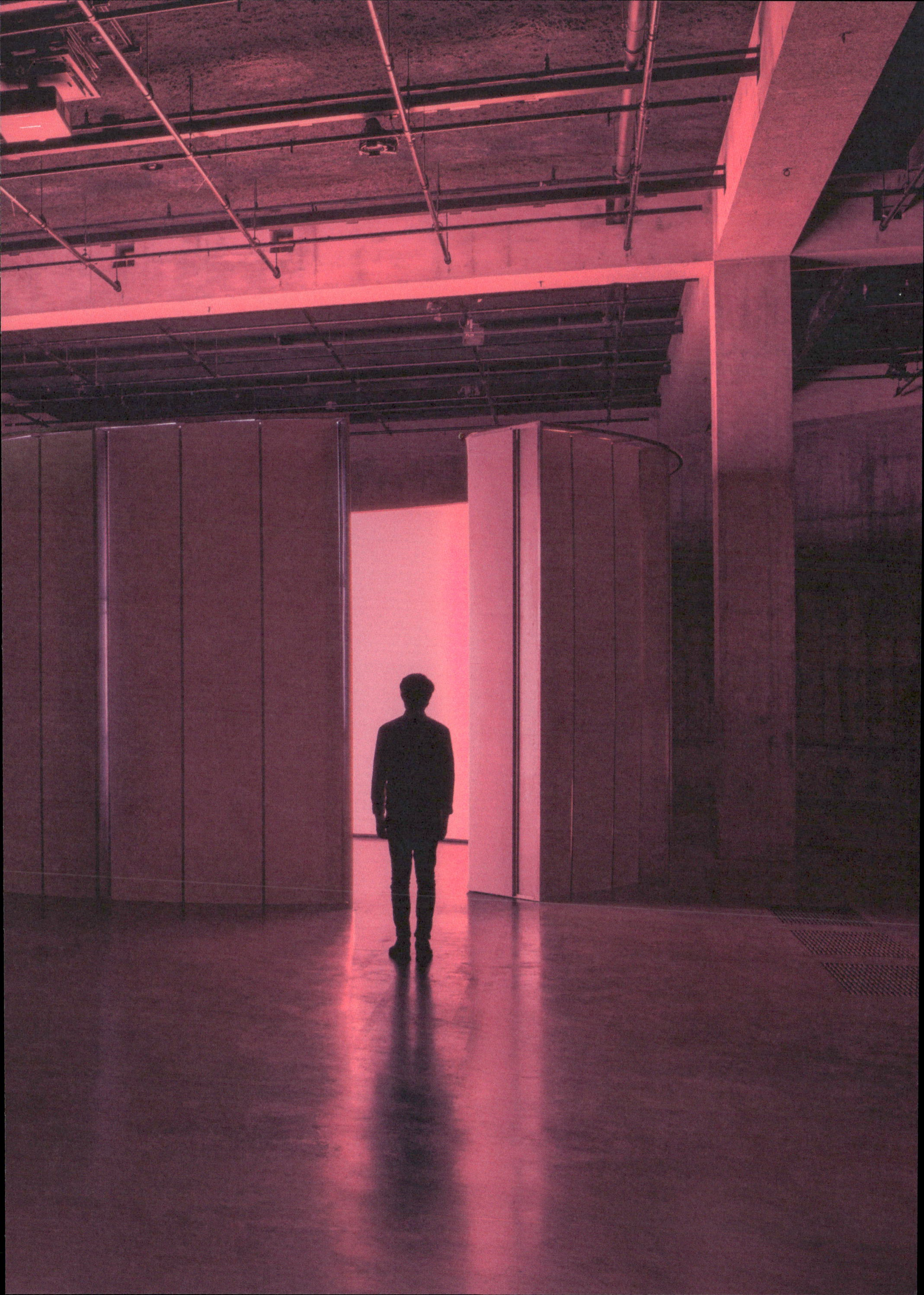

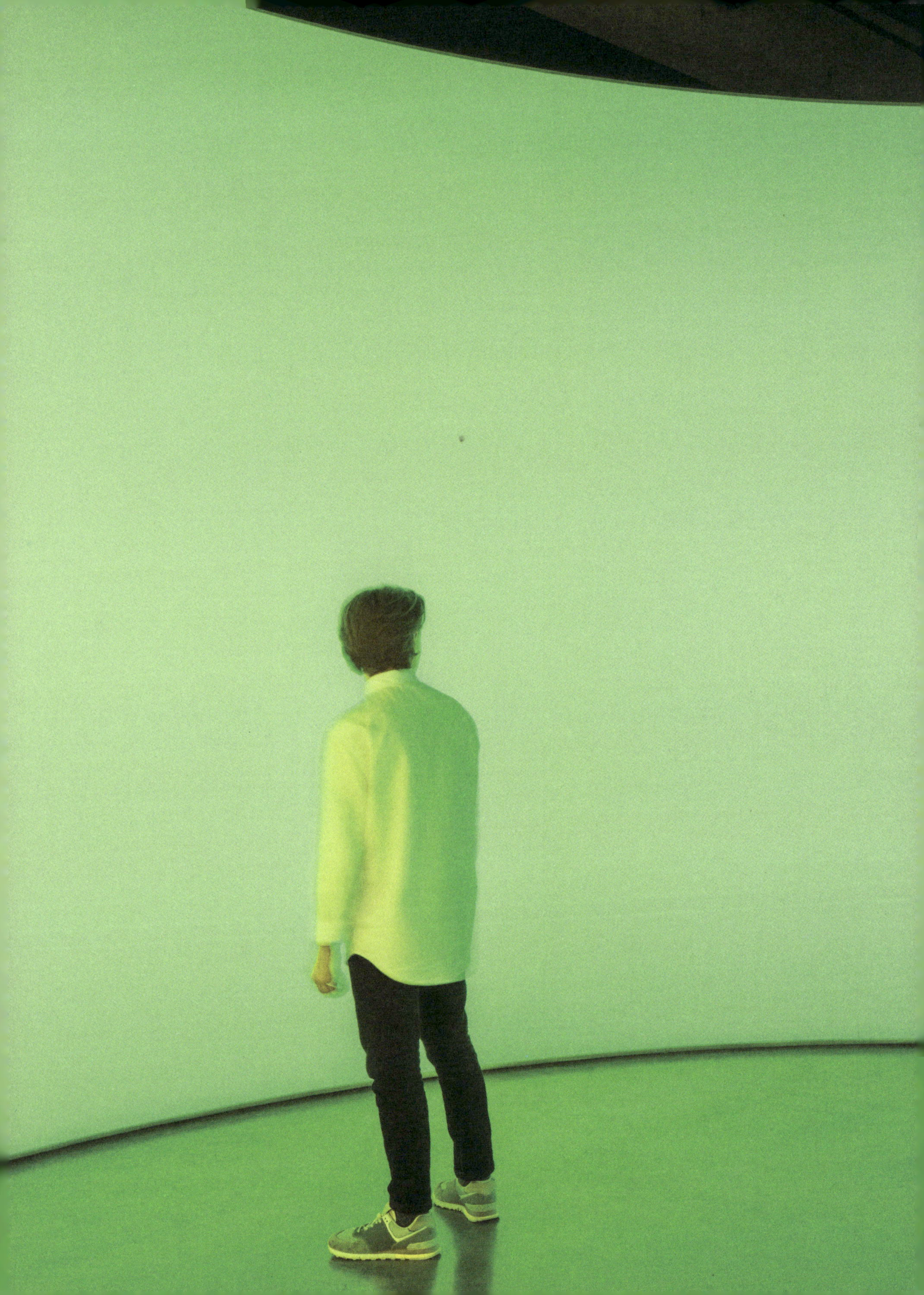

Olafur Eliasson: I'm glad that you could come up this week to work with Sebastian Behmann at our office for art and architecture, Studio Other Spaces, here in Berlin. Over the years, we have become increasingly interested in learning from and addressing questions about local architecture in Ethiopia. We are involved with several different projects in Addis Ababa related to architecture and space, the city and city planning, parks and so on – one being the Meles Zenawi Memorial Park, which is almost done. Our friendship has evolved over this period.
The purpose of your visit this week was essentially to help us, and we are happy to absorb your knowledge and see how we can become better at understanding things that are sometimes hard to grasp at first. Something that strikes me in Addis Ababa is the division between private space – or private property – and so-called public space. Would you start by describing what is called public space in the capital?
Brook Teklehaimanot: I'm also trying to learn more about this, but to start, since Addis is a very young city, this notion of private and public is still being negotiated. It's not really an established cultural truth. Even though it's a city – we call it the capital of Africa – Addis Ababa has a lot of rural cultures within it. The way people act, the way we act, is also partly rural. So that's why we have a strong notion of boundaries and fences. We'll have a fence and a very strong green boundary after the fence. We'll have a dog, sometimes even a guard if you can afford it. So these layers of boundaries tell you that the inside is always very protected, that it is clearly private.
And there is a strong sense of ownership.
Yes. Now public space is, again, different from the European sense of it. What we normally call 'public' is not 'what is not private', but rather 'what we share'. And this is not usually the streets and the squares. It's usually institutions like the church for Christians, which anyone can access, where anyone can go for solitude, not only to pray but also for things like studying. The churches also have a nice atmosphere because they're green, which is sometimes hard to find in Addis. There are gardens around them, and you are not allowed to cut trees. It's a nice environment. The mosque serves the same purpose for Muslims. I think we should kind of redefine what public space really is for Addis Ababa.

PUBLIC SPACE

BROOK TEKLEHAIMANOT is an architect and urbanist who divides his time between his chair in the faculty of the Ethiopian Institute of Architecture, Building Construction and City Development (EiABC) in Addis Ababa and the Technical University of Delft, the Netherlands, where he is a doctoral candidate. He is also the founder and director of protoLAB, a digital prototyping and design workshop. In 2012 he collaborated with Eliasson's Institut für Raumexperimente during the institute's residency in Addis Ababa and hosted an architecture workshop with Sebastian Behmann, who co-founded and runs Studio Other Spaces (SOS), an office for art and architecture, with Eliasson.

And would a museum also qualify as a public space?

Not really. We have few museums and they're very restricted, with hours when you can access them. So they are not part of the urban culture.

Then you have Meskel Square, with the museum at the top of the square and these stairs. There are sometimes gatherings, demonstrations or a big speech, like when prime minister Abiy Ahmed spoke there a few weeks ago. Is that not considered a shared space?

Yes, that's a shared space nearer to the sense of public space you have here in Europe. It's similar in that it's public, very large and widely accessible – but it doesn't actually look like a square at all, formally speaking. I tried to do a film project in Meskel Square a few months ago with visual artist and academic Berhanu Ashagrie.

Oh, my old friend from the Alle art school at Addis Ababa University.

We decided to do a film from all the four different corners of Meskel Square. I was supposed to use my iPhone to capture video, but it was extremely difficult to get footage. It's not that the police came and told us to stop, but there is a sort of social control: everybody is aware that you're doing something different, so people are suddenly uncomfortable, including the police and the authorities. It's not that they're scared of you or anything, they're just curious to know what's happening. People really watch you, so you have to be careful or you will be asked. And it took me a couple of hours just to do three to five minutes' worth of shots. But on the same day, I went to another public space, the Jan Meda race ground, and it was easy to do a small panoramic shot in just five minutes. It was amazing.

Yeah, Jan Meda is a leisure space, for sport. People go there for recreation, whereas Meskel Square is a busy city centre – an intersection of traffic, public transport and so on.

Something else I'm interested in is the space *between* private spaces. When you go into someone's garden, everything is very organised. It's very tidy. But immediately outside, the streets and the side streets between buildings are full of chaos. There are trenches, sometimes even open sewers. Clearly people have no sense of ownership of the street. There are rules – you're not supposed to do this, you cannot drive fast, you cannot open a store on the street without a permit, etc. – but if this space is not public, what is it?

It's nobody's space, actually – a space where nobody belongs. Things like roads are controlled. They don't belong to the public – we'd have to create another term for it. And that's also why, traditionally, people try to push their fences into this space and then acquire more land.

I grew up in Scandinavia, where there's a very strong sense that what is public actually reflects the interest of the public. The street represents a set of values where I can exercise the way I see the world.

So there's a discussion going on in Europe about public space. Is 'the public' actually really public? Is there a discrepancy between how we think about public resources and what we actually have access to? We Europeans – particularly the Scandinavians – think we are infinitely inclusive and welcoming, and the truth is that in the public sphere, in large parts of Europe, there are a lot of phobias and structural challenges. There's racism. You could argue that public space is not in fact reflecting democratic values. I think Addis is in the process of defining the public and the agency that the

notion of the public offers. It has the opportunity to create a kind of bottom-up approach to defining the space that everybody in Addis owns together.

You know, up until recently I thought of Addis as a very young city – it's only 130 years old. That is young by European standards. It made me angry that the spaces I called public in Addis were not as public as I wanted them to be. But travelling to smaller Ethiopian cities – secondary, less populous cities like Hawassa and Mek'ele and others – I saw a totally different story. Hawassa, for example, is a very green city. Everybody takes care of the lawns, though they are not part of their private property; they make sure they're extremely clean. Mek'ele is another city with exemplary urban values. In Mek'ele, people actually clean the streets. They also use public spaces and squares – for example, in [the northern city of] Axum, they use the squares for studying, for sitting together. Even the way they park their bicycles, the way they walk, is totally different than it is in Addis. So I'm interested in why Addis became the way it did. So, though I don't have a finished theory about this, I think something happened in Addis that made it the way it is now.

Addis has a kind of a defensive attitude towards the notion of the civic. Why is that?

I think it has to do with our political history, especially the abrupt jump from the monarchy to the communist regime in the late 1970s. A lot of people died. When you read and hear about it, you can understand why everybody preferred being indoors. It was *dangerous* outdoors. Addis went through that bruising time in history. And again, with the political change in 1991 from a totally communist regime to a partly open economy and another total shift of government, again the old mentality was never welcome. So Addis is always starting out again from square one politically. And I think this has consequences for how we interact with each other. One friend was telling me about a culture in Addis of people sitting inside their cars to have coffee. They buy coffee in the café, but people would rather drink it in their cars in the parking lots. And Addis has nice weather! This is particular to Addis, and I always wondered about it. Somebody told me one theory, which is that during the Red Terror people spied on each other, so you really wanted privacy. Another person told me, 'Maybe it's because it's a new culture, capitalist culture, and you want to show your car off to other people, so having coffee in your car is trendy.' I don't know why it is, but again you still want your private zone. You might throw stuff out the car window, but your car is clean.

I find this so interesting. In Europe, especially in the bigger cities, we have made the mistake of taking public space for granted – as something natural, something that doesn't need to be criticised or, you could say, reinvented as we go along. It is just something we are so used to – just like democracy and our trust in it – that we have forgotten to maintain it. I believe it's a similar lack of self-criticism that's resulting in the current challenges to democracy – the populism, the polarisation. Suddenly you have situations where people are mistrustful and fearful. You have large groups of people who feel marginalised and not a part of democracy. Europe is facing a number of challenges: the EU is more or less crumbling; the responses to the migration crisis are totally ineffective.

I'm inspired by these multiple discussions in Addis of what is public and the effects of successive phases of political rule there, because it teaches me not to take public space for granted. I really very much enjoy going to Addis, despite the fact that I can

see the challenges, the bruises, the oppressive structures and so on – it allows me to take in information. That is why I have been going there: to learn not only about Addis but also about the culture that I grew up in.

Your work as an architect has focused on that kind of an inside–outside relationship. Maybe you can explain that a little.

You know the moderate weather we have in Addis: without harsh winters or summers, the climate is ideal for designing outside space, especially if you have a garden. I am interested in how internal dwelling spaces enter into dialogue with the 'non inside', the 'semi-inside'. It's a typology of its own – let's call it 'typology of the outside' for now. Unfortunately, there aren't many examples of it in our urban areas, but in rural areas you see how outside space is coordinated not only for human beings but for cattle too. You find this in some rural housing typologies in Tigray in northern Ethiopia. This transitional space is sometimes difficult to visualise using traditional modes of representation. The simplest of these typologies could be an outside room: a room with all the amenities of an inside space but maybe without a ceiling, or with half a wall. These are some of the paths I have been taking in my experiments.

I saw the house that you did for your own family and liked it very much. The quality of the small garden, the big garden and the relationship between the inside and outside. Some of it had a modernist twist. I could see that the local circumstances were perfect for making outside space part of the functional programme of the house. The outside is not just a garden; the outside is actually another version of the inside. But tell me, do you think that, taking a longer perspective, global warming will change the climate in places like Addis, and through that essentially change the architecture?

It will. I have seen the difference already in my lifetime. The amount of rainfall is different. The intensity of the sun is different. The rainy season is changing every year. So, yes, this will have implications for architecture. Because we're a poor country, the Ethiopian context requires coming up with materials that are really cheap to acquire and build with, and using fewer imports. This is another experiment we have to do.

You're very active in the architectural school EiABC, and know a lot of students through your teaching. Are young architects very conscious of environmental and economic factors when working towards a local architectural language?

Yes, definitely. But they also need role models and examples. Our biggest challenge is the difficulty of deviating from the mainstream. When the mainstream is always using the same material everywhere – reinforced concrete – it's hard to fight that successfully. Of course, most art and architecture students want to be visionary, but in the end you see this tendency to fall back on comfortable notions and conventions.

These days there is a lot of Asian, particularly Chinese, investment. Chinese real-estate money is flowing into Ethiopia for regional and national projects. This city started out with a sort of modern urban plan, with a beautiful green necklace running through it, which was then turned into parks and so on. But we know that contemporary Asian urban structure is organised around other values, such as optimising profitability. It pays less regard to what we discussed about public space. Do you think the city's architectural evolution, its typology of space, will change now?

The outside influence is clear. The danger right now is more from the industrial parks, for example, where, as you said, it's all about efficiency, and where focus is on the production level. Several industrial parks are planned for the country – about fourteen or fifteen sites, some of which are already built. They are huge parks where the government provides the basic infrastructure – electricity, roads and other such things – and then global companies like H&M and European companies occupy the space. They produce, and then they sell. This is very helpful for the economy and manufacturing sector, but if the land is not well managed the consequences for place-making are dire. While I agree that this phenomenon is being pushed forward by the Chinese, since their construction companies are building these industrial parks, in the end the global market also profits – including Europe's. So I don't agree that China is the sole driver here. I also see a lot of EU money coming in. These industrial campuses will probably look Chinese, but I don't see Addis becoming an Asian city in the near future. I think it's going to take a different trajectory.

I'm excited about Ethiopia's dynamic qualities. The country is thriving, but it is also just moving so fast through so many of the epochs that took much longer in Europe. It's like Addis is a different city every five years. It's incredible. Everything is unsettled, on the move, changing. There's the headquarters of the African Union, there are the various different United Nations offices, there are all the diplomats ... it's really the capital of East Africa, which gives it an interesting global perspective. People are increasingly well educated and often even educated abroad, so there is an interesting cocktail of local skills, talent and knowledge, combined with what people have picked up in other places in the world. It's like a multiverse.

I'd like to ask you a question. My freinds and colleagues and I are always arguing about whether it's possible to identify any specifically Ethiopian characteristics. What is your experience of Ethiopians?

Well, in my experience from teaching at the art school, people are very self-conscious. It takes time to get to know them well. They're also very proud, very robust. The students tend to be good at debating, but they're not especially flexible – they don't readily change their minds.

Do you think they're stubborn?

Maybe you could put it that way. When I teach art at the university in Addis, for instance – which I enjoy a lot, because there are a lot of really talented people – there's often a certain scepticism. I can understand that: my being a white guy from a Western background who has had a lot of exposure within a certain type of art world puts me in a fairly predictable position. But the aim is not to agree or be the same.

The aim, obviously, is to respect that there are different ways and different truths.

This sort of educational format, or debate format, interests me.

I was lucky to have an exhibition in Addis [*Time-sensitive activity*, Addis Ababa University's Modern Art Museum: Gebre Kristos Desta Centre, 2015], and it was an opportunity for me to raise a number of questions without using language.

The artworks spoke for themselves. I think this led to more genuine discussions, because people used their own language to respond to it. I came to really appreciate the views of a number of people, with whom I've since become very friendly. I can see that the more I learn, the less I really know about the country. It has made me more humble.

July 2018

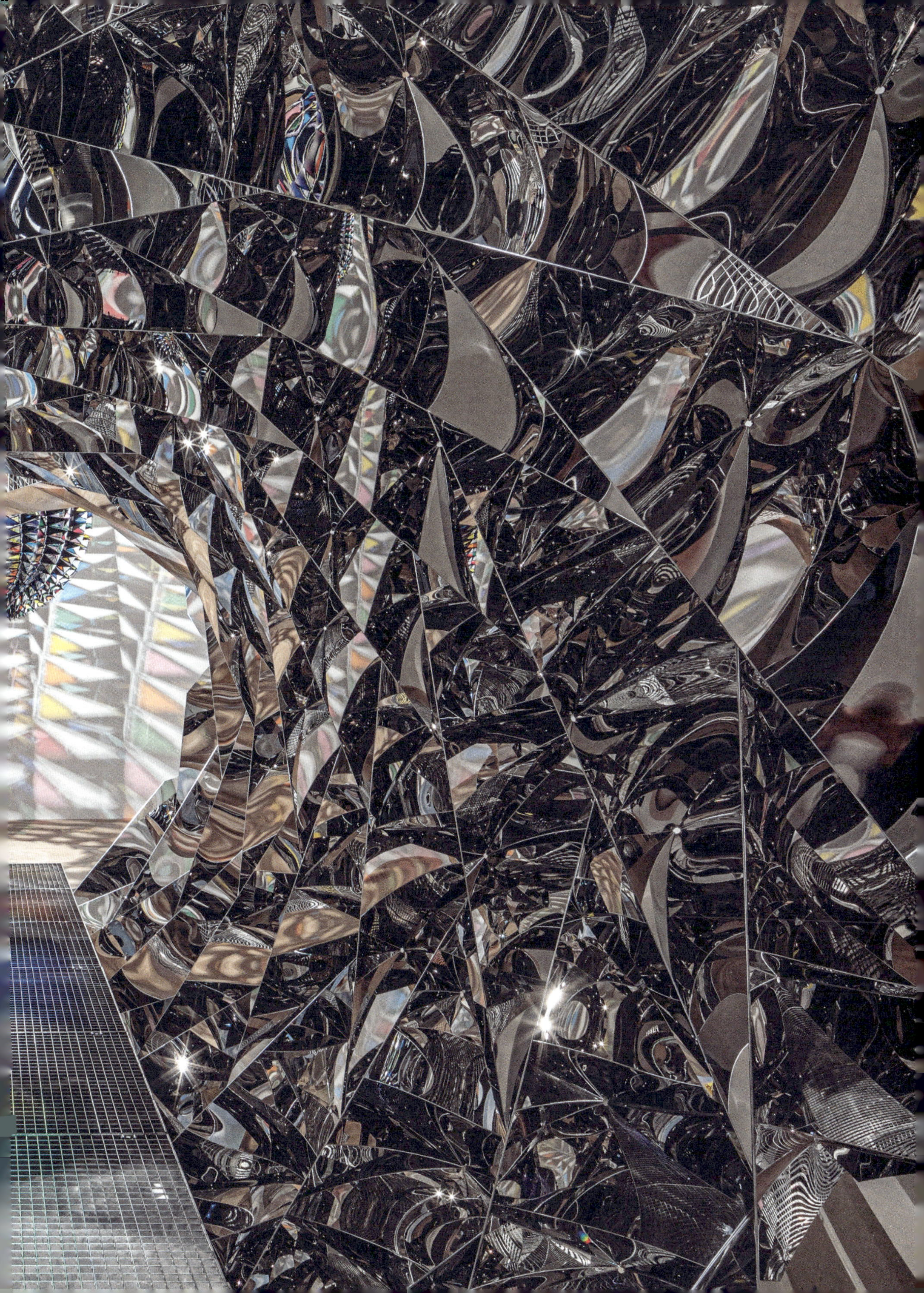

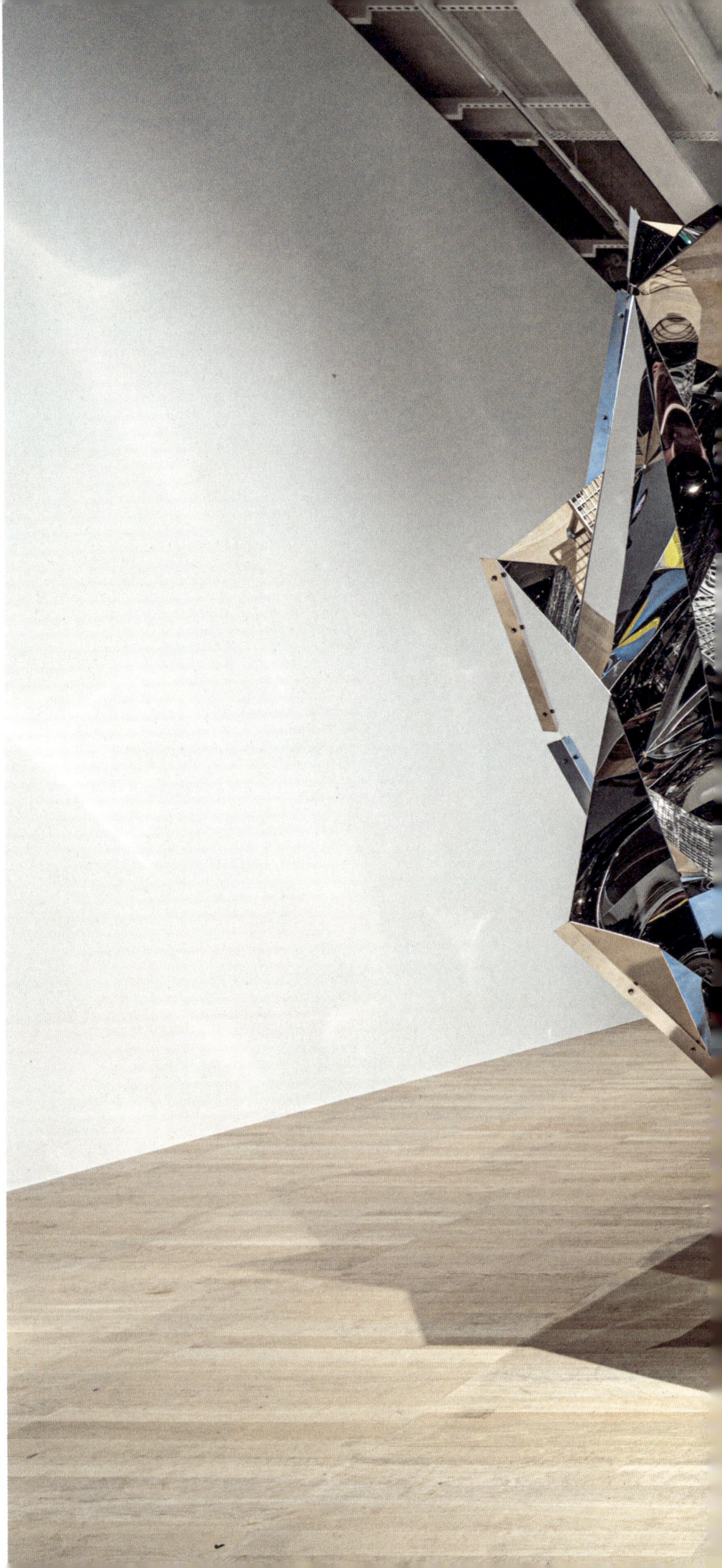

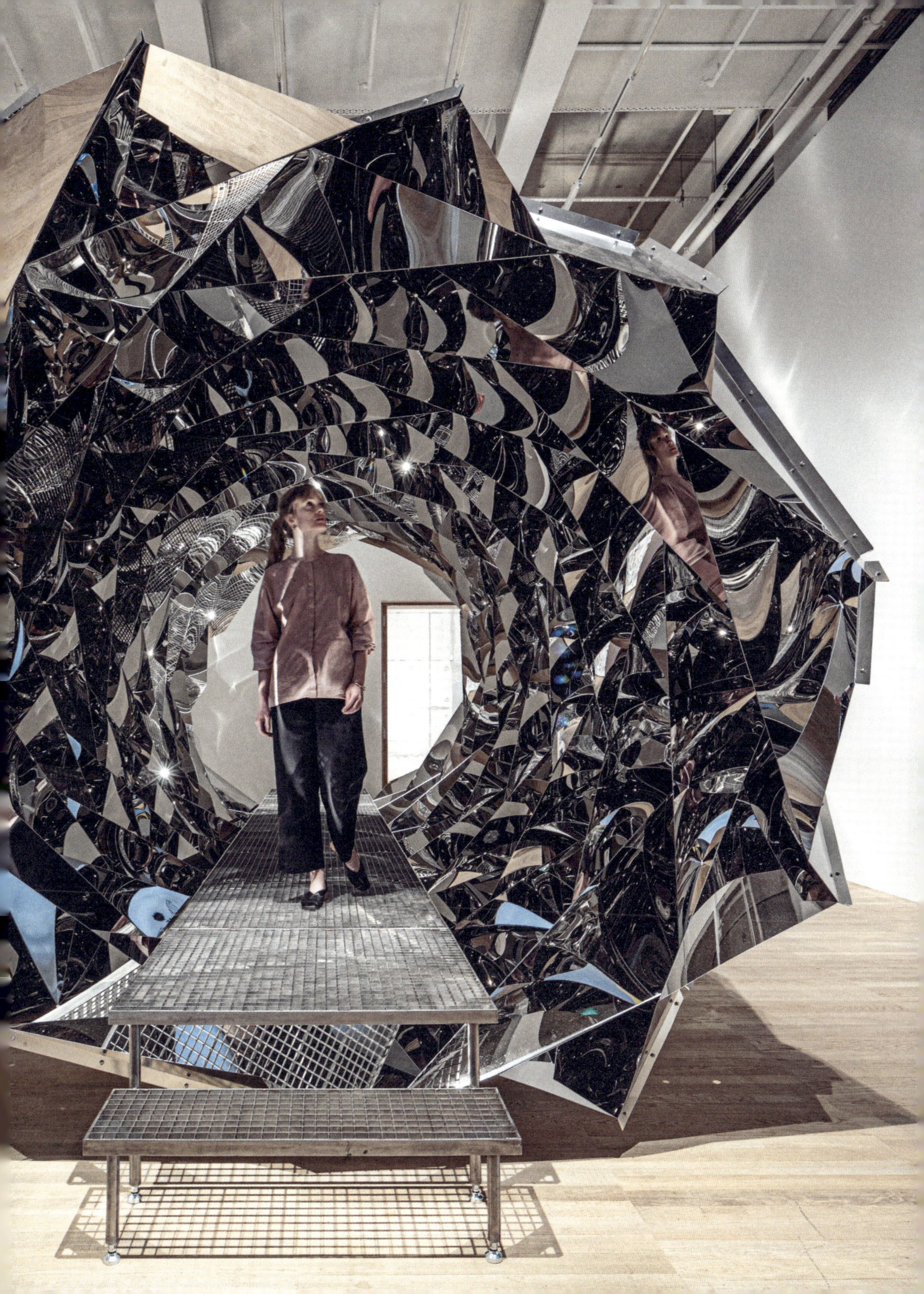

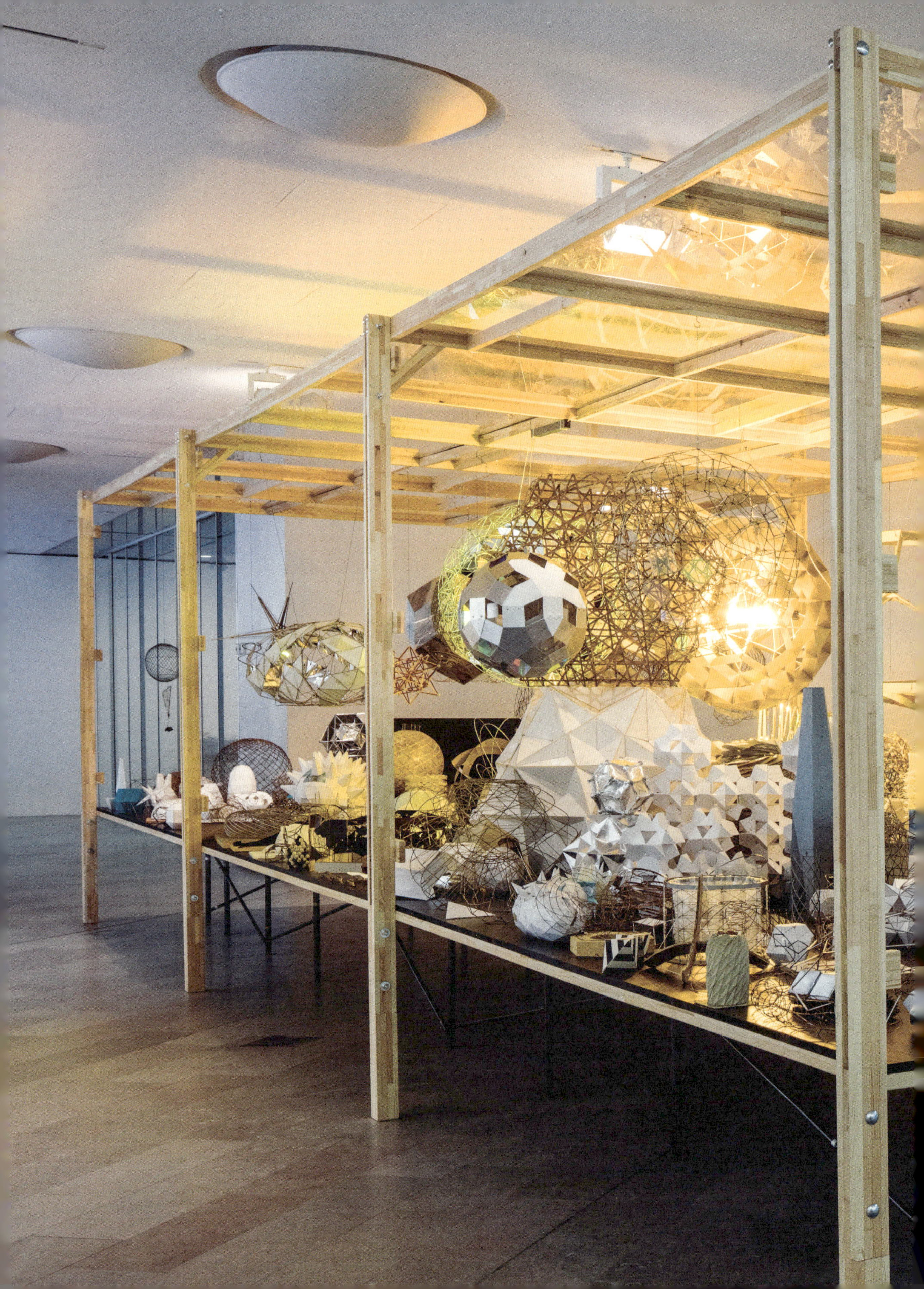

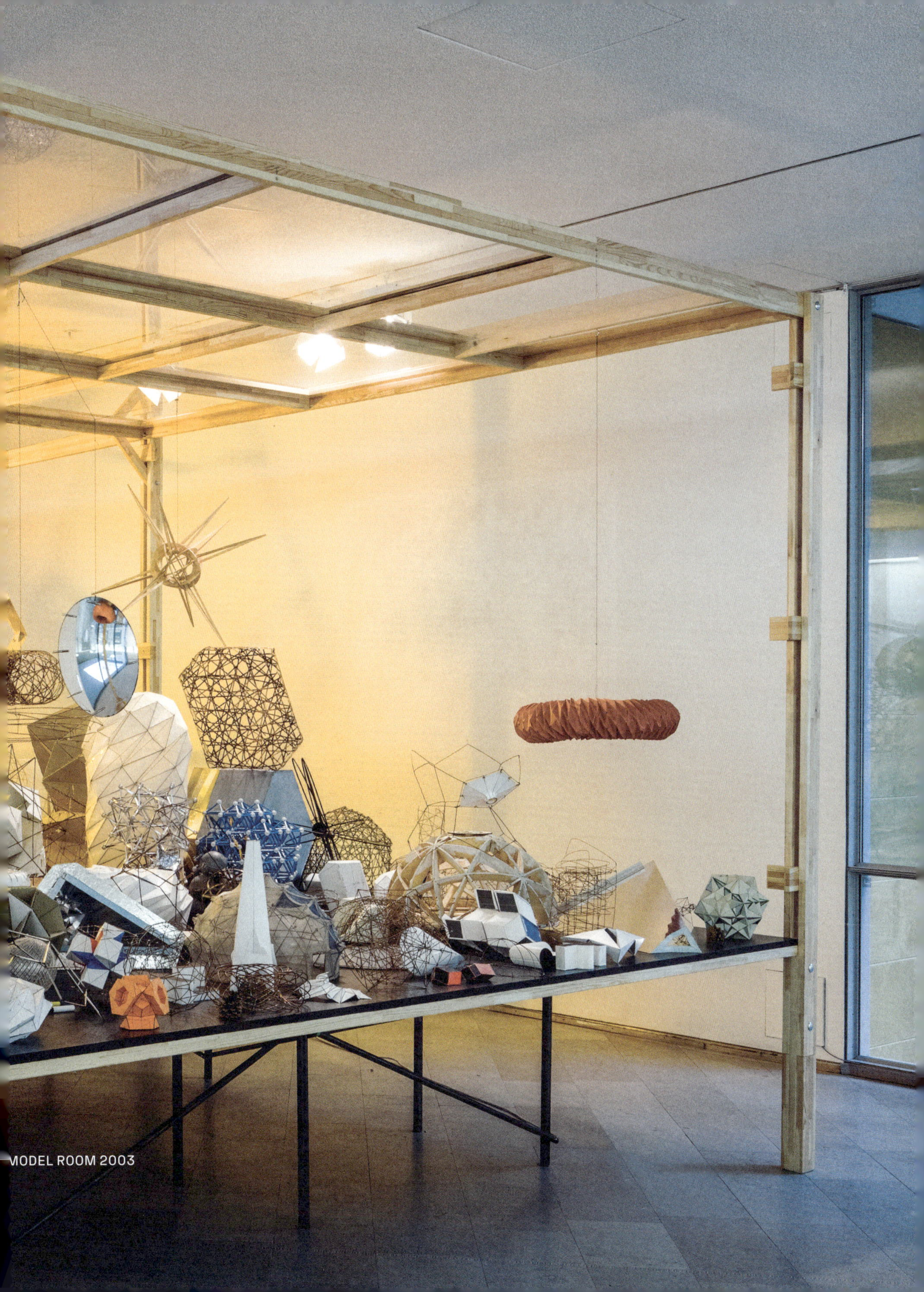

MODEL ROOM 2003

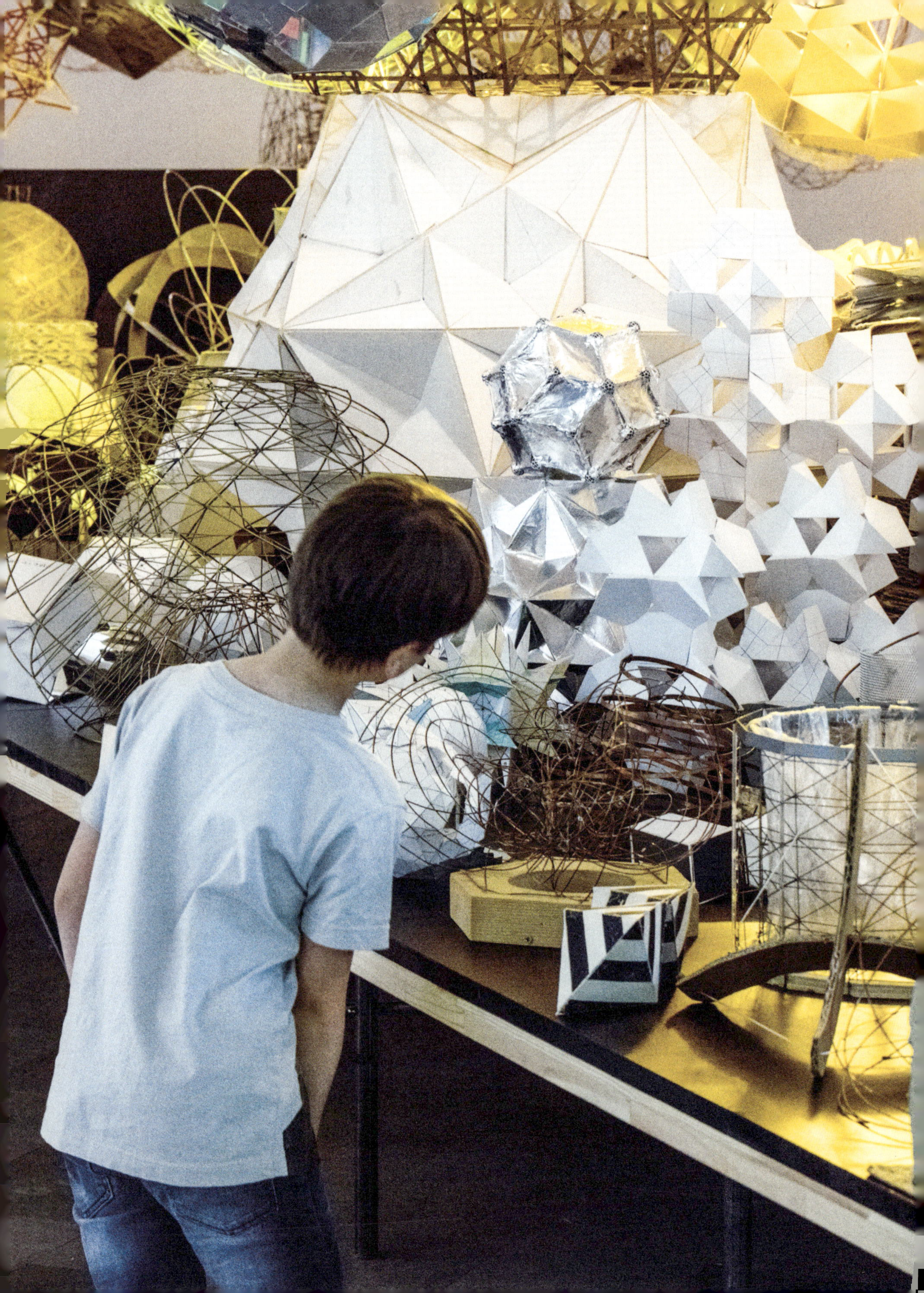

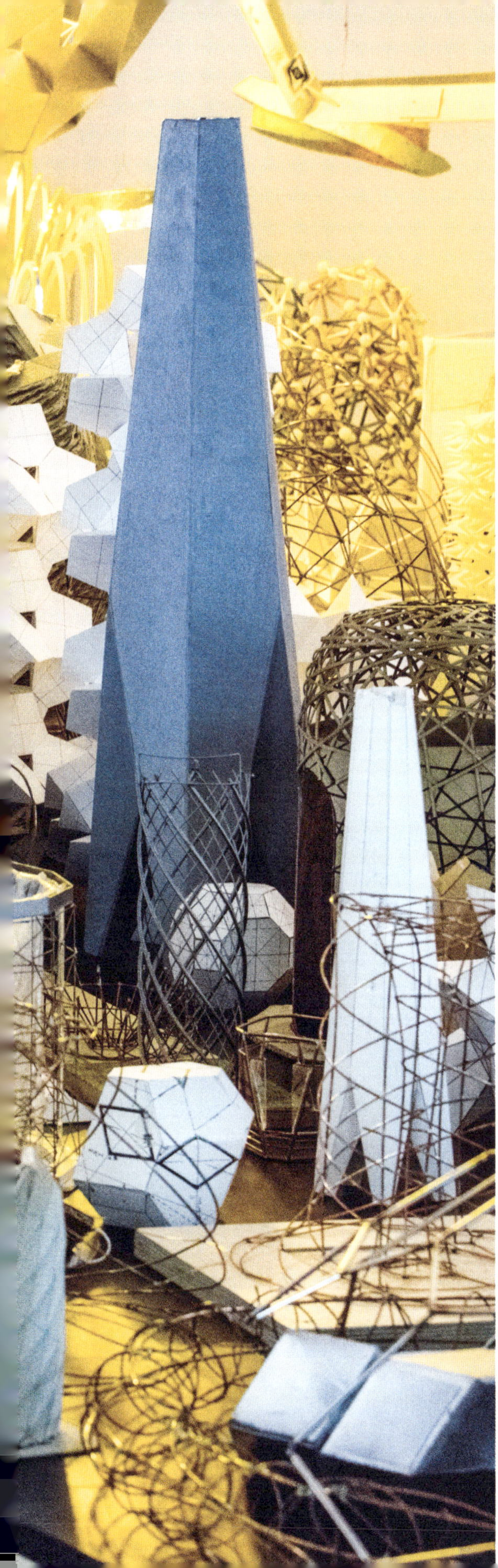
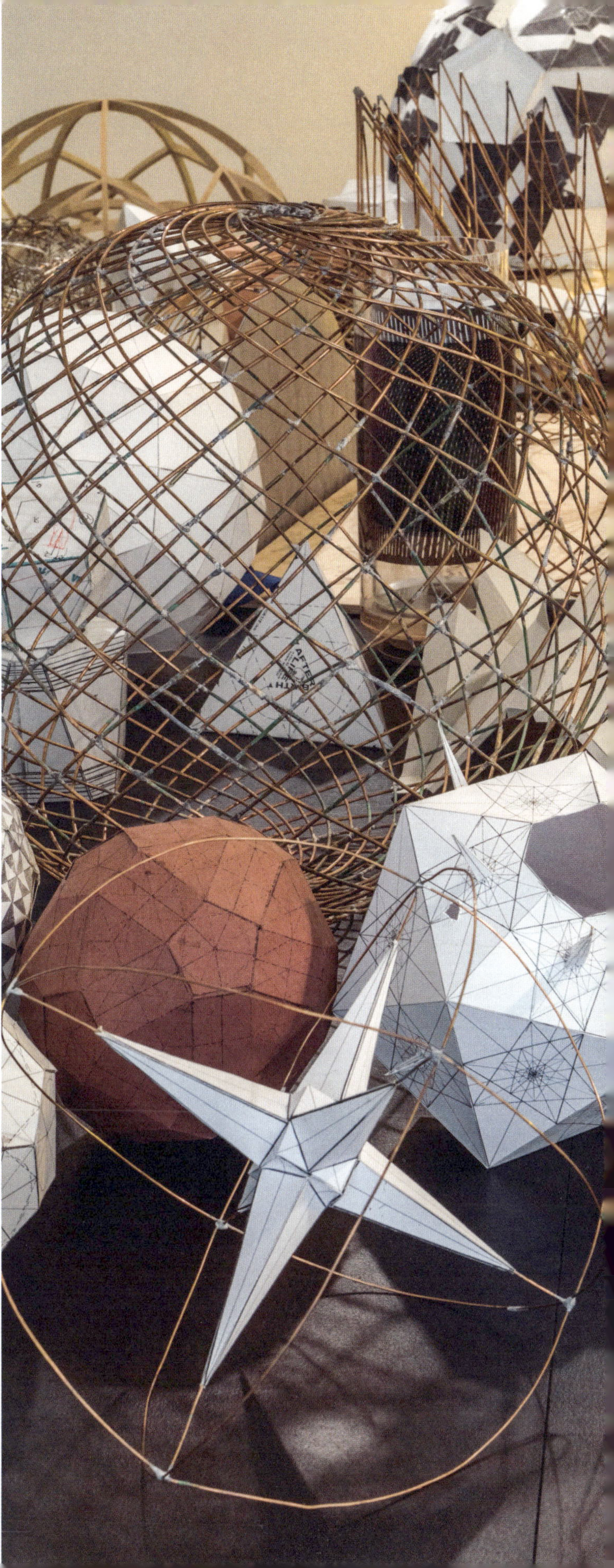

Olafur Eliasson: I really value dialogue that spans many different silos, and this book is a testament to that. It's good to see whether an idea that feels right in one field still holds water when you transpose it to a different field.

Alejandro Aravena: Sure. It makes sense to broaden the conversation out from just talking to your peers. It can be risky too – something I like very much, in principle. In the end, the work I do is not for other architects or other artists – it's a conversation with society.

That's great. What I like about your work, Alejandro, is that although it has a high degree of theoretical clarity, it is also very physical; it's embedded in local environments. I'm interested in this idea of giving body to a thought so that it goes beyond theory and becomes action. How do you work with the body?

I remember once, at a conference about technology and the future, a participant pointing out to me that we're using twenty-first-century software with prehistoric hardware: our bodies. The human body hasn't changed in many thousands of years. A stairway built by the Romans is still comfortable for us today, because our toes haven't changed. So, yes, the body is a fact – one of the facts that my work as an architect takes into account. We're affected by universal forces like gravity. Plus, there's the 'law of minimum effort' to consider – like how a person always takes a shortcut and stubbornly crosses a field on the diagonal because it saves energy. Even across cultures, some things are universal. The human body has that potential to be universal. It's something irreducible that connects a person in Ethiopia to someone in Iceland or Chile.

There are also basic actions that connect us all – for example, lying on the ground on your back. It's hard to know quite what to call this sort of thing – let's say they're 'ineffable certainties'. Something happens the moment you move through those extra ninety degrees, from being seated on the ground to putting your back on the ground and looking upwards. That tree you've been looking at is completely transformed. Look at the sky – and I'm not going poetic here, I'm just trying to describe something fundamental that happens; when you look straight upwards, you feel that you belong to something that is much bigger than yourself.

RECLAIMING CITIES

ALEJANDRO ARAVENA is a Chilean architect and head of the architectural firm Elemental. He is known for his social engagement and shares Eliasson's interests in sustainability, off-grid solutions and the activation of public space. Aravena was awarded the Pritzker Architecture Prize in 2016, the same year he curated the Venice Architecture Biennale.

You're right. There are some fundamental things we all do share. I think that recognising that would help us build a stronger sense of common values.

I also wanted to bring up the values of space. I've been working public space, or, even more broadly put, the notion of the public, into several of these conversations. I'm generalising when I say this applies globally, but these days it seems more value is placed on privatised consumer spaces and the very private spaces like the intimate space of the home than on public space. But public space isn't just what's left in between. I am struggling to see people actually focusing on that, claiming public space as their own, acknowledging that they are its co-producers.

How do you see public space?

Well, I think there may be some good news on that front. When Habitat III [the United Nation's conference on housing and sustainable urban development, which takes place every twenty years] met in Quito in 2016, a major outcome was advocacy for public space. One of humankind's biggest challenges is the massive influx of people to cities. This will have a staggering impact on the built environment. By the year 2035, two billion people will have moved to cities around the world in search of jobs, better education, access to healthcare and even recreation opportunities – that's a rate of about a million a week! If I could synthesise what I heard at Habitat III, particularly from its director, Joan Clos, I would say that for the cities of the future, the biggest value lies in what we are *not* going to build – namely, public space.

It may seem counter-intuitive, but cities are good news. We may complain about the concentration of people, but by every single measurement, living in cities is more beneficial and more efficient. The problem is that rapid migration towards cities results in informal settlements, which have no capacity to produce quality public space. We must find a way to accommodate the new arrivals. If we don't, it's not that people will stop coming to cities; they'll keep coming, and they'll live in awful conditions!

Effective urban development balances the private and the public. Manhattan is a good example; the ratio of private to public space is roughly one to one. So, for every square metre of private, developable space, there is a square metre of public space, including streets, sidewalks, squares and, of course, parks. But when you measure that ratio in an informal settlement like a slum, it drops down to less than ten to one. To me, public space is the most radical physical expression of common good. Private actions, however well-intentioned, cannot guarantee common good, but public space can.

Public space has a huge, powerful capacity of redistribution – not of income, but of quality of life. Many of the problems of living together in cities are created less by poverty than by inequality – that feeling of 'why them, and not me?' One way to measure a city is to look at what you can do in it for free. Cities provide a shortcut towards equality, because they can improve quality of life in ways that don't depend entirely on income. Public space is crucial to this because it has such redistributive capacity in the realm of everyday life. My city, Santiago, is not the poorest in the world, but half its population can't afford to go on holiday. What if we gave those residents the best possible park in front of a social housing project or even near an informal settlement? What if they could go out on the river and have an incredible time in nature? Good public space can help dismantle what could otherwise be a social ticking time bomb.

I don't think enough people acknowledge the agency of public space. You mentioned New York – a city that I love, of course, like most – but I think it is fair to say that much of its public space has in fact been privatised; not fully, but to a large extent. It seems to me – as a Scandinavian – that the economic grid is stronger than what I would call the civic grid. But people don't necessarily realise that public space actually works for them – that it works on the community's behalf, not at its expense. Public space is more than just the negative spaces between positive private units. Could you tell me more about how you see the ownership of public space?

Well, I can start with some very down-to-earth personal experience. I was in London recently for work. And since London is extremely expensive for a South American, I had to enjoy what I could there for free. The parks in London are just stunning. Nobody charges a fee, you don't have to ask for permission. You're just another citizen enjoying the city's quality spaces. It's the same with Central Park in New York. Cities offer a concentration of opportunities, but those opportunities carry a high cost, and public space helps counterbalance the cost. So how can we encourage its creation today? I wish we could avoid using the language of the market, but it seems we need the market's help creating public good. High quality public environments will require the market to do something in its own interest, too.

The good news – to return to the Habitat conference – is that developers, real-estate markets and the market in general are entering a new era and realising that the one-to-one ratio of public to private creates real value. The market will have to become more sophisticated in order to do its thing. The old approach to using land – trying to maximise every single sellable square metre, compressing the footprint, building it up vertically and selling everything – is no longer valued. Developers now grasp – and again, this is counterintuitive – that the economic value of sellable land can be enhanced by what they *don't* sell. Once occupied privately, these spaces will never be able to go back to the public.

But I think it's better to understand each stakeholder's DNA and frame the operation in terms of what comes naturally to each of them. For example: cities in developing countries normally reserve about twenty per cent of the land for public space, more or less. Even for a poor municipality, it's about twenty per cent, when you add up streets, sidewalks and a park here or there. After that, developers and the real estate market leave roughly the same amount of space undeveloped. So, if you add the two together, you are in the area of forty per cent open space. It's important to distinguish between open and public space, however. The private market should make its open spaces fully accessible to the public, not just unoccupied. And a poor municipality should parcel out the land it owns and reserve what I would call civic corridors – like ecological corridors – for future public spaces, in case they cannot deliver them right now. Added up, that already comes close enough to the one-to-one ratio that evidence shows will produce some value gain in the future.

Now, somebody has to give form to that empty land. And here is where the architect comes in – or, in your case, the artist. I was looking at your park in Addis Ababa [the Meles Zenawi Memorial Park, designed by Eliasson and Sebastian Behmann's art and architecture firm, Studio Other Spaces]. Our fundamental, if modest, contribution lies in translating that percentage into form, into space. The form we choose can make a crucial difference in people's quality of life.

I see what you mean about quality of life and the logic behind it. But we know that when real estate interests control public space, these spaces become platforms for pleasing and predictable types of activity rather than catering to critical engagement, as I think public space should. That's why I want to ask about who has the mandate for public space. Who in our society helps shape those pockets of physical space – and even psychological space – where friction, interaction, freedom of expression and self-confidence can co-exist? Because fundamentally it's not really about public space itself but about our sense of collectivity, our shared experience or knowledge. For me, public space should give us the keys to interconnectedness. That's why I'm interested in those behavioural micro-systems you describe in Santiago – for example, the way people use the parks when they cannot go on vacation. I think London's parks are amazing, too, but they are hardly revolutionary; the Romantic vision and values that shaped them were, to a large extent, elitist. We need to find other places in the civic realm where we can say, 'This is our space, we own that.'

I absolutely agree. And, again, I'd say there's some good news in here. A more sophisticated approach to the city is on the way. And it is extremely important to reserve some open space while this kind of thinking develops and becomes more mainstream. Of course, if the market does not get it, public agencies will have to regulate real estate and force developers to do so, because if we don't set space aside now, it's going to be very hard to return it to the public once it has already been privatised.

Recent planning in Colombia offers some clues about what visionary urban planning will look like. The cities of Medellín and Bogotá in particular have seen projects of extremely high quality despite the incredible challenges there. New public space is helping to improve connectivity and promote access to opportunity. It's lowering social resentment and improving everyday quality of life – not to mention things as simple as providing better public lighting and delivering basic security. For most cities, the scarcest resource is often not money, but coordination – namely, getting the different sectors to cooperate: public housing with public works, transportation with infrastructure, and so on. But Medellín's corporation for urban development, the Empresa de Desarrollo Urbano [EDU], controls both transportation and public infrastructure like gas and electricity. The cost of coordination is very close to zero. In Medellín, they found that the city's most dangerous spots were areas around the water tanks. These had been walled in and were very dark at night. In a very bold move, the mayor tore down the walls and transformed these sites of basic water infrastructure into public spaces. Before, there had been almost no single square metre of open land.

And the homicide rate is going down?

Absolutely – in places I wouldn't have been allowed to visit a decade ago. So Colombian planners are merging public space with infrastructure, using cultural institutions and parks to serve as anchors. This is something completely new! We normally see either infrastructure or parks or museums in cities. These projects do all three at the same time. They combine infrastructure – like facilities for managing water, sewage, gas – with transportation, green space and culture. Medellín's incredibly successful 'library parks' are now being emulated all over Colombia and South America. The most important social spaces in those libraries are not the reading rooms but the gathering spaces used after hours, in places where previously there was no public space. These strategies have reduced violence dramatically and improved quality of life. The beauty of the thing is that they're not doing one or the other, but one *and* the other. And this, I would say, gives the rest of us some hope. If they did it against all odds, then there's no excuse for the rest of us not to do it too.

That connects perfectly to something else I wanted to bring up. I work, as you know, in the so-called cultural sector. And I mean 'culture' in the broadest sense – not just theatre, the visual arts, literature and music and so on, but all the way down to neighbourhood associations and local sporting clubs. This sector currently enjoys a high degree of civic engagement in many places; you could even call it civic trust. Without ruling out the relevance of economic factors like employment, I nevertheless see the cultural sector as a 'society machine' – a force at the heart of society rather than at its periphery. It is a force for addressing people's tolerance and sense of inclusivity; for asking questions about belonging and identity – questions of who we are and why we are here and where we are, and so on. But I think the cultural sector has failed to claim its own importance.

Well, culture is crucial, even if the cultural sector is often seen as a kind of 'extra', not a core thing. Politics and the public sector often focus on human needs – 'we work on real, hard social issues', they'll tell you. But culture – whether it's a building, a work of art or a soccer field – leads to moments where you shut up and just experience life. In the same way that food is about more than just nutrition, life is not just needs! On the other hand, the cultural sector often thinks of itself as being about human desire – you know, 'we deal with what makes humans *human*.' But, in the end, life is about both desire and basic needs. It's not a choice between the two; it's both at the same time. The cultural sector connects to people in a very deep way by supplying a crucial synthesis of human needs and human desires.

That's a good point. And those needs and desires are both individual and collective. I think that cultural space, to use spatial terminology, hosts opportunities for us to be together without having to agree. That's why I'm so interested in encouraging culture to leave its own silos and get involved in the mechanics of organising cities, organising public space, organising inclusive activities – even peace talks!

It's no wonder that numbers of visitors to galleries are increasing every year. There's one last thing that's been on my mind, especially since the murder of [Saudi Arabian journalist] Jamal Khashoggi. I've been thinking about how going solar, for example, would take power away from those who do not know how to use it responsibly. Solar power is not just about sustainability and slowing climate change; being off-grid has a democratic potential to correct injustice. Given that cities provide shortcuts towards equality, improving the quality of the built environment is a key tool for remedying social oppression. Well-designed cities can empower people. Then the bullies on the planet would be less powerful.

I completely agree. As an architect, you can execute this in your own work. You're a civic agent. You come with a set of values and you express them by turning them into action.

That's why we call our practice a 'do-tank', not a 'think tank'!

October 2018

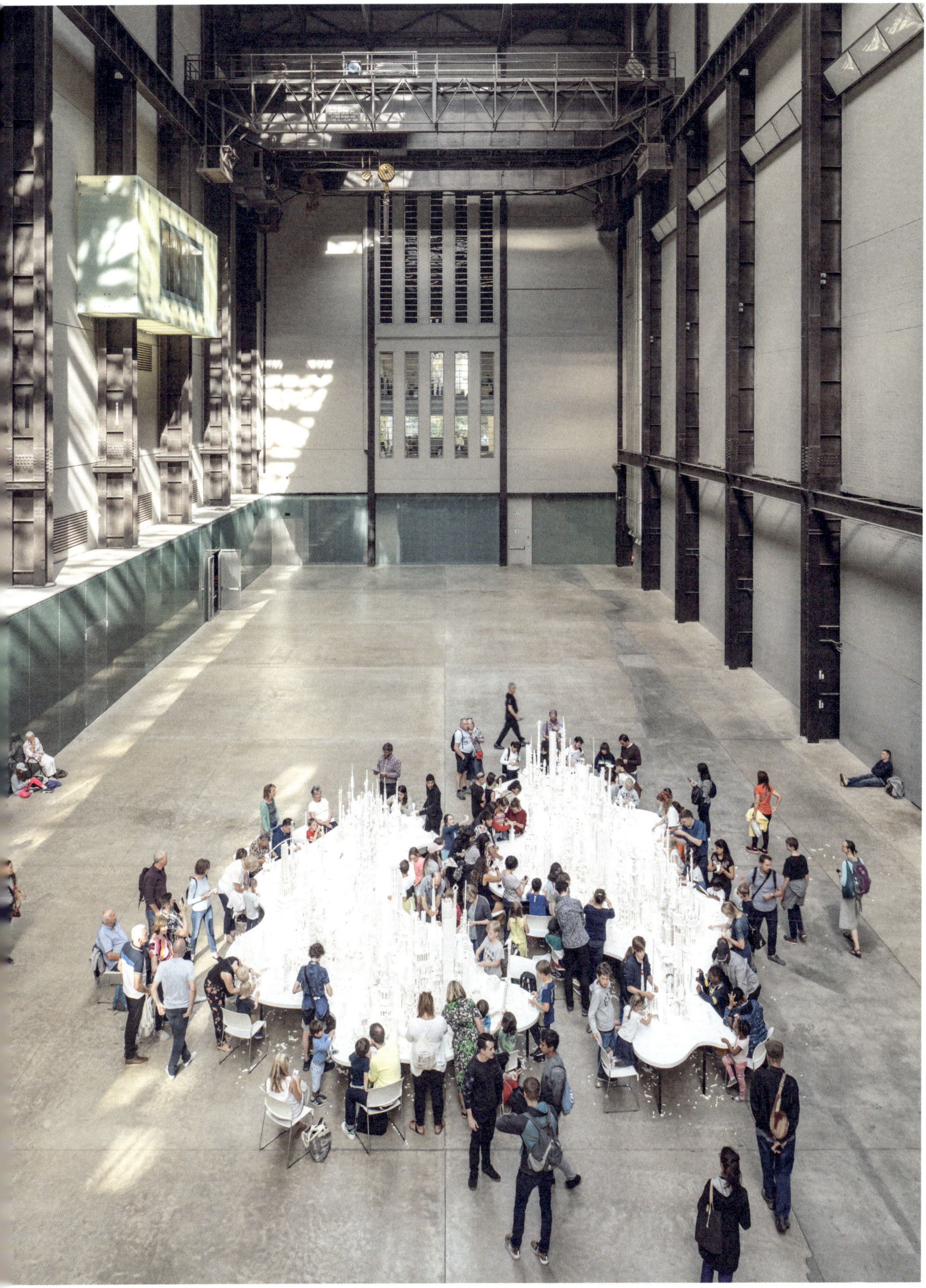

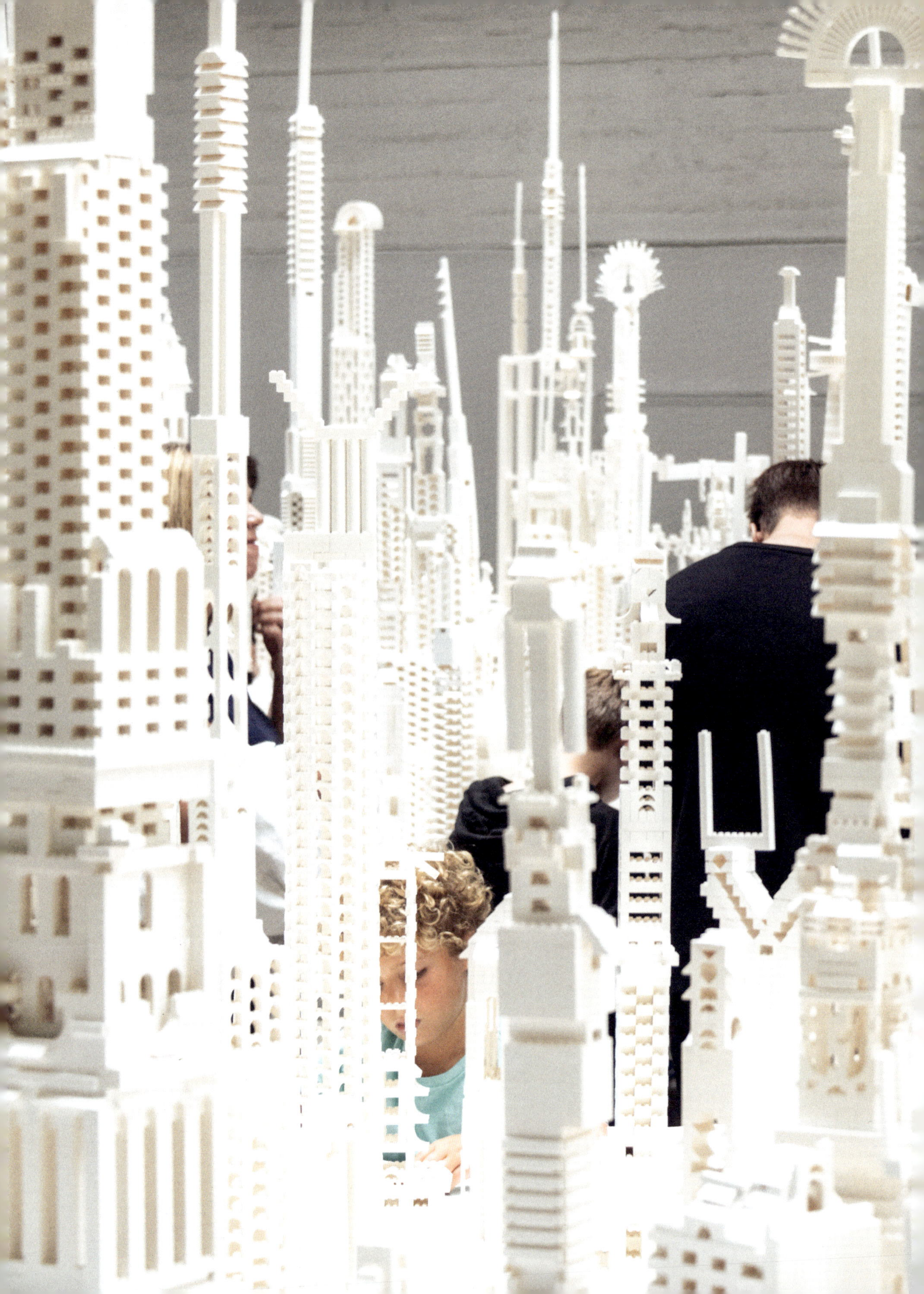

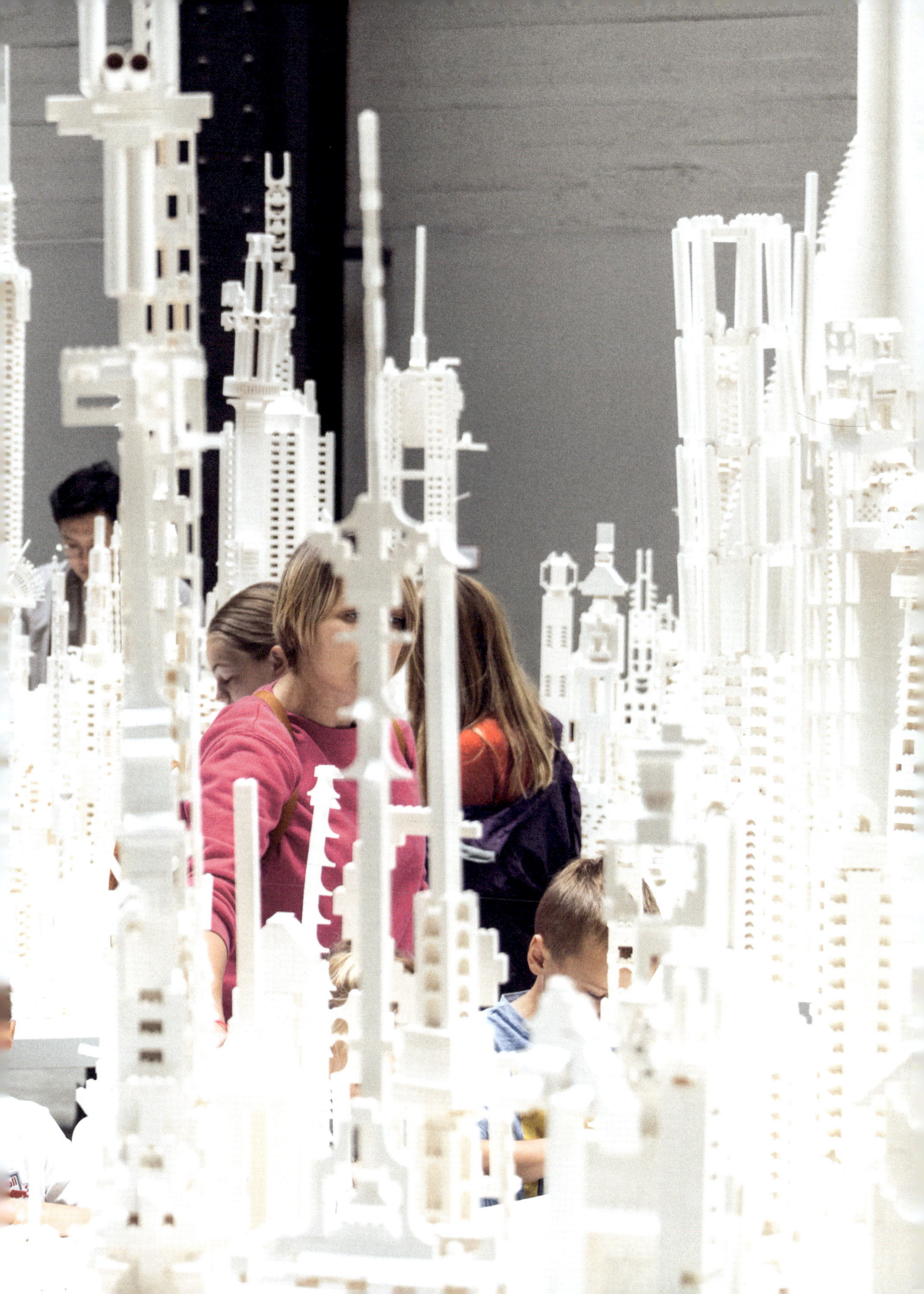

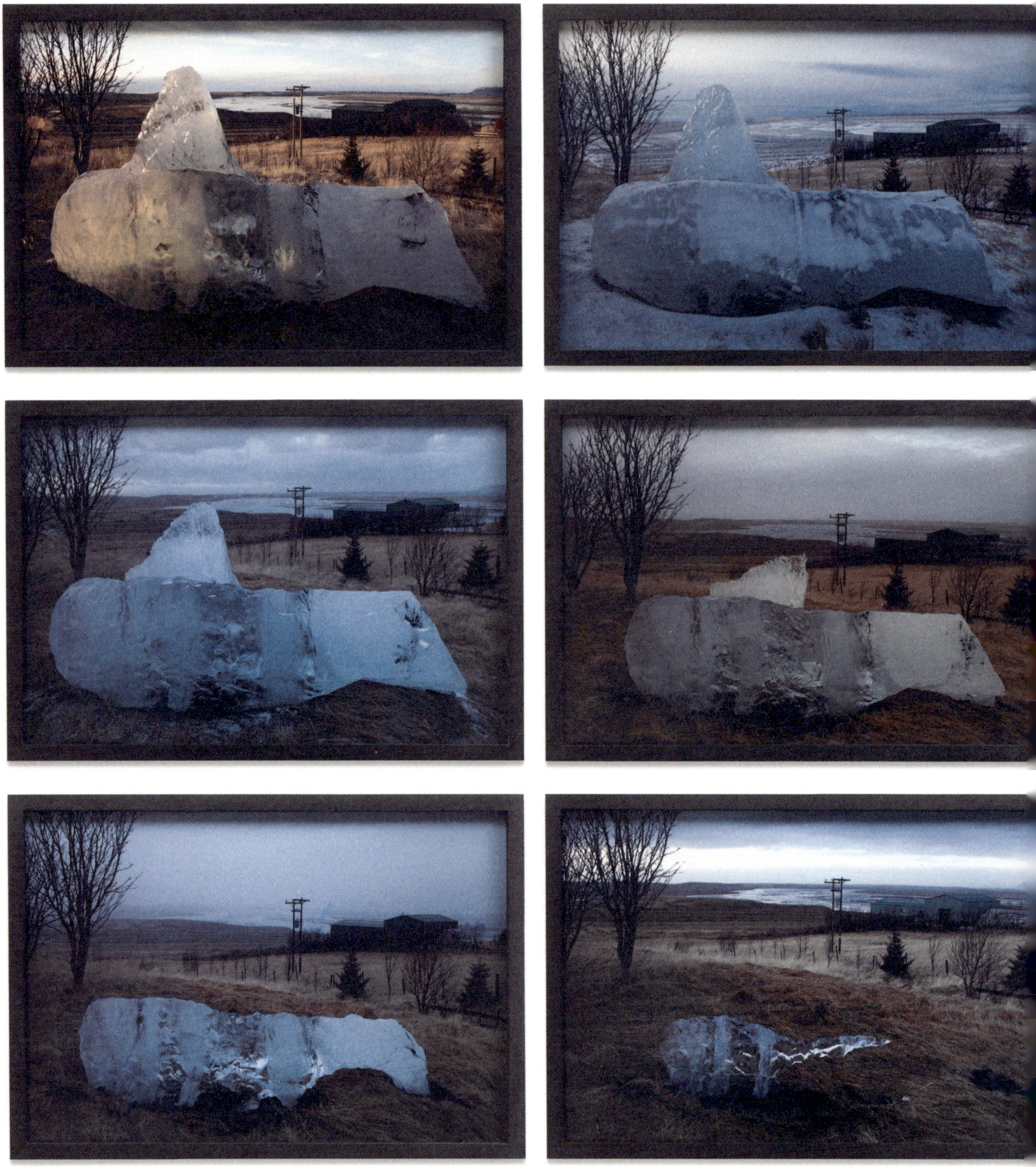

MELTING ICE ON GUNNAR'S LAND 200

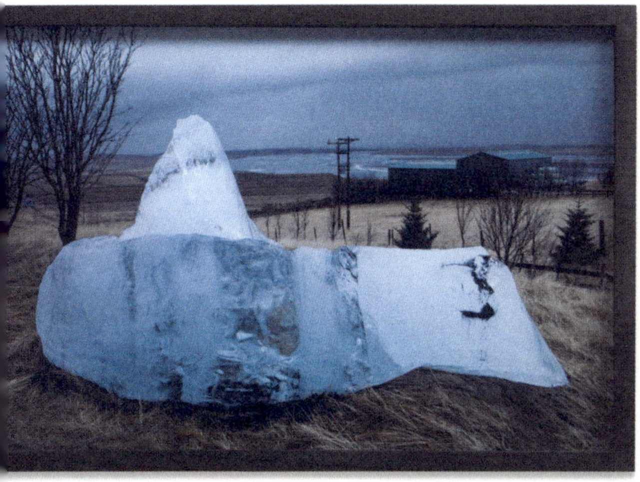
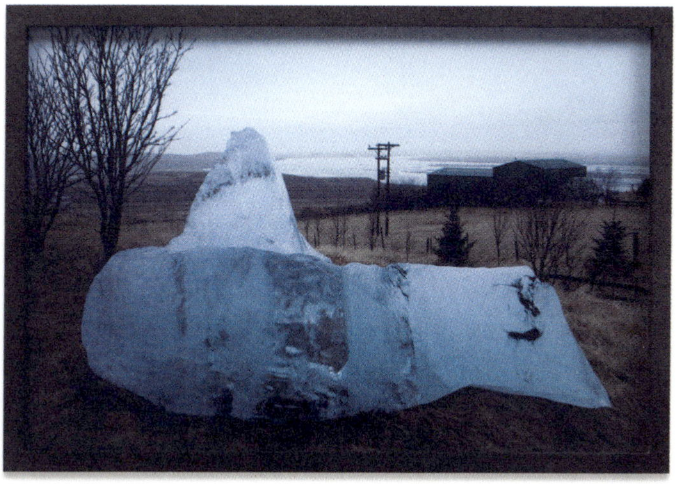
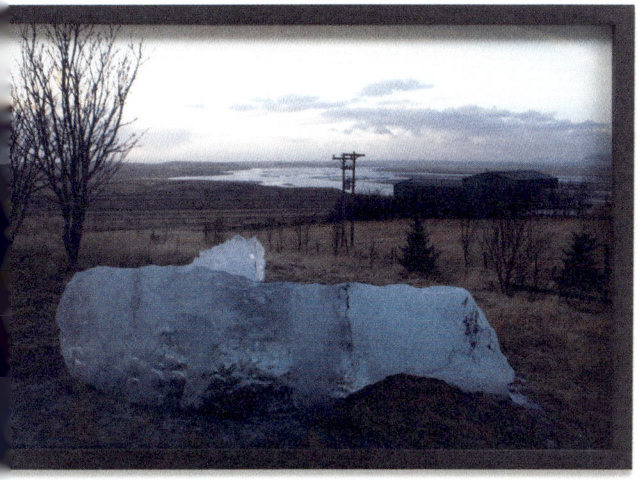
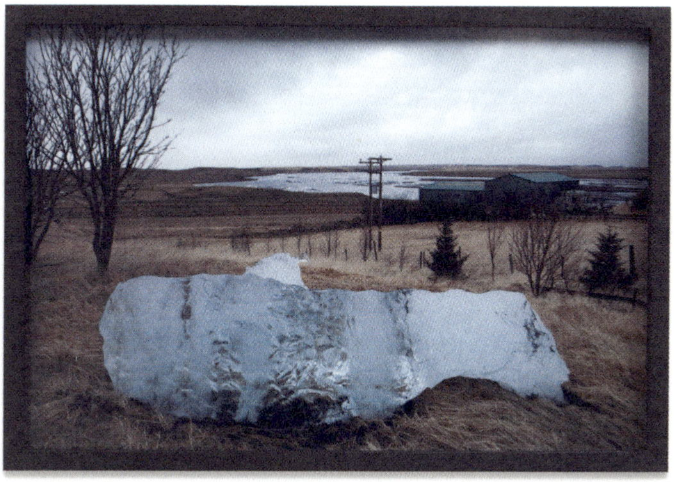
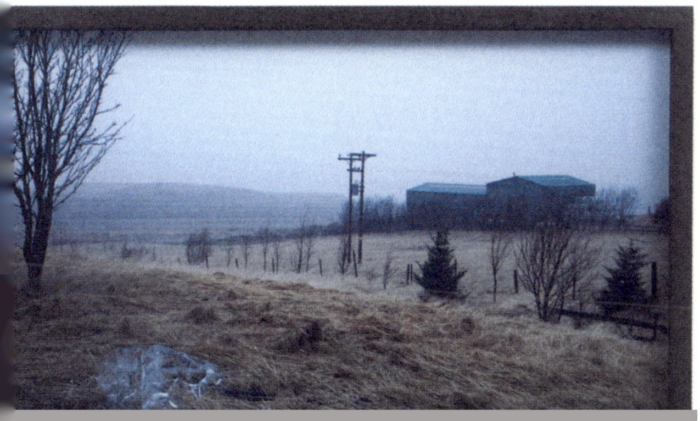
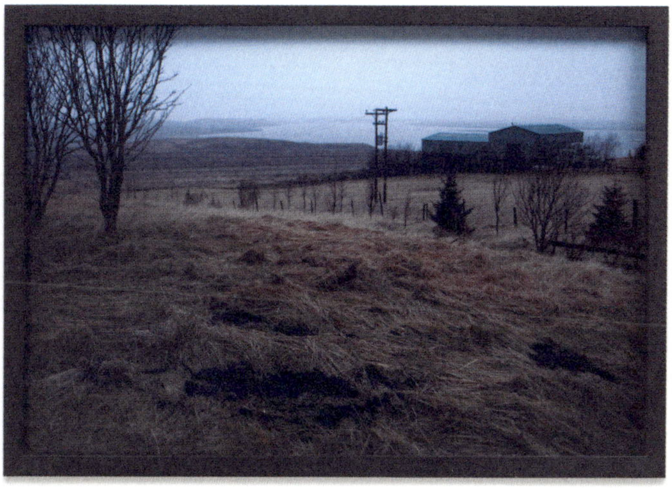

Olafur Eliasson: **Mariana, we have a shared interest in the public sector and in the structural limits of what is known as the public. I come to it from an artist's perspective. How did you become interested in the public?**

Mariana Mazzucato: I come to it as an economist, interested in how innovation drives economic growth in modern capitalism – technological innovation, organisational innovation, institutional innovation. Feudalism was five hundred years of inertia, and then came capitalism, which, as Marx himself said, fuelled innovation and broke down walls. But who creates it? And for what purpose? Ironically, the modern body of economic thought, which is so acritical of capitalism, is not well equipped to deal with innovation. It is too wedded to concepts in Newtonian physics, like centres of gravity, averages and the presence of equilibrating forces. Innovation causes capitalism to be in disequilibrium – or even multiple equilibria. This creates turbulence and, rather than average behaviours, it creates constant differences among economic agents.

Not only do we not describe the dynamics well, but we also don't understand the underlying forces. There are a lot of myths surrounding the figure of the lone entrepreneur and the start-up. But what about the public sector? What about workers? And civil society? As I describe in my book *The Entrepreneurial State* [2013], the history of so many innovations in information and communications technology, energy and pharmaceuticals, would not have happened without patient and strategic public actors. Every technology in the iPhone – the internet, GPS, touch-screen display and even Siri – was initially funded by some sort of state agency. The same is true for three quarters of the most innovative new medicines, and for solar and wind energy. But we don't have a vocabulary to describe that because we pretend that the public sector is at best facilitating, 'de-risking' and 'filling in the gap'. In economics they call it 'fixing a market failure'.

Interestingly, the term 'public value' doesn't even exist in economics. We have terms like 'public goods', but they're just seen as investing in an area that is characterised by too little private investment – from basic research to clean water. It's not an objective, it's just fixing a problem. But I believe public value should be seen as an objective, and one the pursuit of which is characterised by an open process of debate – involving citizens. And we should know how to evaluate the effect of its creation: by asking whether groups in society benefit from that investment and examining the spillovers.

TRUST

MARIANA MAZZUCATO holds the chair of Economics of Innovation and Public Value at University College London, where she directs the Institute for Innovation and Public Purpose. Mazzucato's work focuses on the relationship between innovation and growth, with emphasis on creating a form of growth that is more innovation-led, inclusive, and sustainable. Her book *The Entrepreneurial State: Debunking Public vs. Private Sector Myths* (2013) looks at the role the state has played in the history of technological change – from the Internet to biotech – and her latest book, *The Value of Everything* (2018), explores the differences between value creation, value extraction and value destruction.

So is your ambition to drive agency back into the public sector?

Yes, we need to tell better stories. As Plato argued, storytellers rule the world! The limited ways we describe innovation have helped justify the narrow way in which the returns are distributed. We wouldn't have had the internet without agencies like DARPA, the US Defense Advance Research Projects Agency. But the point is not to copy and paste that experience, but to learn from it. How can public institutions welcome uncertainty and the explorative process that innovation entails? And if the state has the transformative power of co-creating, co-shaping innovation and the associated markets – not just fixing them – what should it foster? What is the area of responsibility? Are you just innovating for the sake of innovation?

A key lesson here is that, historically, innovation has been most successful when it was goal-oriented. In the 1960s, going to the moon and back again in a generation produced many spillovers, most of which are contained in our smart products today. The problem generated the technology. So today we should obsess less about the technology and more about how to frame ambitious problems. Imagine if we applied the moonshot approach to achieving the concrete targets included in the UN's Sustainable Development Goals? I've been working closely with the European Commission on this question and I'm happy to say that they have adopted the concept of 'missions' to guide a part of their future funding for innovation in the European Union's programme for research and innovation, Horizon 2020.

I am interested in how different members of society can contribute to thinking about missions. If the state can be transformative in its actions, if it can actually drive change, the immediate question is: who is making the decisions? And what is being produced? Democratically elected politicians have the responsibility to form institutions and modes of decision making that capture different voices. This includes listening to movements for change. Interestingly, Germany's *Energiewende* – its mission of promoting an energy revolution – involved decades of effort on the part of the green movement, which gave it democratic legitimacy. How movements can be heard and listened to by those framing missions is a key question.

I grew up in Scandinavia, where the public sector has the welfare society as its area of responsibility. Although its success is constantly debated in places like Denmark, the Nordic countries are not actually doing so badly compared to the rest of the world. For instance, there is a long tradition of public support for culture and a kind of overall confidence in the cultural sector. What institutions do you see as belonging to the cultural sector?

I think culture has to be central to how we define these missions. We need poets to help us understand immigration. We need people within academia – in the humanities as well as in the sciences. Artists can help us understand what we mean by a green economy. They can help turn the Sustainable Development Goals into actual missions. This is why I was so struck by your work *Ice Watch* [2014]. You enabled people to experience the difficult concept of climate change by touching those big chunks of melting ice.

The cultural sector can contribute to defining these missions and how we design the process. It is curious however that the narrow framework of fixing market failures also impedes our understanding of culture. In the UK, the BBC is evaluated by the Ofcom regulatory body according to the Television Charter, by which all citizens pay for a TV licence.

During these evaluations, it is regularly told to focus on a small part of the broadcasting sector, such as documentaries or high-quality news. It is then told not to 'crowd out' business in areas that reach the masses, like soap operas and talk shows. And yet its ambition to create public value is precisely what made it bold enough to try to produce high-quality soap operas that would reach regular people. It's the process, not the product.

Didn't *EastEnders* come out of the BBC? Was that the type of project they were not encouraged to do?

Exactly. They were told 'You are crowding out business.' This type of critique, this message to back off, is used against many ambitious public programmes, whether it's a public bank like the KfW in Germany, or an agency like DARPA in the US. We need new indicators to both justify and measure the creation of public value. As an objective, independent of the 'format' – literally, in the case of the BBC and in the case of a bank – it would mean that it's not about what you invest in but how you do so in the most catalytic way, making things happen that otherwise would not have come about.

Art and culture engage at the emotional level without prescribing particular ways of living or acting. A good book can express things that are emotionally familiar but that you had not yet put in your own language. A painting can give visual form to your not-yet-verbalised need. I like to think of the cultural sector as *listening* to you. So when a museum is successful, people leave it thinking, 'I went in there, I was listened to, the museum reflected my emotional need, inspired my imagination and treated me with respect.' To simplify somewhat, I don't think culture tells you what to do, but it listens *to* what you want to do. I like the idea that it's the book that's reading you, the painting that's looking at you, and so on. It's not about a person entering a cultural institution and trusting it. It also has to do with collaborative agency, with creating a space that increases trust – it's about 'we-ness'. At its best, culture hosts critical spaces that are not defined by a market or consumer agenda. It allows you to be a participant – not just to consume but also to co-produce.

Tell me more about what you mean by 'trust' here. Let's say you enter a museum, see a work of art and experience the effect you just described. In such a case, the artist is co-producing an emotion with the viewer. But you are also talking about the space itself? Are you saying that all museums do this, independent of how they're designed? Or that in certain museums, the discussion between staff and visitors helps produce this experience of we-ness? I'm Italian, I can tell you that many museums in Italy don't create any kind of we-ness – at least not when I walk in with my children! So are you talking about the people who get together and think about this co-produced space, or about the art itself?

Both, actually. Of course the work of art must be good enough to enter into a dialogue with the visitors. And if we feel that the cultural sector is actually listening *to us*, we will trust it more. Not all cultural institutions manage that: a museum that communicates in a patronising way with its visitors doesn't show trust. The trust that I'm talking about is like a safe space in which we dare to have discussions and experiences that are difficult to have elsewhere – it's the kind of trust that you might experience in a well-functioning agora. I don't normally draw clear lines between the artist and the artwork, the viewer, the institution or the architecture. Obviously, a great work of art is a great work of art regardless – but it is still influenced by the context in which it is shown. Depending on where you place it – say, in a police station, a kindergarten or in

the street – you'll have three different works. The hospitality a museum extends to the artwork and to its visitors is therefore a proactive gesture.
It's like inclusion. It doesn't happen if you do nothing. If a cultural institution cultivates a trust-driven framework, that is an opportunity for you, the visitor, to be critical and self-critical. A great museum can contain the whole palette of perceptual and emotional responses. For this reason, in the past few years, I've also seen the European Union increasingly reaching out to cultural sector practitioners to investigate and shape a stronger feeling of 'we' in Europe.
Yes, and I think this goes beyond the cultural sector. You're describing a process of creative co-production – but also a trust – that ultimately creates a new relationship between yourself and what you are looking at. It's neither the painting nor the museum; it's the experience. Designing a good healthcare system, or dealing with the word's digital transformation, also depends on these issues. This process of we-ness reminds me of a wonderful video you created on public space in which you said public space should not just fill a gap – a void – but rather that it should be something much more active, intentional and participatory. That is key to driving a more inclusive society. The way you talk about the cultural sector could be applied to how citizens engage with the welfare state. It could apply to how you design a public library, a digital platform, a hospital experience. These can be fundamentally transformative, even beyond the service you're getting. They can shape the relationship you have with the doctor, the nurse, the space, with how you move around. There's a wider need to produce these active, potentially participatory co-created mechanisms through which people live.
I think this must be the way we formulate not just policies but, literally, experiences. Consider the experience of entering a hospital. Our experience of the healthcare system would be very different indeed if it were driven by these kinds of principles. It could be the opposite of what we have today. The healthcare system can either view patients as customers – as clients – or see them as users and participants.
Obviously, I would like to see the cultural sector as a value driver, as promoting a value system that critically examines processes and categories, design and experiences in other parts of society. I do think it offers models of engagement and co-production that could work for society as a whole. Let's say you and I are looking at a painting and that we like different things about it. I like that yellow colour, you like the blue – but we can still be friends, right? We can disagree. The cultural sector offers an opportunity to debate our values within a shared framework that I would like to see evolve elsewhere, too.
Yes. I also love that you see public spaces as places where we can feel safe to disagree. At the same time, I think they should potentially also be places of conflict. Remember that innovations that changed society – like the birth control pill, or even the drugs for AIDS – came about when people fought for them. There was conflict. Democratic values can arise out of conflict – not necessarily people killing each other, but really disagreeing – which then creates change, not just comfort. I'm wary of the perception that somehow we are all in it together. Well, we're not. We didn't get weekends and eight-hour workdays because we were all in it together. People fought bitterly and died for those causes.
Right. And it's an illusion to think that looking at art is only about pleasure. When an artwork is able to reflect an emotional need you might have, it could well be related to

trauma or anger or stress. You listen to some music and think, 'This sound gives my anger a space.' This is why I said it's as if the music, or the artwork, is listening to me, hosting me.

I feel the public sector has mismanaged one of its greatest assets, public space, where it could exercise all the values that it has invested in over the years. In London, for instance, there are many fewer architects employed by the local councils than there used to be. The people who nurture public space have been cut away and, as a result, public space in London has simply become the doormat for private space.

The haemorrhaging of talent and imagination and expertise from the planning system in the UK is really striking. I don't know if you know Public Practice, but they are a not-for-profit enterprise set up precisely to bring high-level architects and designers back into city government. They point out that in the 1970s, over forty per cent worked with city government. Now it's less than one per cent. Planning talent has been outsourced, as in so many other areas. Healthcare has been outsourced, too. And, unfortunately, this is starting to happen in education as well. What happens to ambition and the ability to dream when talent disappears?

I've also spoken with Chilean architect Alejandro Aravena for this book [see pp.110–14]. With his practice, Elemental, he has worked on some really interesting low-cost housing in the poorest areas of Santiago. That commitment to public good is super inspiring.

I'd love to bring you together with Brian Eno to discuss atmospheric issues. His *Ambient 1: Music for Airports* [1978] explores how you engage and create an atmosphere that gives rise to a different experience within an airport. He attended a meeting I organised last week on this whole mission-orientated approach. He said he wanted to write a story of what a street would look like if the kind of investment and industrial strategy and innovation policy that we were advocating were focused on caring. What would it feel like to walk down the street in this caring economy? And how do you produce a more caring economy? What kind of investments and collaborations and innovations might one envisage, working from the bottom up? Artists can picture the very different experiences to be had in a hypothetical society where caring is also an ambition that drives innovation. It's not just about innovation in the tech community but about the way we design welfare state institutions – from housing, to education and health – that can be used to stimulate innovation-led growth. A caring economy, including the government 'purchasing' or procurement that serves it, could itself actually be a key driver of innovation. Imagine the social, institutional, and technological innovations that could create a more caring form of capitalism.

I've been talking about just this with Dennis Snower, an economist from the University of Kiel, and Tania Singer. They've been working on developing the fundamentals for a caring economy. There is actually an increase in value-driven atmospheric research in the fields of architecture, landscape, urban planning and so on. There are a few architecture schools that are simply focusing on atmosphere as a scientific issue: noise, air pollution, air management, seeing the atmospheric as influencing health and levels of stress. And these topics are close to home for me, since atmosphere is a key component of one's encounter with an artwork. Thank you, Mariana!

August 2018

DIN BLIND
PASSAGER 201

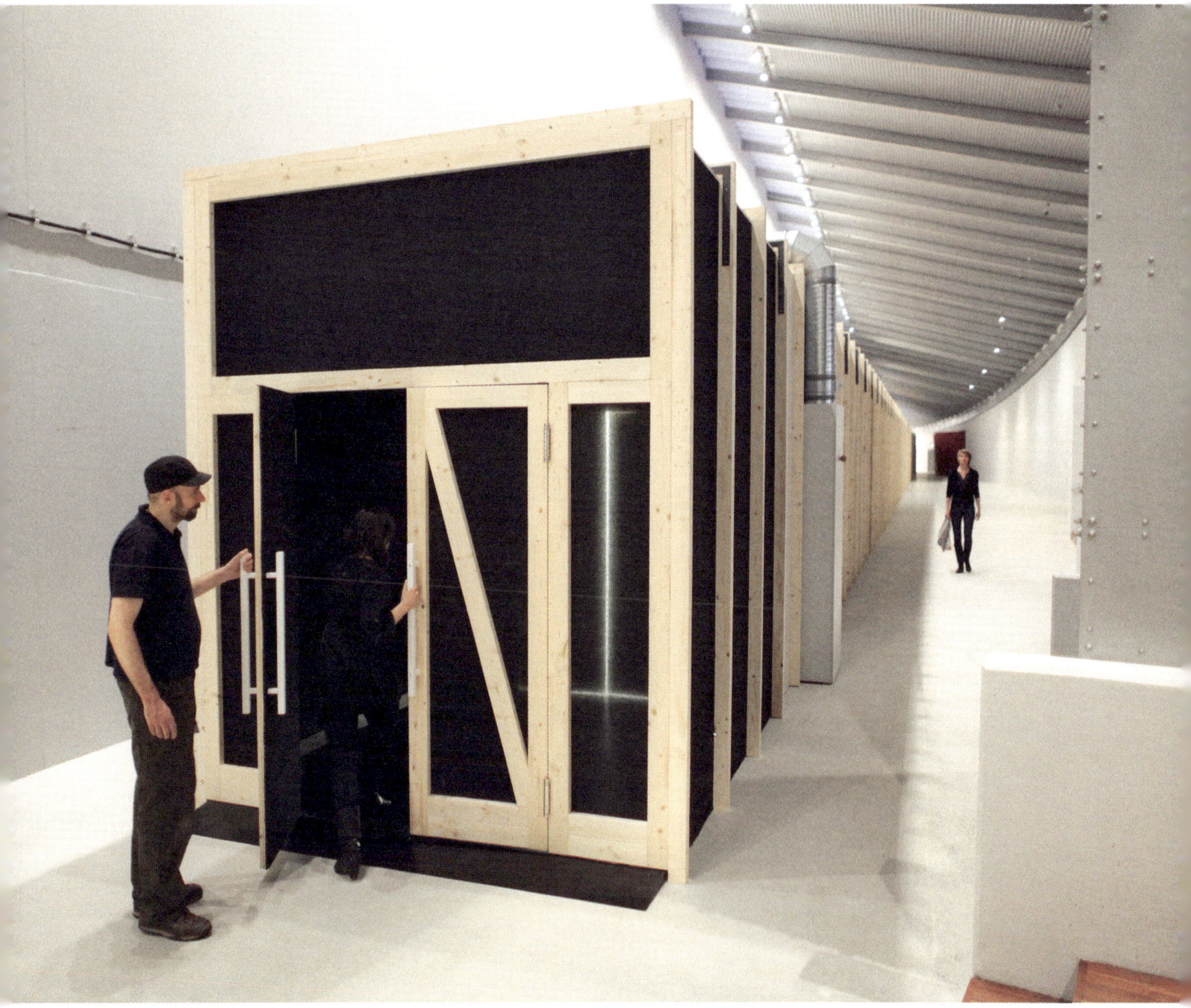

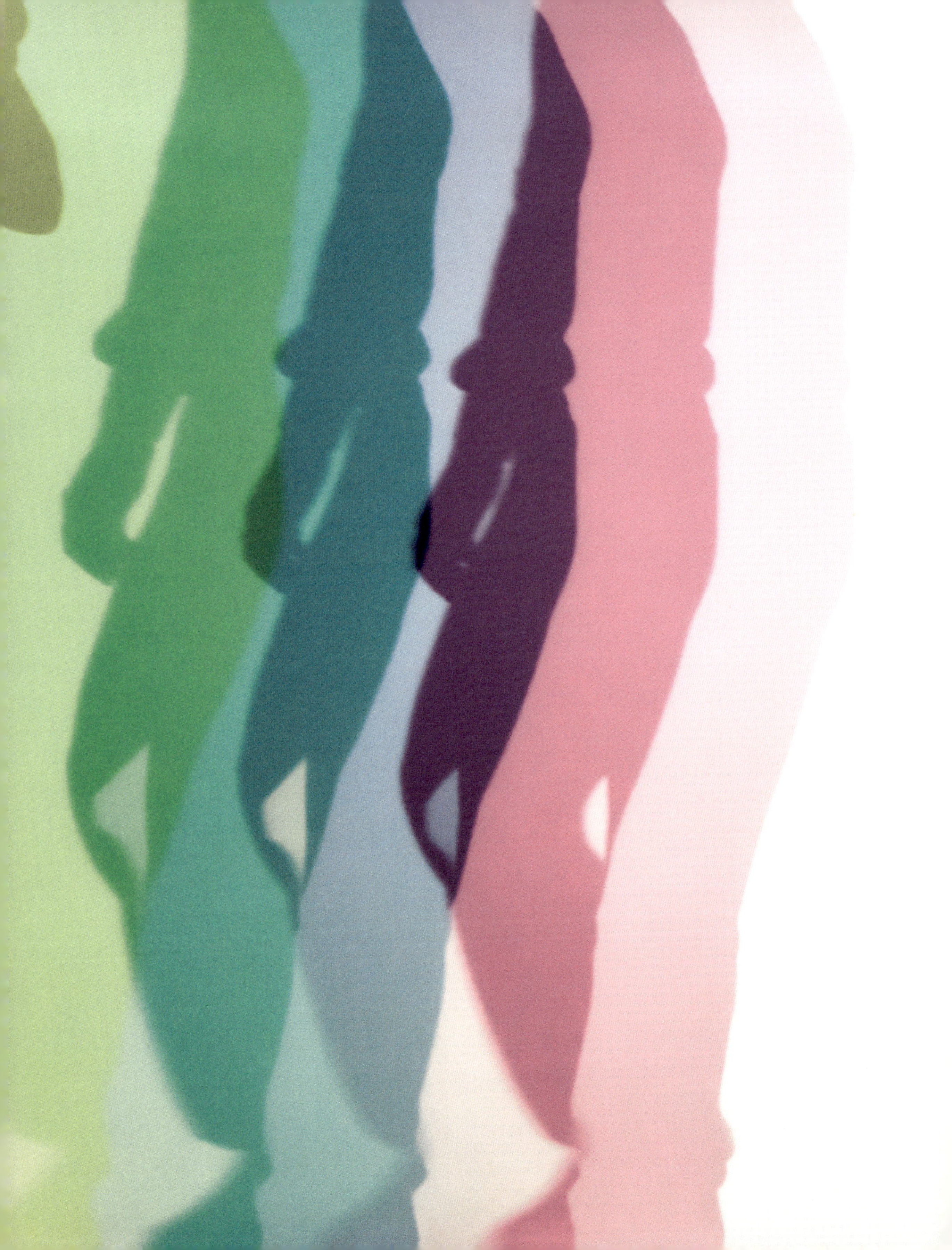

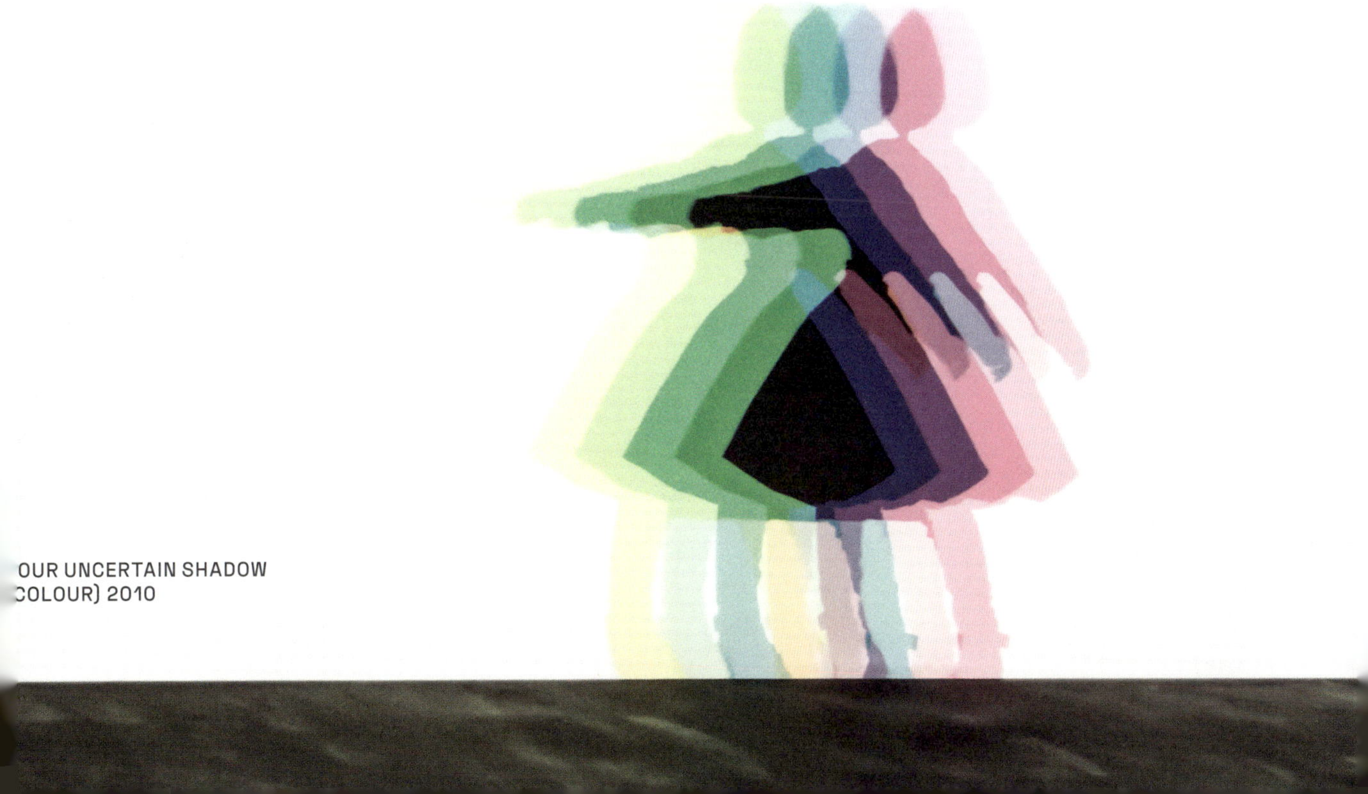

OUR UNCERTAIN SHADOW
COLOUR) 2010

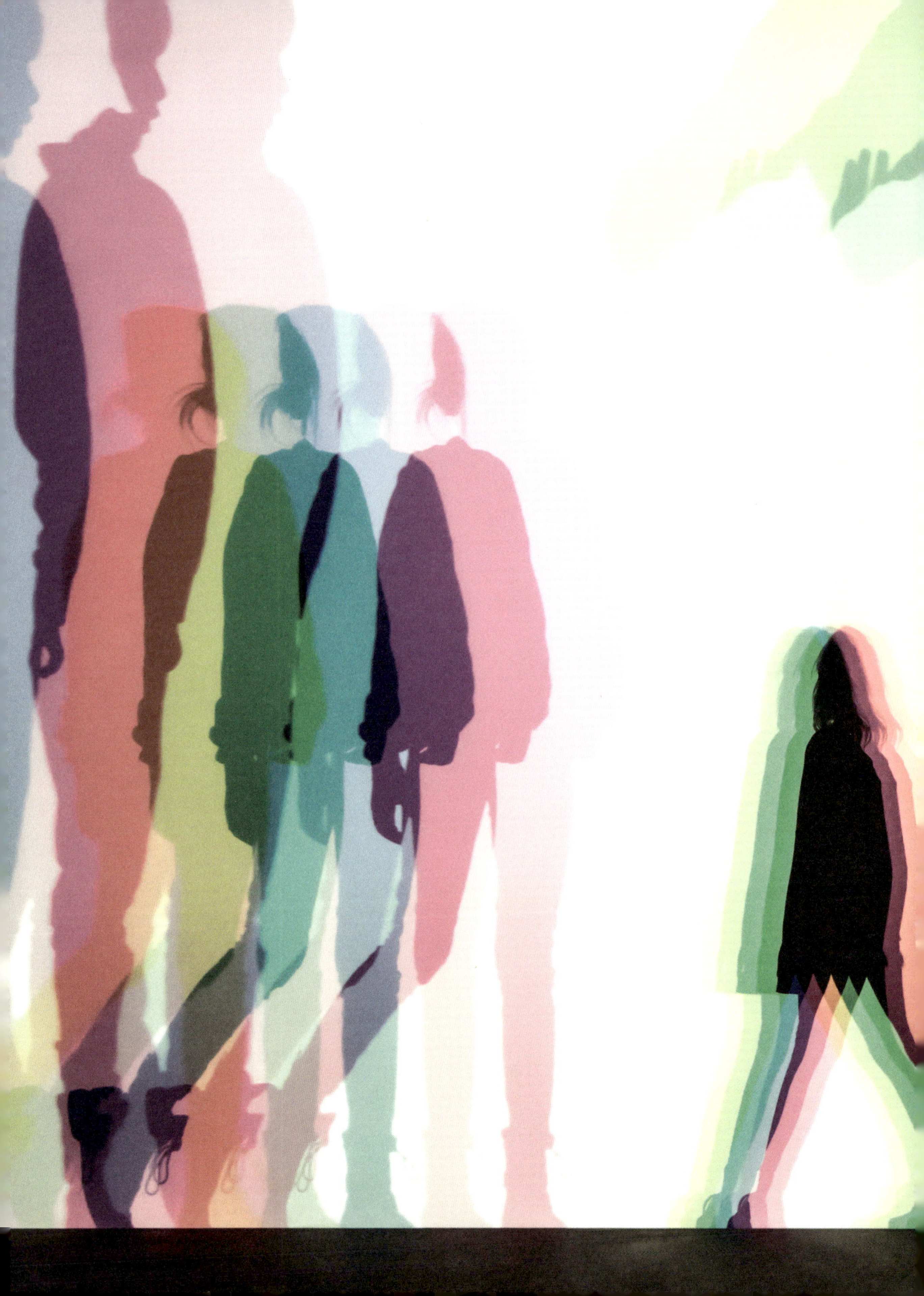

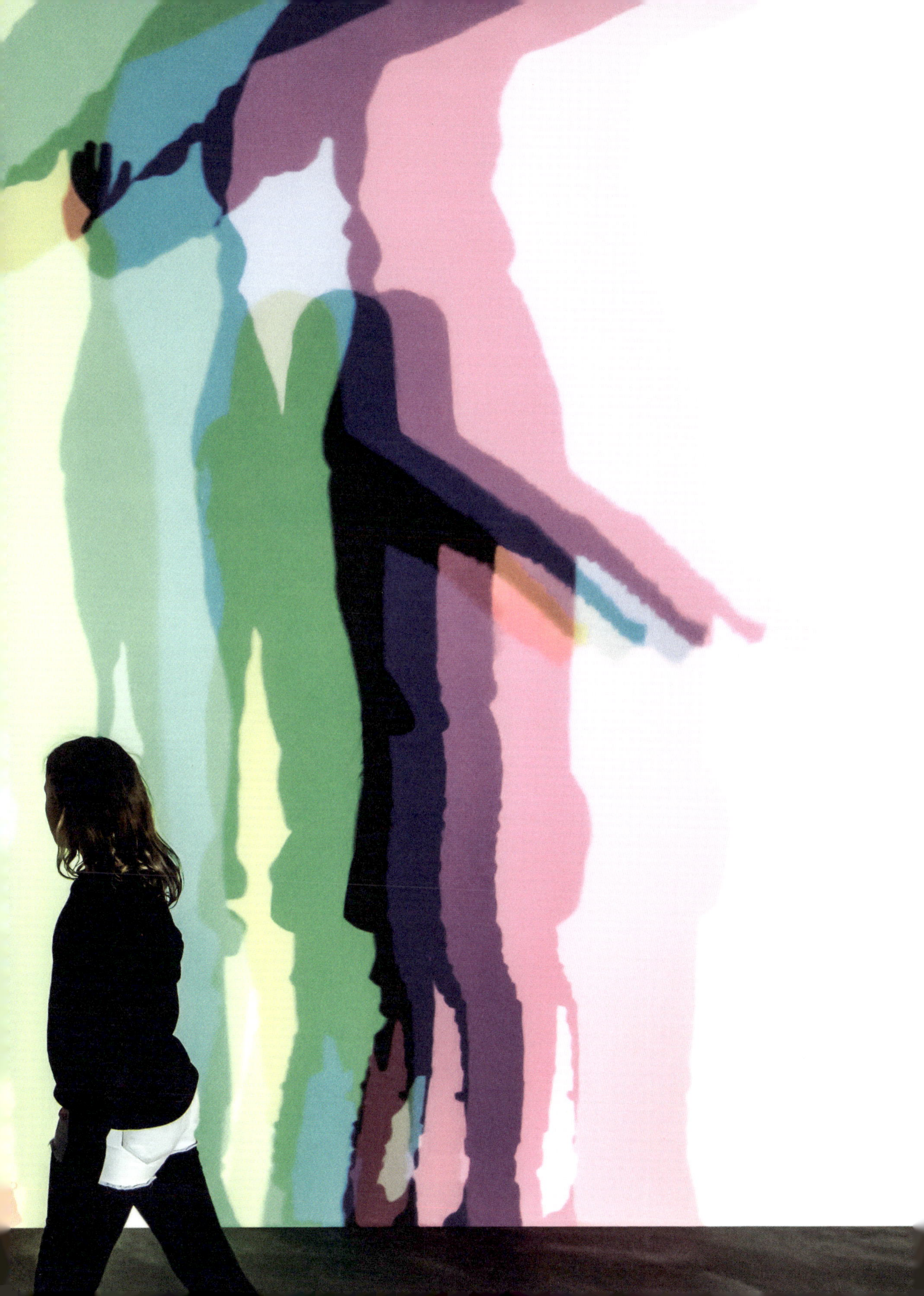

Olafur Eliasson: Sultan, we got to know each other through your interest in art, and I know you have an art foundation [the Barjeel Art Foundation]. I have shown my work twice at the Sharjah Art Foundation, which is run by your cousin, Hoor Al-Qasimi. I was surprised to find I have two friends in this relatively small area. Why, out of the Emirates, and even the Arab region as a whole, is there this commitment to art in the Sharjah region?

Sultan Sooud Al Qassemi: So, Sharjah is one of seven emirates that make up the UAE. Every emirate has its own capital and has other cities within it. As with Kuwait City and Kuwait, or New York City and New York State, you have Sharjah City and Sharjah Emirate, which is a larger area. The reason why you might know two people from Sharjah is that Sharjah was generally the most developed city or emirate in the Lower Gulf. The ruling family there goes back to 1727. In 1820, Sharjah's ruler, Sheikh Sultan bin Saqr Al Qasimi, signed a treaty with Britain, making the area a British protectorate, which lasted until 1971. An airport was opened in 1932, so there was some early investment in infrastructure. Sharjah also had the first educational facilities in the UAE, schools and some clinics. It also saw some sort of leftist activism – it had women's education, for example – earlier than other parts of the region. Sharjah had a fully educated population almost a whole generation before other parts of the Lower Gulf. With education comes a lot of interest in culture and identity and heritage.

And what you and your cousin have in common is a desire to link various aspects of Arab culture – that history – with the international culture scene and the visual arts scene in particular. Culture is essentially about identity. When did you first get involved with the idea that culture is a kind of language that can bridge gaps that would otherwise be hard to bridge?

STORYTELLING

SULTAN SOOUD AL-QASSEMI is a political commentator and art collector. He founded the Barjeel Art Foundation in Sharjah, United Arab Emirates, to exhibit and support art from the Arab world. He writes and tweets prolifically about social, political and cultural affairs in the Gulf States and beyond. Beginning in 2011, during the Arab Spring, he served as an important source of news and commentary on social media. Al-Qassemi has held fellowships and residencies at the MIT Media Lab (2014–16) and NYU's Hagop Kevorkian Center for Near Eastern Studies (spring 2017), among others.

Well, I see myself as a storyteller. I have been writing in a diary, for example, since 1993. I have written short stories and I started performing in plays for the school theatre as well as in television when I was a child. So I have always seen myself in that light. I found that, in addition to lecturing and to writing and performing, art is a way of telling a story, at least a way of telling our story in the Middle East and the Arab world, where I feel that there is still a lot of misunderstanding. Some people don't recognise how far back artistic culture goes in this part of the world. It is important for me to look at the region holistically, everywhere from the Gulf States to North Africa – the region I look at most – but also including some parts of South Asia and East Africa.

I guess you would say that the history of Arab culture has contributed to your notion of identity?

Certainly. Remember that the history of this region was formed through an oral culture – not only due to religion, with, for example, the recitation of the Koran, but also through songs, like the songs that people took to the sea when they went fishing and pearl diving. Poetry, also: there are poetry competitions in the Gulf that go back hundreds of years, even more than a thousand years. These are competitions where people freestyle. They talk and discuss with each other using poetry. This oral tradition has allowed culture to traverse the entire region. And that's why you see people from Sharjah and Kuwait, and even southern Persia and parts of Iraq and Jordan, all the way to Yemen, sharing a lot of cultural attributes. Because the culture was very fluid – the culture was not attached to something concrete. It was easy to memorise – you pick it up, you take it with you and you transfer it to another town a hundred kilometres down the coast, for example. This was something that allowed us to form almost a single fluid cultural identity across the region.

Oral culture and poetry are important to the young people in East Africa, too. In Ethiopia there's a tradition of almost rapping poetry, a sort of performance on stage with a huge audience, and with a high degree of improvisation. It's almost a poetry slam. In Ethiopia it's called the 'wax and gold' principle, in which you can also introduce a political narrative under the safe haven of poetry, or within the frame of culture. Through that you are able to nurture a dialogue about challenges that would otherwise be hard to express. Does the oral tradition in the Gulf have a similar function?

Of course. For example, people used to use poetry to disagree with the tribal chief. And if your poem was very good at the time, it would catch on very fast and spread like fire. Authorities, for example, would be very wary of angering a very famous poet. And so these poets, these intellectuals, would champion certain causes. Like justice, for example: if a poet decided that a leader or a tribal chief was not just, and if he or she wrote a poem about the unjust leader, then that could become very popular and even cause the downfall of that leader. This is a kind of art – to champion causes through an art form.

I'm interested in this because, in my work, I explore the notions of civic infrastructure, of what drives civic trust. When I say 'civic', I mean the feeling of citizenship, of the relation between the individual, society and politics. And civic trust is about sharing values, about a certain societal cohesion, of a coming together of individuals within a structure that we believe in, more or less. And what I see, even in this increasingly polarised world, is an increase in civic trust towards the cultural sector, at least in the

parts of the world that I move in. Culture offers a space for expressing confidence in one another. Would you say that the cultural sector has a standing with the younger generations of today?

I think that there is some kind of standing for culture. But I worry that we are only catching the elite of the Gulf society. I worry that culture is seen as elitist, that it is seen as imported. I fear that we are not allowing young people in the region to take the initiative – that everything is becoming top-down and overseen by government. This is one of the challenges that the Gulf States are facing. And maybe this is by design and not something that is just happening by coincidence. It might be that the Gulf States don't want civil society to feed into the cultural world, because culture can be critical of the government. We see that in some countries in the Gulf, like Saudi Arabia. They have arrested a lot of civil society activists, some of whom are also involved in the cultural world. But in Kuwait, for example, which has the most advanced civil society in the Gulf, there is a great deal of freedom, and I feel that cultural life there can be much more developed – much more critical, and much more interesting. So I feel this should be an example to all the Gulf countries: to have trust in their youth and to allow them even to criticise social matters, using culture. Otherwise cultural production will become stale and the civil society will die out. This would be a threat to us all.

Is the oral tradition taking new forms and shapes? What is the contemporary poetry scene like? There's also an amazing history of writing in the Gulf – the tradition of calligraphy, which is surprisingly contemporary and sophisticated. Is there a sort of popular or contemporary strand of poetry and writing – not necessarily graffiti – that has contemporary cultural agency?

I'll give you an example. In 2007, Abu Dhabi launched a televised poetry competition, *Million's Poet*. It became so big it had millions of viewers across the Gulf and the Arabian Peninsula. It was very popular in the region. The prize money is over a million dollars. Some women's rights activists did make it on to the show, but the show – because it's government-funded and supported – is largely under the government authority. In that sense you cannot be too controversial, you cannot be too critical. And that I think is a missed opportunity. There is another poetry competition in the Arabian Peninsula, which is called Souk Okaz and which goes back, some people say, hundreds if not thousands of years. It's actually a poetry market – an open market in Saudi Arabia – and people go and they do poetry slams. And the poetry that comes out of there is so much more interesting, at least for me, than that on *Million's Poet*.

Now in the Gulf we are also seeing the popularisation of so-called graffiti. You see it in Saudi Arabia and the UAE, Qatar ... everywhere you go in the Gulf. But all this 'graffiti' is sanctioned by the state. This is not really graffiti. Graffiti has a bit of an element of dissidence, a little element of the risqué. But here, you go to the government authority, you get a licence, you show them what the image is going to be, they approve it – or not – there is an organisation that sponsors it, there is an official opening of the mural ... It's fun and it's nice, but it's not graffiti. It's street art.

Right. If I'm looking for cultural statements within Middle Eastern popular culture, is that more diaspora-driven, by people who are not living in the Gulf? How does that influence youth in the Gulf?

Yes, there's a lot of interesting art coming from the Middle Eastern diaspora outside the region. But if you look at cities where there is greater freedom of expression, especially Beirut, you see a lot of interesting art being produced there, including art that is critical of power, art that discusses issues like military drones, like LGBT rights, like women's rights – movements coming from cities that allow more freedom. In the Gulf, artists who do discuss these issues, for example, often only show their work in the studio and don't take it out into the public. Or they might produce it in the region because they need Arabic speakers, or they need local talent to produce the work, but it is ultimately sold internationally. We are definitely missing out on this opportunity. And again, I think the region's governments should give the artists freedom, because if these artists don't create the artwork locally, they are just going to leave and go create it in the West or in another part of the world, and then we lose out. We lose out on the talent, lose out on the creativity. Brain drain is something that affects other industries, and we should not let it affect the art industry, too.

Do you see the cultural sector as actually influencing civil society in the future? I think it is a stabilising influence – one that gives people a sense of worth and identity, that gives people pride in where they are and where they came from, their past and their future. It's stabilising because it's a space in which you can trust each other. You can drive a discussion or debate using culture. You can handle a conflict in a more sophisticated and inclusive, less polarising way than, for instance, you might be able to do from inside a legal system. I know I'm simplifying, but as a principle I'm convinced of this. Do you think what you call the elite will gradually accept that?

Well, I agree with you. I think that the cultural world plays an important role in introducing fundamental issues of human rights to society more broadly. We have seen artists in the Gulf create artworks that talk about labour rights, about human rights, children's rights, the rights of people that are unseen – the labourers, the immigrant workers. I've seen artists do it and bring these issues to the fore. So I think this is a very important role for artists. But when it is seen as coming from abroad, Olafur, then it is rejected completely by the government. For example, we saw how a New York-based coalition of artists and activists called Gulf Labour tried to force Abu Dhabi into introducing human rights reforms and reforms to immigrant rights, but it was completely rejected by Abu Dhabi. The international community should recognise that locals also have agency. And on some issues, we need to be able to move internally, to allow for an internal debate to occur, rather than for it to be imposed on us from the outside. I understand that there must be international support, but it shouldn't be led from the outside. Otherwise it can easily be regarded as outside interference. This is something that can have a negative influence on all of us.

Do you see a trend in the region? Is it getting worse or is it getting better, overall?

Yes, I do see a trend. I'm an optimist, so I do see a trend of things improving. But you have to understand that the way things are improving in the Gulf is through the sharing of non-political rights. So there are more economic rights, there are more social rights – the right to have a job and the right of women to drive, the right to go to the cinema. There are rights in the creative world, too, like fashion shows – you see that happening. You see movie theatres opening in Saudi Arabia. But there is definitely a retraction of political rights. We definitely used to have more freedom of speech in the area, but this has now all but disappeared across the Gulf. We used to have more dialogue, and we used to have more freedom to debate. This is either being eliminated or heavily controlled. So it's like the waves of the sea, the ebb and flow, the give and take. I hope that the governments recognise that you cannot have a thriving artistic sector without a large degree of freedom of expression. I understand that there are cultural issues that prevent us from talking about religion or God or the ruler or leader, but there are other issues to discuss. A greater degree of freedom to talk about these will not only enrich the cultural world but also enrich society as a whole.

On a related note, I know that you are very involved with various architectural histories in the Gulf. When I talk about architecture, I often just talk about space. Space is primarily for people. Why do you follow contemporary architecture in the Gulf?

I'm currently working on a book about early modern architecture in Sharjah, also looking at the region but mostly at Sharjah. The architecture was much more environmentally friendly, for example – these buildings were not glass towers, they were more sustainable. They took space into consideration, and even issues like human rights – for example, the servants' quarters were scaled to accommodate a person comfortably. In the buildings constructed in the last twenty years, however, the servants' quarters are tiny – tiny, windowless rooms. Olafur, when you drive around the Gulf, these towers might as well be in any city in the world. There is less and less local influence, less respect for the environment. There are glass towers, but glass towers act as greenhouses, which means you need more electricity to cool them down. So I feel that architecture is a metaphor for the fast-paced development of the Gulf, which has caused us to lose a small degree of our humanity as we have adopted more and more extreme forms of capitalism. I see this, also, as an important documentation of what happened in the Gulf in the 1950s, 1960s and 1970s. Who were the architects who came here from Europe and South Asia and Africa, and why did they come? What styles did they bring, and how did they adapt them to the harsh climate? I am trying to archive and document and save this part of our history, which is quickly being decimated. In general I am a student of history. I feel architecture is a metaphor for what has happened in the last sixty years across the Gulf.

I look forward to reading it!

August 2018

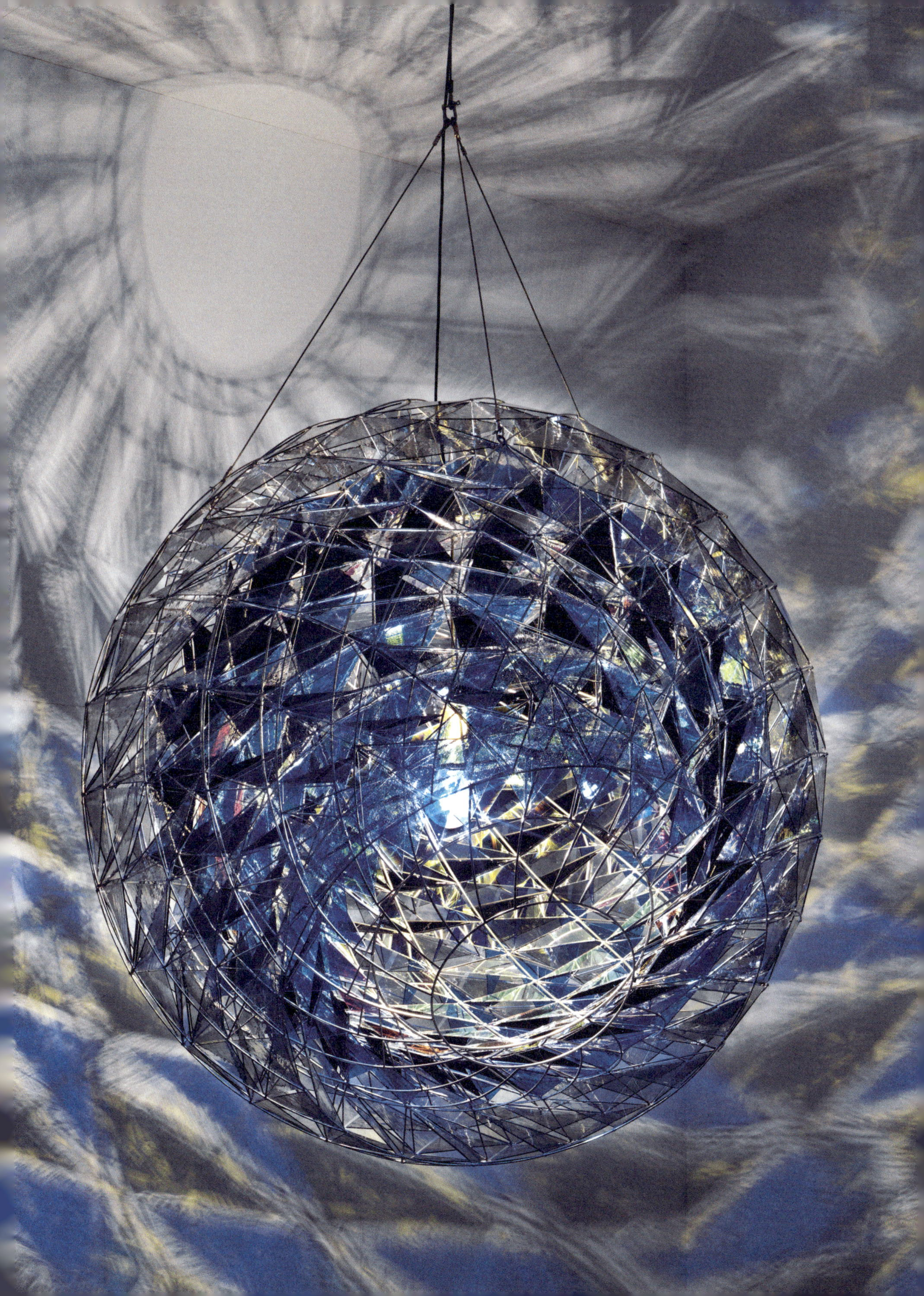

THE EXPANDED STUDIO For some time, Eliasson's practice has extended beyond making artworks, installations and public sculptures. It now includes projects that address questions facing the world today to do with climate change, migration and renewable energy. Studio Other Spaces, Eliasson and Sebastian Behmann's office for art and architecture, has completed designs for projects in countries including Denmark, Ethiopia, Greenland and Mexico, and through his educational research project, Institut für Raumexperimente (2009–14), he explored different forms of teaching and learning.

In order to capture this dimension of his work, the exhibition *Olafur Eliasson: In real life* includes The Expanded Studio, a zone that evokes the environment of the studio in which all these projects are generated. Large panels replicate the pinboards on the studio walls in Berlin where Eliasson and his teams collect articles, images and questions that lead to projects such as Little Sun, *Ice Watch*, and *Green light –An artistic workshop*. Images and videos present new architectural commissions such as the Fjordenhus in Vejle. Visitors are able to sit and look at material on the Studio's website and soe.tv, its video platform. Continuing Eliasson's interest in intellectual exchange and dialogue, every other week a live link-up in this space enables visitors to pose questions about these activities to members of the studio. *The structural evolution project* 2001 is also staged in this space.

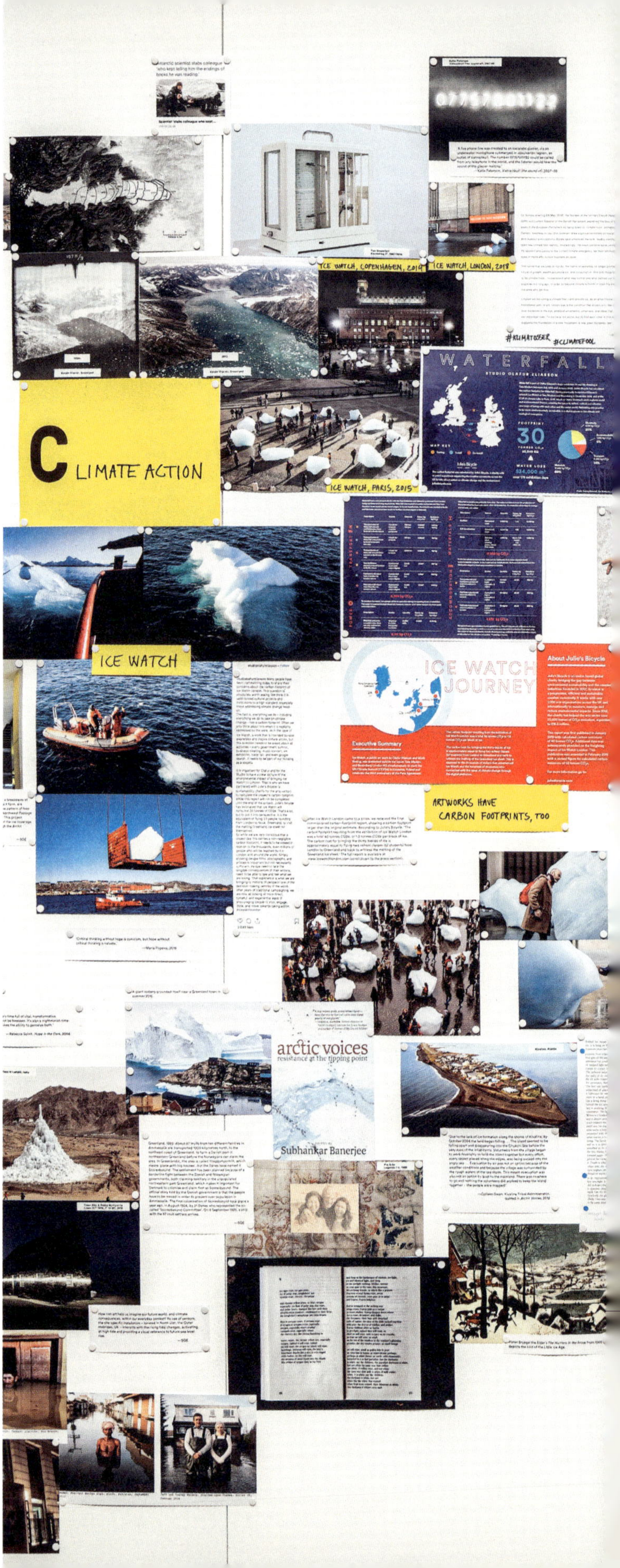

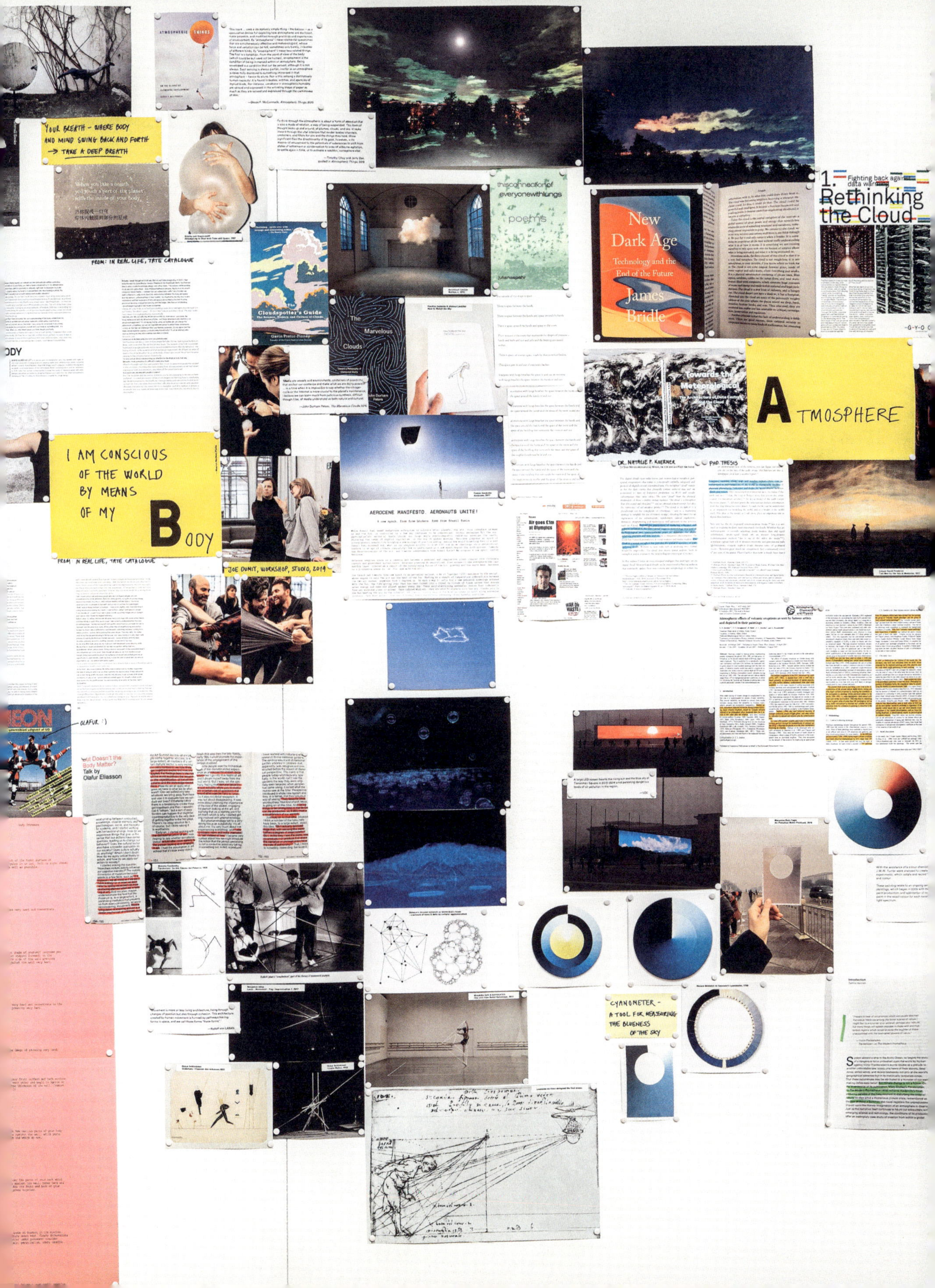
YOUR BREATH – WHERE BODY AND MIND SWING BACK AND FORTH
→ TAKE A DEEP BREATH
FROM: IN REAL LIFE, TATE CATALOGUE
Cloudspotter's Guide
The Marvelous Clouds
thisconnectionof everyonewithlungs
poems
New Dark Age
Technology and the End of the Future
James Bridle
Rethinking the Cloud
ATMOSPHERE
I AM CONSCIOUS OF THE WORLD BY MEANS OF MY BODY
FROM IN REAL LIFE, TATE CATALOGUE
AEROCENE MANIFESTO. AERONAUTS UNITE!
DR. NATALIE P. KOERNER
PHD THESIS
OLAFUR :)
Talk by Olafur Eliasson
CYANOMETER – A TOOL FOR MEASURING THE BLUENESS OF THE SKY

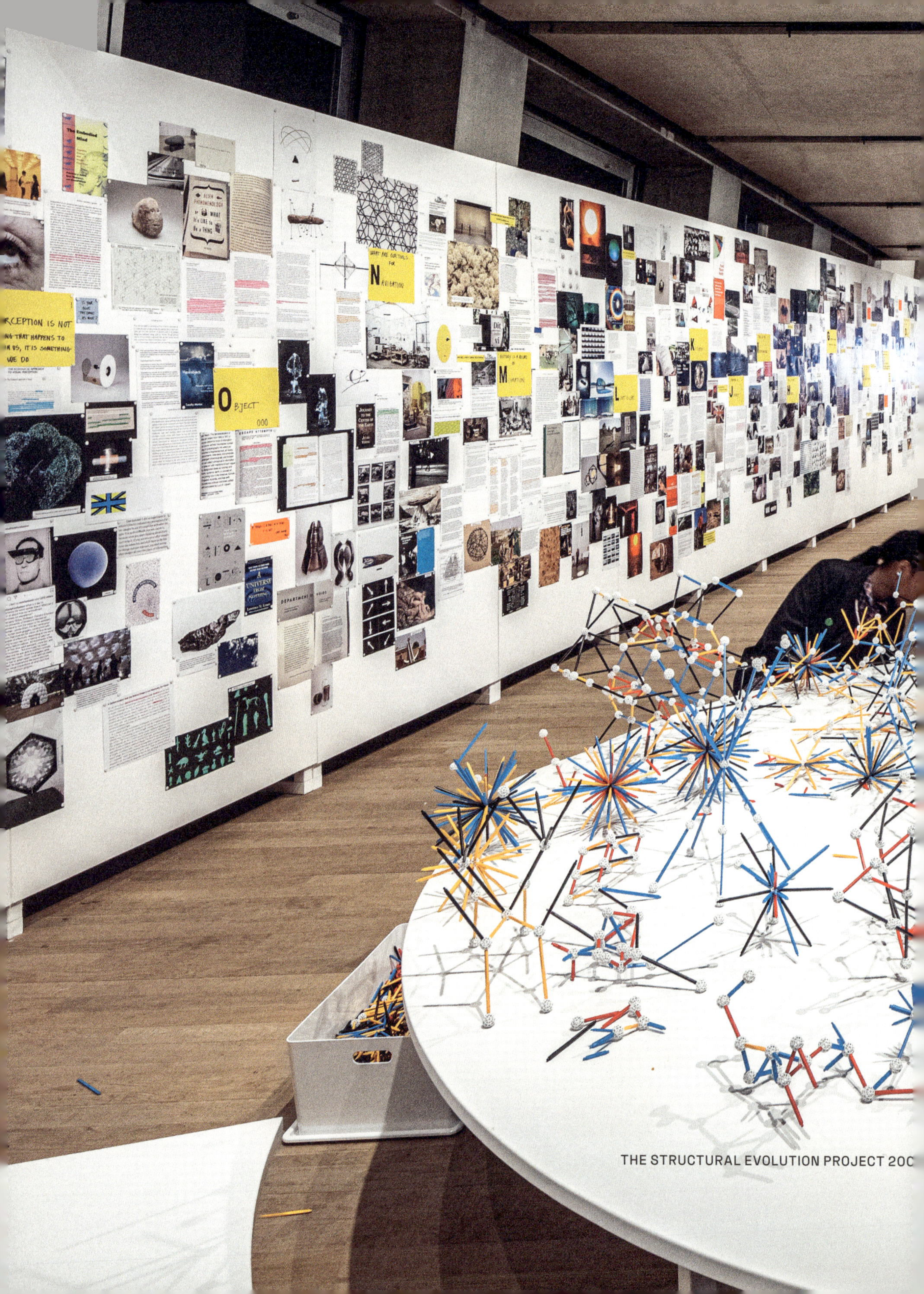

THE STRUCTURAL EVOLUTION PROJECT 20C

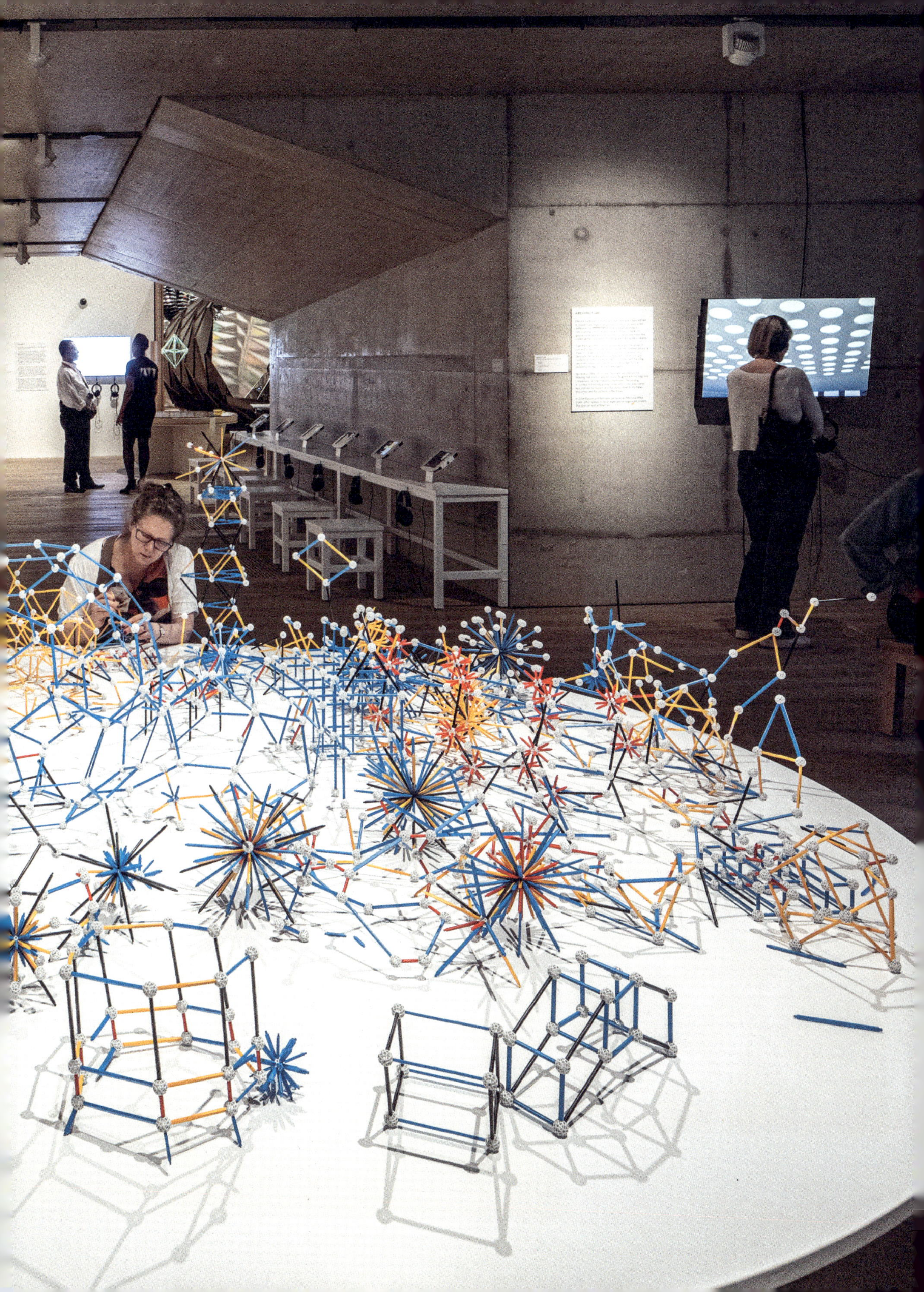

LITTLE SUN Launched in 2012 by Eliasson and engineer Frederik Ottesen, Little Sun is a global project that brings clean, reliable, affordable energy to the 1.1 billion people in the world living without access to electricity, while raising awareness for energy access and climate action worldwide. This not-for-profit venture brings solar light to communities around the globe, especially schoolchildren, refugees and people affected by natural disasters.

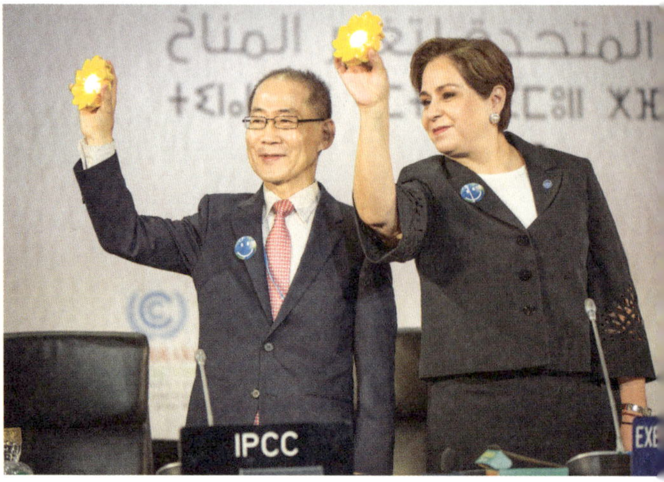

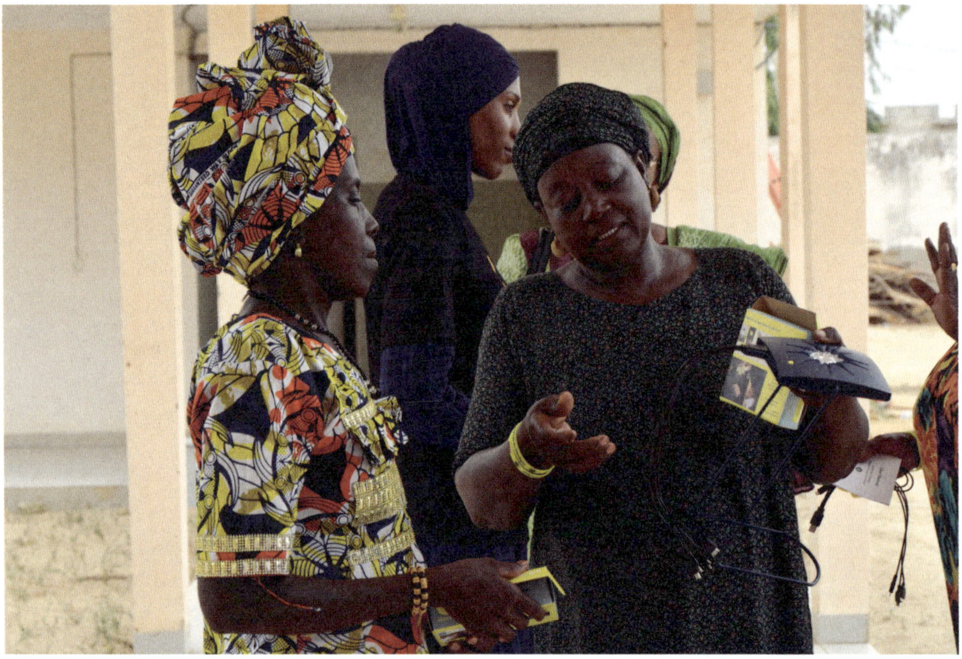

Little Sun's activities to raise climate awareness include participation in events such as the COP22 opening ceremony in Marrakech in 2016 (above), Blackouts and Sunlight graffiti at Tate Modern in 2012 (below) and *Ice Watch* at Tate Modern in 2018 (opposite, below).

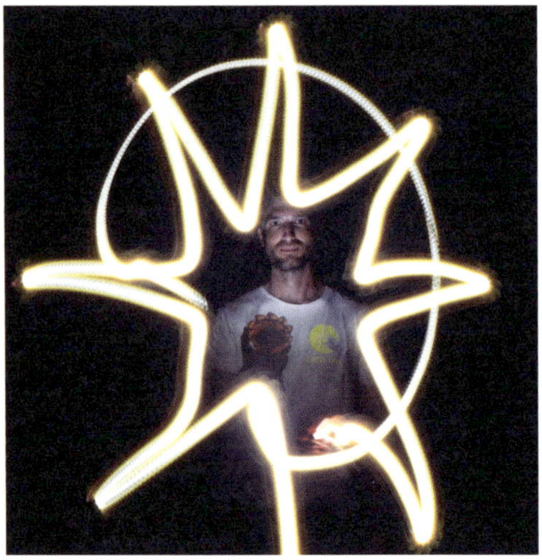

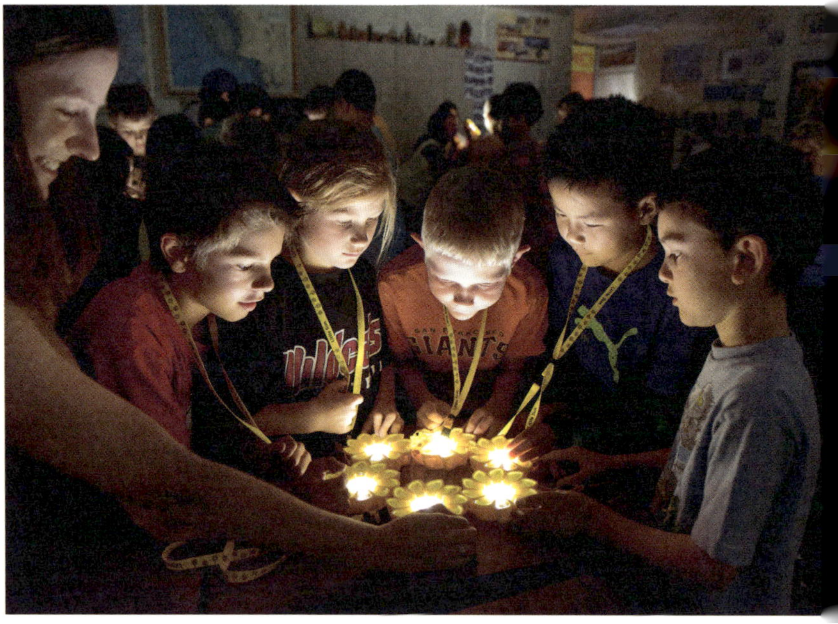

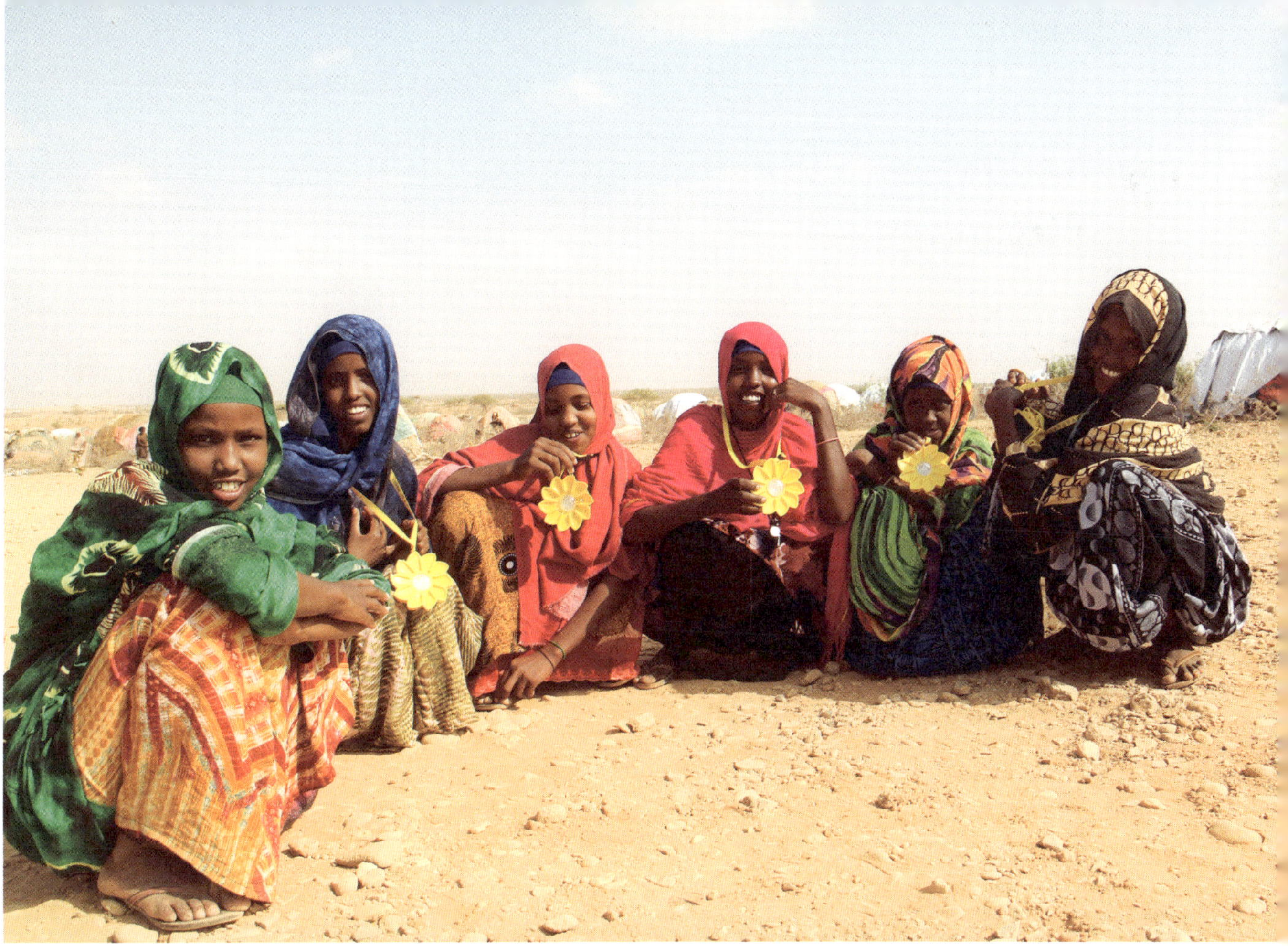

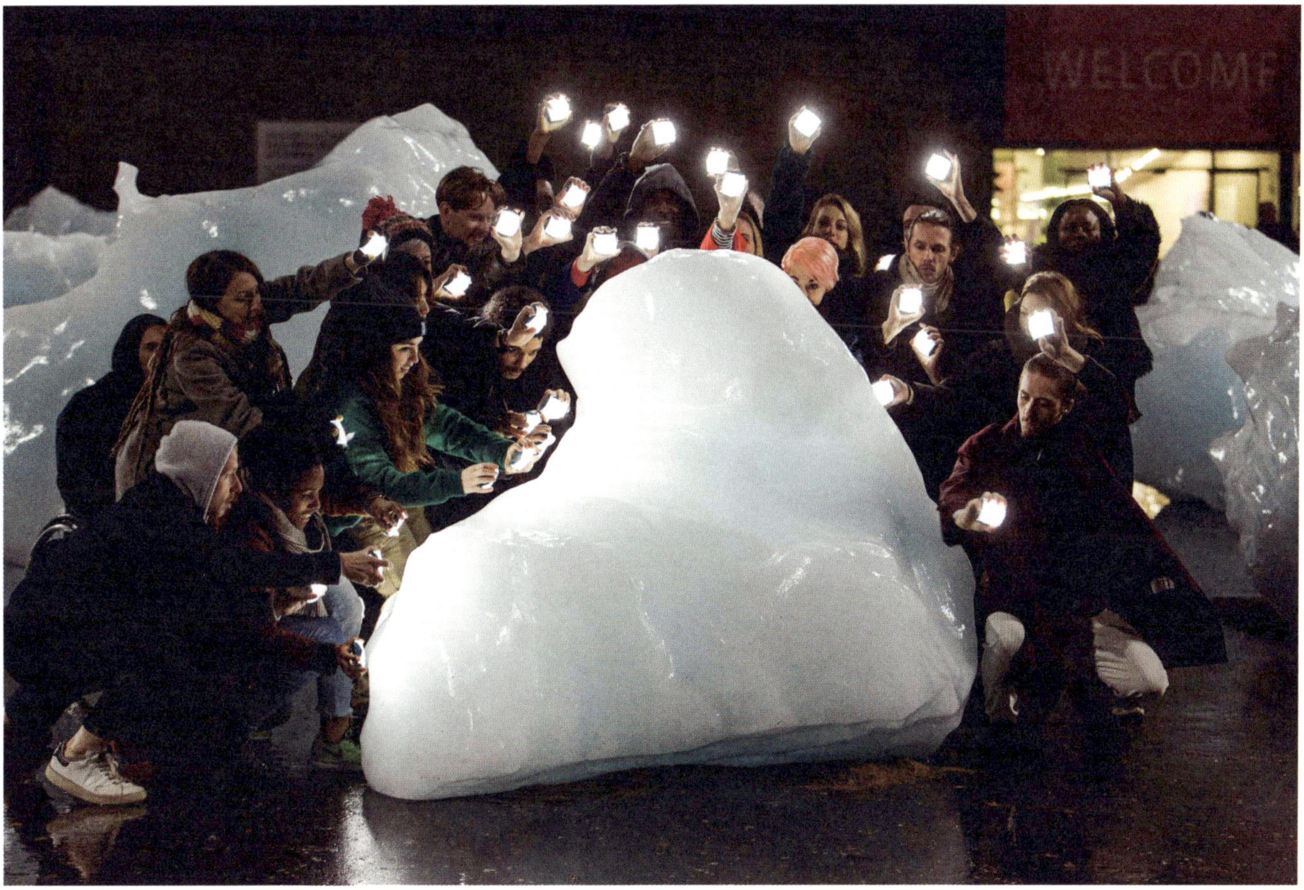
WELCOME

Olafur Eliasson: **I thought we could start by talking about the relationship between art and the world. What I like so much in your work is that when I look at it, I feel I'm in fact looking at my own world. Even though your artworks often deal with a specific narrative relating to the local circumstances with which you are very familiar, I can identify with them. They make me re-evaluate my own local circumstances. How can you be both very specific with a very clear narrative and be very accessible to a global audience?**

Cao Fei: That's an interesting point. I remember you and your son coming to the opening of my MoMA PS1 show in 2016. And even though he was very young – I think ten or eleven – he sat and looked at this very long film for a long time. He almost finished it. Do you remember? The work interested people of different ages – teenagers, young people, even my own kids. So I think this work is for the whole world today. Even though it shows a Chinese environment and location, you can still get a sense of that whether you are watching from Beijing or New York.

You travel so much these days. Do you also make some of your works outside China?

Most of my work is made in my Beijing neighbourhood, but some is made outside. I've recently filmed in Hong Kong, but Hong Kong is quite close to my hometown, Guangzhou, so I'm really familiar with the culture there. A journalist from the *Art Newspaper* asked me recently, 'Why don't you have shows in China?' It's hard to explain. Maybe I'm too young. Maybe it's not the right time. Or maybe it's because I'm Chinese and making films about Chinese stories; if the Chinese watch them, they are too familiar with the environments, the buildings, the people. They don't have the distance.

Sure. When I show my photographs of Iceland in Iceland, it's like showing sand in the Sahara. But I do think you add something – and I hope that I do, too. It's like showing local circumstances in a higher resolution, or under a microscope.

I have a question for you: your work has a sort of psychological, subversive element – maybe it's not a critique, but it offers a re-evaluation of values, of identity. Could this idea of re-evaluating reality be problematic for you in China?

WHOSE UTOPIA

CAO FEI is a Chinese artist currently living in Beijing. Her works have been exhibited at a number of international biennials and triennials and in major museums around the world. In her art she reflects on the rapid and chaotic changes that are occurring in Chinese society today, mixing social commentary, popular aesthetics, references to surrealism and documentary conventions.

I don't think so. Most of the works don't have that kind of issue.

No, your work is not *conventionally* critical, not in an oppositional way. But, it is still about reconsideration of what is good and bad. It offers me a subjective opportunity to re-evaluate things. It shows that the world is not static, that it can move. For me, you are reorganising reality.

All Chinese artists face the interview question about censorship. Foreign journalists always ask, 'How do you feel as a Chinese artist – and as a female artist? What kinds of censorship are you facing?' That is why many artists, including myself, reconstruct a sort of society, or create an alternate reality to parallel our lives. It's like a film – like fiction, not reality. It looks like our reality, it resembles how we live, but we also use dramatic means to reconstruct reality.

I'm interested in the mechanism of change, because I think culture changes the world. How do you change reality, even on a small scale, with your work, with your films?

My film *Whose Utopia?* was filmed in 2006 in a lighting factory for Osram in Guangzhou. It followed the workers there for half a year and was about their dreams and their reality.

Yes, I know this work. It's fantastic.

Well, this year I finished another project, *Asia One,* which follows the smart logistics centre of a really big internet shopping company. It's like eBay and Amazon – it delivers to your house in twenty-four hours. You can shop for everything on the website – water, household goods, mobile phones, everything. So I filmed it. I went into the factory, which is almost fully automated, robotic, and then I set a fictional story in it, a love story. In the twelve years between these two films, there's been a change. When I filmed in the Osram factory, it was all about making products to export on the global market. Today, people can shop online, everything's automatic, factories don't need as many workers and they don't need to make as many products to export to the West. They can sell and earn money on the domestic market.

They are more independent.

Now leaders from Germany and France are coming to China to meet the CEO who created this smart logistics company; they want to do business with him. So you can see that China is stronger now, and also how important the technology of the next era will be to China. So that's what my interests are: global change, economic change, the changes in Chinese industry. When artists focus on this, it's not documentary, but it can transmit information. Even early work that I made in China opened up to the world – from *what* we produce to *why* we produce. One of the workers in *Whose Utopia?* – the lady doing the peacock dance in the film – is now a CEO. She contacted me two years ago and said: 'I was eighteen years old when you came to my factory. You filmed and did workshops with us, and I think it opened a door. Because I came from a village, and when I saw you do all these things, I just wanted to leave the factory. I went to university, studied English, joined a company and did translation, moved to Zhuhai city, and now I am a CEO! I'm married!' It's life-changing. So when you ask me about art's potential, I think people can get a sense of something from the project. *Whose Utopia?* can give hope, can open up a door to the world. And then something happens. It's like magic.

I understand that increased wealth has created a large middle class in China. Fewer people live in poverty, more have an education. I can also see that there is this idea of freedom, of access to everything in consumer-driven environments. But I also think your work is about identity and belonging – and also happiness, about being happy with your life.

Actually, many of my works are about love. Love, and also hope. My work is about conflict – hope and hopelessness, dream and reality; it is always going between the two points.

Yes. And do you think that the way you show your work in collaboration with a museum – say, in Düsseldorf, or at the Guggenheim in New York, or another institution – and being part of culture also plays a role in this?

As a Chinese artist, I think it probably does. Maybe when North American or European artists show in those places, visitors don't think this, especially if the collections are Eurocentric. But when these institutions show work by a Chinese artist, there's a contrast. People might see my work by chance in such places and say, 'Oh, this work's great ... Oh! It's *Chinese*!' I think it probably means something when works are shown this way. What do you think?

For me, there are also different levels of engagement. One level is direct contact with the work of art, for the people who go to a museum, a concert or a cinema. Then there is also the cultural institution and how it positions itself in relation to artworks. And then there is the whole network of cultural institutions and how they are integrated into society. I ask because your work is very much about the world, and even though you are clearly inspired by Chinese culture, you use a language that people from many different cultures can identify. For me, your work is also about connecting culture with society and showing that there is a dynamic relationship between the two.

Well, I feel many institutions – some big, some small – are sometimes genuinely interested in what I am doing. But sometimes they're interested in 'a Chinese artist' doing things that don't look Chinese. Do you understand what I mean?

I think of you as an artist who started in China. But the questions you explore – about love, identity, culture and society – are not just Chinese. They are *also* Chinese, but these are questions we have everywhere. When someone like my son responds to your work, he is actually thinking about his own life, and that, I think, is what makes it such a success. Art introduces something like a pair of glasses through which you can see things you cannot normally see.

Let me ask you a question, now. You are doing a lot of different things, not just works for museums. You're doing a virtual reality project with [VR research hub] Acute Art, and your solar project, Little Sun. You're trying out all these different things, worldwide, with different modes of distribution. You're open to new things. Not all artists want to try VR, for example, or to try working on a BMW car [both artists were invited to produce a car for the BMW Art Car Collection, Eliasson in 2007 and Cao Fei in 2017]. You and I are similar in that we love new things, and sometimes doing these projects leads us to other topics – for example, pollution. The results are different, of course, but for both of us, the goal is not just to finish a car, for example – 'I'll finish this project and give you a product' — it's more the issues that attract us. I wanted to go to the BMW factory and I wanted to do another

project in the factory, and then I wanted to understand what people in business are thinking.' What interests us are all the things behind the project. That's a meeting point for us.
I agree – the so-called art world is sometimes too small, too interested in itself. Sometimes it is good to find a balance between the inside of the art world and the outside of the art world. You mentioned the Art Car project for BMW. Yes, I'm interested in questions of mobility, society, the climate and also innovation. BMW has a commitment to art and culture, and I think it is because BMW understand they need art and culture in order to survive in the long term. The same goes for politicians. More and more politicians, more and more people in the public sector, are consulting cultural practitioners, and I'm very interested in this type of collaboration, too. So I work with both the private and the public sectors. I think it is always super important to be honest. And to take risks. Whoever collaborates in this way should be very honest – should be both positive *and* very critical. After all, we are not 'doing business' with them. We're doing art. And art can be pretty resilient.
You mentioned VR – what fascinates you about it?
I tried out VR very early, on the computer. I created the artwork *RMB City* in Second Life in 2007. We didn't have glasses or headsets yet, but you still had your avatar in this virtual world. Various art institutions ran some of RMB city's buildings, carrying out cultural activities in that virtual world. There was my avatar, and Hans-Ulrich Obrist's, and all the other people in the audience, sitting in the big city hall. We'd see the city, the sky, the digital ocean; we could float into the sky and fly over those spaces ... It was a kind of pre-VR experience. Twelve years on, the technology has developed, and I still really want to understand what's happening today, what the technology is, what the possibilities and limits are. I'm trying augmented reality now.
Me too. On one side I'm trying to do some artistic experiments in VR, but I also use it very often for practical things. For the show at Tate Modern [2019–20], my team made the whole exhibition in VR for the first time. We just bought an architectural supplement for the programme Rhino and drew the space very quickly. It's very minimal, only black and white, but just this morning while I was walking through the exhibition in VR and placing the works in the space, I realised I had to move a door from the left side to the right side. I realised, 'Oh my god, if the door is on this side, visitors will miss a room!'
I wanted to ask you: what do you think is reality and what is real life? What do you want to do in VR? I tried out your VR *Rainbow* at Acute Art. It was very beautiful, but we already have waterfalls and rainbows in real life. What can you experience *differently* in virtual reality?
I am not sure yet. But I like to challenge the technology, so I choose what is most difficult to make, which is to recreate natural phenomena like water, rainbows, mist, ephemeral experiences. I told the great people at Acute Art, 'I want to make natural phenomena.' It was really hard, but I liked the process. Our conversations taught me so much about colour, movement, programming. For me it was an educational opportunity. I have all the VR instruments and technologies here – the headsets, the interface systems. I am following it quite carefully, because even though I don't know exactly what I want to do yet, I'm sure VR will be part of the future.

I'm so interested in what VR or AR can do. Right now they usually just offer people a sort of Hollywood experience – illusion, magic, deception. You look at a Hollywood film and then play some game, and afterwards you have no memory of it.

Yeah, you have Hollywood, gaming and the sex industry. In a way I think we only see the commercial side. But medicine now has some advanced systems for teaching surgery. And there's probably a lot of secret VR being used by the military: for airplane simulation, counterstrike simulation, military training. Often, innovation is more about defence and offence than about creativity.

Also consumerism and online shopping.

One area that I think is developing a little faster now is the feeling of collectivity. In VR, more people can be inside my artwork at the same time. If you are alone it's one thing, and if you are with somebody else it's different. Now, the other person could be in China – it could be you in Beijing! We could have a conversation in virtual space, together with the artwork. It's evolving very fast.

Yes. But compared to the experience I had with Second Life more than ten years ago, I'm still waiting and looking for the big leap in VR.

So am I.

I wanted to ask you about the audience's reaction to your recent show in Beijing [*The unspeakable openness of things*, Red Brick Art Museum, 2018]. I know your earlier show in Shanghai [*Nothingness is not nothing at all*, Long Museum, 2016] was very successful. Two years later, they said your Beijing show was hot because a lot of people went to see it. Many were posting photos on social media, which is interesting, because your work has lots of mirrors, and a lot of reflection from the materials – so the people taking photos with their phones added another reflection to the work: selfies. A reflection of this reflection ...

It's a challenge, but it's also an opportunity. I have been talking very closely to Mr Yan, the collector and founder of the institution, and his very good team at the Red Brick Art Museum. It's actually my fifth solo show in China, and my second big show. Gradually I am coming to understand the local conditions better and better. It was really special for me that such a high percentage of the audience consisted of young people. A very large number of visitors were under thirty. Visitors were well-versed in technology.

But it's a challenge for my work if people only look at it through their phones. When I asked people informally about this I found that many of them were first-time museumgoers. I like that my shows appeal to them. But I also understand that that first time is the hardest – that art, books and theatre can sometimes be very abstract. I need to concentrate to watch a film for thirty minutes. And maybe I need to go to a museum three times before I realise that this is not about consumption – this is actually co-production.

It brings us back to the idea that an artwork allows you to see a part of yourself in it; it hosts you. For the opening at the Red Brick Art Museum, a journalist mentioned that he found my show to be very Chinese. It had to do with my use of the circle, of emptiness. I found that so interesting.

August 2018

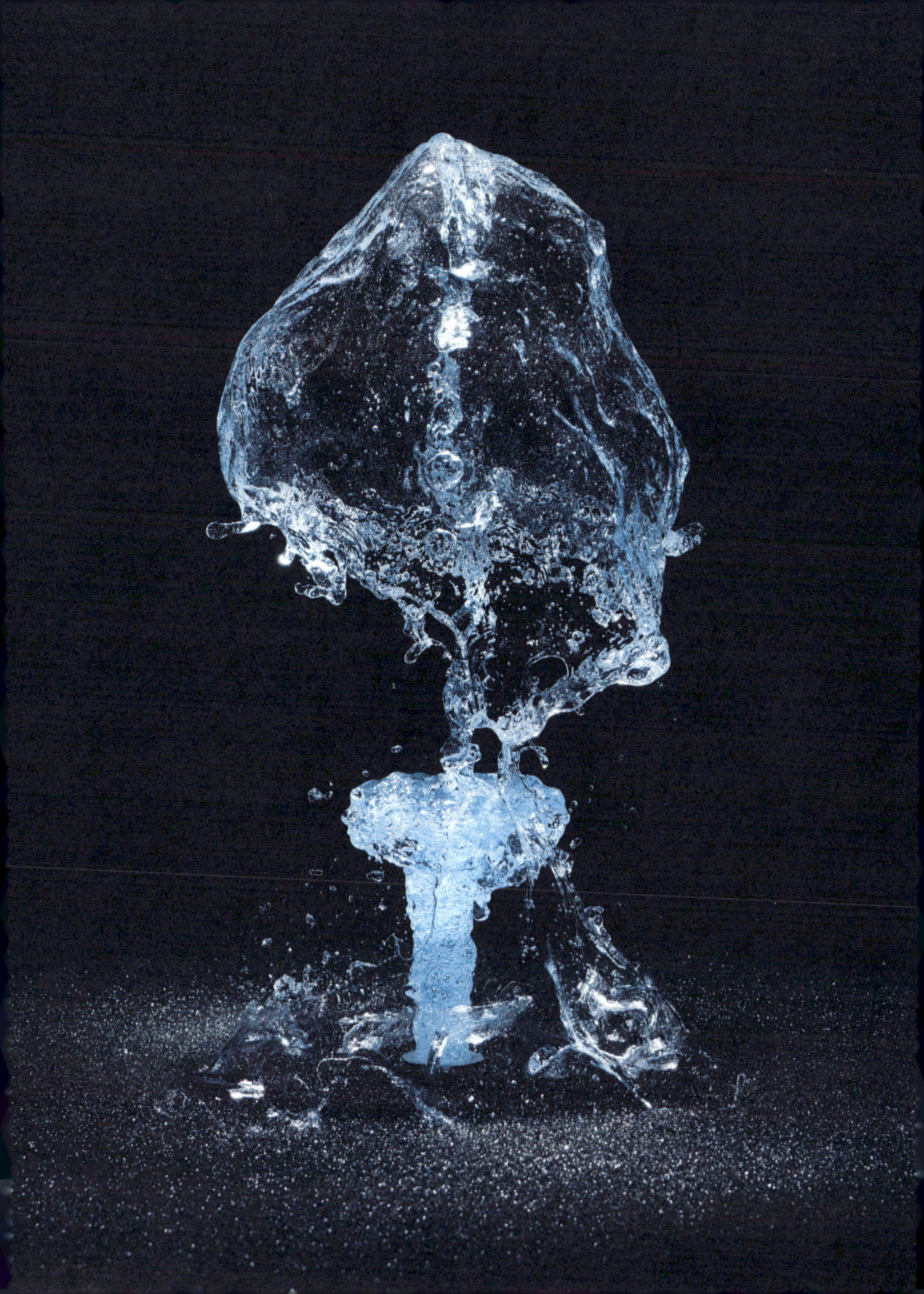

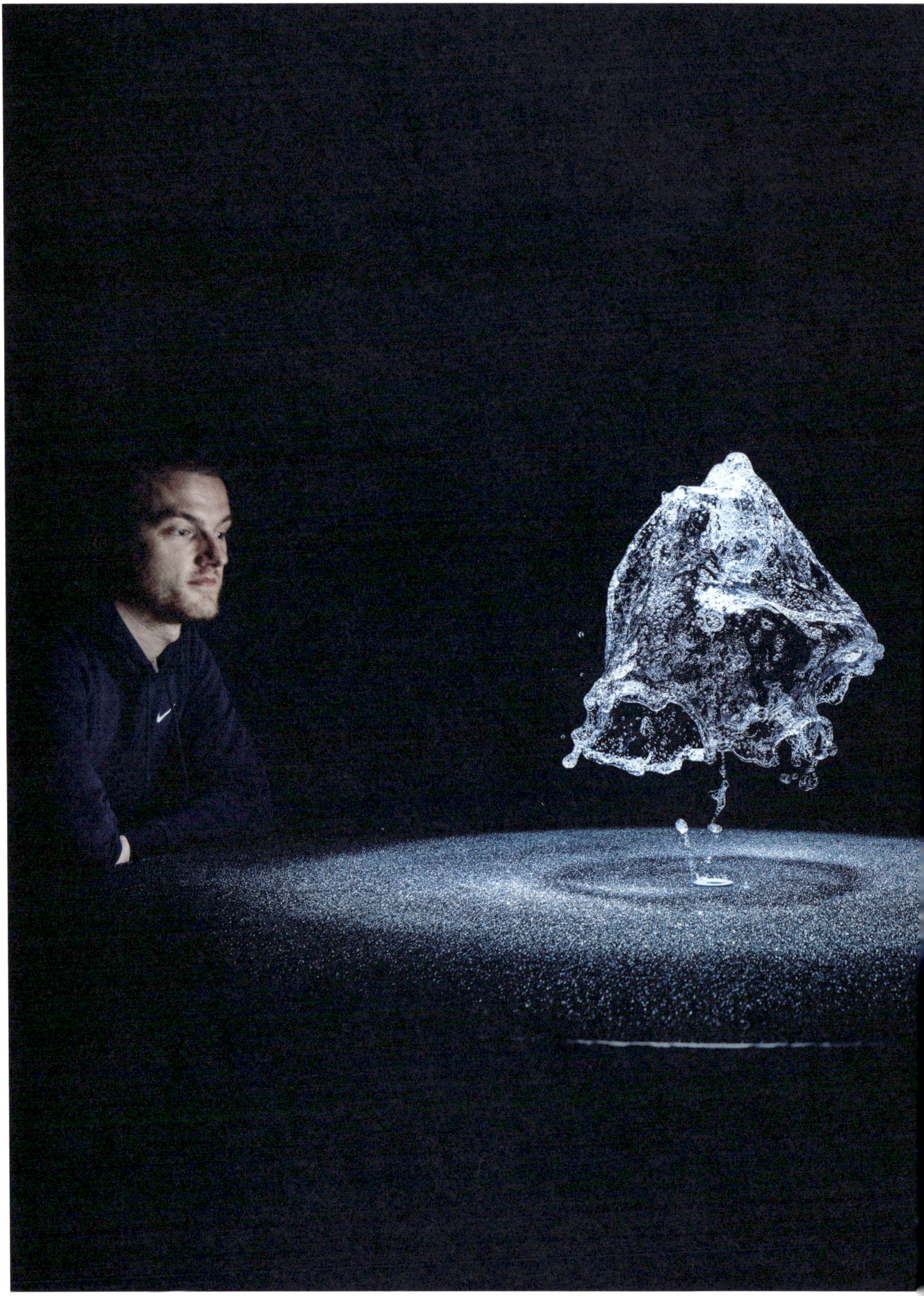

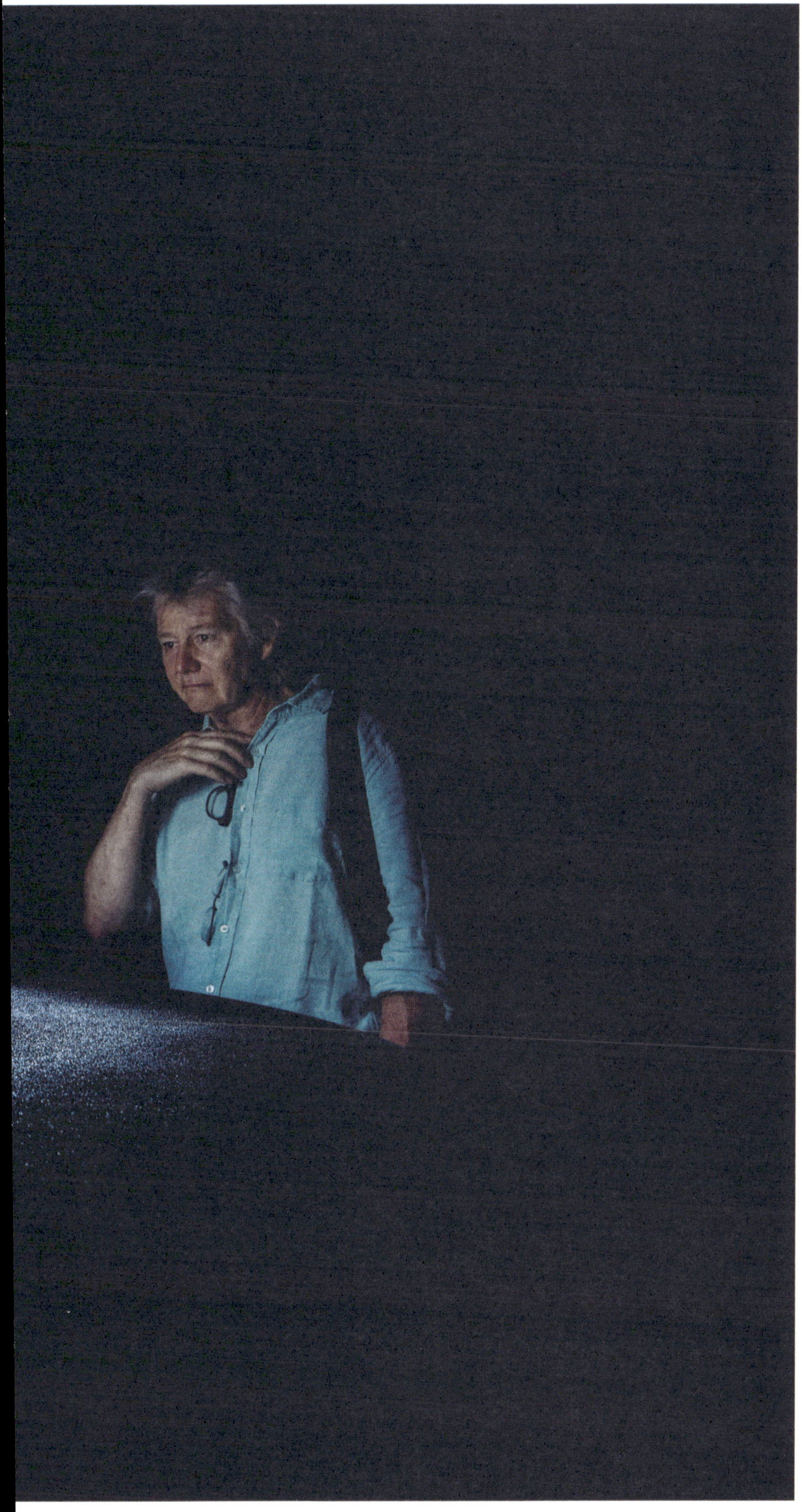

STARDUST PARTICLE 2014

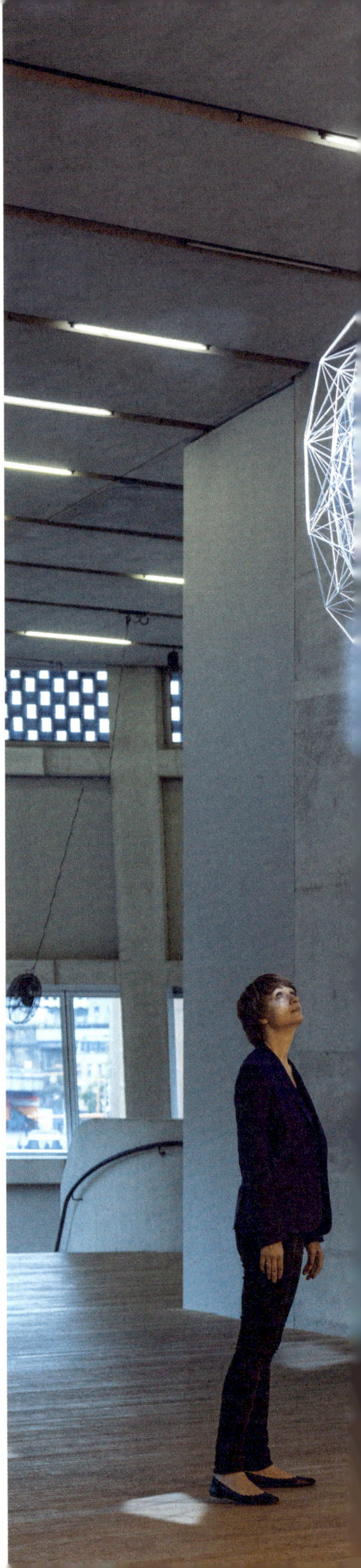

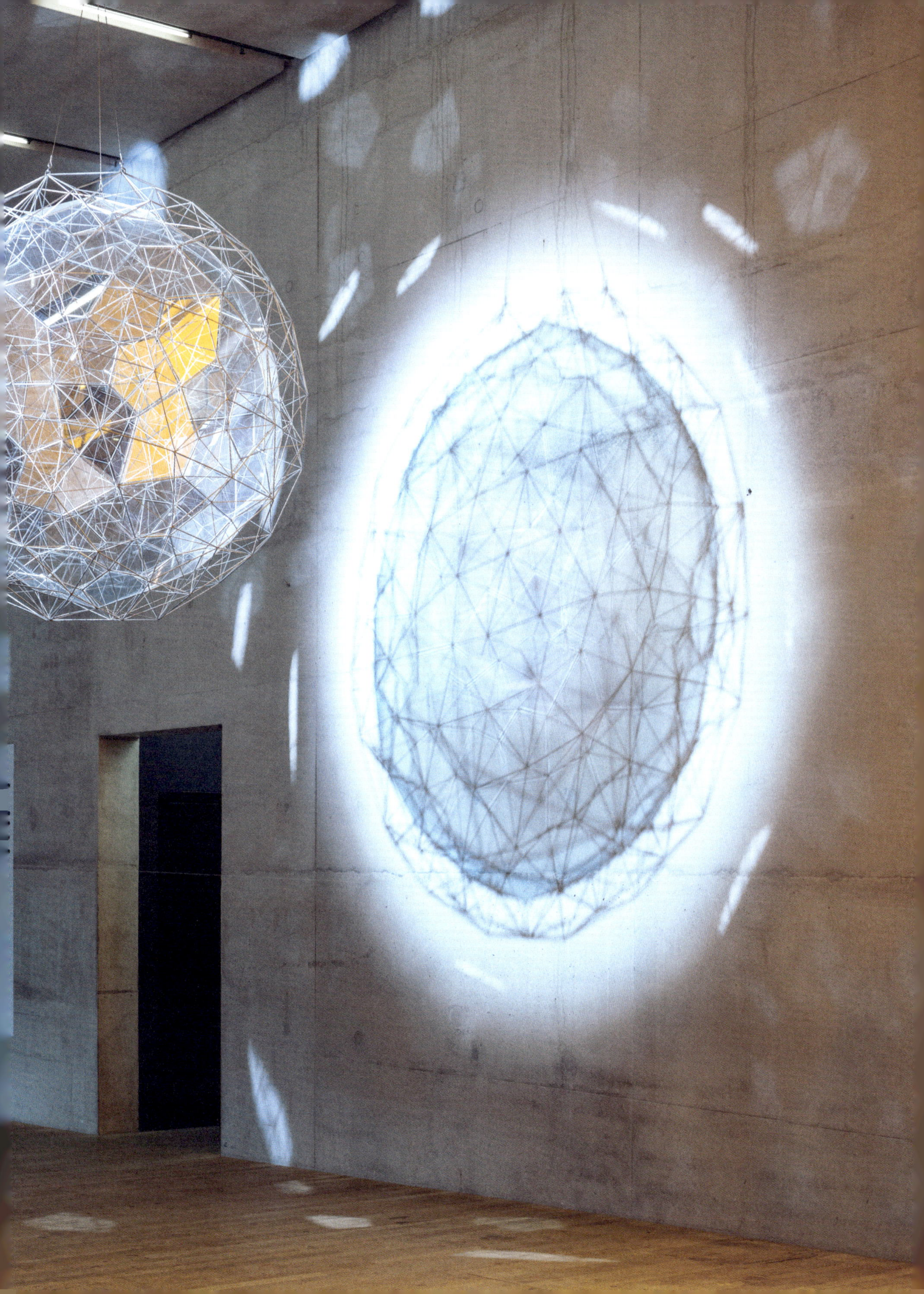

Andreas Roepstorff: Why don't you start by telling me more about what you'd like to accomplish with this exhibition.

Olafur Eliasson: There are many levels to this: first of all, I see the accompanying book and its conversations – like this one – almost as a small artwork. The catalogue isn't supposed to *represent* the exhibition; rather, it's a part of the exhibition. It should offer readers access to how my artworks, both in the studio and when shown in an exhibition, reach out to a lot of different people and experts and draw on many different areas of knowledge. I'm speaking with people who interest me – people from widely different fields with whom I am regularly in touch in one way or another. These contacts are an invaluable source of new ideas for me.

The exhibition curator, Mark Godfrey, has been very interested in those activities of mine that relate *indirectly* to art. These include advocacy – for climate action, for example – and my social business Little Sun, which promotes access to renewable energy; also architecture and food. You might say these interests lie on the periphery of the traditional art world. Getting this to fit into the exhibition has been quite a challenge, for a simple reason. My artworks typically bring about a kind of experience-contract with the visitor. You walk into the exhibition with certain expectations; you leave it with certain memories; and when you engage with the artwork, it's a very bodily and direct experience. This has a lot to do with using your senses and with being conscious about using your senses. My work with architecture, with sustainable energy, with migration and climate action takes place outside the museum, however. So how can I prevent something that has been unfolding outside from turning into an oversimplified representation of that activity within the museum? It's surprisingly difficult to get these different activities to speak to each other within a single space.

EXPERIENCE

ANDREAS ROEPSTORFF is Professor of Anthropology at the University of Aarhus, Denmark, and the founding director of the Interacting Minds Centre, also in Aarhus. His research explores cognitive neuroscience, interaction, play, collaboration and intersubjectivity. In June 2018, Roepstorff and Eliasson conceived and hosted a workshop at the studio entitled 'Experimenting, Experiencing, Reflecting: Art and Science at Work in the Public Realm', exploring convergences between social science and art. Roepstorff also participated in the programme of lectures and seminars that accompanied Eliasson's *Green light - An artistic workshop* in Vienna in 2016.

I thought it might be fun to speak with you, Andreas, about what an experience actually is. What's going on when one experiences something? Of course, I am aware that it is a mingling of culture, biology, a great deal of psychology, and so on. But how would you dissect, or describe, what happens? This could be in relation to art, but it could also be an experience of something completely everyday. I don't aspire here to turn the process of having an experience into an object. An experience has a before and an after; its importance lies in this continuation, this *flow*.

In my own reflections on what an experience is, I have moved through three different phases. I think these may represent more general trends in how people think about experiences more generally. Let me start this way: for a long time, I subscribed to what is known as a naïve realism – that is, the idea that an experience is when the world inscribes itself in me. Experience, accordingly, is a way for the information that is present in the world to become accessible. To experience means being as faithful as possible to what is happening in the world.

In the past few years, however, I have become much more aware that I harbour – as body or as brain, as a biological being – certain *expectations* about what's happening in the world. In this understanding, experience contains a large element of predicting what may be happening in the world – a prognosis. These predictions converge with what is actually a rather thin stream of information coming from the world. This somehow turns the relation upside down. Suddenly, it's as if the rich and faceted part of experience actually lies within the self. This can be biological, it can be cultural, it can be all kinds of things. What the world provides, first and foremost, are correctives to the cognitive perspective – refutations of assumptions about what is happening, that again are invitations to remodel the world. This approach is currently known as 'the predictive mind' – one of today's big buzzwords in philosophy and cognitive science; Andy Clark's *Surfing Uncertainty* [2015] and Jakob Hohwy's *The Predictive Mind* [2013] are two excellent books on the topic. In this understanding, the functions of consciousness and the brain and, perhaps, all of biology are an attempt to predict the world, with its actions, events and underlying causes. In a certain sense, an experience scenario thus becomes a form of simulation about what is happening in the world, and the experience is not so much situated in the world but rather has largely to do with what one *expects* from the world. This may unfold at various levels of detail, or granularity, and with various degrees of precision.

And the third phase?

Right now – together with Claire Petitmengin, whom you also know – we are carefully following what happens when you direct your experience back towards experience itself, when you direct your attention back towards attentiveness. Claire and some of her colleagues have worked a lot with a particular way of posing questions related to subjective experience. This has become formalised in a technique – called the 'elicitation interview method' – in which one asks questions leading back to an experience. The method may appear deceptively simple. However, strange things often happen in this process, as you suddenly come to realise that you can gain access to many more levels under one apparent layer of momentary subjective experience. So, an experience seems to be neither a passive stream of information into the body nor a set of expectations about the world; it is closer to being a form of space that you can delve down into. And, as you go back to it, your experience may be radically transformed.

When you're part of such an elicitation interview, or when you hear somebody else being put through this type of interview, it's like stepping into a landscape. There are just levels upon levels upon levels of nuance. In this third model, experience itself is thus a kind of universe that one can be helped to enter in order to revisit the experience and deepen and transform it.

You could consider the three ways of experiencing as movements. In the first, you are consuming the world – taking it in. In the second, you are taking on a more active role; instead of consuming, you become a kind of producer, and you produce reality through your predictions. This activity carries with it a concomitant responsibility. In the third, through the elicitation interview, we have a way of establishing augmented contact with the surrounding world, even though, paradoxically, it might sound as though you were actually isolating yourself inside your experience. Instead, you enter in and you fine-tune your sensitivity, and thereby also your contact with the surrounding world. By virtue of this kind of consciousness-expansion, or fine-tuning, your experience almost becomes spacious. Indeed, this is also a kind of action. Opening up for subjective experiences is also opening up for actions. I'm tremendously interested in the hinge that allows an experience to swing back and forth without any friction between one's inner world and the world outside.

I'm following you. You see, if the first model consists of my *representing* the world and the second consists of my activity of *constructing* the world, then the third has to do with *sharing* a world with each other. For it appears as though access to this level of experiences almost demands that the experiences be unfolded in a loop: the experience makes contact with – and affects – other people, only in order to come back to me again, through the elicitation interview. The world and subjective experiences are something we share, and I find this element of sharing fascinating.

Apropos of sharing: over the years, we've hosted a number of different workshops at the studio, like when we had slow-motion dancers visit us. The act of watching them dance is not necessarily the central issue for me, even though it's really cool – rather, it's the consciousness that you acquire of your own body and your own speed. When I'm watching a person dance, I can sense a wholly concrete physical reflectivity. I'm dancing along, but I'm also matching the dancer's movements with my own *potential* movements, keeping an eye peeled for differences, for similarities. And I'm asking: what world is the dancer creating with his or her body? Would I be creating a different kind of world with my dancing body?

Right. It makes you think: 'Wow! You can be present in the world in so many different ways.' And you can learn so much about the world by taking a look at how others are in it.

Dealing with another person's construction of the world is super interesting. Your own way of relating to the surrounding world moves from being one that you take for granted to being a construction, and that's a really healthy experience.

Since we're speaking about construction, another theme that comes to mind is the relationship between culture and nature. The idea that culture and nature share a space, are intertwined, is one that can also be seen in the writings of French philosopher and sociologist Bruno Latour and in his way of dealing with environmentalist James Lovelock's ideas about Gaia, which go back to the 1960s. Gaia is Lovelock's name for the earth, which, as he has it, consists of all the consequences of

all the actions that have been carried out by everything that is living. As human beings, we cannot place ourselves outside of or above this.

For instance, it is important that we humans acknowledge that we are nature, too, and only by appreciating this will we fully sensitise ourselves to our effect on the climate. There's something of this in what you and I have been talking about – that nature is not an 'Other', something external. In the same somewhat holistic way, I sometimes say that we do not walk into a museum in order to step out of reality. We walk into a museum in order to see reality in higher resolution. Or, for that matter, let's take my studio: this is also a place where you see concrete and non-concrete processes in high definition that, incidentally, are not specific to my studio but are, in fact, happening everywhere. *Connectedness* is the crucial element here, as it is for Latour. We are infinitely bound up, whether we want to be or not. One institution relates to another; people and things are inextricably linked together. They are no longer 'entities', they are 'agents', and the consequences of all their actions constitute our world.

The metaphor you've come up with here is really nice: that we don't step into a museum in order to step out of the world. No, in a way, we walk into a museum in order to step into the world. Bruno Latour's book *We Have Never Been Modern* [1991; published in English translation by Catherine Porter in 1993] also deconstructed the nature–culture dichotomy. To me, the book was a revelation. A key point in it is that our whole way of thinking is based on the idea that culture and nature are the antitheses of each other, and that this epitomises the modern. But Latour says that we never have been modern, because if you look into the world, you'll see that culture and nature are getting more entangled than ever. The idea that culture and nature can be separated is an illusion.

Of course, it's not just a philosophical question about the relationship between nature and culture – it's also largely about the Anthropocene era. The climate debate is being driven by a polarisation of nature and culture. Unfortunately, this stalls climate action and locks us into a highly inflexible system. Latour has become one of the most exciting and radical theorists when it comes to the thinking on the Anthropocene. Philosopher Timothy Morton is another really interesting voice.

Andreas, in previous conversations, we've talked about the concepts of cohesion – about identity and 'we-ness' in different orders of magnitude: a small and locally anchored 'we'; a larger 'we' – for us, the European 'we'; the global 'we'; and so forth. I am fascinated by the notion of trust and trust systems. When does trust increase? When does it decline? You might say that the polarisation we are now seeing in European and American politics – via populism and nationalism, the lack of empathy we are witnessing in connection with the migration crisis, for example – signals a decline on the we-ness graph. Are you looking into these ideas at the moment?

I'm working at the Interacting Minds Centre at Aarhus University. Its name inherently contains the notion that we should not only be studying cognition or psychology – or anything else – in isolation but that we've got to see these fields as being situated *between* human beings.

In fact, we've just run a series of experiments examining the idea of trust. As a model, we took an incredibly simple economic game, which is known as the 'common goods' experiment. Together with other participants, you have to invest money in a shared pool. You've got to decide for yourself how much you'll invest. Then the common pool, somewhat magically, accrues. Afterward, you divide it up equally among yourselves. As far as the whole group is concerned, it's advantageous when everybody throws everything into the pool, as this generates maximal growth and, when this happens, everybody gets richer. But as far as I am concerned, the best situation *for me* is when you and the others throw in everything you've got, while I hold on to what's mine. Because then I get a piece of what you've all contributed, in addition to getting to keep 'my own'. However, if we all follow this logic, none of us would contribute to the common pool. Such experiments have been used by economists as simplified proxies for how much people trust each other.

Our assumption was that trust is something that can easily be eroded but is difficult to build up. We therefore conducted an experiment where people alternated between playing with computer agents, or bots, that were either quite willing to share or really unwilling to share, and with other people who had had similar experiences. This allowed us to create particular environments of high and low trust. Our assumption was that if one starts out in a scenario of high trust, one may be able to remain in that state. However, if one were so unlucky as to begin in an experiment under conditions of low trust, it would be very difficult to build it subsequently. In fact, this was not at all what we found. People appeared to be enormously responsive to the environment they were in, here and now. When they were playing with 'trusting bots', they would also display a high degree of trust. And if the bots showed a low degree of trust, then the participants also displayed a low degree of trust. Furthermore, when they interacted with other people, participants were actually rather unaffected by what had gone on in the previous round. Thus, the picture that emerged was that people seem very sensitive to the specific environment and rules of interaction that were applicable at a given time. This is potentially a very positive story – if it holds – because it appears that trust may breed trust, just as distrust breeds distrust.

Can you say some more about 'we-ness'?

In almost all of these economic games, people are not given a chance to talk to each other. Shared reflection is actually regarded as a form of contamination because one is supposed to inquire into 'human nature' and into how one would immediately react. The interesting thing is that sharing experiences about the environment one is in, and about the game one plays, may create an entirely different way of setting a frame of understanding. We have not looked into that enough yet, but talking together appears to allow us to meta-communicate, to share uncertainty, to gauge the environment, to coordinate and negotiate complicated patterns of trust and collaboration.

It seems crucially important *both* to explore subjective experiences *and* to create a language about what that experience consists of. At the end of the day, that leaves me in something of the position of the cultural optimist. It does inspire confidence in the idea that creating spaces for reflection matters. When we speak to each other, we may come to a position of being able to share each other's perspective and seeing what that does to our own understanding. This seems often to be a deeply bodily experience.

September 2018

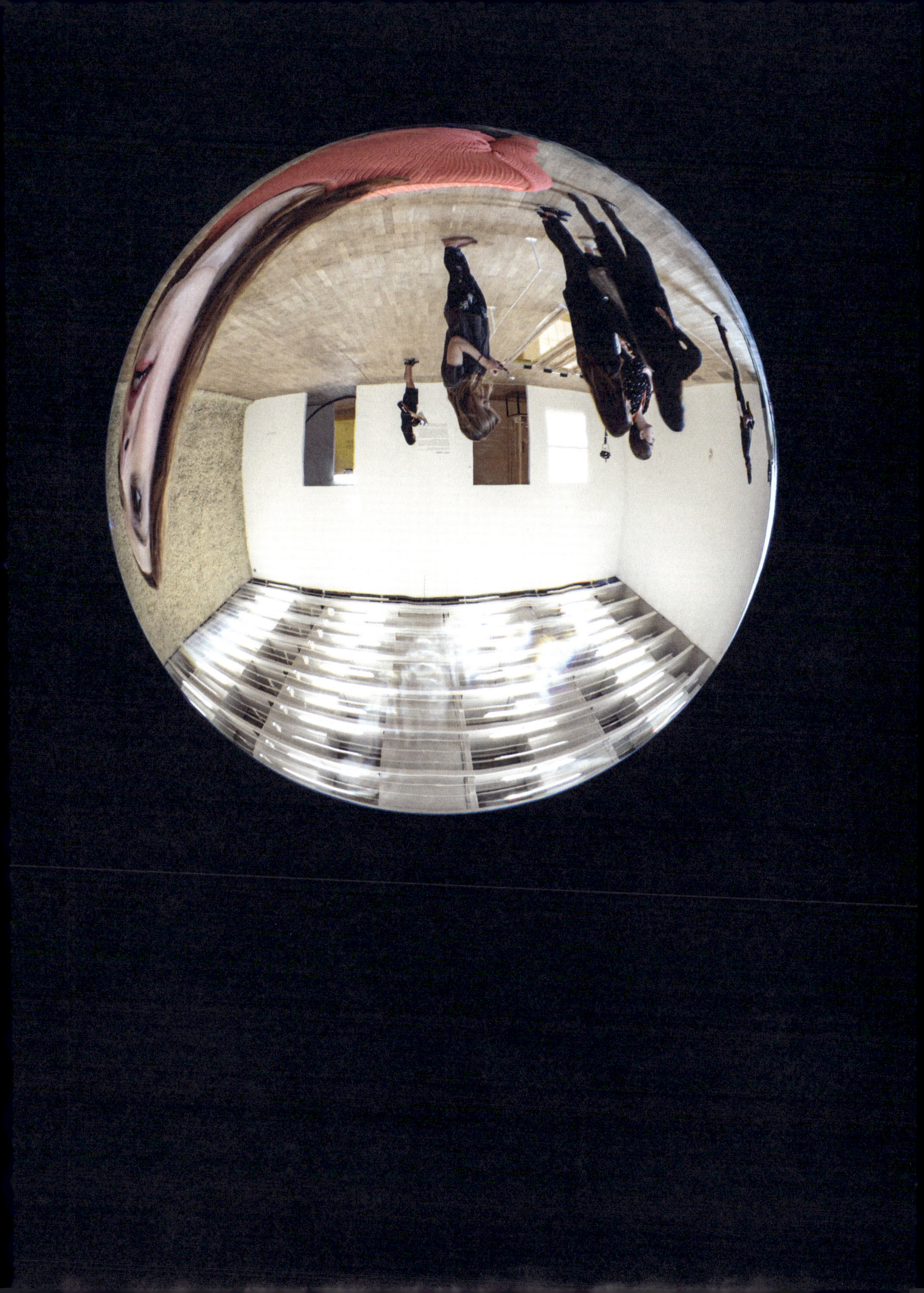

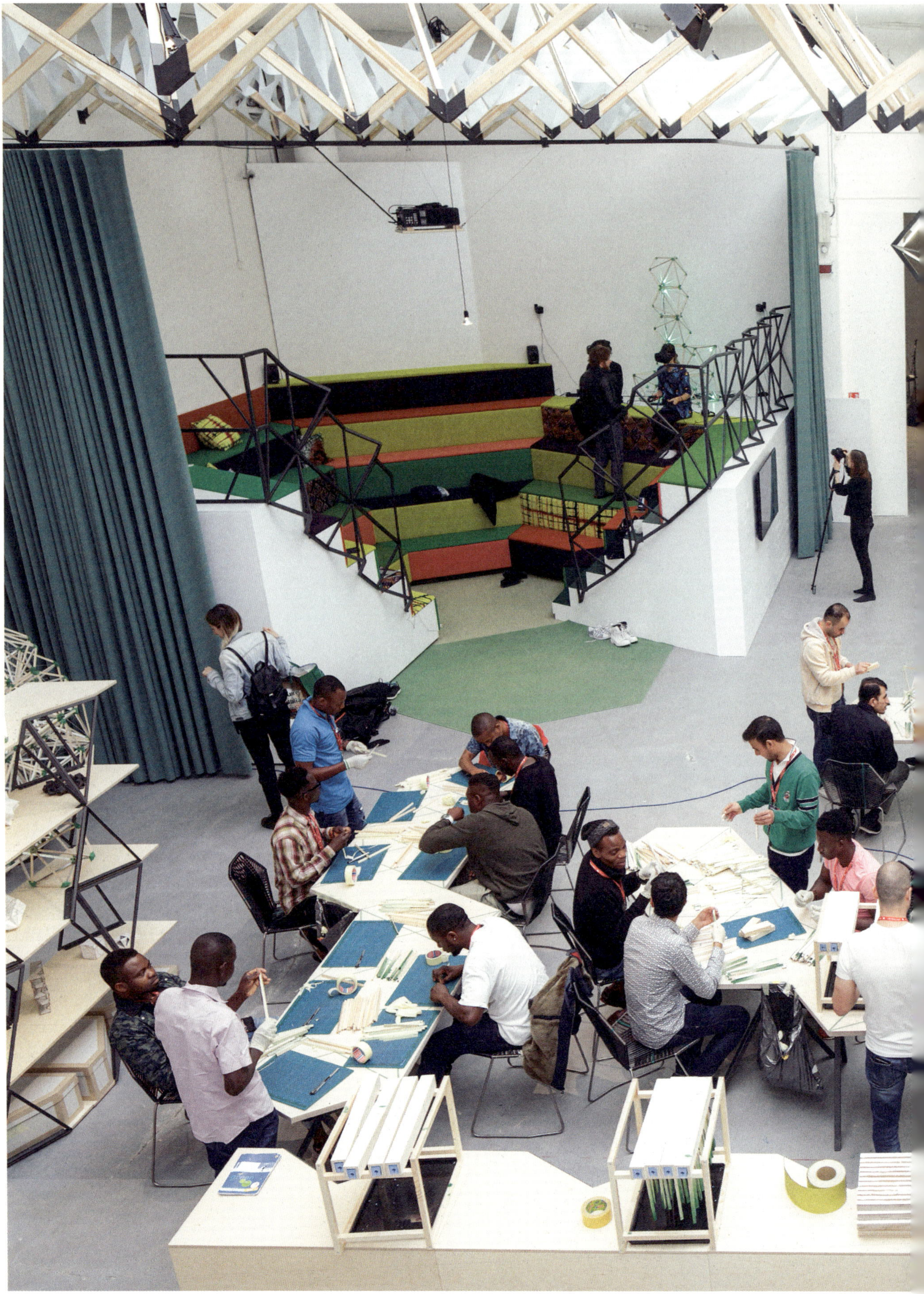

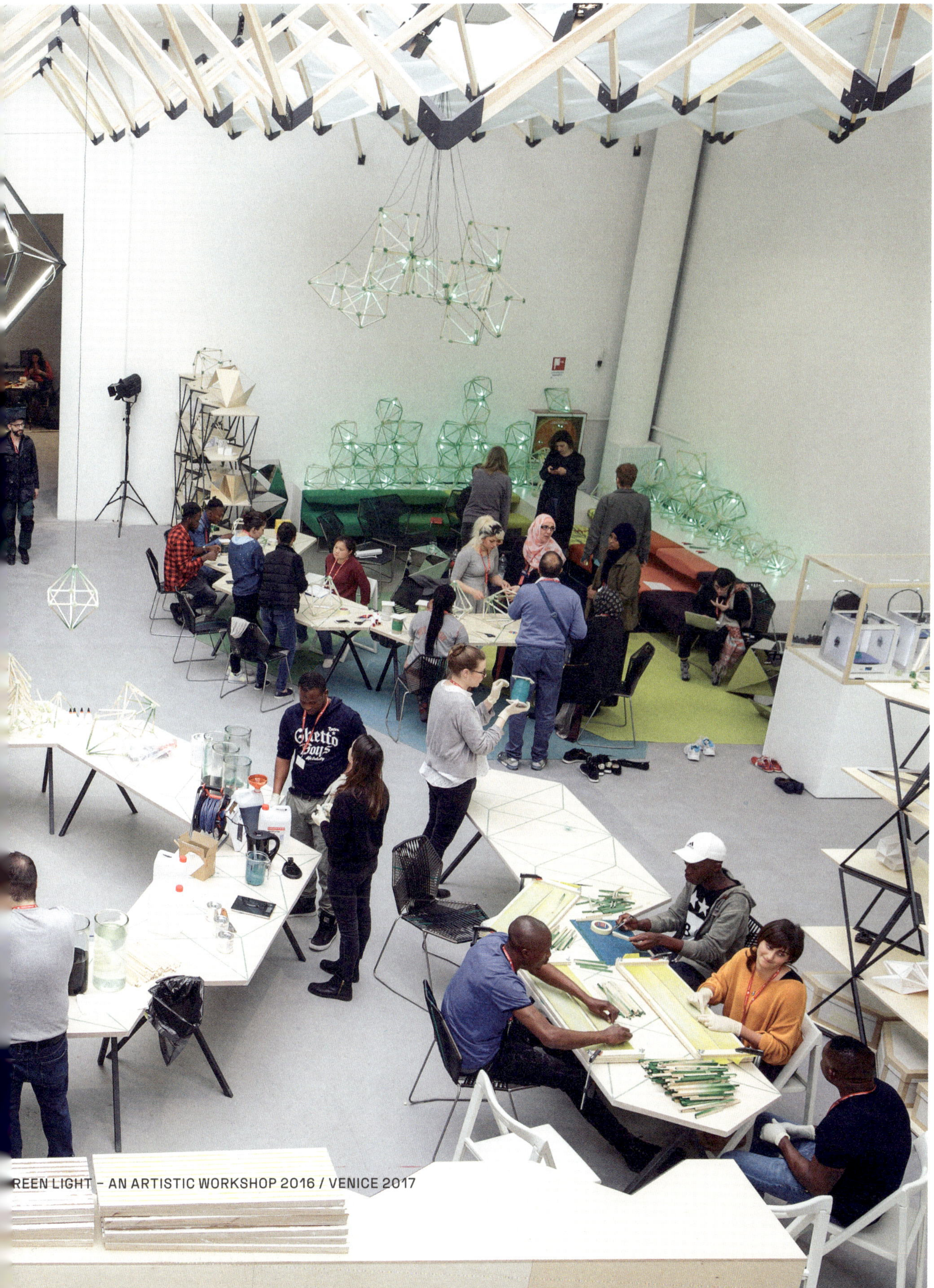
Ghetto Boys

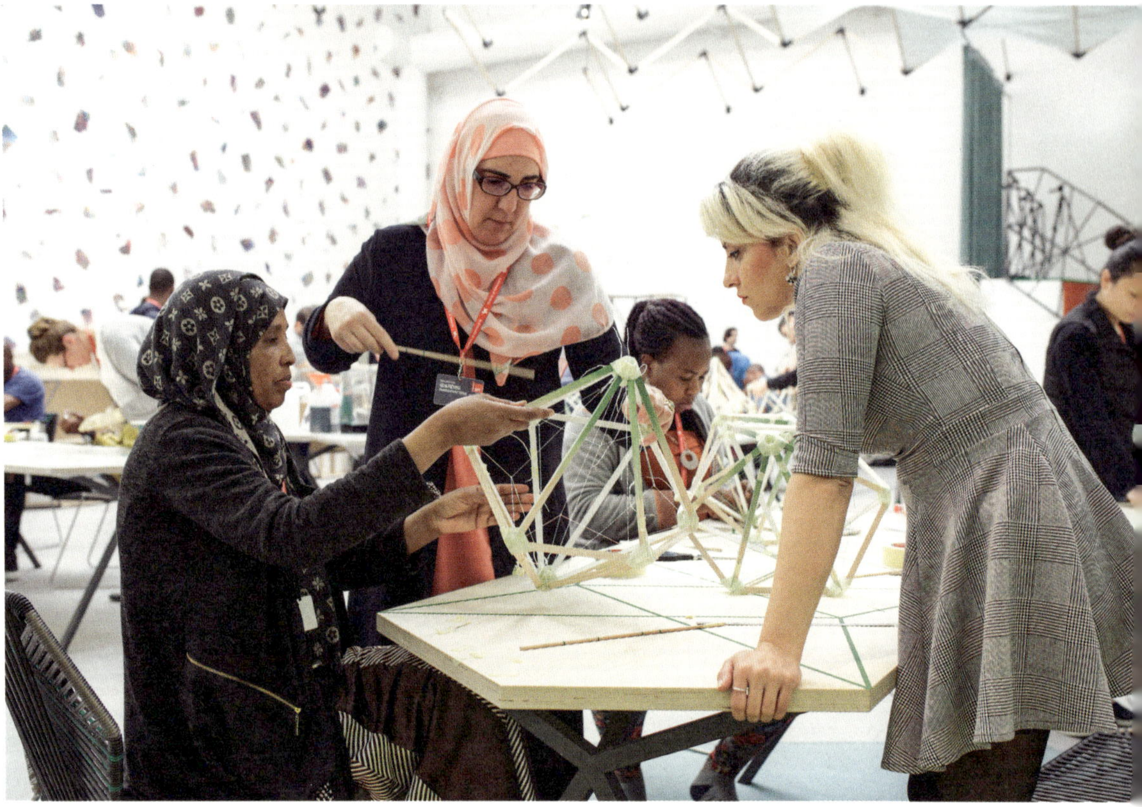

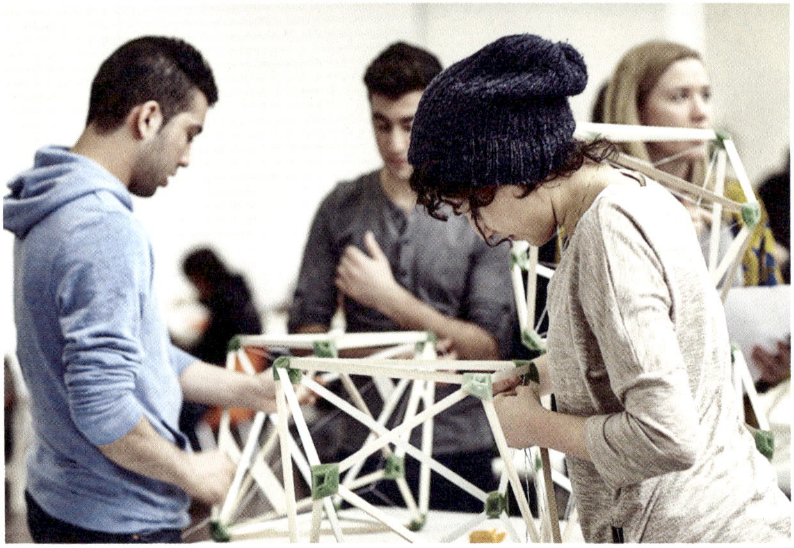

GREEN LIGHT Initiated in Vienna in 2015 in partnership with TBA21, *Green light – An artistic workshop* is an act of welcoming, addressed both to those who have fled hardship and instability in their home countries and to the residents of the cities that have received them. Working together in a creative process, participants build a modular light – proceeds from the sales of which go to benefit refugee communities – and construct a communal environment in which difference is not only accepted but embraced. The project includes an educational program, called Shared Learning, which comprises seminars, lectures, artistic interventions, psychological and legal counselling, and creative workshops. *Green light – An artistic workshop* has also been hosted as part of the Venice Biennale in the summer of 2017 and in other venues around the world.

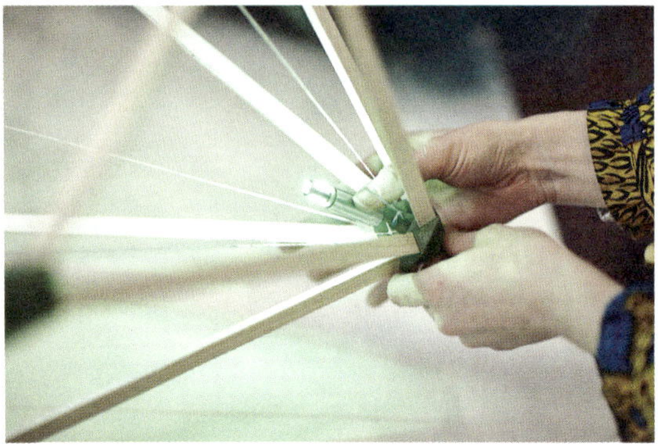

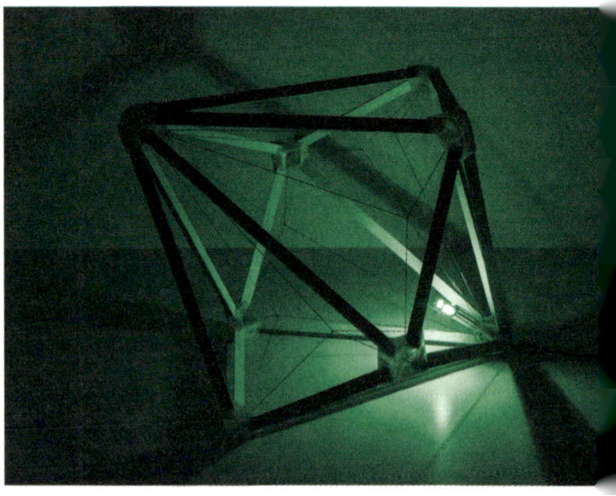

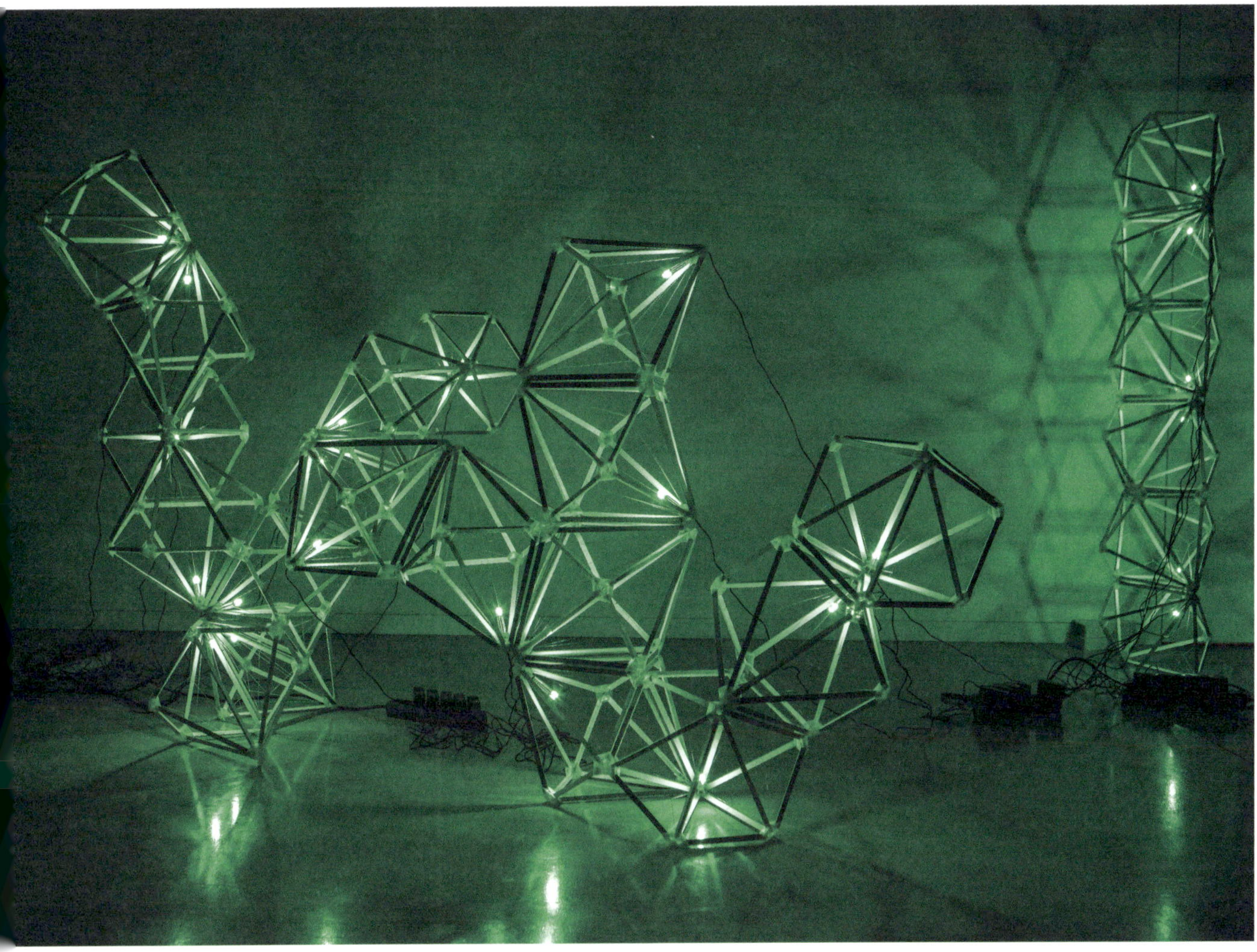

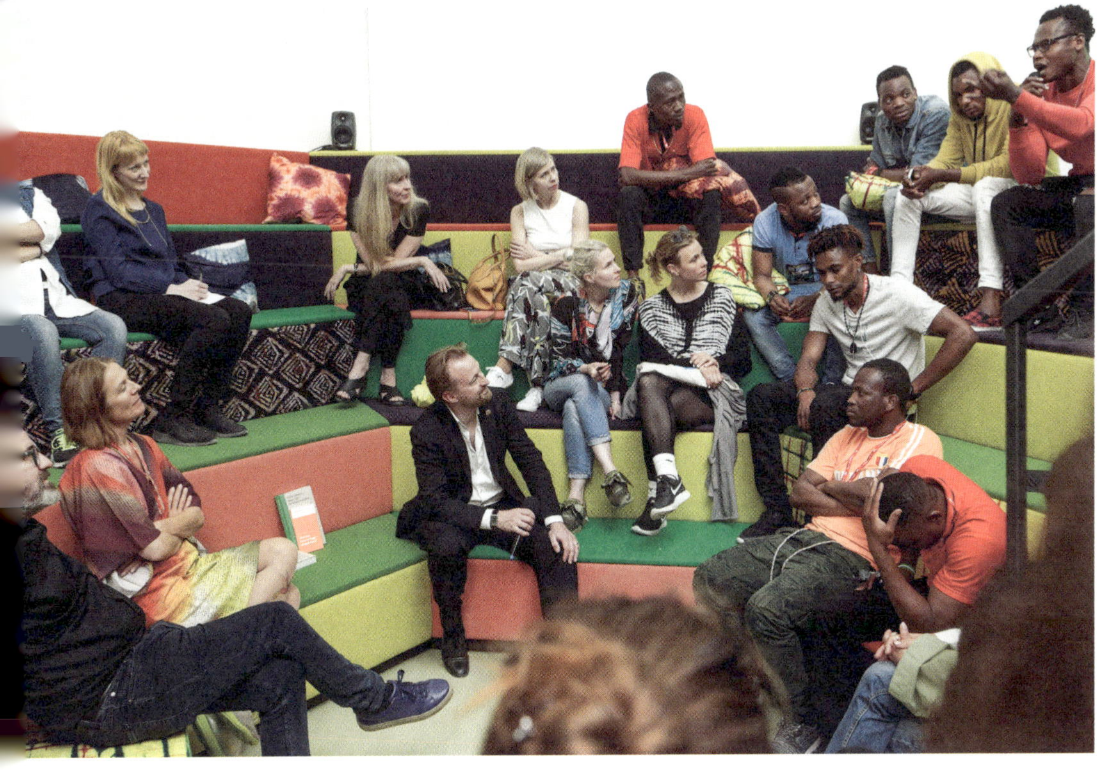

Olafur Eliasson: The last time we met, Tania, we met in a theatre, and I always forget that you were trained in theatre before you went into psychology and neuroscience, right?

Tania Singer: Yes, I studied psychology in Berlin, and during my studies I worked in theatre and opera in order to become a director. But when I started my PhD I had to make a choice. Both jobs take more than a hundred per cent of you – you can't do a PhD in science and become an opera director at the same time! These are two worlds that take everything from you.

They do! But you have somehow preserved this interest in different fields of work – I've felt it strongly in our conversations. Your interest in art and your work with non-scientists and people from the political sphere situates your pioneering work in the study of compassion. At what point did compassion emerge as a theme for you?

I guess it was around 2000, when I had completed my PhD in classical developmental psychology in Berlin and moved to London to join a very exciting new field called social neuroscience. Social neuroscience was about asking how the reality of other people comes into your brain, how we become intersubjective beings. When I'm empathising with your suffering, I can feel your pain; unless we are psychopaths, we all can share the suffering of others. But how does the brain do this? How does it know what others are feeling or thinking? In cognitive neuroscience up to that time, the brain had always been investigated in terms of the isolated individual, but not in social interaction with other brains.

Yes.

In London, we published the first studies on empathy – that is, on the brain circuitries underlying our capacity for emotional resonance and for feeling what another person is feeling. We were also making a distinction between empathy and compassion: compassion is not just feeling *with* someone but feeling *for* someone. Compassion is rooted in a feeling of unconditional love and concern for others – it's a strong motivation to help others, not just a resonance with their feelings.

COMPASSION

TANIA SINGER is a Professor in Psychology and Social Neuroscience, scientific head of the Social Neuroscience Laboratory of the Max Planck Society in Berlin and an honorary board member of the Mind & Life Europe Institute. Singer has long studied the neuronal, hormonal and developmental foundations of human social behaviour, with particular interest in social and moral emotions such as empathy and compassion, envy, revenge and fairness. Her projects include the ReSource Project, a large-scale study of mental training and compassion. In 2011, she organised the workshop 'How to Train Compassion', which brought together neuroscientists, psychologists and contemplative scholars at Olafur Eliasson's studio in Berlin.

And then there is emotional contagion, which is, in a way, a precursor of empathy. We can, for example, be infected by the stress of another person or group, or by laughter. The difference between empathy and emotional contagion is that in emotional contagion you are not aware that you are feeling the emotion of another person. It's unconscious, and similar to a virus. In empathy, on the other hand, when I feel your pain I'm aware that your pain is not my feeling. I know that this is your suffering and that I'm suffering with you, but also that it's not *my* suffering.

It's about levels of awareness, really. And the more aware you are, the easier it is to separate yourself from a feeling like stress. That's why I am so interested in awareness – it helps you develop tools to tackle whatever situation you are in.

Compassion is yet another social emotion. If I have compassion for you when you are suffering, I don't necessarily have to feel your pain or share your pain – I just feel a strong, warm feeling of concern and a desire to help, to go into action. So it feels very different, too. Empathy is a good thing, and it's usually our first reaction when we are confronted with the pain or suffering of others. But empathy alone can turn into what we call 'empathetic distress'. It's like, 'You are suffering and, because I'm empathic, I become so miserable myself that I am not able to be of any use to you anymore.' In social neuroscience we always emphasise that relating adaptively to the suffering of others means taking this first empathic response, which connects us to others and their suffering, and transforming it into compassion.

You mentioned how stress can be increased or decreased by the social situation we are in – does your research also address how the context of our interactions affects our capacity for empathy and compassion?

One of the constraints in neuroscience is that of course we can't just transport a brain scanner to a public space to see what's happening in interacting brains in natural situations. But we can create somewhat social situations in the lab by manipulating the context a scanned person is in. In one of the classic empathy studies, for example, someone lying in the scanner is made to feel pain in their hand and the pain circuitry in their brain is measured. They then see other people in the lab also being made to feel pain, and we measure their empathic brain responses. And we can change the context in which the other people are perceived by, for example, telling the person in the scanner that the other people receiving pain are members of an 'in-group' or an 'out-group' – either part or not part of their political party, their nation or their football club, or someone who has another religious background, or whatever. When witnessing a member of an out-group suffering pain, the subject's usual empathic neural response to their pain is basically blocked. Some people even experience reward signals – they almost rejoice when someone who they dislike or perceive as a member of an out-group receives painful little shocks. They experience schadenfreude. So, by manipulating the context, we can see how empathy comes and goes in seconds. It's a very fragile emotion.

This is incredibly interesting. Would you say that the distinction between in-group and out-group is a cultural construct? Or is it also biological?

It's both cultural and biological. Little children already show a strong in-group/out-group bias. There's usually one child in every school class to whom the other children are cruel. They are influenced very early on by the idea of either belonging to or being outside of a group. It seems to be an inbuilt evolutionary mechanism for group cohesion, although, of course, the specifics of what makes someone in-group or out-group are cultural. Why do some people think Muslims are different or Christians are different or Jews are different? Why do we form boundaries? That's a cultural belief system that is built up into a collective narrative. And because such cultural narratives correspond to an evolutionary-formed basic mechanism – the propensity to quickly create in-group/out-group distinctions – they are very easily formed and maintained.

I think it's important to address the difference between biology and culture, because people sometimes think that culturally constructed systems are natural, which can be dangerous and reductive.

I totally agree about the dangers of confusing culture and biology. It's a very important distinction to draw. When we show pictures of the brain, people often think what they are looking at is biology and thus somehow genetically determined – that the responses we see are inborn. But this is wrong, because the brain is very plastic. Of course many features of the brain are genetically predetermined, but most of all it is a learning device; it's a big sponge that learns from the culture in which it's embedded.

I wonder whether physical presence plays a crucial role in developing an empathic response to someone – can we also empathise with people we see on social media and in the news?

The same empathic brain responses are captured when you show people movies, or even when they read books or see BBC news clips, but this response can be stronger or weaker. When your partner or someone else very close to you, such as a family member, is nearby, their presence boosts the empathic signal, while when you have a very abstract text, the empathic signal gets much lower. But if you have strong visual images – like wounds or crying babies – then the empathic response is of course stronger again, and the media take advantage of this mechanism.

It can flip into a feeling of numbness, too. Can our empathy pool be filled up, so that we have empathy for the first refugees we hear about having drowned in the Mediterranean, but gradually lose our ability to empathise through growing accustomed to such stories?

Over-exposure can indeed influence the empathic response. Nurses and doctors, for example, who are exposed to suffering every day, develop coping strategies to distance themselves from it. If they always went into empathic resonance, they would burn out. And that is a huge problem in the helping professions. You get into empathic distress, and then you burn out because it's just too much to bear. Or you become cynical, which happens to a lot of surgeons, medics and doctors – their patients just become objects they work with. Obviously these coping strategies are not very adaptive. But we can train people to transform their initial healthy empathic response into compassion – into a caring, loving attitude – and you can't burn out on love. And of course, compassion is always good for the patient – you cannot receive too much love and care!

This is connected to how we got to know each other. In 2011 we did a workshop, which you organised and I hosted in my studio, called 'How to Train Compassion'. What made it special is that it brought together people with contemplative backgrounds, like Buddhist monks and other contemplative thinkers, with clinical psychologists, neuroscientists and social scientists all working on compassion. This range of people wouldn't normally work together. As I said, what has always fascinated me about your work is how you successfully bridge all these different fields.

Well, I don't always succeed! Bringing practices from traditions like Buddhism and Christianity into a more reductionist natural science environment is not easy to do. I am part of the Mind & Life Institute, which, back in the 1970s, began sponsoring dialogues between the Dalai Lama and Western scientists to investigate how Western sciences – reductionist biological sciences – could be in dialogue with contemplative philosophical traditions to explore how meditation, training the mind, cultivating inner spaces of consciousness, and so on, could serve humanity. These dialogues bring together people who are experts in what is called the first-person perspective – who can talk from their inner experience of meditating and cultivating their heart and their mind – and scientists like me, who measure what we call the third-person perspective – the body, the brain, the immune system, and how these markers change when we engage in mental training or meditation.

This neuro-phenomenological approach – bringing together the first-person subjective perspective with the third-person objective measurements – forms a core part of contemplative sciences. In contrast to this, the predominant approach in science has been very much influenced by behaviourism: 'We don't believe what people tell us about their own conscious subjective experience, which is biased. We only believe in what we can objectively measure in observed behaviour.' So contemplative sciences try to find methods to bring first-person subjective phenomenological experiences together with the objective measurements. It's a very interesting field, but also a challenging one.

What brings people from these different fields together is the wish to bring compassion and secular ethics back into science and into society at large. There is a strong interest in exploring how we can train and cultivate secular ethical values and intersubjectivity – 'we-ness' and not just 'me-ness' – which is what we discussed and practised at your wonderful studio during our four-day gathering there. It was such a special experience to be able to hold this workshop in your studio.

I do hope the activities that my studio is engaged with generate the kind of trust that allows people to take more risks and be less defensive. In terms of the question of 'we-ness' versus 'me-ness', your work has really inspired and influenced me. I have shifted my attention more and more towards our collective experience – towards our interdependence and how we influence each other. And one theme that goes through the conversations in this book is the idea of being connected and acting on your beliefs, particularly in relation to climate. I've been talking to another scientist, the behavioural psychologist Elke Weber [see pp.196–200], who is a specialist in decision-making theory, about the difference between knowing and not acting, and knowing and acting – these two types of knowledge. So I would like to talk about what I think you have called 'presence' and 'perspective-taking', which have become really important for my work since I learned about them from you.

Perhaps I can explain what is meant by perspective-taking. It comes from a nine-month intervention programme, the ReSource project, which was meditation-oriented but also based on Western psychological knowledge. It comprised three mental-training modules: 'Presence', 'Affect' and 'Perspective'.

In the first module, people learned to become present and focused on the now. In 'Affect', the second, compassion-based module, we taught practices that help activate what you just spoke about – compassion and the motivation to act. Just saying 'Oh, I feel your pain!' doesn't necessarily help. You also have to practise acting on your feelings: 'There is someone who needs my help – what can I do?'

Perspective-taking, which comes in the third module, addresses the ability to take a bird's-eye perspective on your thoughts, aspects of your own personality as well as the minds of others. It also speaks to overcoming the in-group/out-group distinction we spoke about before. Compassion is easy for in-group members, but feeling compassion for an out-group member is much more difficult. There's an evolutionary bias towards caring for people of your in-group while not caring about out-group members, the whole planet, or something abstract like the climate.

So perspective-taking is necessary if you want to move towards global compassion – if you want to develop a strong motivation to act, for example, for the climate or for people who are very far away. To understand beliefs of people who are foreign to you, you have to take a bird's-eye view and disconnect first from your own particular belief system so that you can cognitively go into the mind of another. Their actions might at first seem strange to you, but, if you're able to perform this jump in perspective, you can see that their actions usually follow logically from the beliefs they hold. So, while the compassion-based 'Affect' module is essential to generating love and pro-social motivation, you also need to have perspective-taking to be able to resolve conflicts, to develop global compassion and act on it.

When we talk about turning perspective-taking into action, do you think positive narratives are more motivating than negative ones, like threat- and fear-based narratives? I'm thinking of my conversation with Mary Robinson, who talks about the necessity of creating a positive argument to stimulate action, rather than a fear-based one [see pp.78–81].

A negative, fear-based narrative activates our stress system, which narrows down our field of action considerably. When you're under threat, your whole system is focused on saving your own little self. You don't see the bigger picture – the common good, the global world – it's all about your own immediate survival. So a fear-based narrative will never invite a wider perspective. In terms of climate change, it therefore seems to me essential that scientists say: 'Look, on the one hand there is imminent danger – if we continue like this we will encounter these problems – but, on the other hand, the good news is that you can do something about it, and what you can do is A, B, C ... ' and then give concrete examples about what individuals can do in their everyday lives. Such narratives and positive encouragements could create a movement, which is what we need if we want to tackle huge challenges like climate change.

Let's go back to when you started out, when you were still working within the cultural sector. It seems to me that the cultural sector is different from the private sector, which commercialises our attention, and also different from much political discourse today, with the rise of fear-based rhetoric and populism, and the polarisation that results in blaming out-groups that we've seen in the EU and elsewhere. How do you see the cultural sector?

It is essential that fundamental science connect to real-world problems, and the same is true for the arts. Art can have a strong self-referential side – my previous experience of the world of art was sometimes that artists would only surround themselves with artists; you always interact with the same people, day and night, without ever connecting to the larger society. And this can really limit the cultural sector's potential. But when it goes beyond being self-referential, art has a huge potential to motivate change – as we have seen with some of the big movies about climate change, which were certainly more efficient in changing attitudes than all the scientific paperwork that, unfortunately, often never reaches the public.

So I do think that artists – and scientists – need to make the effort to translate their knowledge into understandable language in order to enter the public conversation and public space, and to reach people, including politicians and change-makers. A good example was when you brought your art into the middle of the climate conference in Paris by positioning blocks of glacial ice from Greenland in front of the Pantheon [*Ice Watch*, 2014]. Actions like that bring important ideas into public space as tangibly embodied experiences that can really change how people think about significant issues.

November 2018

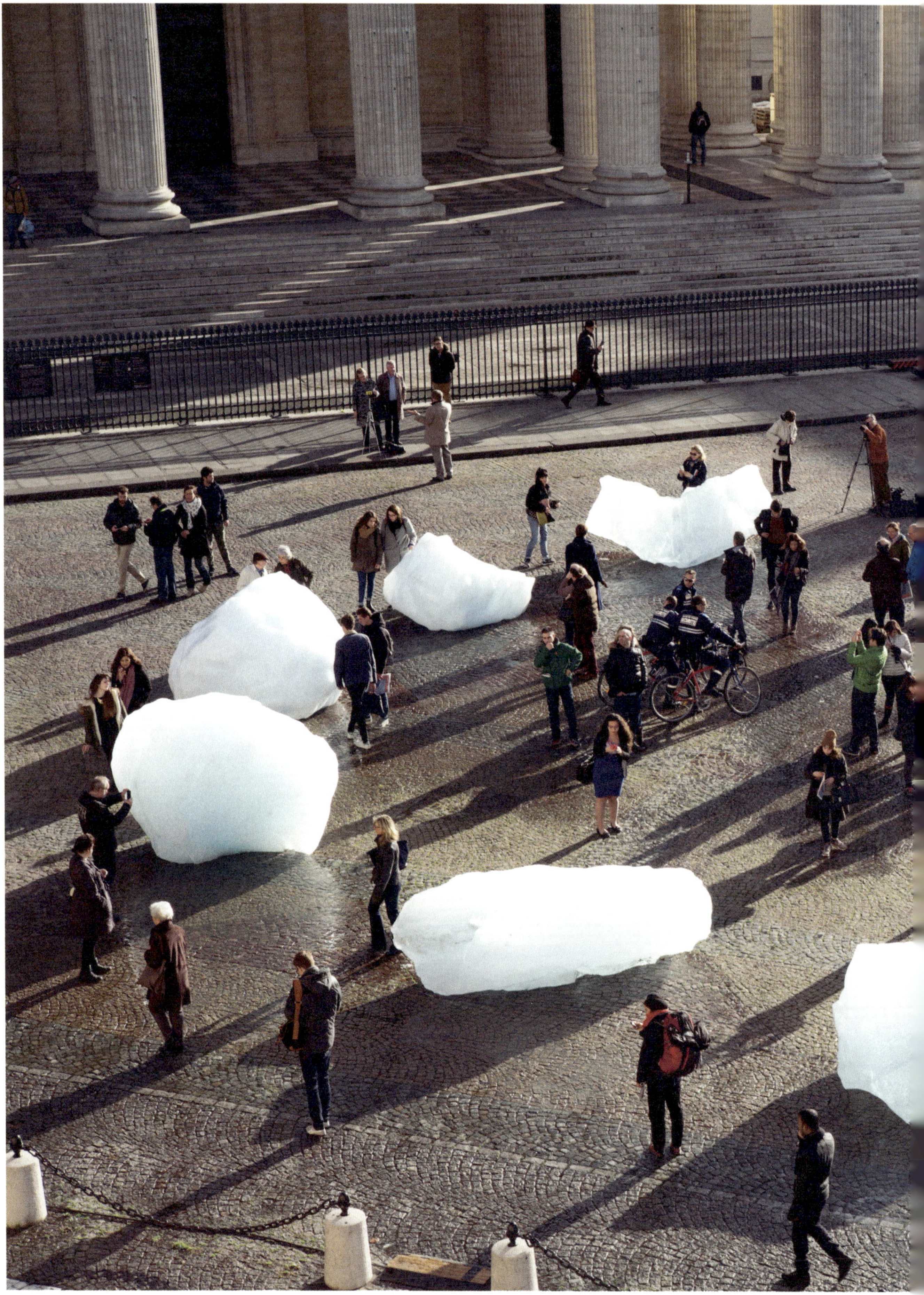

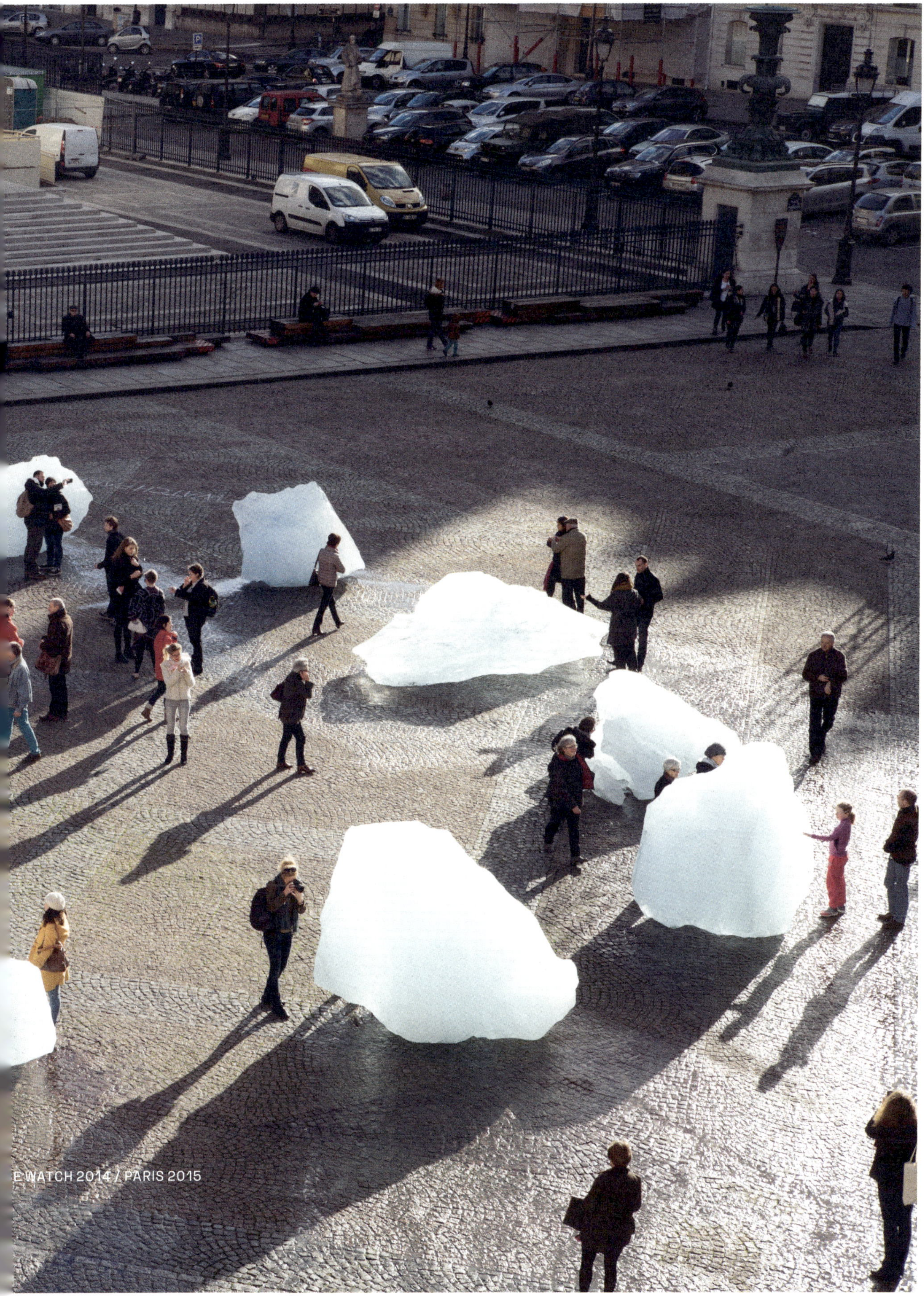

E WATCH 2014 / PARIS 2015

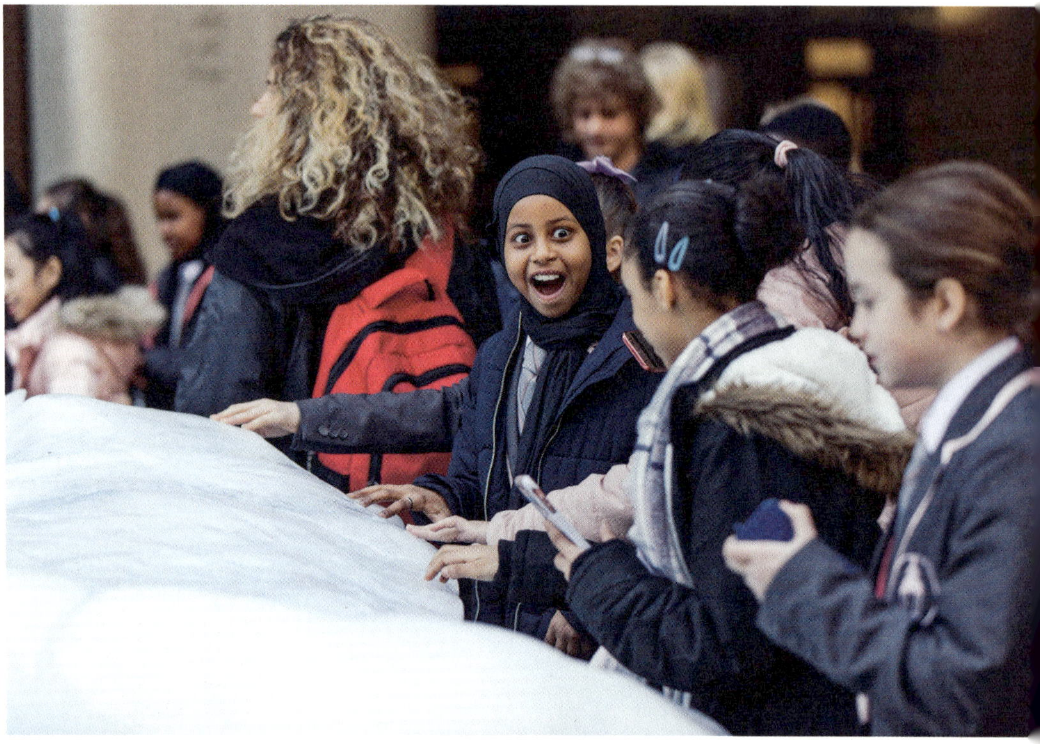

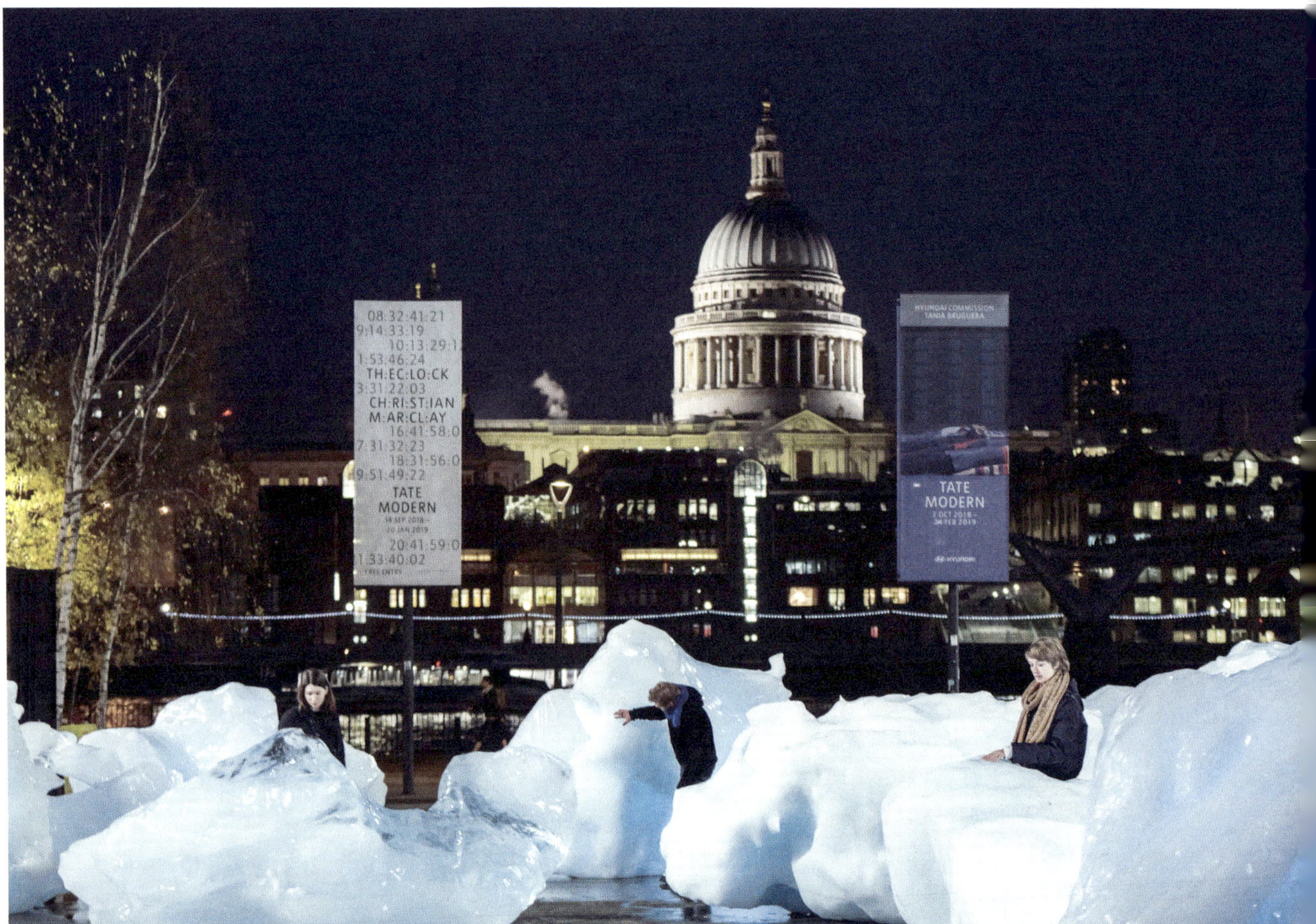

08:32:41:21
9:14:33:19
10:13:29:1
1:53:46:24
TH:EC:LO:CK
3:31:22:03
CH:RI:ST:IAN
M:AR:CL:AY
16:41:58:0
7:31:32:23
18:31:56:0
9:51:49:22
TATE
MODERN
14 SEP 2018 –
20 JAN 2019
20:41:59:0
1:33:40:02
FREE ENTRY
HYUNDAI COMMISSION
TANIA BRUGUERA
TATE
MODERN
3 OCT 2018 –
24 FEB 2019
HYUNDAI

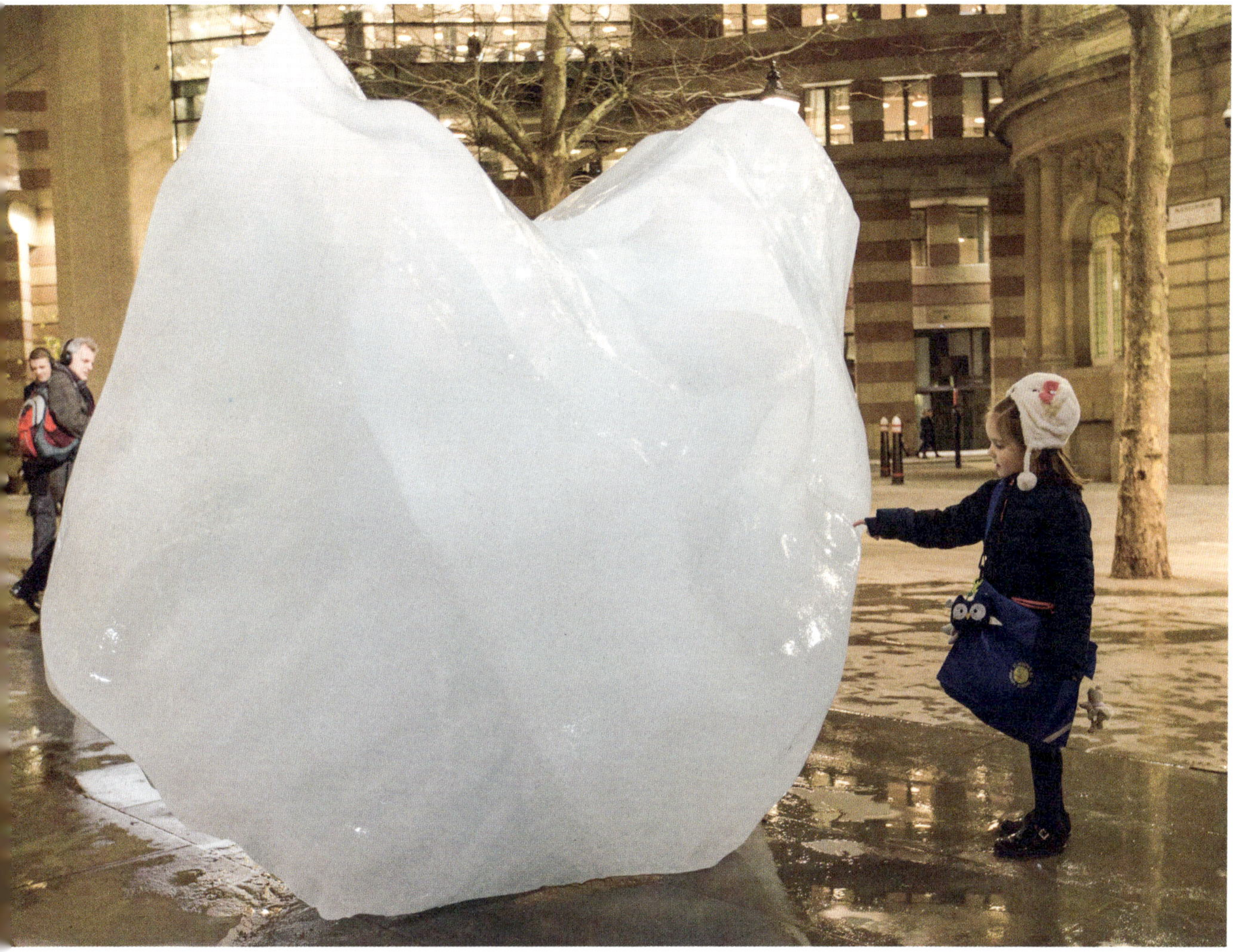

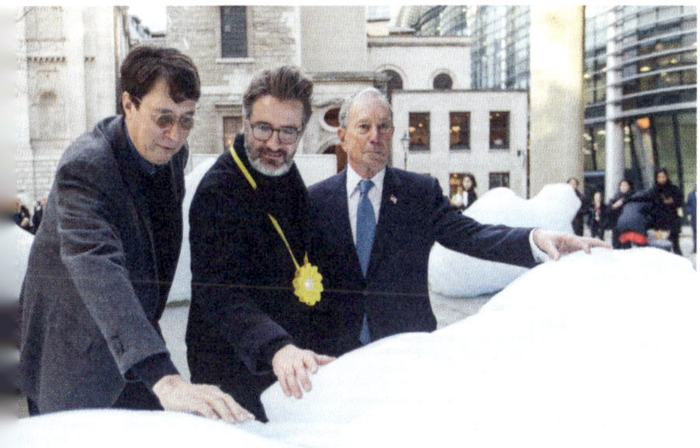

ICE WATCH A collaboration between Eliasson and geologist Minik Rosing, *Ice Watch* seeks to communicate the urgency of climate change and to raise awareness of the need for concerted global action. Large blocks of Greenlandic glacial ice, harvested from the sea, are presented in a prominent location to provide a direct and tangible experience of the reality of melting Arctic ice. To date *Ice Watch* has appeared in 2014 in Copenhagen to mark the publication of the UN IPCC's Fifth Assessment Report on Climate Change; in 2015 in Paris on the occasion of the COP21 UN Climate Conference; and in 2018 in London, with the support of Bloomberg Philanthropies, in front of Bloomberg's European headquarters and Tate Modern to coincide with COP24 in Katowice.

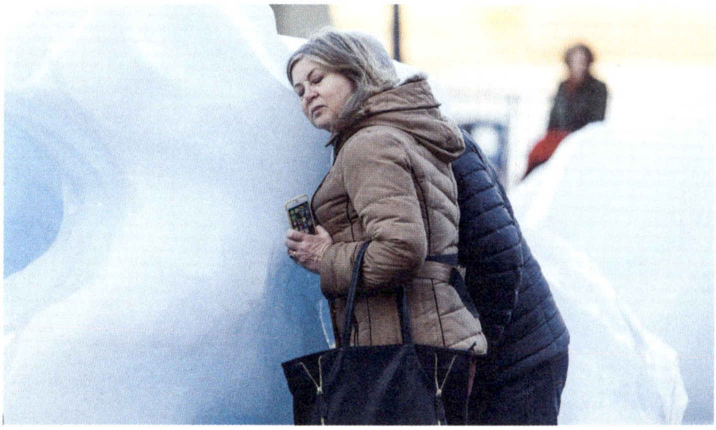

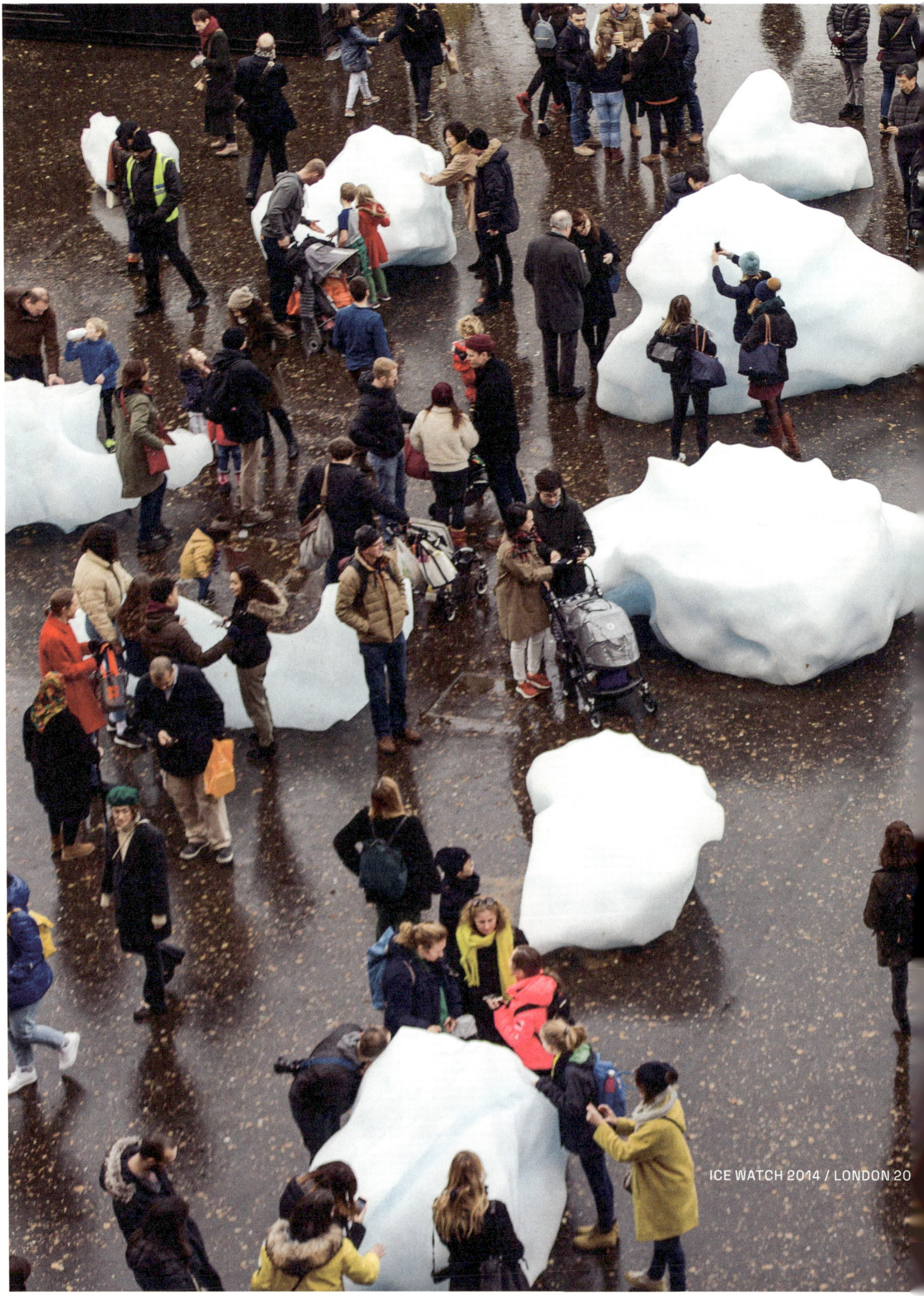

ICE WATCH 2014 / LONDON 20

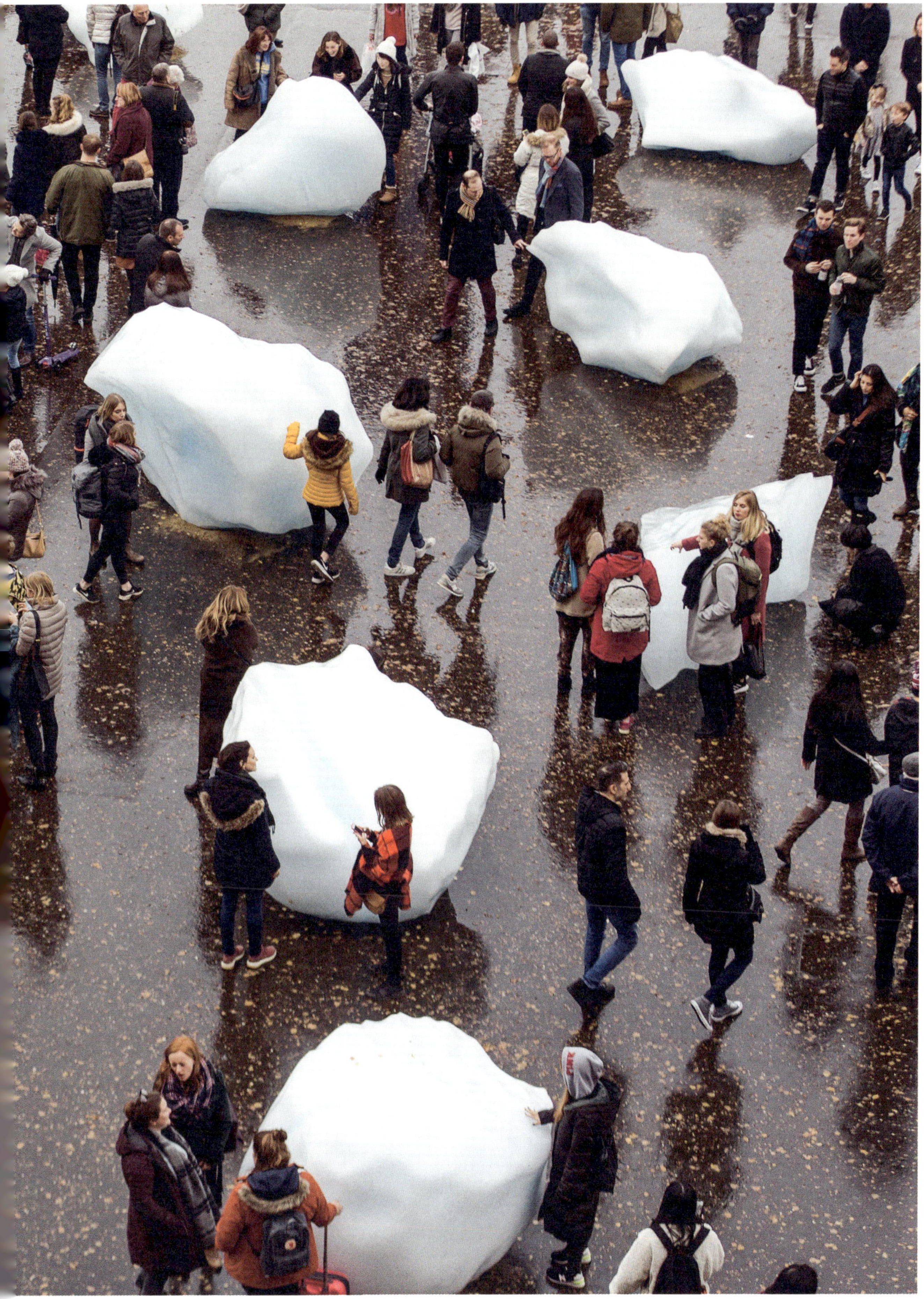

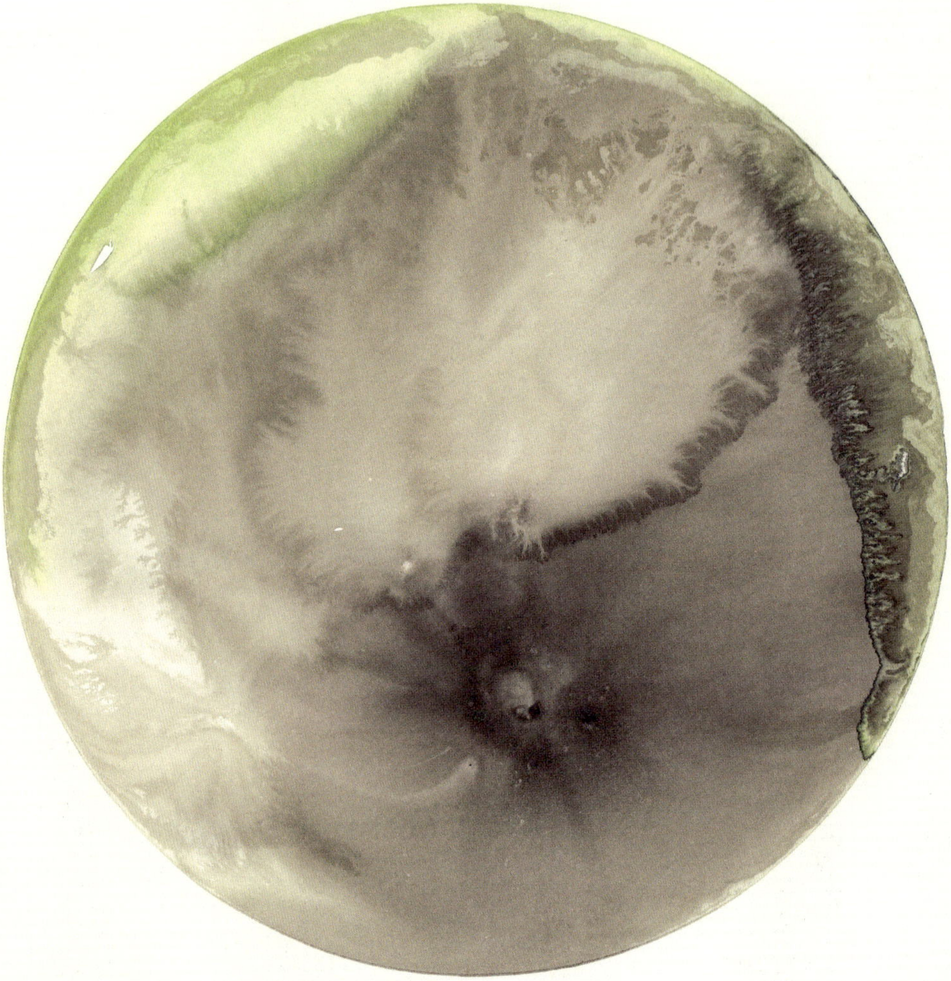

GLACIAL CURRENTS (BLACK, GREEN) 20

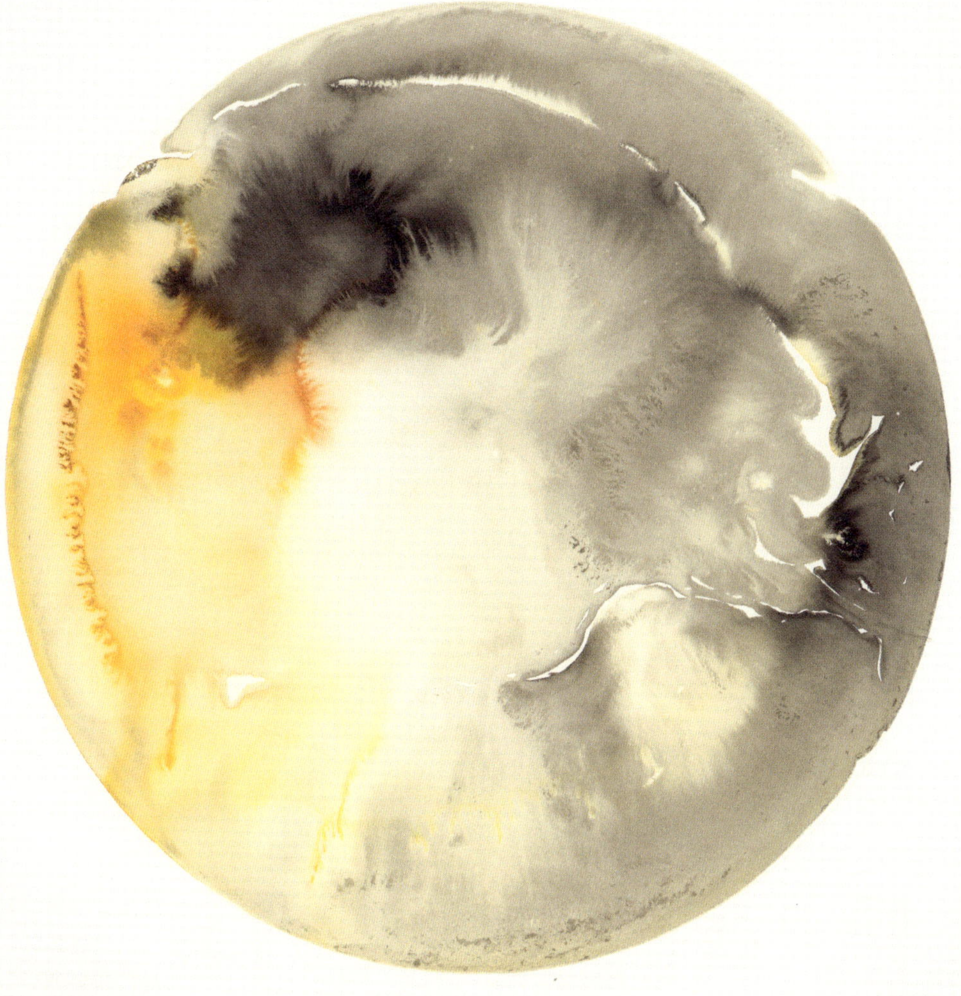

_ACIAL CURRENTS (YELLOW, SIENNA) 2018

Olafur Eliasson: **Mary, your book *Climate Justice* has just come out. How do you define climate justice?**

Mary Robinson: Climate justice is the link between human rights, development and climate change. It's about making how we talk and think about climate very people-centred. It's about asking, how does it affect people? That then brings you to the justice issue, because climate change disproportionately affects those who are least responsible for greenhouse gas emissions: people who don't drive cars, don't do major manufacturing, don't have central heating, et cetera. And yet they are already severely affected, and they have been for years – on food security, access to water, having to move from where they live because of intense flooding or intense drought. That fact is very hard to get across to people living in more temperate climates like Europe and the United States. Even though we see more shocks, it's still not something we take as seriously as we should.

The other side of climate justice is that in order to address its injustice and unfairness, we should prioritise getting clean, renewable energy off-grid to the billion-plus people who have no access to electricity.

In early 2011, at a very early stage, my foundation brought together a group of people who used the term 'climate justice'. We came up with principles of climate justice that relate to the essentials of human rights and gender equality. They're not rocket science – they're very clear and very easy to identify. What I'm finding more and more is that business – especially The B Team, the non-profit that brings together business leaders who believe that business should be a driving force for social, environmental and economic benefit – is intent on going net zero on greenhouse emissions by 2050, and doing it in a way compatible with climate justice. That means a just transition that takes into account, for instance, the concerns of workers in the fossil fuel industry, who mustn't bear the brunt of the switch to clean energy. We have to have a just transition for them. That's all part of climate justice.

CLIMATE JUSTICE

MARY ROBINSON was president of Ireland from 1990 to 1997 and served as United Nations High Commissioner for Human Rights from 1997 to 2002. She is a member of the Elders, an independent group of global leaders brought together by Nelson Mandela, and of the American Philosophical Society. Robinson visited Eliasson's studio for a dinner in 2017, where a diverse group from the cultural and political worlds came together to discuss the implications of climate change. She returned to the studio in 2018 to launch her new book, *Climate Justice.*

I feel everyone can identify with your book's focus on the individual, on people's actual experiences. The climate challenge often seems so abstract that it's hard to imagine what one can do as an individual; your approach is important in asking 'How does this affect me as an individual? How do I, as a member of society, recognise that I have individual power, and that I don't need to wait for systemic solutions?' It's not the opposite of the systemic, but a finer, more detailed version of the systemic.

Yes, that's a part of it. I deliberately chose stories to illustrate the different ways people show resilience in coping with situations. I intentionally included two stories from the United States. One was about Sharon Hanshaw, who had a hair salon in East Biloxi, Mississippi, before Hurricane Katrina. The other described a native Alaskan scientist seeing the erosion of her people's way of life. I also chose a head of state, Anote Tong, former president of The Republic of Kiribati. And then I chose Natalie Isaacs of Australia, because she's an average middle-aged professional woman who felt she needed to do something and formed the movement 1 Million Women [whose mission is 'fighting climate change through our everyday lives'].

Now, there's a big link between my book and the podcast that I do – *Mothers of Invention*. We interview a whole range of women, mainly, and they're doing an enormous number of things like this on the more innovative side. Ultimately I'm trying to promote empathy and solidarity for people who are suffering but who are not sitting back and waiting as victims; they're making a difference, they're fighting back, making themselves resilient. We should admire what they're doing, we should support them, and we should understand that we'll all be in this situation unless we have more solidarity and focus on strategy. But, of course, individual action alone won't solve the problem. We have to make people more conscious of the need to use their voices and their votes and their marching and their activities in order to push for changes in government policies – the price on carbon, the removal of subsidies, all of that.

You also emphasise the importance of bringing the small, island states to the table. As you say in the book, they were on the right track from the beginning by setting a threshold of 1.5°C rise in average global surface temperature above the pre-industrial level.

In Paris at the 2015 United Nations Climate Change Summit we didn't at first understand what it meant when the small island states and the poorest countries, like Nepal and Bangladesh and Ethiopia, insisted on having the goal of 1.5°C written into the text. At the time I think most of us thought that this was in order not to have small islands go under. But actually, the new UN report that was just published says that this goal makes it a safe world for all of us, and that we have under twelve years to get on the right track [the Intergovernmental Panel on Climate Change released its 'Global Warming of 1.5°C: An IPCC Special Report' on 8 October 2018]. That means a forty-five percent reduction in emissions. There's a clarity to this, an urgency, that has completely galvanised me. I was in Belfast yesterday, I'm travelling to Galway tomorrow, and I've been working in The Hague with One Young World [a global, not-for-profit forum for young leaders] – really talking about how we need to be grateful to those small island states and to the least developed countries for insisting on having this in the text. The scientists then were asked to explain the difference between 2°C and 1.5°C, and how we could keep it to 1.5°C. And we've never really had scientists tell us that before. We should be very grateful to those small island states.

You seem to be positive despite the gloomy nature of the most recent report. How do you manage?

It's a lesson I learned from Archbishop Emeritus Desmond Tutu. About eight years ago, when he was still chair of [non-profit peace organisation] The Elders, we were on a panel together in New York, moderated by an American journalist. The journalist said to him, quite sharply: 'Archbishop Tutu, why are you such an optimist?' And he looked at her in surprise and he shook his head, and he said, 'Oh, my dearie', he said – and he called her 'dearie'! – 'I'm not an optimist, I'm a prisoner of hope.' Now I'd known Archbishop Tutu for a very long time. I knew him during the very difficult days in South Africa when I was part of the anti-apartheid movement, I remember him chairing the Truth and Reconciliation Commission in South Africa and I remember him crying on television because some of the evidence was so hurtful, so terrible. And this remark about being a 'prisoner of hope' is important, because it means you may not see that the glass is half full, but you find something in that glass that you can work with. And that's what each of the stories in my book is about: life is very difficult, it's unjust, but you don't spend too much time thinking about that. You think instead, 'Well, what can I do? What can I do to address this?' Whereas if you just describe how terrible that report is – which it is, because it says we're not on track for a safe world and we don't seem to be capable of turning around – if we just talk about it in terms of how serious it is and how terrible it is, and we've only got twelve years, and we're not doing it, then all the energy goes and you're left with no capacity to really do something. So it's very, very important to have that hope – to be prisoners of hope.

I agree. Research into decision-making also shows that you cannot get people to commit to climate action over time if they are scared, if there's too much fear – it makes them numb instead. You have to find optimism within the climate challenge to really motivate people. I think it's important to add to this notion of hope ideas for what people can do that are actually within reach. What change of behaviour is within reason? Don't you think that it's necessary for the people who wrote the UN's IPCC special report on the climate to come up with a list of things people can do? The need for systemic changes is clear. It's also clear that the politicians are not necessarily acting. As an artist I am very interested in what is within my micro-systemic reach. Why is there not a report on this?

What I've been doing for some time is to say we need to change our habits. It's about what we eat, the amount we consume – that we shouldn't package and build our economies on a false hope. We need to be much more intelligent about how we get well-being and a better life. And I think culture and cultural thoughtfulness and intuition would be extraordinarily important in that space.

I could not agree more. But I also think the UN could take a stronger role in guiding civic society and guiding the individual. Because clearly they offer systemic solutions, but the confidence from governments in actually adapting these is very low. And maybe we have more leadership in the private sector.

We do, really surprisingly. I've been working on a letter from The B Team leaders to the European Union – to heads of state, prime ministers and also the relevant ministers – saying that the EU must first of all greatly increase its ambitions for 2030, and, secondly, that it must make a declaration as the EU that it will achieve net zero greenhouse gas emissions by 2050. And you know the countries that have done that? The Marshall Islands, Fiji – small island states – and Costa Rica and Ethiopia. Not the United States, obviously – forget that, under Trump. But the EU has to show that kind of leadership. If they do that and actually say, 'We will be net zero greenhouse emissions by 2050', then you work backwards. It's like the space race! I was talking to One Young World in The Hague, and I had this nice anecdote about when John F. Kennedy announced that the United States would put a man on the moon, in 1961. The average age at NASA eight years later, when they landed the man on the moon, was twenty-six; that means that their average age when they were listening to Kennedy in 1961 was eighteen. So that was my message to these young people in The Hague, who were talking about what they were doing on plastics – we had a whole session on plastics, and they were doing an extraordinary amount on addressing how to clean up plastics and how to invent alternatives. They were only there because they were champions of this. And it was quite impressive.

To come back to culture, Mary, we've talked about the public sector and the private sector. I think culture enjoys a high degree of trust within society in general. I'm referring to culture in the broadest sense – not just the elites, but local poetry clubs and hobbyists, everything. And in that sense, I think culture can verbalise human emotions and ideas that are otherwise not listened to. Why do you think culture is still most of the time seen as a peripheral activity, also within the UN? You are such a champion of the public sector. Can you tell me why culture is not seen more as the beating heart in the physical body of civic society?

Well, first of all, I'd make a comment on participation, if I may. Promoting my book has taken me to a number of arts festivals – arts festivals, not book festivals – and they've been wonderfully participatory. I've found audiences to be very lively in questioning – the Q&A sessions have been absolutely active. Now, for some reason, the UN has never really captured that spirit. It does have quite a vibrant culture but it is rather – how would I say it? – a kind of 'insider' civil society. Inside the tent, they have their own acronyms and their special UN-speak – and that's not much good [laughs]. We need to get to both the local and the creative in a very new sense out there. And I certainly do think the recent UN report is so clear that any group will take it on board when you talk about it – that's my experience. I've been talking to people who haven't really thought about these things, and they are absolutely taking it on board. They are in listening mode much more now, because somehow we know that something is happening that we can't fully understand. Also, you're right that culture is much more trusted – I think something culture really can do is help make those links.

It's important to say something but not to try to prescribe it. For example, what we say on the *Mothers of Invention* podcast is that 'climate change is a man-made problem that requires a feminist solution'. And then I explain, because I think it still needs to be explained, that 'man-made' includes women; a feminist solution definitely includes men. But we're not prescribing what the feminist solution is. The podcast explores, in a very open way, what guests say about paternalism, about Black Lives Matter, about all these kinds of things. It's very exciting, because we're not prescribing, we're just listening. And there's humour, because the person doing it with me, Maeve Higgins, is a comedian. Humour is also very helpful.

You are completely spot on, saying that it's actually not about telling people what to do. Through my social solar-energy company Little Sun I have come into contact with a lot of people who can relate to the climate justice question. You put it in a way that has helped me verbalise some of the reasoning behind Little Sun and the notion of empowerment. For instance, in Little Sun's case, it's not about telling Ethiopians what to do about their climate solutions. It's about listening to them, hearing the solutions they have.

Exactly.

There are a handful of strategies in culture that could turn out to be practically helpful to the application of some of the UN recommendations. I would say that if the UN has to send peacekeeping forces somewhere, as traumatising as that obviously is, it is because they failed to send cultural agents twenty years or ten years before. Though I am aware that I am simplifying a little, of course. We should be careful about saying it's just about democratisation, but by all means the cultural component is an active and not a passive one, and that's why I'm pleased that you are using cultural platforms – like my own studio – to launch your book later this month.

Yes, I'm very appreciative. It's wonderful to return to that great studio of yours.

October 2018

FJORDENHUS
2009–18

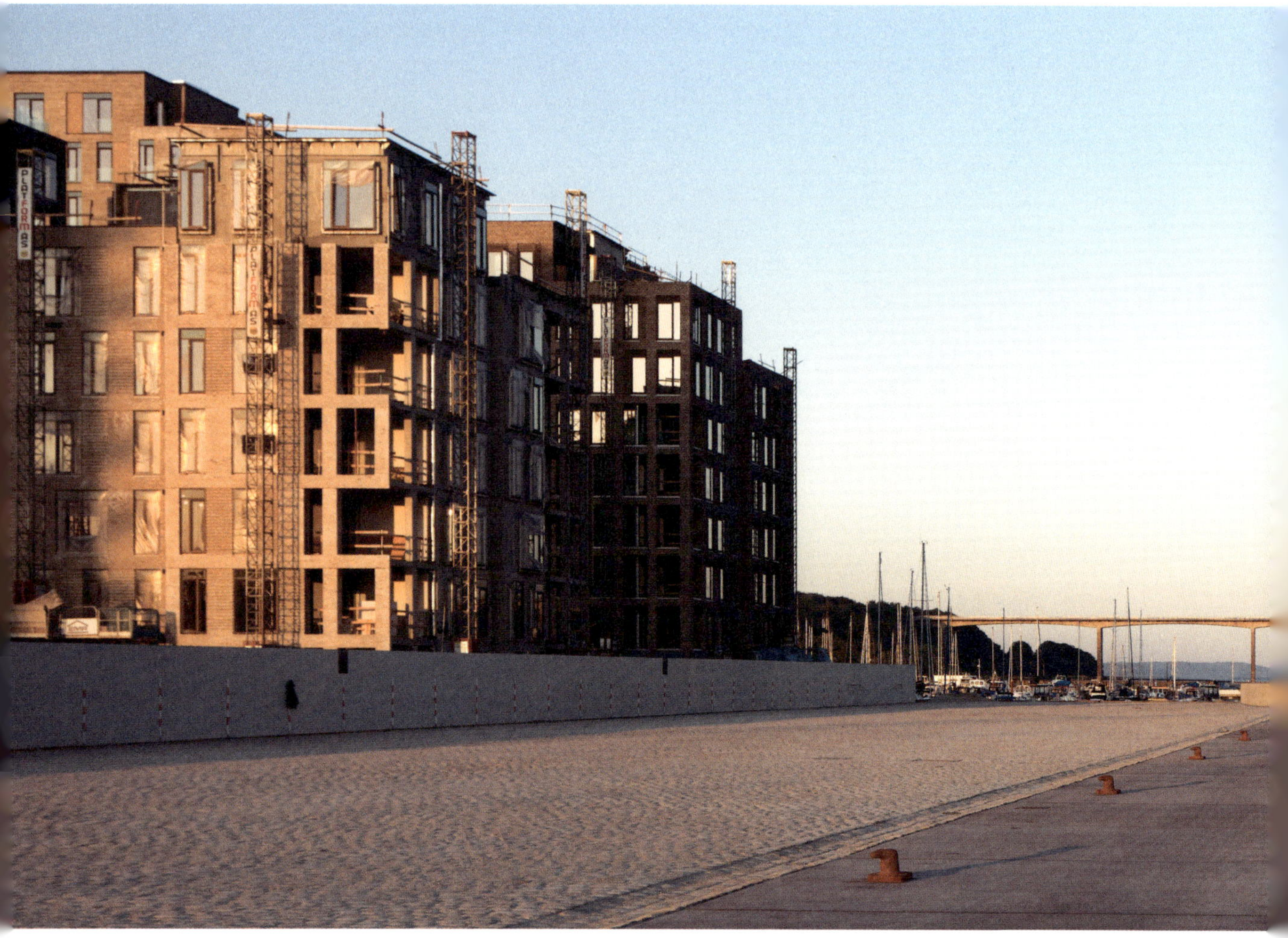

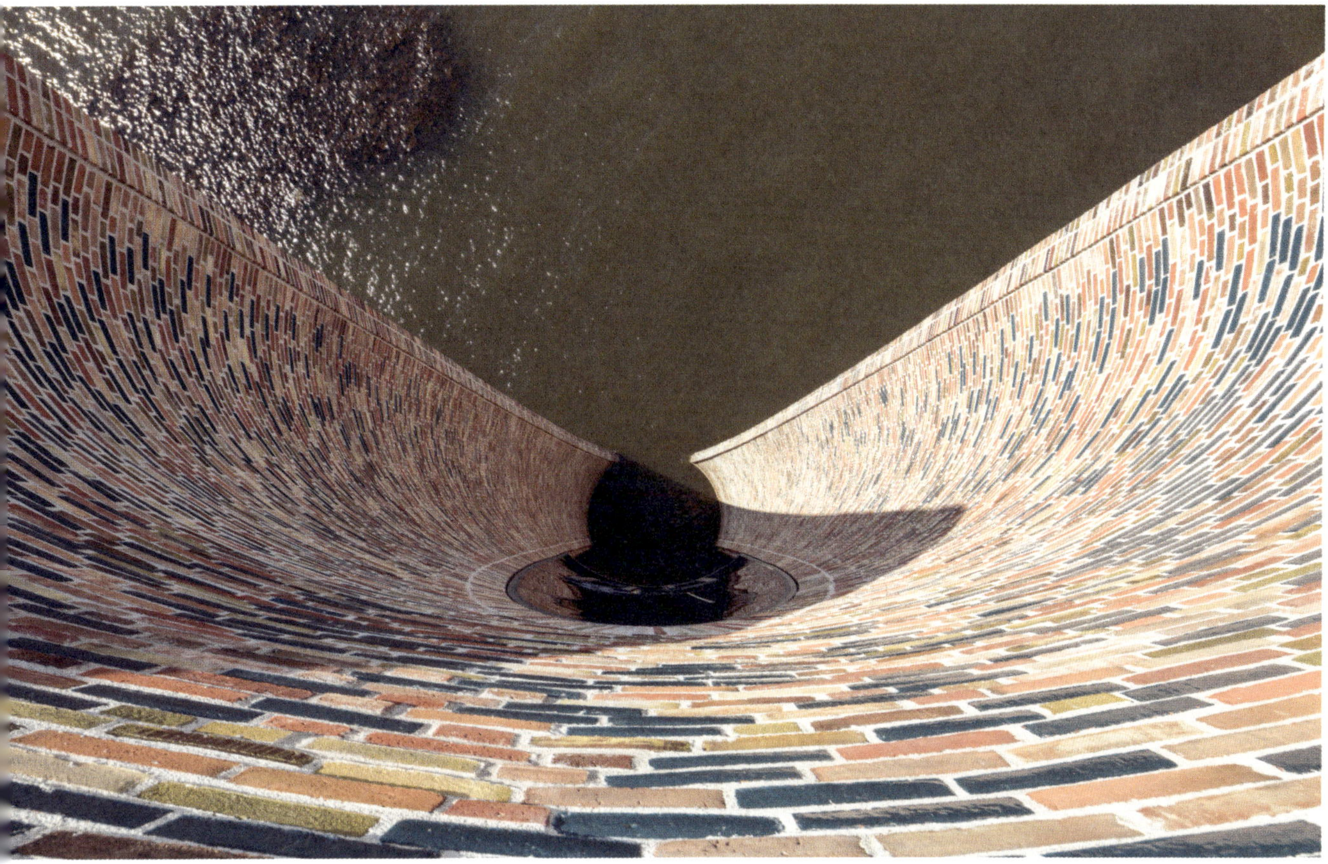

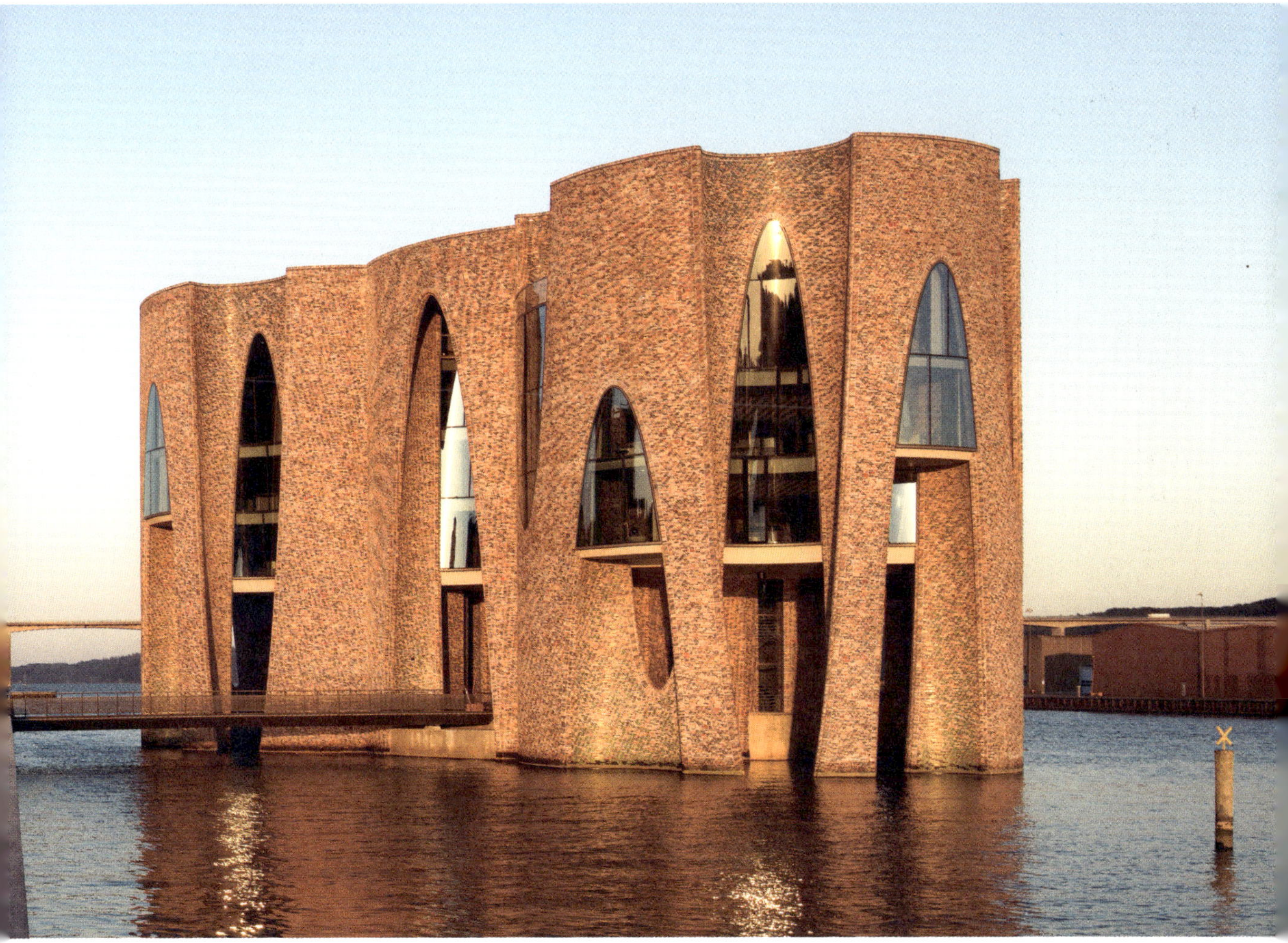

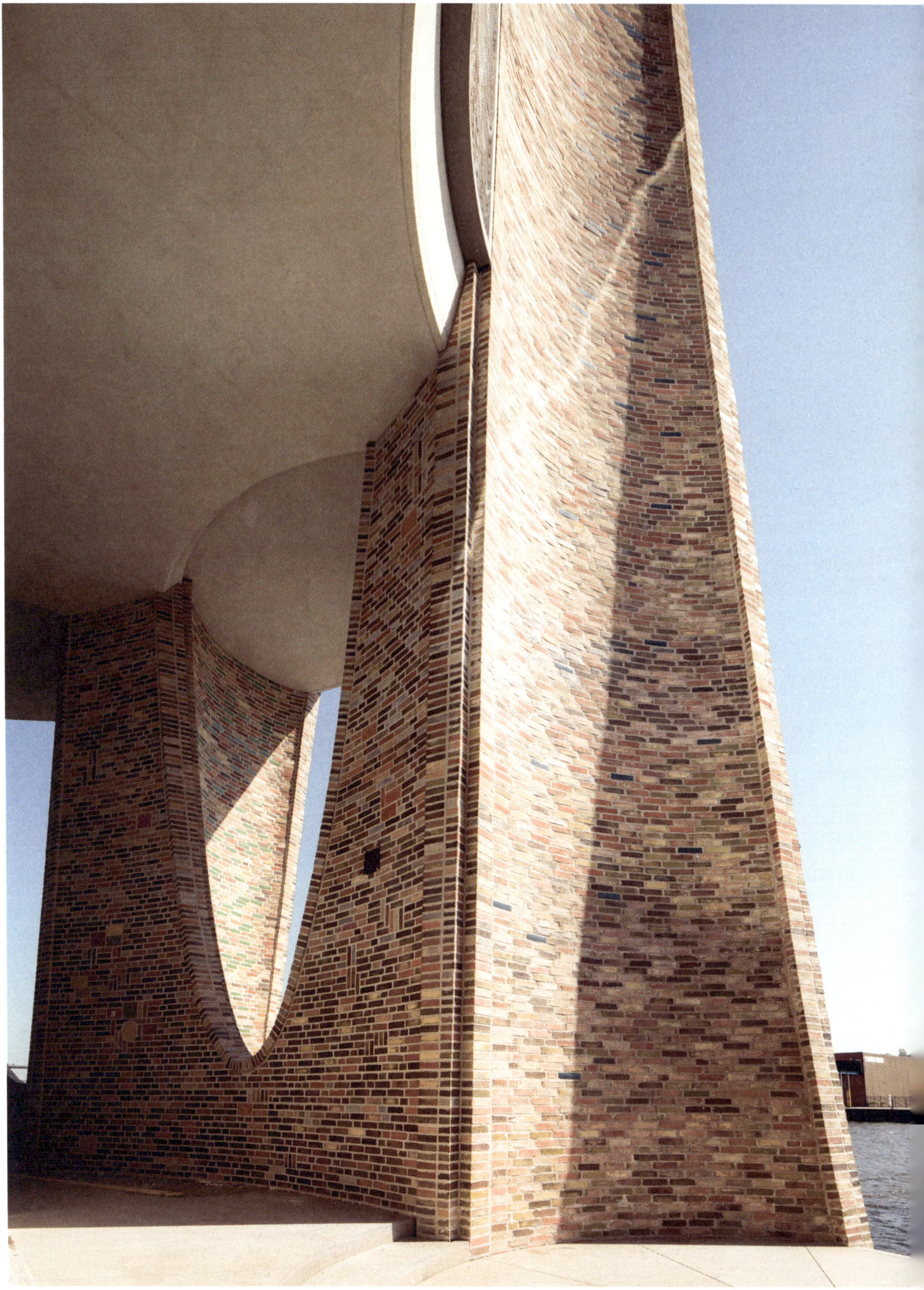

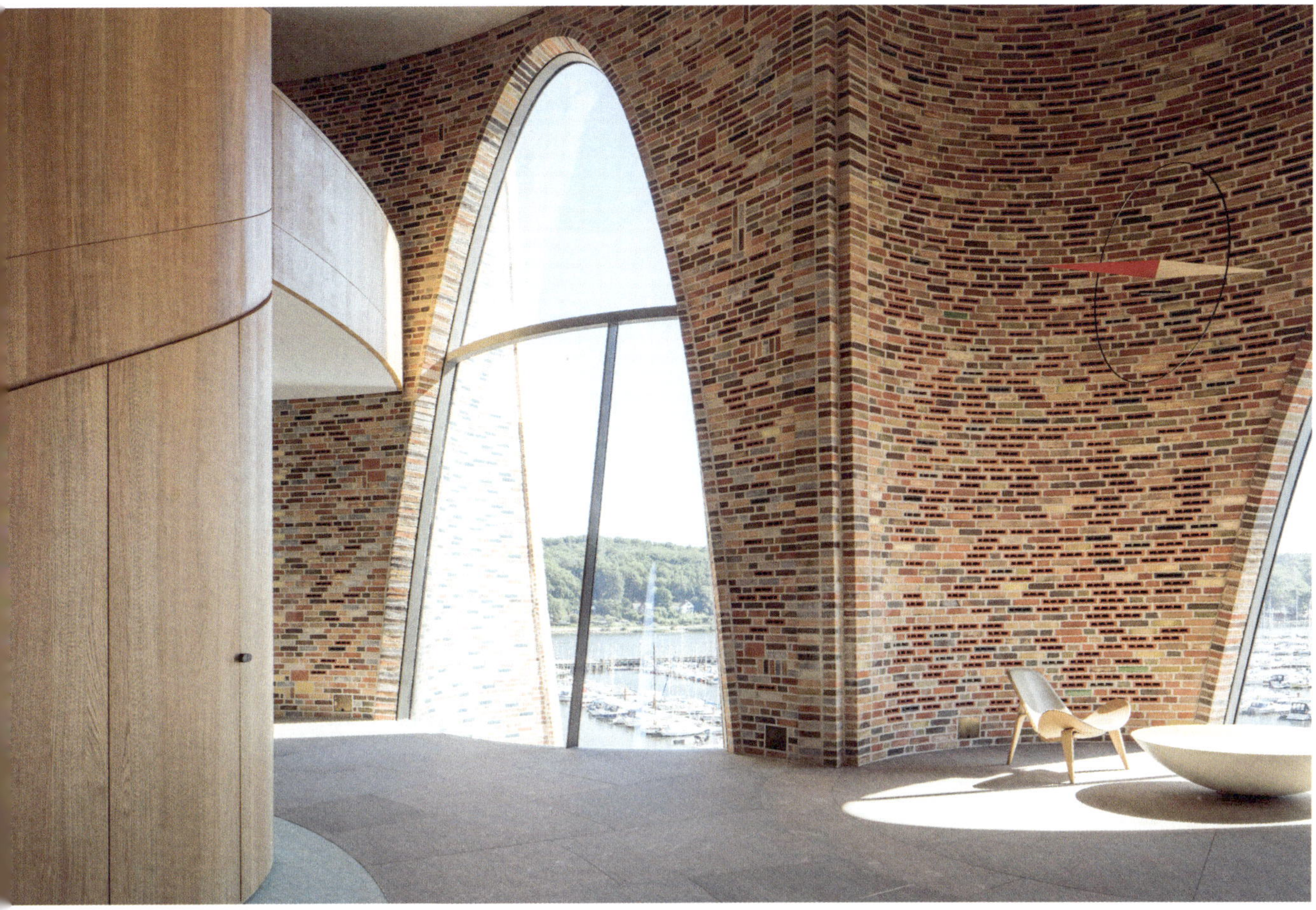

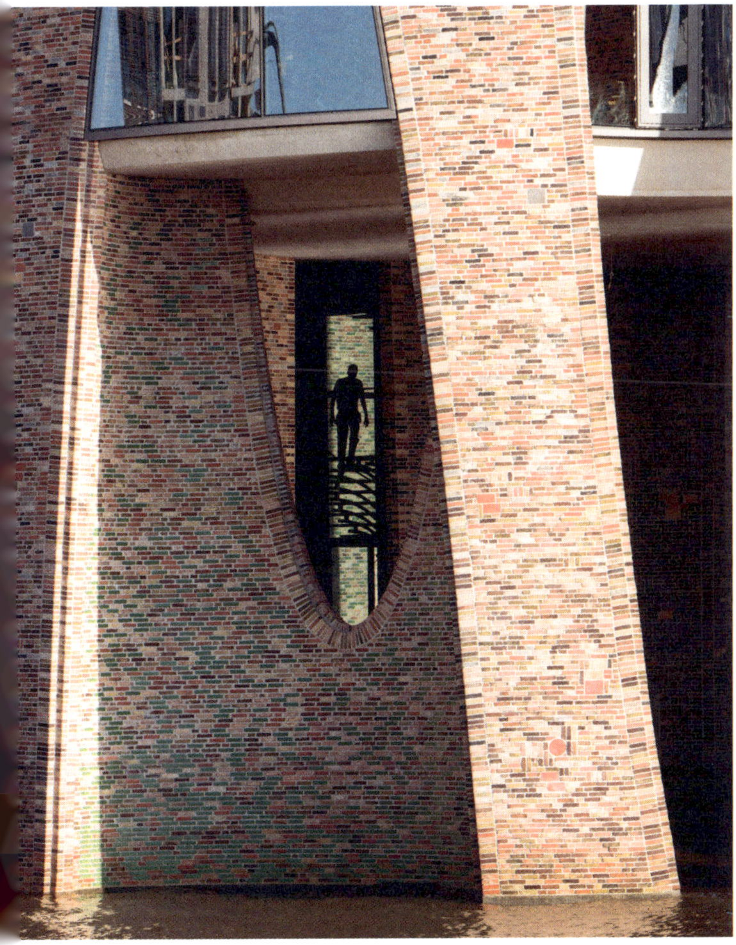

FJORDENHUS 2018 Fjordenhus (Fjord House), commissioned by Kirk Kapital, is the first building designed by Olafur Eliasson and Sebastian Behmann with Studio Olafur Eliasson. Rising out of the water of the Vejle Fjord, Denmark, the building is formed by four intersecting cylinders with brick facades from which ellipsoidal negative spaces were removed to create complex curved forms and arched windows. The building together with its artworks and furniture were designed as an integrated whole.

Olafur Eliasson: Josefine, you are able to put into words things that are otherwise difficult to articulate – to give a voice to things experienced largely through the senses. I'd like to begin with something from a talk you gave a month ago in defence of the Amager nature reserve, a talk that was later printed in the Danish newspaper *Politiken.* It was tremendous! In it, you emphasise values associated with nature as being held in common – you don't utilise the traditional split into subject and object, or the idea that nature resides outside of us while culture resides within us as human beings. The nature reserve is a large, still undeveloped green space in Copenhagen that, unsurprisingly, investors and politicians have been trying to develop for a long time. It hosts a variety of flora and fauna, and a human presence has also established itself amid the plant and animal life. Copenhageners use the nature reserve as an extension of themselves, and that, I think, is very exciting, for that's just how I have always used Iceland. Maybe we could start by talking about your vision of nature.

Josefine Klougart: The talk dealt with why I think it's a bad idea to build upon a common natural space like the Amager reserve, and it took as its starting point the description of a fallacy that I think is central to the problems we're facing today, both as individuals and as a society or culture, both locally and globally: the fallacy that it makes sense to draw a distinction between people and nature as something radically *other*, something located 'out there', something for us to investigate and observe. I think this is an illusion – an illusion that prevents us from experiencing ourselves as existing in an intimate connection with all life, as being part of all life, an illusion that paves the way for an instrumental relation to nature in and around us.

WE ARE NATURE

JOSEFINE KLOUGART is a Danish novelist, the editor of the literary journal *Den Blå Port* (The Blue Gate) and the founder of the independent publisher Gladiator. Eliasson and Klougart first crossed paths in a conversation on memory and inner landscapes in relation to *Your glacial expectations* 2012, a site-specific outdoor work by Eliasson and landscape architect Günther Vogt. The work resonated deeply with Klougart, who grew up in the area of rural Denmark where it is located.

You can go back in history, of course, and see how the separation and marginalisation of nature appeared, how it has evolved, the different consequences this has had in different periods – how nature has gazed back at us with different faces. And we can imagine how that face will look at us in the future, as temperatures rise and nature responds to our increasingly harsh treatment. It's particularly intriguing, I think, to look back at the Enlightenment, when the hierarchisation of different forms of experience achieved a new radicality. People wanted to emerge from darkness, but what they overlooked, perhaps, was that every light you shine into the world also calls forth new shadows, so that something else ends up lying in the dark. Nature – the entire concrete world, almost – came to be seen merely as a resource rather than as an entity in its own right.

My contention is that sensitive experiences – characterised by their circular nature and the interplay between sensory perception and reflection – are particularly beneficial for letting us discover our own essential condition, our connection to each other and to nature. As living creatures in the world, we're not merely a part of the same cycles as rivers and trees and insects – we simply *are* nature. Instead of looking at poetry, philosophy, mathematics and science as things that set us apart from nature, we have to start seeing them as nature's way of reflecting on itself.

Our cultural history is the history of nature itself thinking, of nature itself trying to understand the world – in the words of poet Inger Christensen, 'nature's effort to understand itself'. Rather than seeing culture as an indication of the distinction between humanity and nature, we need to see it as the manifestation of an intimate connection. When we speak, we are nature speaking; when we think, we are nature thinking; when we control nature outside of us, we are nature controlling something within itself.

That's a beautiful way of putting it.

The Enlightenment is particularly interesting for us as artists, I think, because the revolt against mystical thought and religion also undermined, in a way, the conditions for our ability to experience art. Aesthetic experiences share something with what used to be called mystical experiences. Aesthetic experience shares something with religious experience. So when you make a break with religion, it's dangerously easy to make a break with our ability to experience the world aesthetically. But aesthetic experience is a fantastic path to a very rich realisation that balances the sensory and the reflexive in a way that enables us to see very complicated patterns as a whole, and thereby gives us, at a glance, a chance to understand something new about ourselves and the world.

You're right that the potential for emotion, experience and realisation was denied in the service of rationality. Do you think that's still the case?

Yes, in part. I feel we approach aesthetic creations with a lack of openness and, to some extent, a lack of a sense of form – an inability to observe the work and to see it as an ordering of material. We don't really learn how to look at art or how to read literature. Our educational system instrumentalises art and literature by presenting them as difficult systems of signs that we're supposed to translate into another language through an intellectual manoeuvre – a bit like a rebus we have to solve, an accumulation of symbols that need to be translated into concepts. In the same way, we diminish our cognitive abilities; the freely circulating interplay in which we both reflect and perceive, feel and observe, is short-circuited by the fear of not being able to figure something out.

The thing that's so exciting about this to me is that you're engaged in a form of literary activism.

A lot of politically engaged art today invalidates itself as art. I've always regarded my work as being engaged, but not in an explicit way. I try to write in a language that opens itself to a sensibility, a sensitive experience, that I feel is a radical corrective to the kinds of instrumentalisation and rigidity in thinking that have led to some of the national and global crises that we're in the midst of.

I think it's completely legitimate to call that activism, because culture is part of society, not something you step out of society to practise. When culture is seen as peripheral, it can be hard to understand its political potential, but culture is critical to a society's ability to be reflective, and thus to reinvent itself. We've talked about emotions; you said that the political resides where we become sensitised and inspired to act at the same time. Can you say more about that?

I think there are times when it succeeds and times when it doesn't. When it doesn't succeed is when you're reading a novel, for example, and you're directed to the concepts, the analysis – when you're prompted to read the book as if it were a rebus or an allegory. Then your intellect is activated, which can be quite pleasurable, because there's something pleasurable in being able to see signs and translate them into ideas, but there's another way, which is what I think you're talking about. That's when literature succeeds in opening up the person who's reading, initially to the independent world that literature brings to life, and then to the world in which we exist. Poetry and art are always creating a new language from fragments of the familiar. This new language opens us and opens the space of art, and we take that back with us when we return to the world. The new language reveals to us something new and strange, allows our consciousness to access a new experience of our basic condition, our ultimate connectedness. And really, how often does that happen?

I suppose it happens when readers feel that their emotional needs are being reflected – when the book articulates something that they, without necessarily knowing it, needed to have expressed, as if the book were listening to them. That's how I think an artwork succeeds – by that connectedness: to feel that it means something if I vote, means something if I demonstrate; to feel that my caring for others actually makes a difference.

I think that the way art opens us up in itself helps prepare us to make better collective decisions, simply because we develop a sensitivity that we can use to experience our interconnectedness with everything – with each other, with the earth, with nature. There's a real need for this type of experience, a need that I believe has settled into our culture like a sorrow – a sorrow that carries with it a great deal of suffering: aggression, depression, addictions of all kinds, simple turmoil, a decline in our ability to see complicated associations and think with complexity. More and more, we allow ourselves to be entertained and we become emotionally and intellectually lazy – or rather, anaesthetised. And this at a time when we really need to be able to think in a clear and nuanced manner, a time when we need to understand abstract relationships. It's a basic condition of modern life that we can't immediately see the consequences of our actions. It used to be easier, because if you poured poison into a lake and went back and fished, you'd get sick; the effects were more direct. Now the effects, at least initially, are exported to Third World countries where they aren't immediately visible to us. Artists don't have a greater responsibility than other people, but I think we do have the important ability to provide access to experiences that can open us up.

How do you see the way you work as part of the cultural sector? You've also helped to start up a publishing house?

You have to look at it on different levels. There is, as you say, the individual's personal experience of an artwork or a book, where the revolutionary potential lies in forming a person who is capable of experiencing their own existential condition, their time and their possibilities more completely, with more complexity and nuance – giving them a refreshed starting point from which to go out and change society and the world. You could say that anyone who devotes their time to art is, in fact, an activist. Art is by definition a language of resistance, an effort to develop new understandings of ourselves and the world, a laboratory for the development of new thoughts that can shape a new reality and a new vision for what we should do together. At the same time though, there is a system outside of art that normalises the language that art speaks with, blunting the revolutionary potential of art's language. Our sensitivity is up against such powerful forces – capitalism, for instance, into which are built mechanisms that challenge our sensitivity in different ways, and the powerful political forces that speak to our fear, which causes us to avoid contact with others and restrict how much of the world we can see.

Philosophers and artists and citizens need to unite to try to talk about this field of experience. That's one of the reasons we founded Gladiator – not only to be a publisher but also to be an institution for cultural education. That's the way we see ourselves – as a space where people can talk together about literature while it's being created. We're opening the publishing house up to the world through a range of different course offerings, so that people can enter into conversations with their fellow students and teachers, who are primarily authors, artists, editors and musicians.

Coming from Iceland, I grew up with the idea that there isn't really any nature in Denmark. Yet it turns out that there is in fact a little pocket of nature, which is where you come from – the moraine landscape of Mols. You've written quite a lot about it, and reading your work has helped me understand my relationship to Iceland.

It's clear that the landscapes we have intimate relationships with get folded into both of our artistic practices in various ways. Creating art is essentially about becoming nature – nature understood as a creative energy, a form-producing energy. How do you do that? By listening to the forms you see around you, especially those forms that resonate because you know them so well – forms that have taken root in you. In childhood we have the aesthetic openness to see the potential for beauty in forms that, later on, we walk right by without noticing.

I grew up partly in Denmark and partly in Iceland, and when I looked at the natural landscape in Iceland, I felt like I wasn't quite sure what it was I was seeing and that the only way to figure it out was to engage it physically. I had to walk through it, crawl up it, roll down it, swim in it. It was totally corporeal. Walking through the landscape turned into measuring it with my body. So when I go to Iceland, I rediscover not so much the landscape as myself and the way I perceive.

When I wrote my first book [*Stigninger og fald* (Rise and Fall), 2010], I was quite unaware of the degree to which it was a book about nature, and the relationship between nature, language and the mind. When it came out there was discussion about whether it was problematic to publish a book with so much natural beauty in it in 2010 – at a time of nationalist, Romantic stirrings on the political scene. Was it a problem to depict the beauty of the Danish landscape, even though the book portrays the darker, more brutal side of nature as well?

That may very well be.

But at the same time, I think there are all kinds of problems in avoiding minute description of those landscapes that are, after all, the starting point for our first investigations into our connections with the world around us. It's part of the human condition that we never signed up for a particular landscape – or a particular family for that matter. Our native countries are always points of identification, of experiences of oneness with the world, as well as the opposite – points that mark our existential alienation from nature and the family we're a part of. They hold such power for us, no doubt because the balance between feeling at home and feeling like a stranger in itself reflects one of the basic conditions for any aesthetic pursuit – namely, that in creating, we're transported to a state between perfecting a form we don't understand but sense intuitively, and facing something radically foreign that rises to meet us from the paper's pages, or from the sight of how the light is refracted by a large constructed waterfall.

If there's something you think is beautiful, you should claim it, otherwise your opponents will take it. You write in that way, too, don't you – there's a kind of deconstructive effort in the narrative.

If you manage to make something that truly becomes art, then the work itself is armed against, is born with the antidote to Romanticism inside it, because there simply has to be some resistance somewhere in the work. The new tendency of right-wing nationalists is the polar opposite. Their comprehension of nature doesn't seem to me to have very much to do with nature itself – they just use it as an unchanging symbol. Art's engagement with nature itself, however, has an utterly different significance. Art investigates nature not to use it as a symbol but rather as a formal inspiration or as a picture that casts a new light back upon the world so that the world itself, the landscape itself, can reveal itself to us with greater complexity. As long as we're interested in the landscapes we inhabit and that inhabit us, as long as we let them enter into works that help to open us up and sensitise us, they'll be a corrective to dogmatic instrumental thinking – with respect to other people too. If we give nationalist, right-wing politicians a monopoly on engaging their countries' landscapes and wildernesses, then not only are we surrendering our landscapes to them, we're also relinquishing an opportunity to counter the increasingly instrumental relationship to nature that these politicians are themselves producing.

October 2018

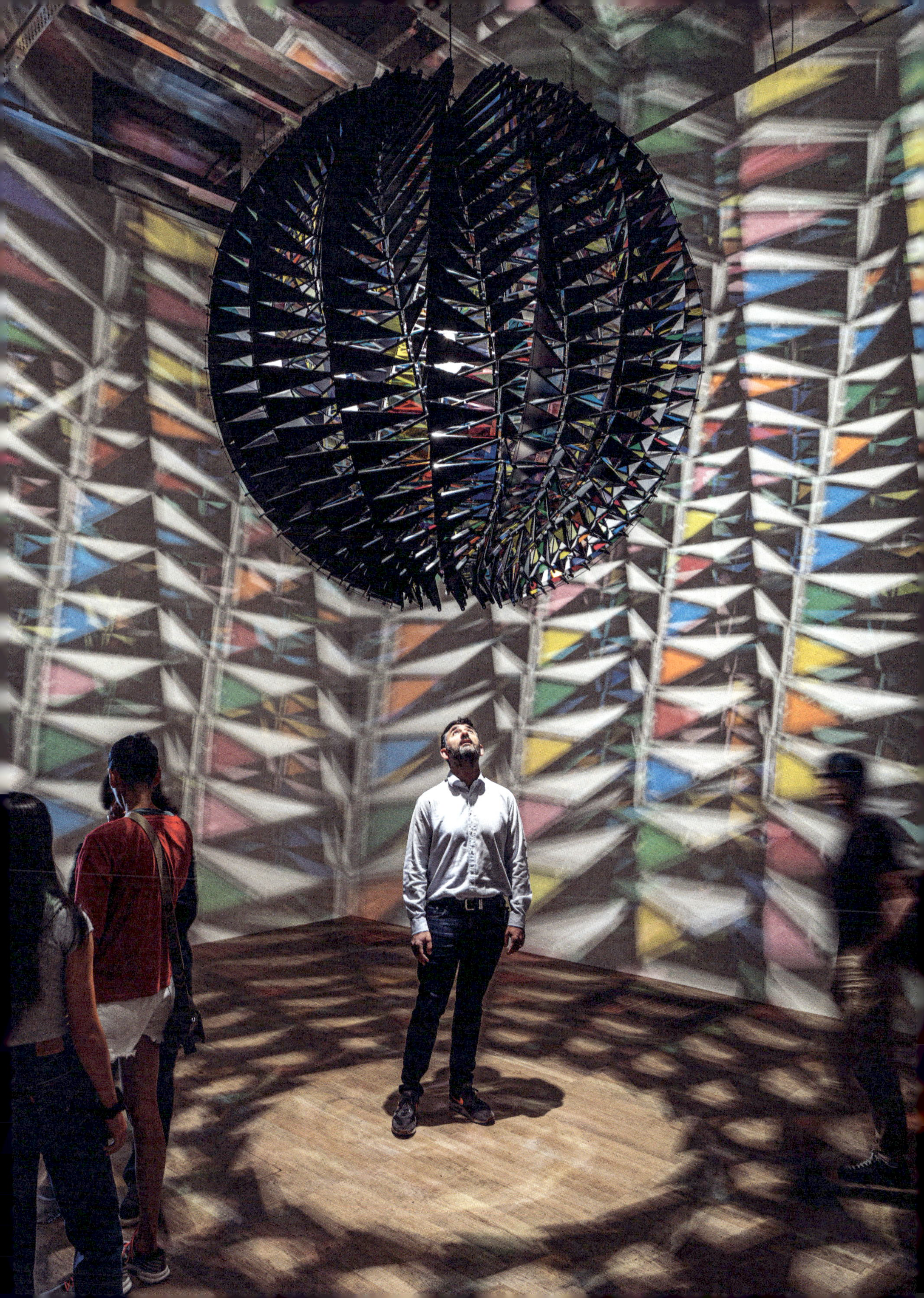

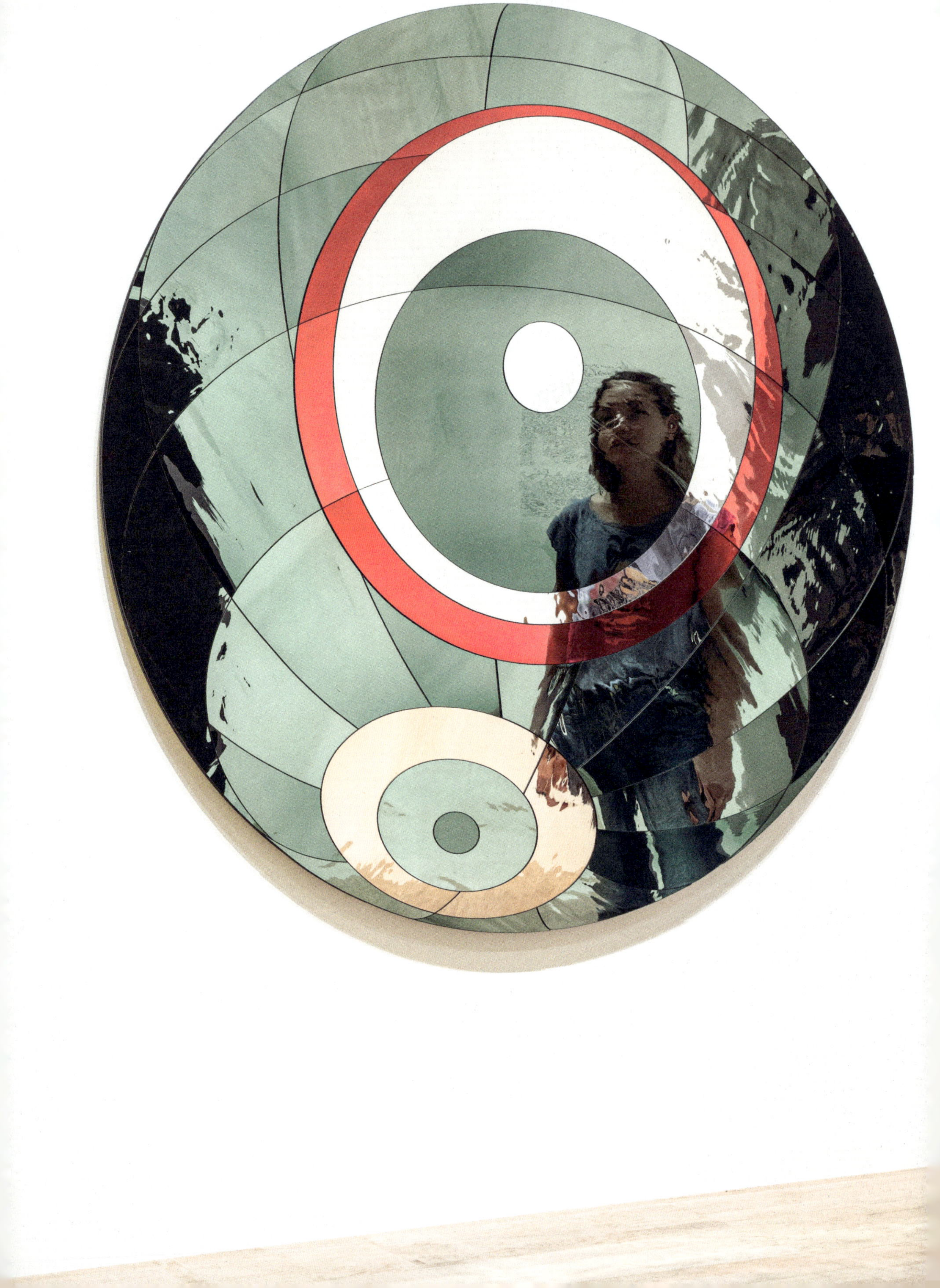

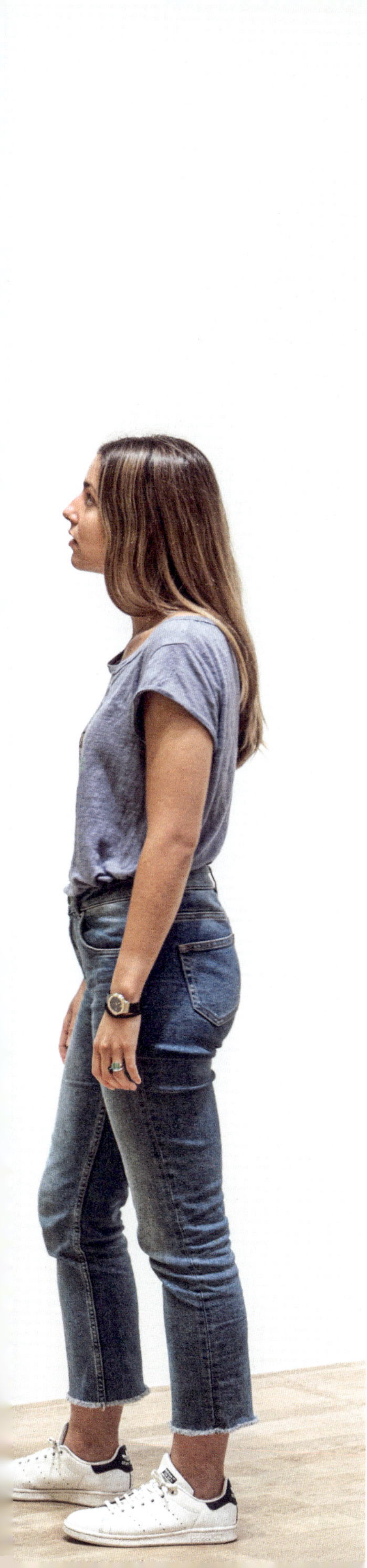

GLACIAL SPHERICAL FLARE 2019

COLOUR EXPERIMENT NO.80 20

OLOUR EXPERIMENT NO.81 2019

Olafur Eliasson: Since we last spoke, the United Nations Intergovernmental Panel for Climate Change [IPCC] has come out with a new report on climate change. Why don't we start by talking about the content of that report?

Elke Weber: The report basically looks at the consequences of having either a 2°C [average global surface temperature rise] target for 2100 or a 1.5°C target. The 2°C target had been considered a safe scenario in terms of global warming – something to aspire to, even though it's actually not that easy to achieve. But this report shows that even warming of 1.5°C by 2100 would have quite serious consequences for the well-being of the human species and our planet, which shows how critically impacted we are by changes in temperature, both as an ecosystem and on the level of human well-being. I think it's quite a wake-up call for all of us!

Back at the UN Climate Change Conference, COP21, in 2015, when the Paris Agreement was made, wasn't the 1.5°C target sought by the small island states, who were not invited to the main meetings?

That's right.

And now it turns out they were right.

Yes, they were right – and even their request for 1.5°C as a safe level doesn't look so safe anymore, which is very disturbing.

I'm very interested in your work on the relationship between experience, affect, emotion and changes in behaviour. As an artist, I work a lot with the question of what an experience is, with the psychological construct of an experience. So I thought we could talk a little bit about this, because I myself have become increasingly involved with the question of how our emotions influence our evaluation of whether or not we should do something about the climate. You have verbalised quite precisely why it is that some people, though they intellectually understand the concern, still have a way to go towards actually taking action, and one of the factors is whether people are emotionally touched by it. How do you verbalise that?

RISK AVOIDANCE

ELKE WEBER is Professor of Psychology and Public Affairs and of Energy and the Environment at Princeton University. In her research on judgement and decision-making, Weber studies the behaviour of individuals and groups as they deal with uncertainty and making trade-offs in their personal and working lives. She explores how choices impact the environment, with implications for environmental and energy policies. In spring 2015, Eliasson invited her to participate in the first workshop to develop content for the UN Live Museum for the United Nations, which was held at the Louisiana Museum of Modern Art, Denmark.

I coined the term 'risk-as-feelings'. We often know intellectually, analytically, about a particular danger that faces us, but the risks can seem distant in time and in space. For instance, on a personal level, we know that we should save for our retirement. There's a body of research from the 1960s on the psychological dimensions of risk, according to which certain risks strike us at an emotional level – like nuclear radiation, for example – while other risks – like climate change and sea-level rise – just seem like statistics and don't activate the same feeling of dread. The absence of that feeling means that although we know about the risk, we don't take any action on it. We have to be frightened of something to take action, to protect ourselves from it.

Isn't it the case that being scared can also make us less likely to take action, because there's a tendency to withdraw?

You've put your finger on a really important problem! You could argue that if climate change doesn't scare us naturally, we should use visualisations of future consequences, the way Al Gore has done in his movies – scare people into doing something about it. In general, scaring people, or making them feel guilty, is an effective prompt to action when there's something simple they can do in response. If your mother makes you feel guilty about not seeing her for Mother's Day, you can go visit her to free yourself from that negative emotion. So if there were something simple and immediate we could do about climate change – if we could just make a donation and be done with it – then scaring people would be a good way of activating them. The problem with climate change, however, is that we need to change so many of the things we do, over such a sustained period of time – things that affect us individually at a psychological level as well as at a social and political level – and this type of sustained action is not effectively motivated by negative emotions, because nobody wants to feel scared or guilty for an extended period of time. We just turn away.

That brings us to the idea from decision-making theory of the 'finite pool of worry' – that once we are occupied with a certain amount of worry, we tend to leave other concerns aside.

Yes, we do have a finite pool of worry. There's a lot of evidence that if we worry more about, say, our family or the economy, we worry less about other things. In 2008 and 2009, when there was a major economic global meltdown, concern about climate change measurably decreased; people were worried about other things.

But wouldn't you say that people's worries about Donald Trump have produced a strong progressive movement – that precisely *because* people are so worried, they have begun all kinds of initiatives – on migration, say, and climate? Does it sometimes work the other way around?

It certainly can work that way, especially when we see the risks as related; if you think about the connections between them, then one worry can activate another. But if there's too much worry and people don't see a way out, they feel powerless. And when we feel a lack of power, a lack of agency, we freeze.

I think it's fair to say that Trump is a master of using emotion, albeit abusively. Since affect is a great motivator for change in behaviour, it can be misused.

Of course! And Trump uses fear very effectively. He knows how to elicit it and how to tell people what to do about it, which is to vote for his party.

How would you calibrate a healthy balance between data and emotional input?

It becomes problematic when you tell people not only that they need to vote for the right people, but also to travel less, use less energy, switch the kind of car that they drive – fifteen or twenty different things they need to do. In this case I think eliciting positive emotions, as well as providing information on what people can actively and effectively do, is the right direction. Because we don't just have a finite pool of worry, we also have a finite pool of attention. How many things can you deal with at the same time? We do things one at a time, and often the order in which we rank them isn't right. Climate change could put an end to our existence on this planet. Why aren't we paying all of our attention to it? Whatever else there may be to worry about, we certainly shouldn't be ignoring climate change, as we currently are, on both individual and political levels.

I think culture has an important role in society because it so strongly values exchange and debate. It's different from the private sector in that it's not interested in selling – it doesn't commodify experience; it's a very individual experience to watch a play or read a book. At its best, culture prompts us to consider fundamental questions about ourselves: how we are in the world, what we long for, what happiness is. That's why I'm such a strong believer that the cultural sector – the arts – can inspire feeling and action. When scientists – many hundreds of scientists, I understand – work on these reports for the UN, do they show applications for the data? Because to turn data into action we need someone to show us a route to application, which is something that your work addresses.

There have been some small, small steps in that direction. These risk assessment reports are issued every five years or so, and the assessment in 2015 was the first to mention any literature or evidence on how people actually make decisions. Before that, everything had been premised on the assumption that we simply make rational economic choices – like that we will switch to solar electricity when it becomes cheaper than coal-based electricity, or that we'll buy electric cars instead of fuel-powered cars when they become cheaper and more efficient. But that's not the case – there is some evidence that people are afraid of new technology, for one thing – and that last report was the first to mention non-rational, human sorts of decision-making processes. And because people realised that this was an important contribution, I expect the new assessment report, on which work began this year, to again place an emphasis on it. I expect there will be more emphasis on how to influence the demand side, not just the supply side – not just on the new technologies and solutions that will be developed, but also on how to stimulate human demand for these things. There will be an emphasis on the human response in addition to the economic and political factors. So we are making some steps in the right direction.

Let me also say a few things about the importance of culture, because you're absolutely right that the arts – the work of novelists or playwrights or visual artists like yourself – have a very important role to play in helping people engage with this issue. Culture is neutral and non-threatening – it doesn't feel like it's didactic, like people are being talked down to – and at the same time it is concrete and experiential. I had a discussion recently about risk as a statistic, about how people don't respond to statistics, but they do respond to stories and individual fates. People do respond to an experience – like seeing your work, *Ice Watch* [2014], which brings icebergs to people; the way it allows people to see pieces of the Greenland ice sheet disappear before their very eyes is a very successful example of this approach.

At the same time, I think we need more examples of what an active and constructive response could look like. There are so many novels these days that get classified as 'cli-fi' – sci-fi that relates to climate change – but they're nearly all dystopias, horror stories. 'Here we are a hundred years from now, and the sea level has risen and we're being attacked by tropical storms, and how do we deal with that?' And while that is dramatic – and I love a good dystopia as much as anyone – we also need utopias. We need stories about how we got from the current moment to a future that's a lot more positive, a future in which we have learned our lessons and have done what needed to be done to prevent the disaster from unfolding.

Art is good at conjuring up utopias. It can even be a little too utopian! But to go back to something we were discussing before, I'm curious about the UN taking on the issue of how to apply the data. We would expect the public sector – specific governments and politicians – to determine how to apply the scientific reports from the UN, but we don't see politicians doing that. Do you think there is more leadership in the private sector? And if so, why? What's happening? Why are politicians not taking a lead?

These are really good questions, and there are no simple answers! Campaign finances are often determined by companies – by political donations made by vested interests. Certainly in the United States, the oil industry and companies that do not want action on climate change make enormous campaign contributions. Another factor is that these days politicians seem to be afraid of appearing paternalistic. Paternalism has become a dirty word, which is odd, because most people would agree that parents have an important role to play! We elect politicians because we realise that as individuals we have neither the knowledge nor the time to make the kinds of long-term strategic planning decisions that affect what the world will look like in fifty or a hundred years. That's precisely the kind of thing we need to delegate to politicians. But politicians have become more interested in re-election and in the fate of their parties than in the public good. They determine their positions with public opinion polls, and the public doesn't seem to have the same visceral response to climate risk as towards perceived threats like immigration, crime or terrorism. So, rather than guiding public opinion and public action, politicians have become followers – and I think that is a problem.

Now, nobody likes change. If you tell people that they have to change their immediate comfort level and standard of living for the sake of future generations, or even for the sake of their own long-term well-being, you shouldn't expect them to embrace that; we are just too focused on our immediate needs. But politicians sometimes have to say, 'This might look like a sacrifice in the short term, but you'll be better off in the future.' And research shows that when the public experiences the benefit of these actions, then, within a short period of time, they often feel quite positively about the same thing they had previously opposed. So I think we have to educate our public officials – first to remind them of their duty, and secondly to remind them that they can lead public opinion, that opposition is not necessarily permanent.

What makes me so excited about your work is how you talk about solutions in a very positive way, rather than focusing on the negative. There *is* a positive narrative to be told – it doesn't have to be all doom and gloom. I'm very interested in how you focus on the need to use emotional, experience-oriented communication if we want to motivate people to change their behaviour. Let me ask you one last thing. It's easier to motivate people to change when the change comes across as the more enjoyable option. Do you think there can be a kind of hedonistic climate agenda? It sounds almost counter-intuitive, but do you know what I mean?

I've often argued that you should never let a good crisis go to waste – there is always a silver lining. One way to think about the current climate change crisis is that it allows us to rethink the basis of human happiness. Material and economic comfort and security are important at a very basic level, but once those are established, acquiring more and more goods – more vacations and bigger houses and more expensive cars – does not really make us happy. What makes us happy is hanging out with friends, doing things for others. Yet this lesson goes largely unheard. Instead we are all on a treadmill that depends on the exploitation of our planet, and which our planet can no longer sustain. There's a body of research that looks at our current crisis as a wake-up call that requires us to re-examine what actually makes us happy and to develop, especially in Western countries, new lifestyles that are less focused on material consumption and more focused on community experiences with loved ones. These are changes we can make in our own lives. They don't have to happen far away. Showing how to make these changes, showing what is really important through stories and examples, this is where culture and art can help the world tremendously.

October 2018

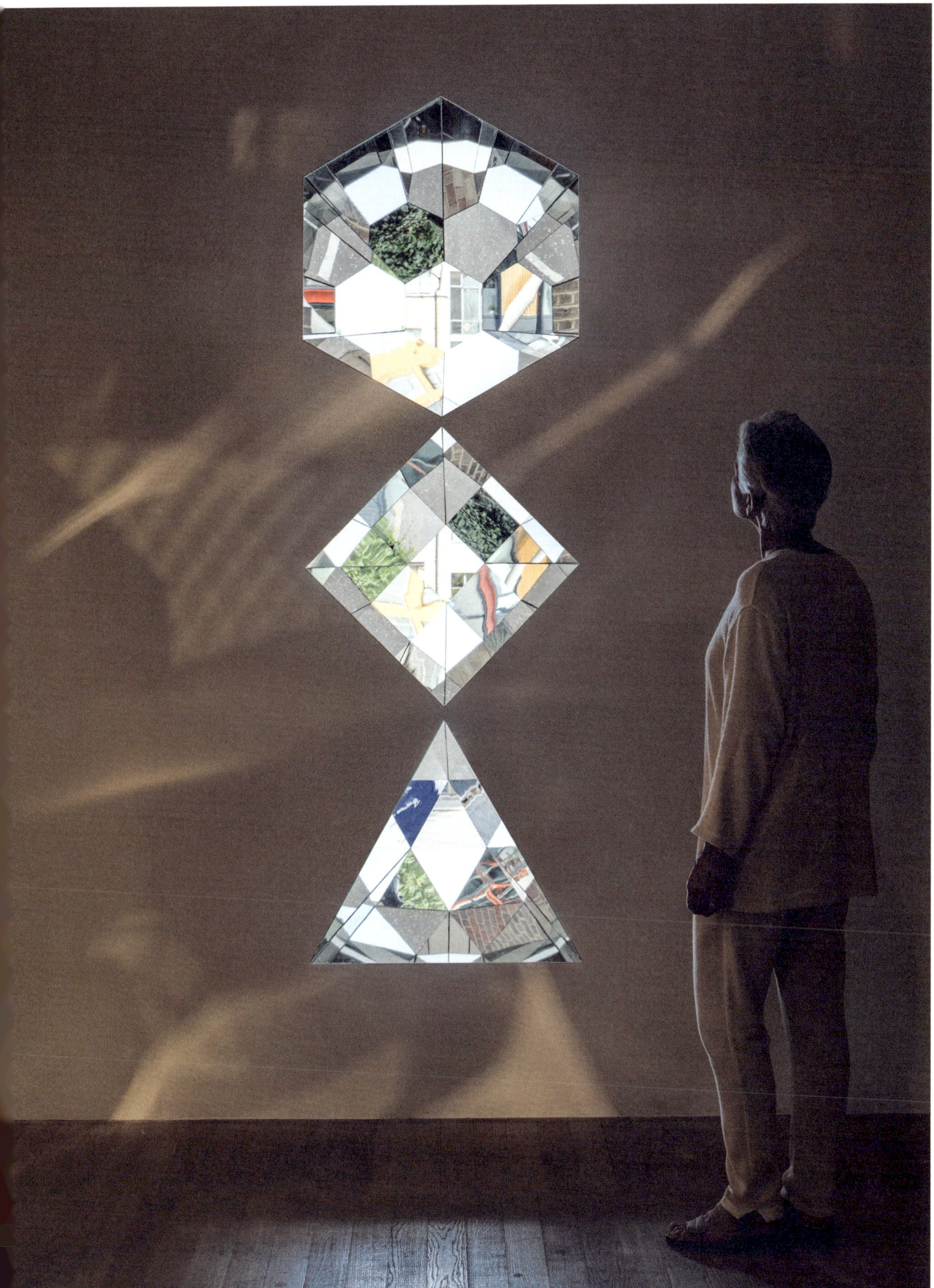

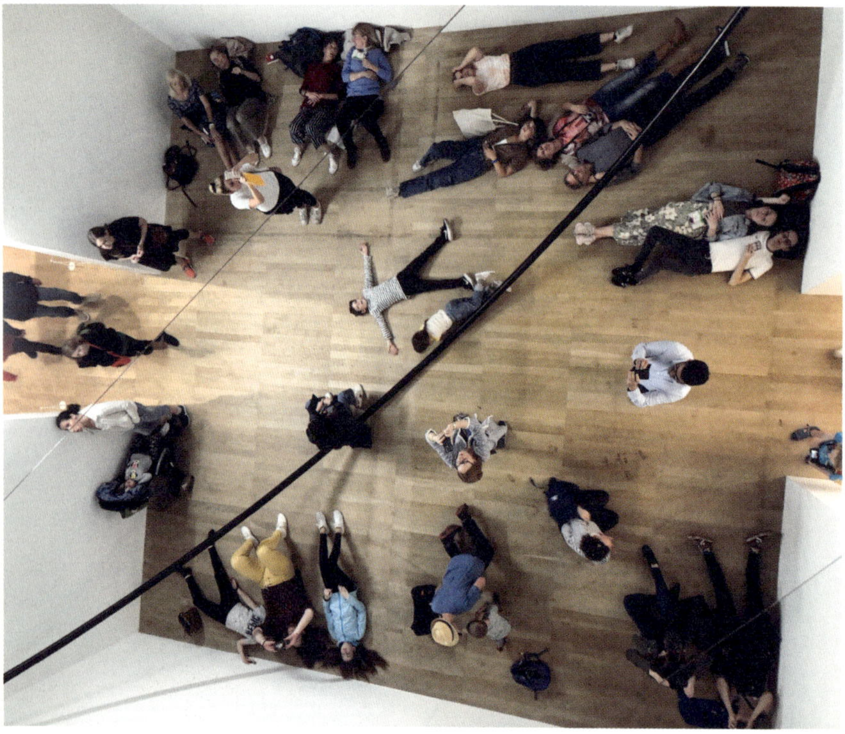

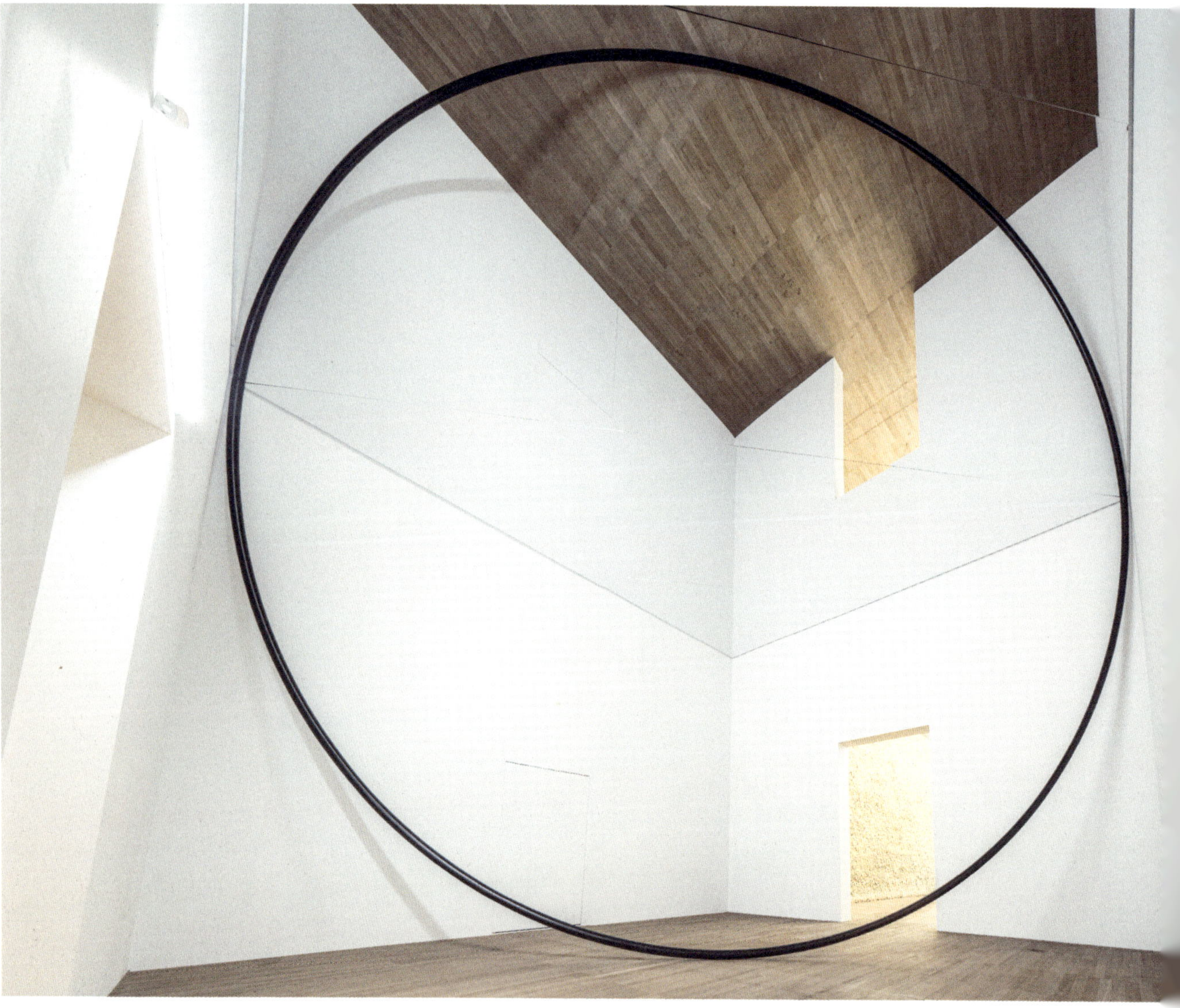

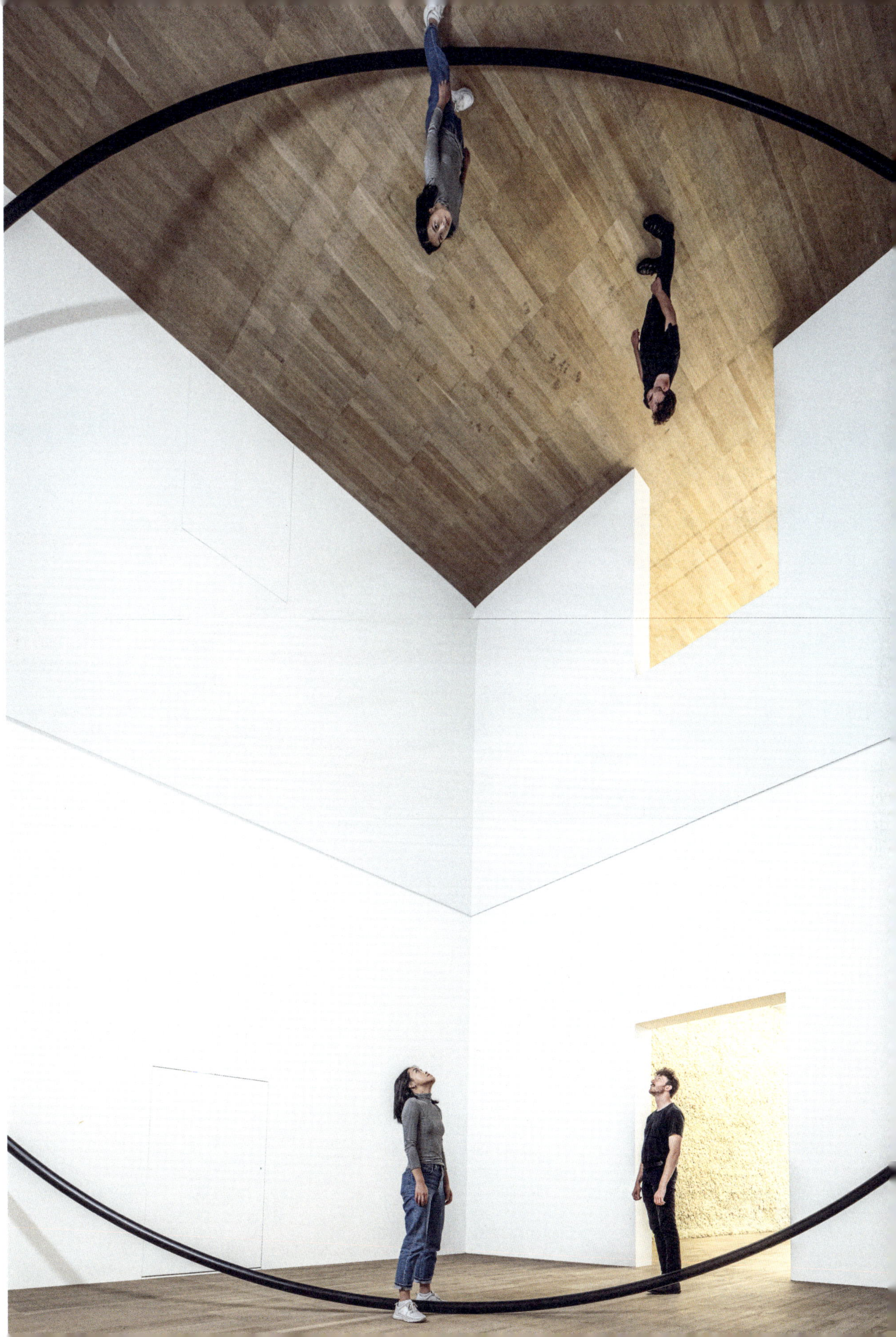

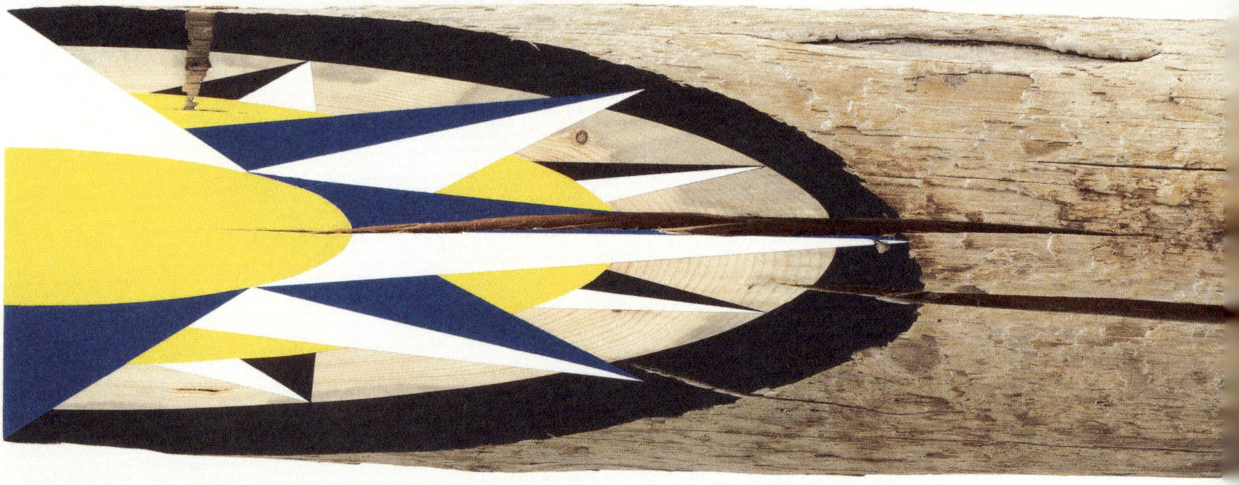

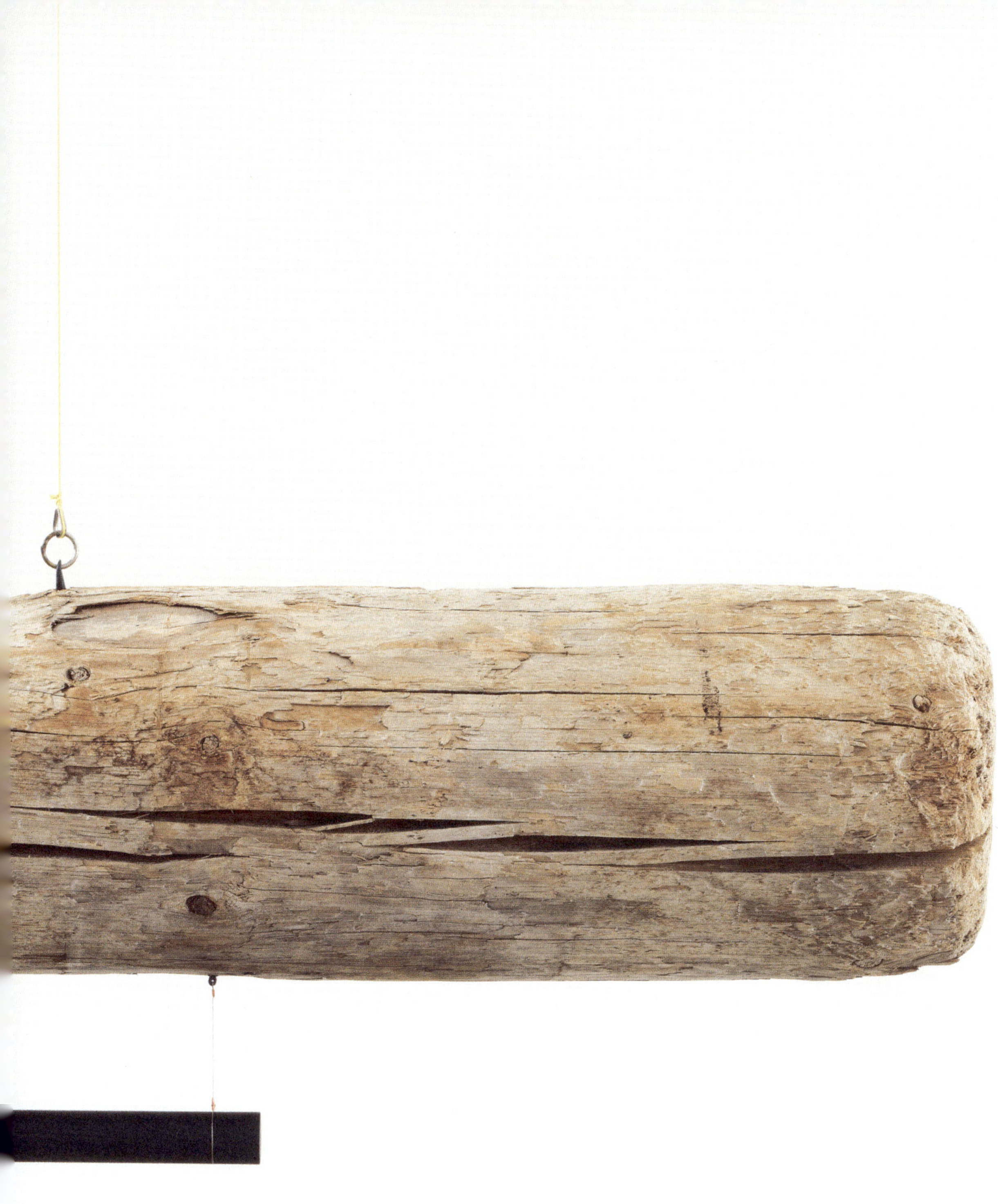

Olafur Eliasson: Zubaida, thank you so much for speaking with me. Since we first met, in Venice in 2017, during the *Green light - An artistic workshop* project, I've been thinking about the path you've travelled. You were born in Afghanistan.

What brought you to Italy in 2015?

Zubaida Tahiri: There were a lot of factors that contributed to my leaving Afghanistan – life there had become very difficult for me personally, and I no longer felt safe. I grew up as a refugee in Pakistan, so I knew that Pakistan and Iran, another neighbouring country, weren't good options. The United States was so far away, and Australia was difficult to reach, so, for me, the best was Europe. But I knew very little about Europe then, and even less about asylum procedures. Fortunately I received permission to stay in Italy for five years.

What route did you take to Italy?

Actually, I travelled by air. It was fairly simple: I flew from Kabul to Istanbul and from Turkey to Italy on another flight. I didn't come in the difficult way that so many people do.

I understand that you were attending university in Kabul; once you got to Italy were you able to continue studying?

In Kabul, I was studying Political Science and Public Administration at the American University of Afghanistan, with the support of a scholarship for Afghan women from the US Embassy. It took almost two and a half years from the time I left Afghanistan before I could enrol again. At the time it seemed like a big gap. Now I have a scholarship from the Italian government and I'm working towards my master's in Green Economy and Sustainability at the University of Ferrara.

GREEN INNOVATION

ZUBAIDA TAHIRI was born in Afghanistan and is currently working towards her master's degree in Green Economy and Sustainability at the University of Ferrara, Italy. Tahiri arrived in Italy from Afghanistan in 2015, after working in Kabul and studying finance, public administration and political science at the American University of Afghanistan. She met Eliasson at the Venice Biennale in 2017 where she participated in *Green light - An artistic workshop*, a project begun by Eliasson and Thyssen-Bornemisza Art Contemporary (TBA21) in Vienna in 2015. Tahiri contributed to *Green light* with, among other things, a personal blog post and an original short film about her experience as an asylum seeker in Italy. She worked as an intern for Eliasson's Little Sun solar lamp project in 2018 and 2019.

How did you come to join the *Green light* workshop while you were in Venice – and what was your experience as a participant in the project?

I was living in an apartment belonging to a project that provides support for refugees living in Venice. We heard that there was a project in the Biennale that we were invited to participate in. We knew that it would be in the Central Pavilion, which would give us a lot of opportunities to see the other artworks in the exhibition, and I was curious about the project itself as well, though we were only told that it was to do with the construction of a green lamp and I didn't know anything about you at the time – I'd never heard of you or about any of your artworks or projects. But I was living in that area, in Giardini, so I knew about the space, though I had never been inside.

What did you think of the group of people who came together? People were quite different, with different backgrounds.

The most interesting thing for me was to see a lot of people like me, who were in situations like mine – people from so many different countries, whose differences looked so beautiful there together. We all worked together and learned a lot of things together – language classes, film editing ... Another really positive and interesting thing was our interactions with the visitors who came and the students who were working with us. Many people would come and sit with us and ask about our countries and how we had ended up here and what we were doing in the Biennale. We had a lot of opportunities to share our own points of view with the people who came to the exhibition.

Was it easy to talk to people who came into the exhibition?

In the beginning it was so crowded. There were a lot of cameras, a lot of media, which wasn't so comfortable for some of us at first. But later it got much better, with the visitors who joined us, who worked together with us or just sat with us to talk. It still took some time to get used to it, but once we did, we enjoyed it. And it wasn't only about us sharing with them – they would tell us about how they had come to be there too.

I think this aspect of spending time together is interesting. Most visitors didn't know what to do either, especially at the beginning. 'Am I just supposed to look, or am I allowed to engage?' And you had to create a space where dialogue was actually possible.

Yes, some visitors were really surprised to find out that they could join us!

In a blog post you wrote about your experience with the project, you mentioned an open atmosphere, which allowed people to talk and understand each other. I'm actually very interested in this idea of atmosphere and the openness of an atmosphere; I think we tend to underestimate the degree of impact that the atmosphere of a place has on our feelings. With *Green light*, I was hoping that we could establish a generous atmosphere.

Right. And we were really given the feeling that it was our place, a space for us. It wasn't like 'We just come here to work.' It wasn't particularly structured. We had the freedom to choose what we'd do, and whenever I'd feel a little bit bored doing one thing, I'd switch to another station to work on something else. We were very free and comfortable with each other, and would have long conversations while we were working. There were many options available to us, like the film-making project that came later, and all the classes that were offered. So the resources the space offered and the way it was set up were very important.

That's actually great to hear because, when designing the space with my studio team, I wanted to encourage the feeling that you could navigate where to go, who to work with, when to study, when to teach. And for Christine Macel, who curated the Biennale, it was important to create a studio-like atmosphere. But we only really learned how it worked once the project was up and running, including the presence of visitors. Do you think this kind of openness, where you have both freedom and responsibility, could be transferred to other spaces?

I have been thinking about how these principles could be applied in communities that host refugees. When I lived in a camp in Sweden, the hundreds of people living there were so all aimless – we had nothing to do. Maybe projects could be undertaken in such camps that would give everybody an opportunity to be productive, to work. I think it would also help build relationships between the people in such camps to have this kind of shared project – it would make those environments more friendly and better for the people there.

I agree. There is a tendency, when we talk about integration, for it to mean that you integrate so-called strangers into a predetermined, fairly static environment. But I believe it's more about the quality of an encounter – of meeting up and exchanging knowledge – rather than one person having to be integrated into an unchanging situation, which is not at all productive and completely misses any potential for reciprocity. That's why I wanted to emphasise a space that allows for the meeting up of histories, identities and narratives.

Now that you're here in Berlin, you are working with us at Little Sun, my solar energy project. You've been studying green economy and sustainability, and of course Little Sun is very much about those subjects.

It's interesting to think about the impact of solar energy. Projects like Little Sun make visible how many people in the world, how many millions of people, don't have access to energy. Everybody has their own perspective on helping the planet – whether they are using recycled products or going vegan or even choosing not to have children – and I think Little Sun can make a great contribution to that. The most important thing for me is that we have the ability to help people who are in need. When we collaborate with each other and bring our resources together we can really benefit the world.

Is there anything you are particularly interested in working on at Little Sun during your time here?

Right now I'm doing research into the use of solar-powered lights in refugee camps, where they can increase the safety of women and girls, and I'm working with a colleague on a project to distribute lamps in Afghanistan. I've also done some calculations about the contribution Little Sun's lamps make towards reducing emissions – calculating the emissions that are reduced by each kerosene light that is replaced by a solar lamp. It's an opportunity for me to learn.

What do you hope to do when you finish your studies?

I would love to start working in my field right away – I really love research into green innovation, for instance. But most jobs need people who already have experience, and although I worked for four years in Afghanistan in finance and administration, the jobs I've had in my home country don't count for very much on my CV here. So I'll start at a very basic level, gain some experience and hope for a job in the future that's related to the green economy – ideally combining it with finance.

I'm curious whether you think it will be possible for Afghanistan to have a green economy in the future, when the situation improves.

Yes, definitely! Currently our GDP is very low, clean water is not available for everybody – we don't have access to even very basic necessities. The people in my country have so many worries in their lives about the political and economic situation and their basic safety that they don't have much space to think about things like sustainability.

As an individual, I am very concerned about climate change. We will all suffer. I have been giving a lot of thought to how, when peace returns to my country, consideration of climate issues can play an important role in determining how we restore our society and economy. And the younger generation are becoming more aware of and informed about climate issues. Recently I saw a report about a very small and quirky but inspiring thing. I was watching a video from a television station in Afghanistan about a man who'd designed a dustbin made from plastic bottles – he was collecting plastic bottles and using them to make dustbins that he put in different parts of the city. So it doesn't take millions of dollars to invest in a project; very small waste-reduction and recycling projects are important too.

November/December 2018

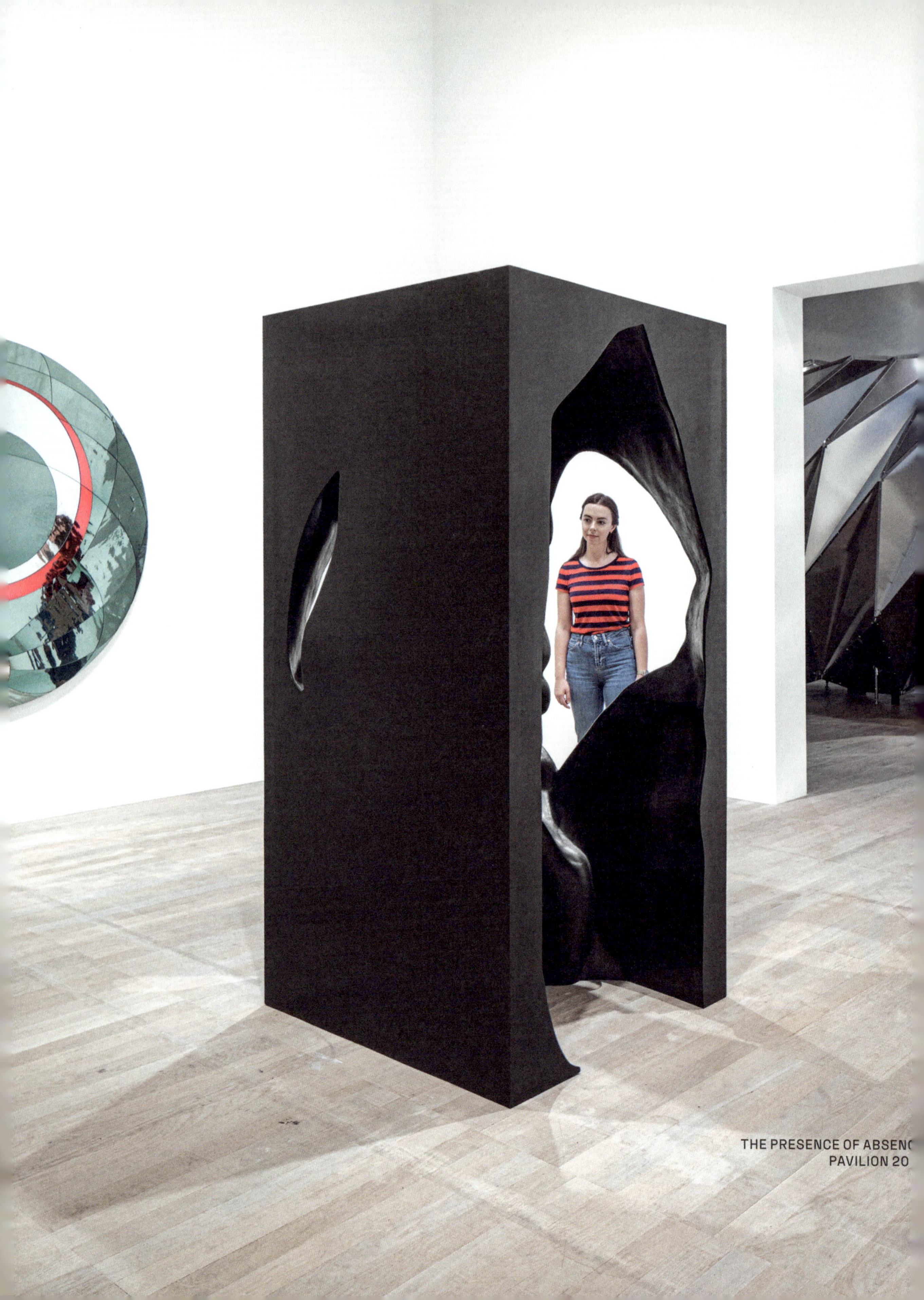

THE PRESENCE OF ABSENC
PAVILION 20

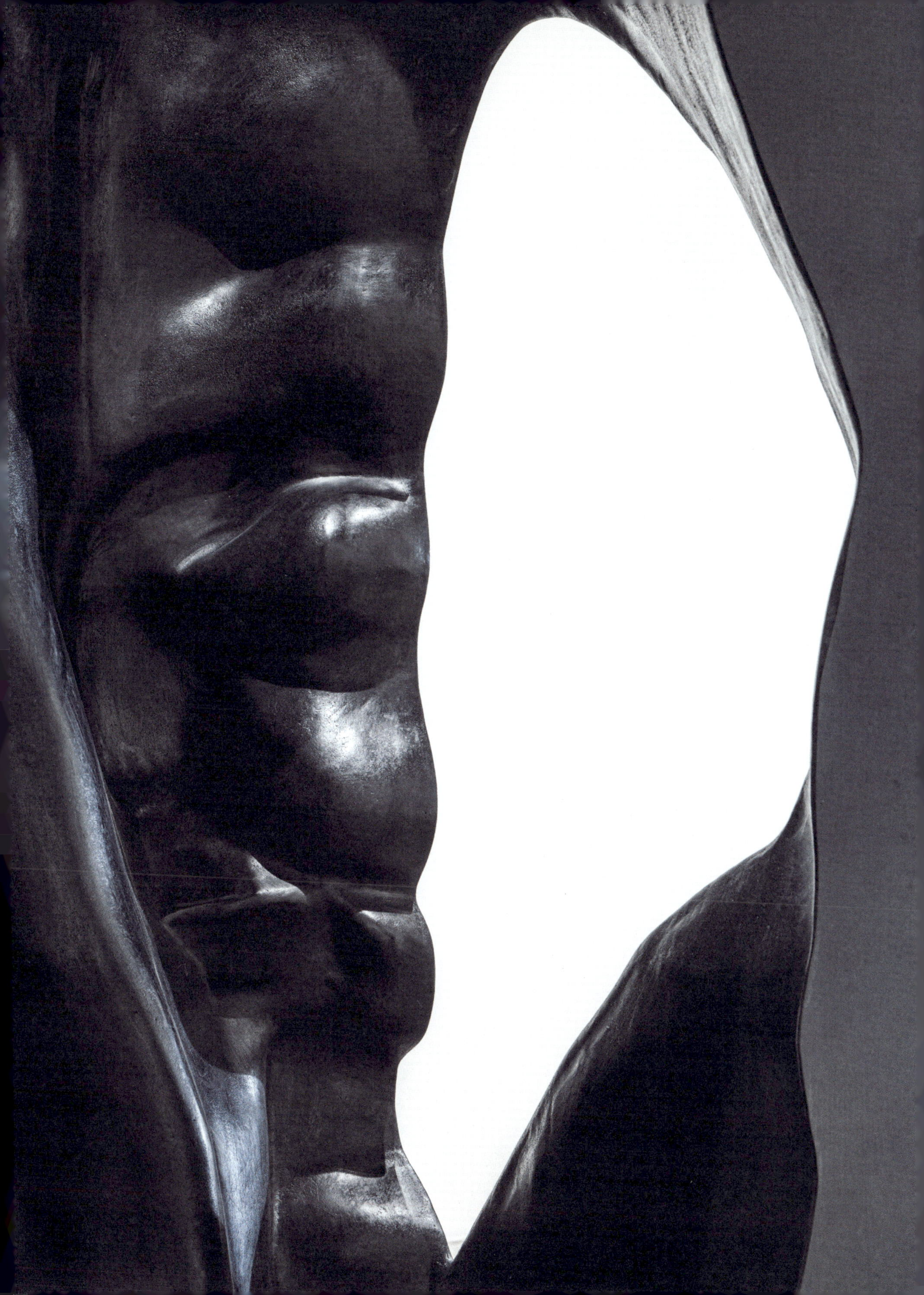

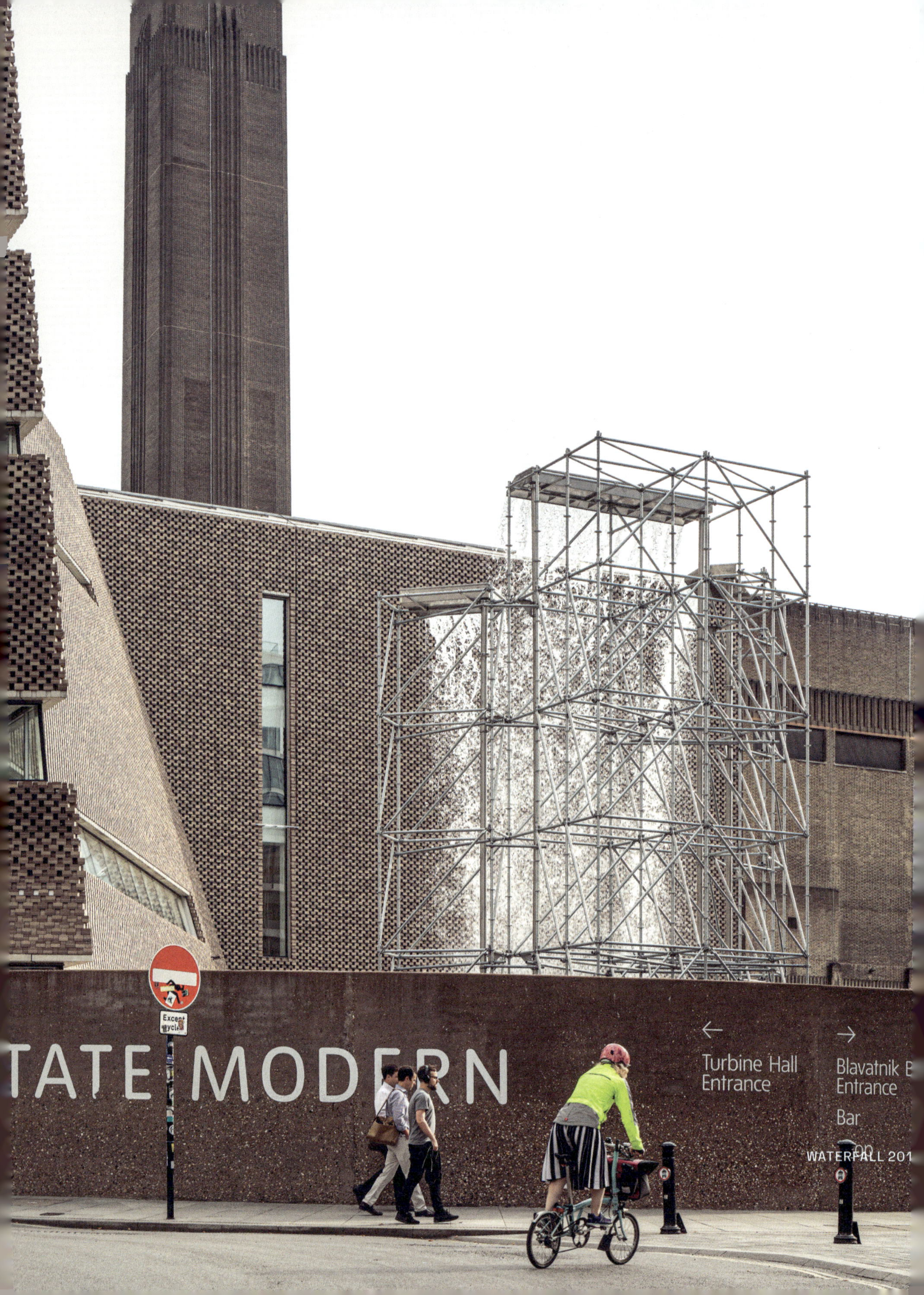

WATERFALL 201

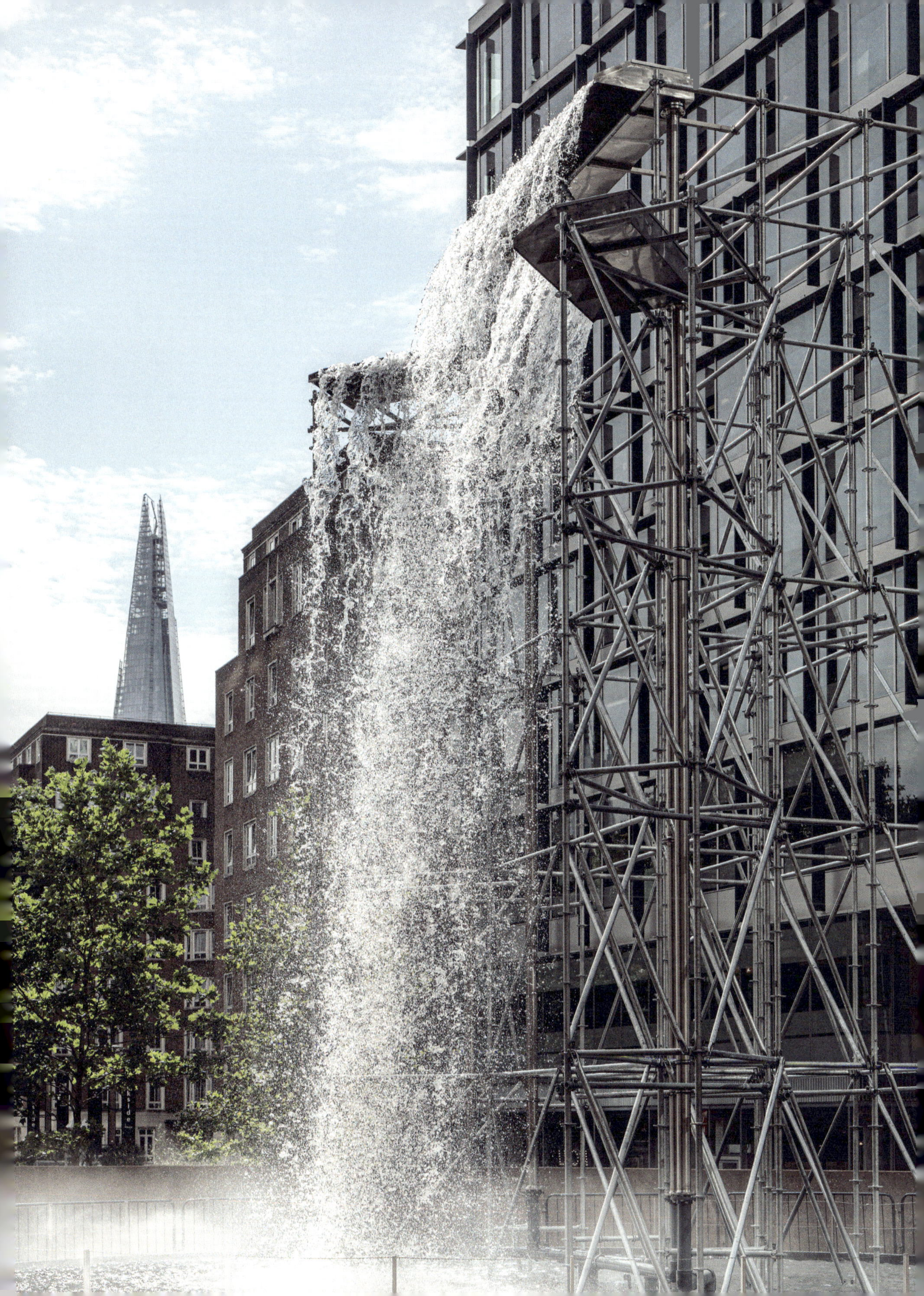

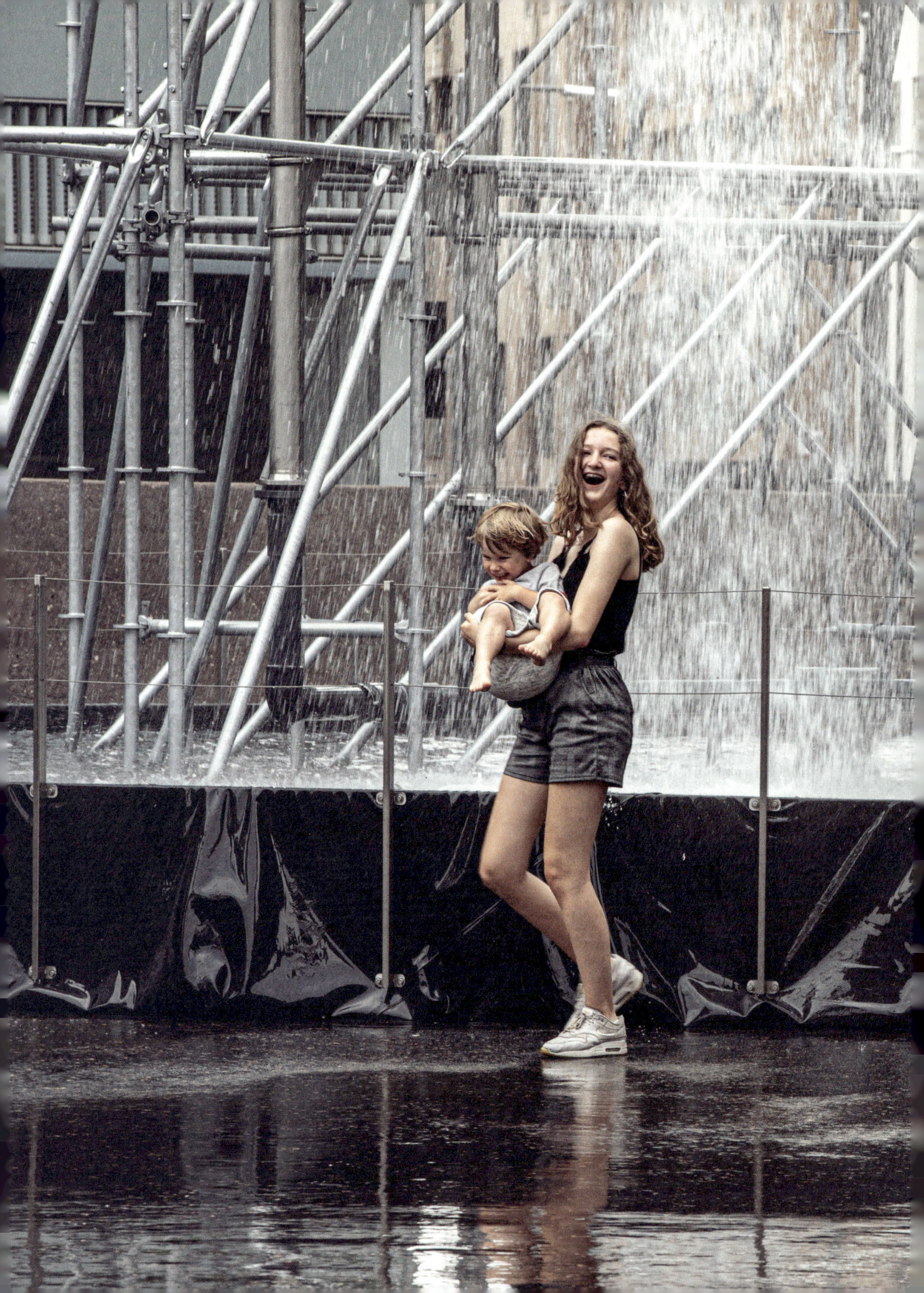

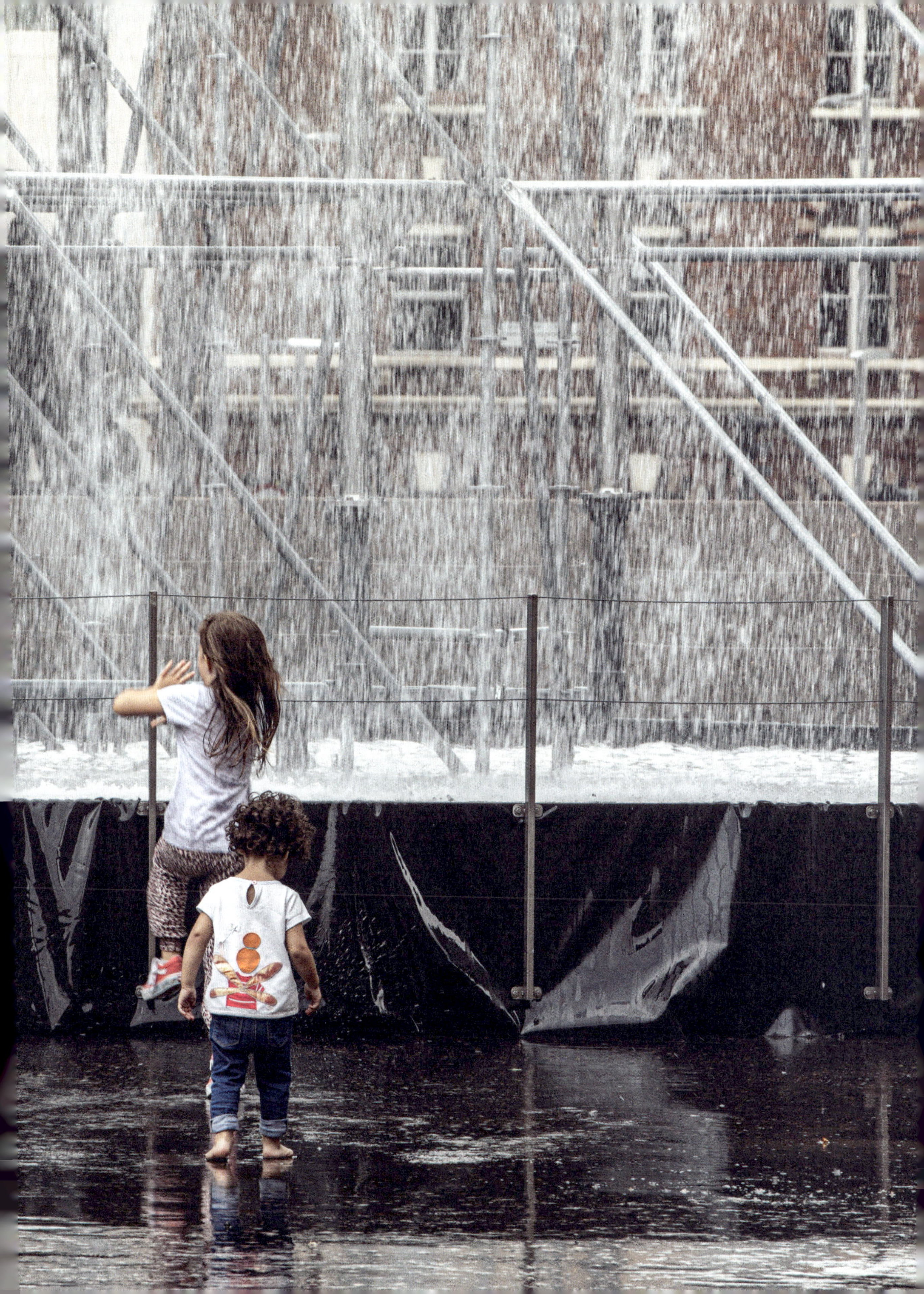

Olafur Eliasson: **Your many years at IKEA give you a unique insight into how the company operates in the world, and I hope you'll tell me more about that, but I'd love to start by talking about materials. On the table in front of us is what might look like crumbled cement or something . . .**

Marcus Engman: It looks like sand from the moon!

That's true, but it's actually called glacial rock flour. It's a dense mineral mud that's left behind when glaciers recede – essentially it's pulverised mountain. It turns out to be extremely nutritious for the earth, very enriching for the soil. In the last Ice Age, the glacial belt went across North America and Northern Europe, leaving this substance behind in pockets of unbelievably fertile earth, defining the affluence of this region. And now, as Greenland's glaciers recede due to climate change, my friend Minik Rosing, who discovered the beneficial effect of the mud, is looking into the possibility of distributing this rich mineral powder all around the globe to kick-start soil fertility. I've been incorporating it as a raw material into some of my works; it makes a lovely green-blue glass, for instance. I've also used the glacial ice itself.

That's interesting and surprising! How do you get into new materials? How do you research the materials themselves and test production techniques and so on?

I'm mostly interested in the agency the material communicates. In design, I'm interested in the extent to which the design of an object embodies a sense of agency. If it's a piece of wood, it can bring together what we see and what we *feel* about what we see. If, say, a particular material comes from an area that's full of conflict, that may influence how we experience it. Materials carry embedded psychosocial narratives. Here we are sitting at a granite table, but these particular granite slabs actually came from a Berlin sidewalk. So the table's surface was smoothed by feet, by the weather, by the whole life of the city; the stone has certain qualities as a physical material – it's a lovely granite – and at the same time, you can tell there's a story embedded in it. For me, it's interesting to address materials from the double perspective of what you might call their data and the narratives that emerge through experience.

CURIOSITY

MARCUS ENGMAN is a Swedish designer. From 2012 to 2018, he served as head of design at IKEA, where he oversaw the company's shift to a more collaborative and transparent way of working with design. During this time, he met Eliasson, with whom he found common ground on Eliasson's Little Sun project. Together they launched a collaboration, dubbed LS X IKEA, which will develop and distribute a number of new solar products. Shortly after this conversation, in October 2018, Engman left IKEA to form the creative collective Skewed Productions.

A lot of work in design is about material excursions, and this tension comes up from time to time. People talk about 'honesty towards materials' – if it's wood, it should look like wood and feel like wood, and so on. But sometimes we want to challenge that, to do something different that makes people react to the material. If you put veneer over metal, for example, you'll have something that is 1.5 mm thick but is as strong as a thick piece of solid wood, and that disturbs your perception of wood, which I think is interesting as well.

When people realise that this is a thin layer of wood applied on metal, their next question may be, 'Is the company behind this trying to trick me?' Or do they understand that this is probably the best use of wood because it uses much less wood to make something much stronger?

I think the latter. To me that's the obvious choice. One thing I'm interested in is the work you've been doing at [social energy business] Little Sun to empower small businesses. It's the right kind of thinking, but it's really ambitious. I've worked in retail all my life, and I know how hard it is! To build that on the other side of the world is super-complicated, and I'm very intrigued by how you do it.

I freely admit how naïve I was to think I could solve the issue of 'last-mile retail' [the need to deliver product the 'last mile', from centralised hubs to individual consumers] in one stroke with one product! Still, we haven't given up.

Being a little bit naïve is a good starting point for changing anything.

Developing Little Sun reminded me of being a young artist, when I had to do everything myself. I was out there on my own, knocking on doors, talking to people who were not necessarily interested in talking to me. When I knock on doors as an artist I'm usually welcomed, so it was very instructive to find myself back in the position of starting from scratch.

We've talked about how large areas of the world still lack access to energy, and about how Little Sun is so good at forging an emotional connection. That's something you've always been good at. It's not just a functional product. And it's not just the connection between energy and education that Little Sun highlights by enabling children to study at night. I remember when we discussed the ways people would use energy: light was first, but second was music, which made me glad. Energy is actually about life, and for me that's what music represents.

That aspect of the conversation also made me think in a different way. Historically, IKEA is a hugely function-oriented company. We connect to people by solving their problems – by asking 'What are the functional needs here?' We do home visits. That's something I loved about you; you weren't just looking at another part of the world to solve its problems. You actually went there, spoke to people – you did home visits as well!

Well, I'd spent a lot of time in East Africa and Ethiopia and know the huge impact that access to energy has on people's livelihood and well-being.

That's taking the home visits to the next level. When we actually live with people instead of just asking them questions, we can see their emotional needs. After that, you go about your design and communicating what you do – and why – in a completely different way. The discussions we had with you early on opened up my mind for that larger scale. The way you work, as I understand it anyway, is by putting a lot of effort into the narrative of things, so you get that connection. Few designers are so skilled at that, and it's not a topic you talk that much about, but it's such an important thing if you want to change behaviours, not just adapt to them!

I believe it's fair to say you represented that kind of change at IKEA, taking the company in a more emotionally driven direction. Rather than just adapting to behaviour, your team has actually been pushing a change of behaviour, especially when it comes to sustainability and the environment. You've also said that IKEA is reaching more out to other kinds of creators ...

Yes, to musicians, fashion designers, and other people who are not so much in our niche. You know, the topic of the home doesn't come up as factor number one when we ask people to name what they think most contributes to a better life. What comes up are things like travel, music, art, fashion. And those of us who do believe – firmly – in the importance of the home need to be curious about those factors, too. We have been inviting other creatives in so we can learn from them. For instance, the fashion industry is really good at constantly reinventing itself to make things important every season. The music industry has changed itself completely in the last ten years; it was going down the drain and has now come up with a completely new way to collaborate on and produce music, so I wanted to see what we could learn and bring into design from that.

Do you think that furniture retail and design – and the whole machinery behind it, from sourcing to customer relations – will go through similar changes?

Absolutely. How we produce things will change a lot. The biggest cost for a product these days is not raw material but logistics. Soon it won't be efficient to produce where the raw materials are. It may be more efficient to produce closer to where you're going to sell the goods. That would be a better value chain. Another thing is that we aren't very good yet at production-on-demand on a bigger scale. That's still maybe ten years off, but it will change the game totally. I'm not predicting the death of mass production – things like components are still well-suited to mass-production. So it's a mix.

You're describing on a macroscopic, global scale the very thing that Little Sun is going through on a microscopic scale. Obviously, we'd love to simply source and produce and sell Little Sun locally and not have to ship it around the world. That would be most sustainable. But the components, which come from companies in different countries, are not available everywhere. We haven't cracked that yet. The past year of working with you has taught me a lot about the science that goes into sourcing, and about a value chain that also includes elements of sustainability, without ignoring the fact that we are very interested in affordability.

I was struck by an idea you presented about sourcing and producing completely locally using open-source design, with no intellectual property, so that if the local chair-maker were able to produce the chair better or more cheaply – and maybe more beautifully, say, in a better colour – they could do that, which would give you a healthy sense of competition.

I myself believe firmly in the open-source approach. It changes things. I think it's a way forward for design. Looking at it from an IKEA perspective, if a competitor comes up with a similar product that costs less, the only thing that says is that we haven't done our work right. It shouldn't be possible to do it for less. It shouldn't be scary to work with open-source just because someone might steal your ideas. You have to be good enough to do it at that scale and always be the best.

I'm intrigued by this idea of open-source. It is part of the times, but how do you see it connecting to intellectual property? How will it pan out? As an artist, I'm very conscious that if somebody copies one of my artworks and sells it a lower price, I have a legal backup system to protect me. I really like the democratic notion of open-source, but where is the threshold in terms of intellectual property? Would you 'retrofit' open-source legislation onto everything? Could you just start producing Eames chairs?

I don't think you can retrofit it, but it's different if you do something completely new. It has to do with why you design and produce stuff. If you really want to change things, then you want it to touch as many people as possible, because that makes a bigger change. For me it's about reach. But I'm conflicted about this myself. Having worked creatively all my life, I really can't understand why you'd make great design ideas available to only a few people.

In my case, I make a work of art that somebody buys. There is only one work. They might take it home, or, if I'm lucky, they'll bring it to a museum and more people have access to it. I can also prioritise working more in public space and less in private space, or I can direct my studio more towards architecture and projects that are publicly accessible.

Don't you want your work – or the idea of your work, even when you do a single piece for someone – to encounter as many people as possible? Or do you want to reach individuals?

It's not either/or. Sometimes the work is in a highly intimate relationship with one person; I can achieve things that would be difficult within a more complex group dynamic. But I'm also very interested in collective experience. I'm very interested in public space, in the felt feeling of sharing, in the idea of trust – civic trust and 'we-ness'. IKEA interests me because it is so big that there is a civic component to what it does, and your design agenda relates to social issues. I'm a big believer in social cohesion and trust-driven systems, and so naturally I want to know who is shaping our civic systems. It makes a big difference whether everything is presented in a monolithic way or whether, instead, it's communal agendas that facilitate our seeing each other, getting together, sitting across from each other, sharing with each other.

At IKEA you're going through a robust transformation – changing strategies, adapting to the new world. I would say the cultural sector is undergoing something similar. IKEA is now collaborating with the cultural sector, too, and some of the designers you've worked with lately, like Walter Van Beirendonck, are kind of radical! Am I correct in thinking that you are harvesting trust from the culture sector?

I've never looked at it like that. It would be sad if people thought we were just trying to harvest their trust or doing something like co-branding. It's not about that at all. IKEA is the market leader in what we do, all over the world, and my view is that, if you are the market leader, you should lead the market. That means making excursions into the unknown. It's an approach based on curiosity.

I've tried to encourage craftsmanship – the actual skill of making things – at IKEA. A big change I've seen over the last few years is that some of the once-great design agencies have totally lost their sense of craft. They've turned into something more like management consultants that sell design-thinking. My idea has been to actually bring in creatives and put them together with our internal designers and other specialists to make something new. We have done an amazingly diverse range of stuff that way, including excursions into completely new materials and production techniques – even into realms like gaming, for instance, or working with you on our Little Sun project. To me, that's just taking responsibility as a leader.

Being a cultural-sector person I'm interested in how I can offer something that has an impact on how we live on this planet and how we behave towards each other. I believe that, through IKEA, I am able to reach people in a different way and probably have an impact on a much larger group of people than I could by working only in the cultural sector.

For me it's not just about who you could reach through IKEA. It's more about what we wouldn't be able to do if we didn't do it together. This coalition of brains is the main thing when you collaborate with someone – you want to have some kind of friction, a good friction between people. So the question is: what is it that is not apparent in Little Sun on its own or in IKEA on its own, but could spark something interesting if we put them together? That's what I'm looking forward to seeing emerge from our collaboration.

September 2018

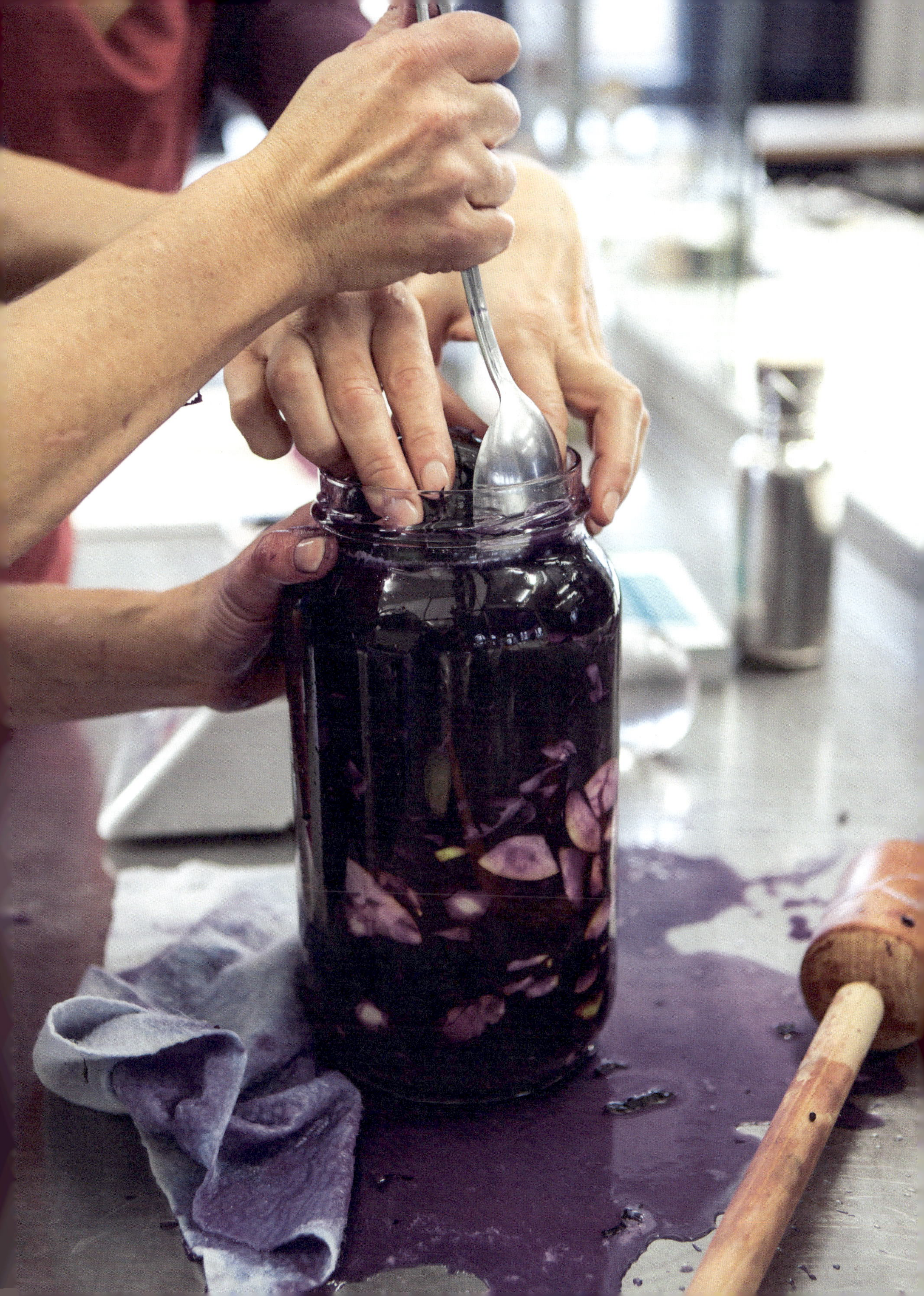

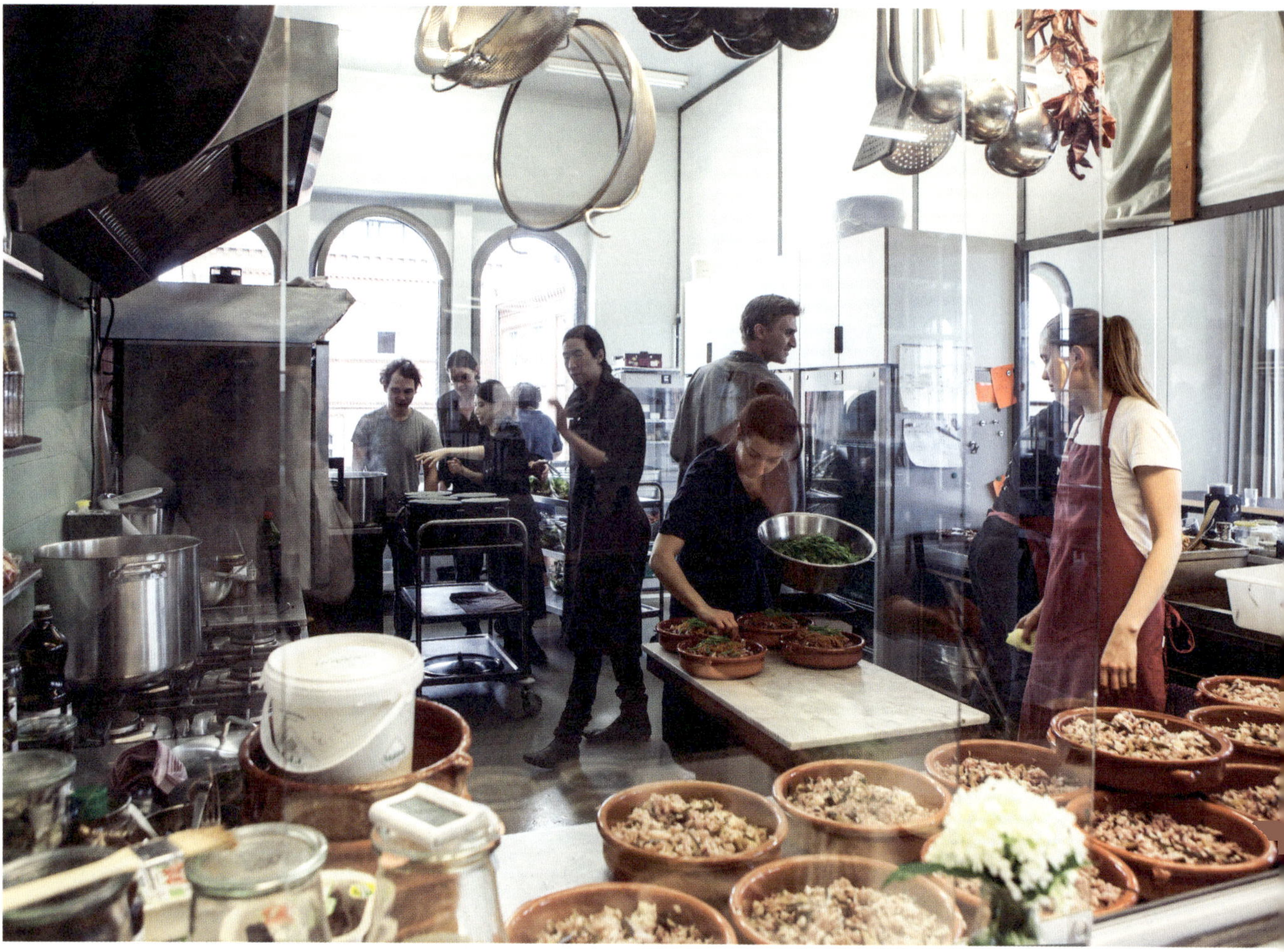

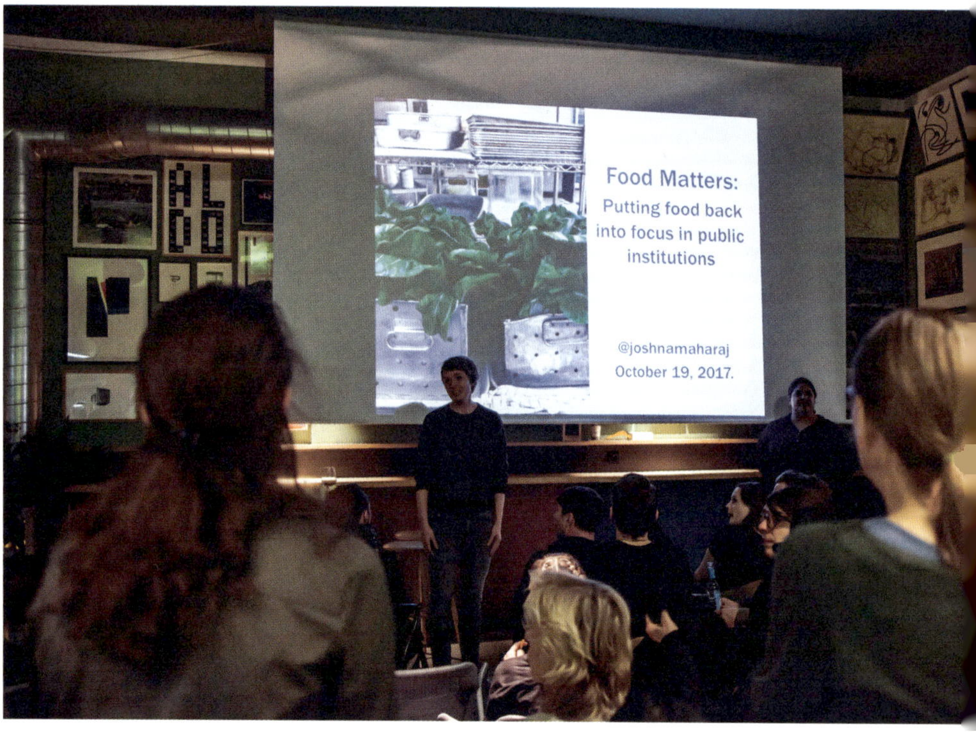
Food Matters:
Putting food back into focus in public institutions
@joshnamaharaj
October 19, 2017.

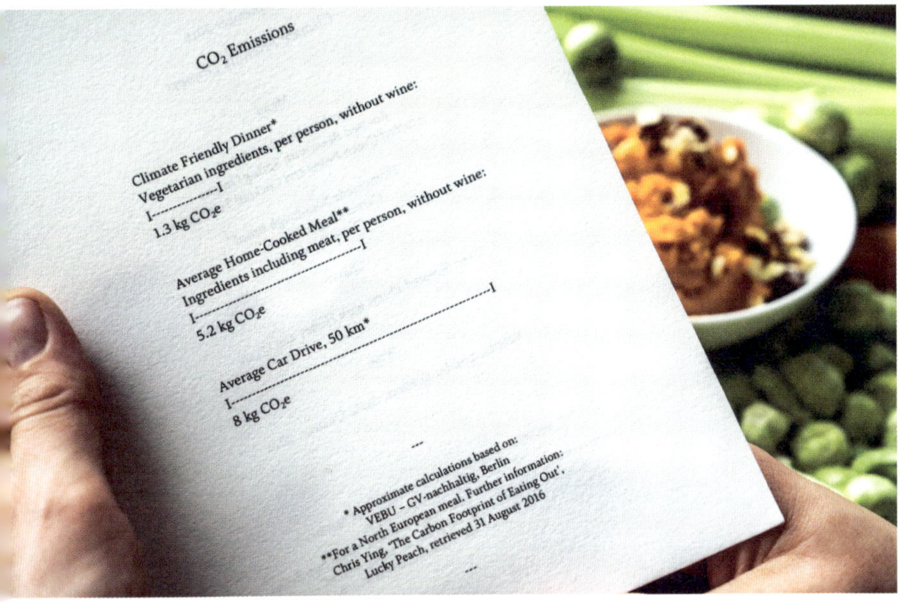

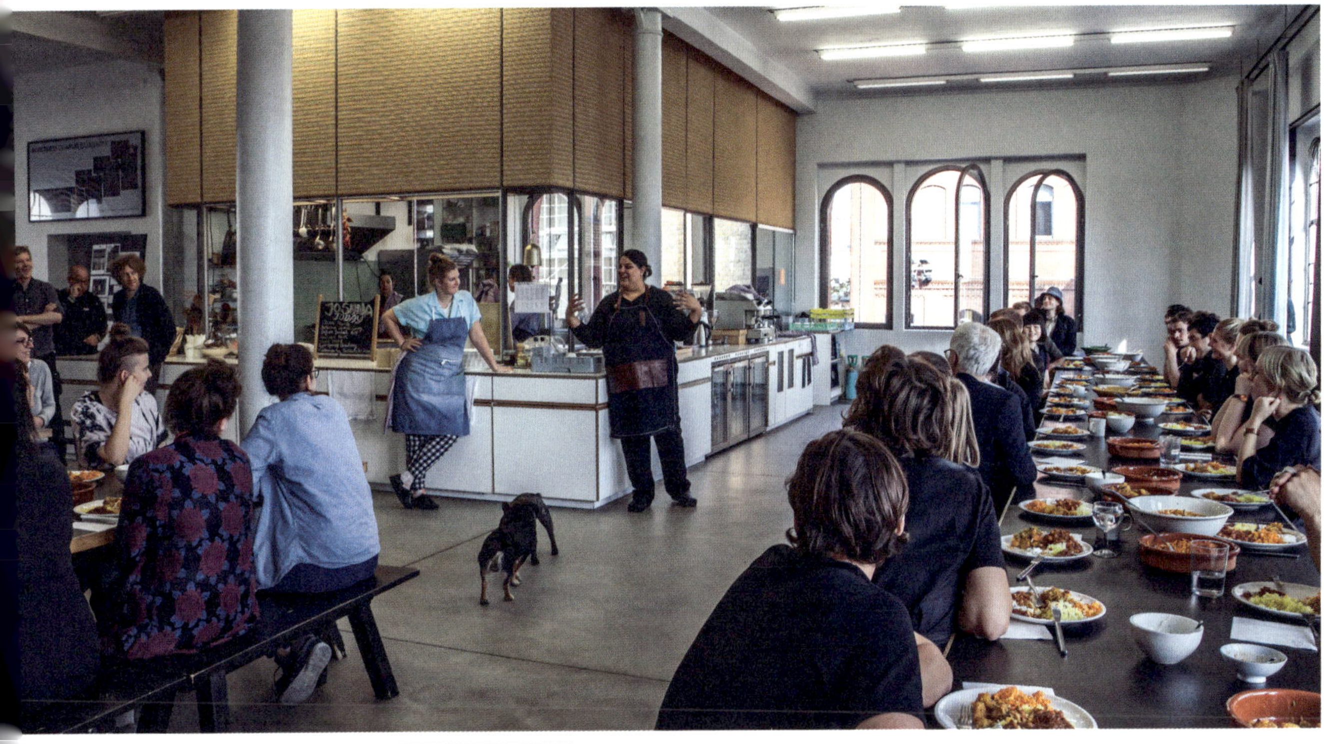

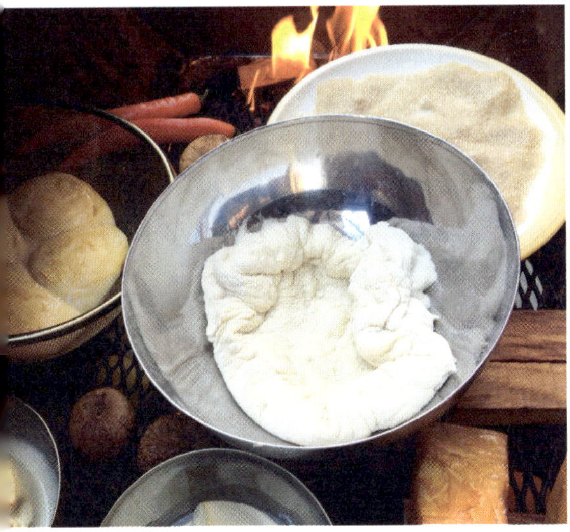

SOE KITCHEN The kitchen at Studio Olafur Eliasson was established in 2005 to provide family-style lunches for the studio team. Driven by the interests of the cooks, the kitchen has developed into a space for eating and thinking, food experimentation, and exploration of climate-conscious cooking. The kitchen frequently collaborates with artists, food activists and chefs. In 2018 the kitchen team spent three months in Reykjavik for SOE Kitchen 101, a project led by Eliasson's sister Victoria Eliasdottir and hosted by the Marshall Restaurant, where they served a locally-sourced menu and ran a programme of events.

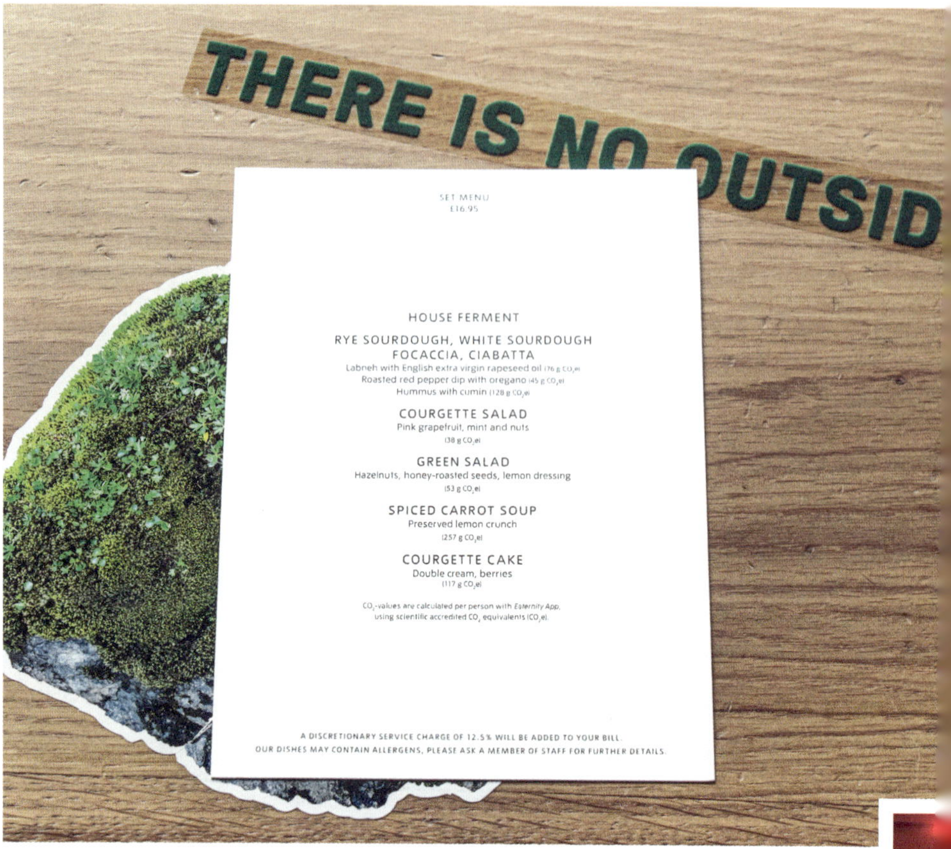
THERE IS NO OUTSID
SET MENU
£16.95
HOUSE FERMENT
RYE SOURDOUGH, WHITE SOURDOUGH
FOCACCIA, CIABATTA
Labneh with English extra virgin rapeseed oil (76 g CO_2e)
Roasted red pepper dip with oregano (45 g CO_2e)
Hummus with cumin (128 g CO_2e)
COURGETTE SALAD
Pink grapefruit, mint and nuts
(38 g CO_2e)
GREEN SALAD
Hazelnuts, honey-roasted seeds, lemon dressing
(53 g CO_2e)
SPICED CARROT SOUP
Preserved lemon crunch
(257 g CO_2e)
COURGETTE CAKE
Double cream, berries
(117 g CO_2e)
CO_2-values are calculated per person with *Eaternity App*, using scientific accredited CO_2 equivalents (CO_2e).
A DISCRETIONARY SERVICE CHARGE OF 12.5% WILL BE ADDED TO YOUR BILL.
OUR DISHES MAY CONTAIN ALLERGENS, PLEASE ASK A MEMBER OF STAFF FOR FURTHER DETAILS.

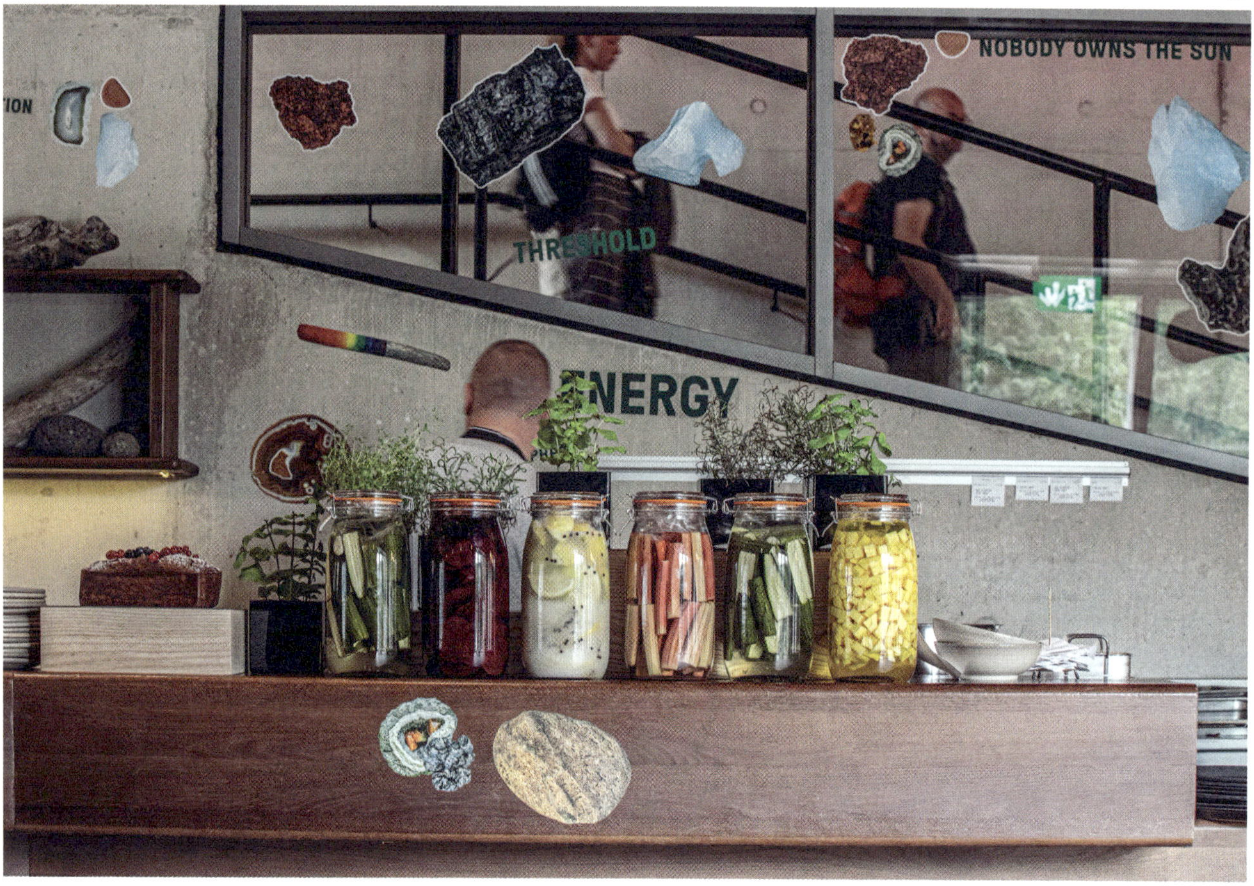
NOBODY OWNS THE SUN
THRESHOLD
ENERGY

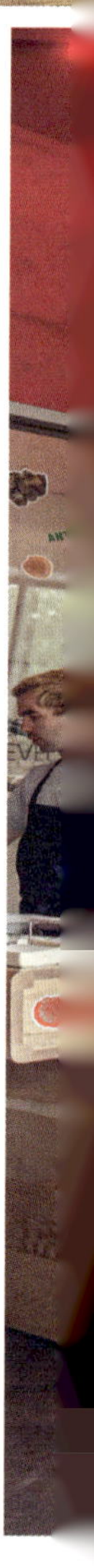

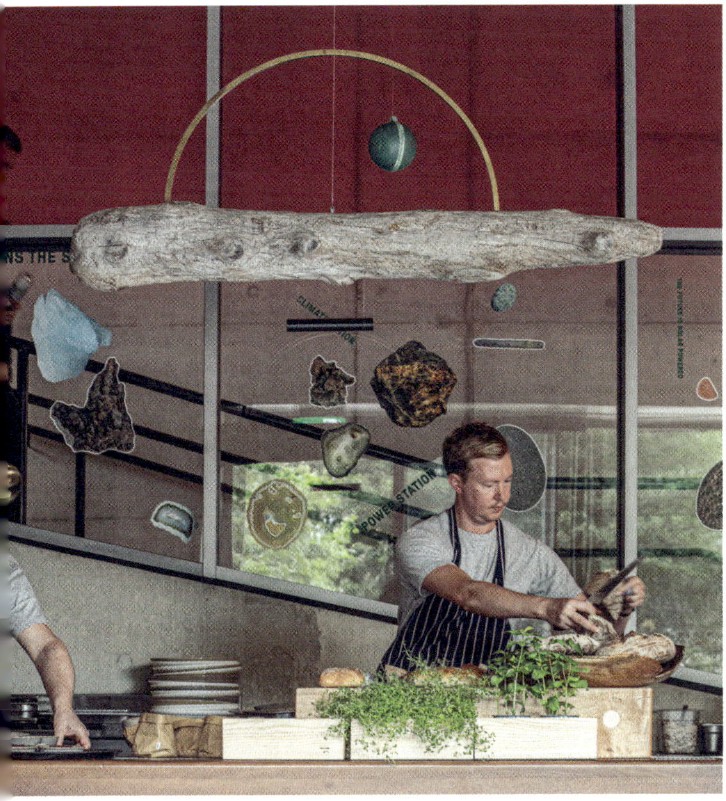

TERRACE BAR X SOE KITCHEN On the occasion of *Olafur Eliasson: In real life,* Tate Eats collaborated with Eliasson's team to turn the Terrace Bar in the Blavatnik Building at Tate Modern into an offshoot of the SOE Kitchen. The space was transformed with pink gels on the internal windows and stickers Eliasson designed for Rimowa; long tables encouraged visitors to eat together. *Shore compasses* 2018, made with driftwood and other materials found on Icelandic beaches, were hung from the ceiling together with examples of *OE Quasi light* 2019, designed by Eliasson for Louis Poulsen. The menu, based on the dishes served in the studio in Berlin, comprised breads, dips, soups, salads and cakes. A carbon footprint was provided for each dish, and a series of programmes was organised around issues including food, cooking and climate.

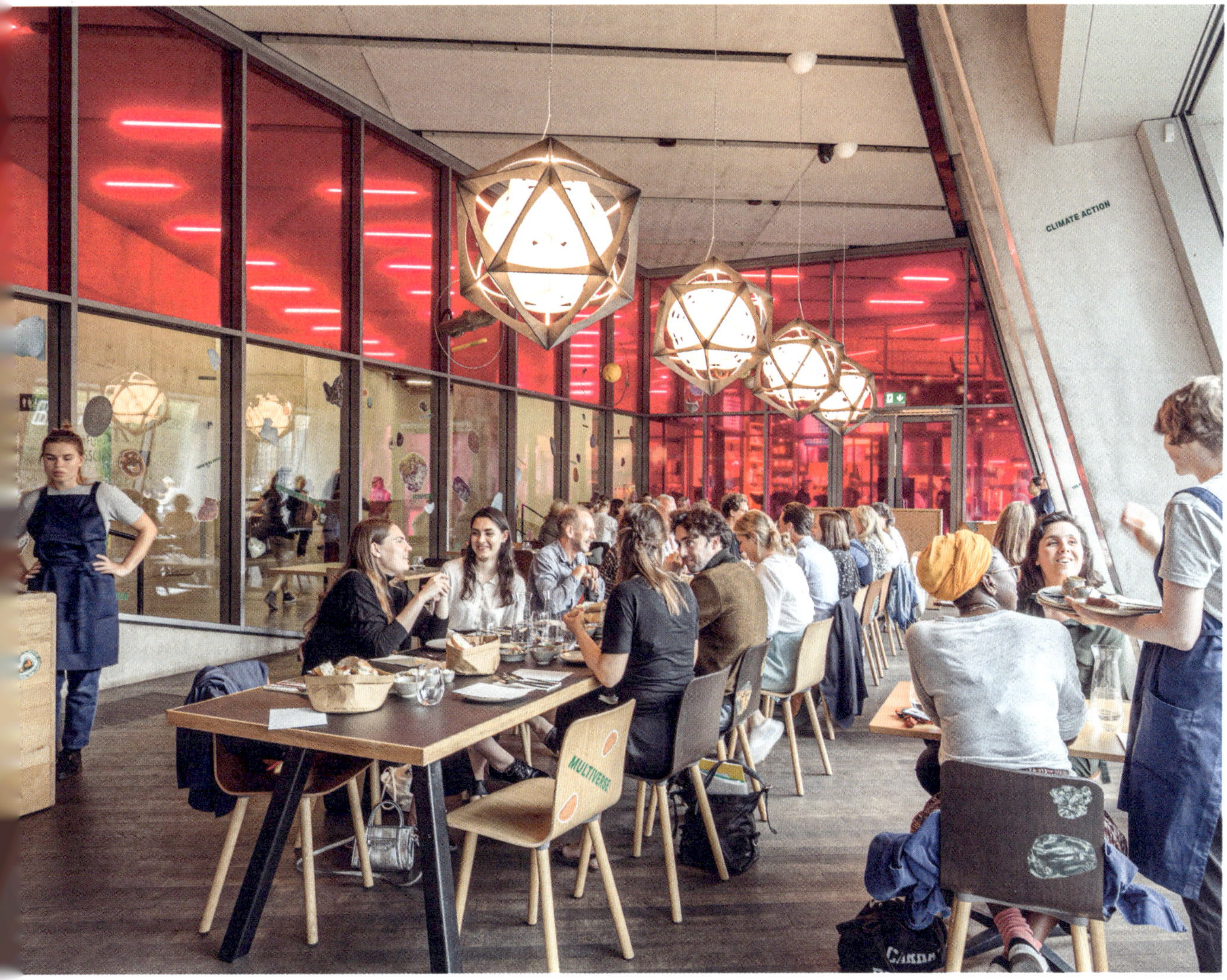

NOTES

1 'Olafur Eliasson in Conversation with Daniel Birnbaum' in *Olafur Eliasson: Reality machines*, exh. cat., Moderna Museet, Stockholm 2015, unpag. **2** Conversation with the author, Berlin, December 2018. **3** 'In Conversation: Daniel Buren and Olafur Eliasson', *Artforum*, May 2005, p.212. **4** Eliasson's title was based on his idea that the installation, as well as the viewer, had agency, and that the 'garden' could look back on the viewer as they passed through the space. **5** http://olafureliasson.net/archive/artwork/WEK101537/5-dimensionel-pavillon. A recent work using this form is *Map for unthought thoughts* 2014, where a powerful light is installed in the centre of two half-rings based on this lattice, creating shadows on the walls beyond; viewers pass between the rings and walls to contribute to the shadow play. **6** One of the first times Eliasson used this phrase was in the interview for his show in Dundee in 1999. See Marianne Krogh Jensen and Olafur Eliasson, 'What we have in common is that we are different' in Katrina Brown and Olafur Eliasson (eds.), *Your position surrounded and your surroundings positioned*, exh. cat., Dundee Contemporary Arts 1999, p.18. **7** Eliasson took this phrase from Yvonne Rainer's autobiography *Feelings are Facts: A Life*, published in 2006. **8** Hal Foster, 'Six Paragraphs on Dan Flavin', *Artforum*, Feb. 2005, p.161. See also James Meyer, 'No More Scale: The Experience of Size in Contemporary Sculpture', *Artforum*, Summer 2004, p.223. Meyer writes: 'We lie down – and lose ourselves, become part of, indeed *become*, the spectacle before us. *The weather project* delivers a mass audience that cannot fail to be overwhelmed by the magnitude of the installation itself. The museum is not so much "revealed" as transformed into a destination, an event.' **9** Hal Foster, 'Dan Flavin and the Catastrophe of Minimalism' in Jeffrey Weiss (ed.), *Dan Flavin: New Light*, New Haven 2006, p.146. **10** Hal Foster, 'The Spectacularization of Art' in Hal Foster, Rosalind E. Krauss, Yve-Alain Bois, Benjamin H.D. Buchloh and David Joselit, *Art Since 1900*, London 2004, p.656. These debates were the subject of the conference 'Rethinking Spectacle' organised by Claire Bishop and myself at Tate Modern in 2007. **11** Madeleine Grynsztejn, '(Y)our Entanglements: Olafur Eliasson, The Museum, and Consumer Culture' in *Take Your Time: Olafur Eliasson*, exh. cat., San Francisco Museum of Modern Art 2007, p.22. **12** Ibid., p.14. **13** Ibid., p.21. **14** Ibid., p.23 **15** Ibid. **16** Olafur Eliasson, 'The Experience Machine – The Artist Interviews Himself 1995/2015' in Christiane Maria Schneider and Christian Boros (eds.), *Olafur Eliasson: Boros Collection*, exh. cat., Boros Collection, Berlin 2015, p.57. **17** 'I think it is possible to initiate a dialogue with politicians using the language of art ... Sometimes working in museums is maybe good for the art career, but I am also slowly realising that it carried with it an element of disconnection. Sometimes I think it's better for me to be at a business forum, although I know the moment I get there, my language has problems, and if I say I am an artist, they are just not going to listen to me. So I have to find out how to speak and show them my work and give them my work, so that they think, oh, I can use that in what I am doing. I want to work against marginalisation.' Olafur Eliasson, 'Lecture One' (2012), in *Turning Thinking into Doing into Art: Four Lectures in Addis Ababa*, Berlin 2015, p.23. **18** Quoted by Richard Benson in 'Olafur Eliasson: Art will change the world', *Wired*, 30 Sept. 2019. https://www.wired.co.uk/article/olafur-eliasson-creative-manifesto **19** Hans Ulrich Obrist, *Hans Ulrich Obrist / Olafur Eliasson: The Conversation Series*, Cologne 2008, p.86. **20** Addressing the work he made for the Munich shopping centre, Eliasson wrote 'Beneath *Sphere*, consumption rules. But if you lean back, look up and out, you leave the consumer horizon; a greater perspective emerges.' Eliasson in *Studio Olafur Eliasson: Unspoken Spaces*, London 2016, p.200. **21** Obrist 2008, p.86. **22** Eliasson quoted by Rob Alderson in 'It's OK to Disagree: The Divisive Work of Artist Olafur Eliasson', *Printed Pages*, Autumn 2014. https://www.itsnicethat.com/features/its-ok-to-disagree-the-divisive-work-of-artist-olafur-eliasson **23** Chantal Mouffe, 'What Could Be Agonistic Art?', talk given in Eliasson's studio as part of the Institut für Raumexperimente, 24 June 2010. See also her book *Agonistics: Thinking the World Politically*, London 2013. **24** Olafur Eliasson, 'But Doesn't the Body Matter' in Daniel Birnbaum and Michelle Kuo (eds.), *More than Real: Art in the Digital Age: 2018 Verbier Summit*, London 2018, p.160. **25** Quoted in Alderson 2014. https://www.itsnicethat.com/features/its-ok-to-disagree-the-divisive-work-of-artist-olafur-eliasson **26** https://littlesun.com/wp/wp-content/uploads/2016/03/LS_Facts_and_FAQs.pdf **27** 'It is my hope that *Green light* will shine light on some of the challenges and responsibilities arising from the current refugee crisis in Europe and throughout the world. *Green light* is an act of welcoming, addressed both to those who have fled hardship and instability in their home countries and to the residents of Vienna.' Olafur Eliasson quoted in https://www.tba21.org/#item--greenlight_workshop--1226 **28** Moses's project involves recycling agricultural waste material into fuel briquettes; these are then sold in small enterprises usually run by women. For more on such projects, see Alice Rawsthorn, *Design as an Attitude*, Zürich 2018. **29** https://littlesun.com/wp/wp-content/uploads/2016/03/LS_Facts_and_FAQs.pdf **30** Jackie Wullschlager, 'Venice Biennale Round-up: A Rainbow Thread of Optimism', *Financial Times*, 12 May 2017. https://www.ft.com/content/2f810520-3584-11e7-bce4-9023f8c0fd2e **31** Cristina Ruiz, 'The Road to the Venice Biennale is paved with good intentions', *Art Newspaper*, 16 May 2017. https://www.theartnewspaper.com/review/the-road-to-the-venice-biennale-is-paved-with-good-intentions **32** Javier Pes, 'Creative workshop is just the job for Venice Biennale', *Art Newspaper*, 20 June 2017. https://www.theartnewspaper.com/comment/creative-workshop-is-just-the-job-for-venice-biennale **33** Renzo Martens's views on art serve as a useful contrast to Eliasson's. 'The question really is what we want art to do. Is it to offer little exceptions to the status quo? Can it suffice to show our morals, to undo wrongs or depict them in morally right ways? In my mind, depicting immorality, racism, exploitation, as if they were phenomena outside of our lives, as if they existed only on the other side of our lenses, relieves us, but it also relieves such a depiction of any claim on reality. I think that if art limits itself to the morally acceptable, it conveniently obscures the production processes that pay for our lifestyles.' Renzo Martens in T.J. Demos, 'Towards a New Institutional Critique: A Conversation with Renzo Martens', *Atlántica*, no.52, Feb. 2012. **34** As *LA Times* critic Christopher Knight noted, the colours of Eliasson's 'film' contrasted with those we see on screens and in cinemas, which are now digital and made of tiny pixels. Here the light here was analogue and 'pure'. Christopher Knight, 'Artist Olafur Eliasson built a *Reality projector* of smashing beauty', *LA Times*, 2 March 2018. **35** *Reality Projector* also evokes early experimental film such as Hans Richter's *Rhythmus 21* 1921, and the 'expanded cinema' of the 1970s, especially Anthony McCall's 1974 *Long Film for Ambient Light* where, without using a projector or celluloid, McCall turned a room into a 'film' that involved the changing light conditions created by a single bulb and the windows of the space as daylight changed to night. Like those two precursors, Eliasson's work opposes the commercialisation of cinema.

BIOGRAPHY

Olafur Eliasson was born in 1967. He grew up in Iceland and Denmark and studied from 1989 to 1995 at the Royal Danish Academy of Fine Arts. In 1995, he moved to Berlin and founded Studio Olafur Eliasson, which today comprises more than one hundred team members, including craftsmen, architects, archivists, researchers, administrators, cooks, programmers, art historians and specialised technicians.

Since the mid-1990s Eliasson has realised numerous major exhibitions and projects around the world. In 2003 Eliasson represented Denmark at the 50th Venice Biennale, with *The blind pavilion.* Later that year, he installed *The weather project* in Tate Modern's Turbine Hall, London. *Take your time: Olafur Eliasson,* a survey exhibition organised by SFMOMA in 2007, travelled until 2010 to various venues, including the Museum of Modern Art, New York. *Innen Stadt Aussen* (Inner City Out), at Martin-Gropius-Bau in 2010, involved interventions across Berlin as well as in the museum. Similarly, in 2011, *Seu corpo da obra* (Your body of work) engaged with three institutions around São Paulo – SESC Pompeia, SESC Belenzinho, and Pinacoteca do Estado de São Paulo – and spread out into the city itself. In 2014 *Riverbed* filled an entire wing of Denmark's Louisiana Museum of Modern Art with stones and water, emulating a river in a rocky landscape; later that year, *Contact* formed the inaugural exhibition at Fondation Louis Vuitton, Paris. *Verklighetsmaskiner* (Reality machines), at the Moderna Museet in Stockholm in 2015, became the museum's most visited show by a living artist. In 2016 Eliasson created a series of interventions for the palace and gardens of Versailles and mounted two large-scale exhibitions: *Nothingness is not nothing at all,* at Long Museum, Shanghai, and *The parliament of possibilities,* at Leeum, Samsung Museum of Art, Seoul. *Green light - An artistic workshop,* created in collaboration with TBA21 (Thyssen-Bornemisza Art Contemporary), offers a response to the challenges of mass displacement and migration. Originally hosted by TBA21 in Vienna in 2016, the project was part of *Viva Arte Viva,* the 57th International Art Exhibition – La Biennale di Venezia, in 2017. Eliasson's site-specific installation *Reality projector* opened at the Marciano Foundation, Los Angeles, in March 2018, the same month as his solo exhibition *The unspeakable openness of things* at Red Brick Art Museum, Beijing. *Olafur Eliasson: WASSERfarben* opened at the Staatliche Graphische Sammlung in the Pinakothek der Moderne, Munich, in June 2018.

Eliasson has also produced numerous projects in public space. *Green river* was carried out in various cities between 1998 and 2001. Eliasson designed *Serpentine Gallery Pavilion 2007* together with architect Kjetil Thorsen for London's Kensington Gardens. *The New York City Waterfalls,* commissioned by the Public Art Fund, were installed along the city's waterfronts in 2008. *Your rainbow panorama,* a circular coloured-glass walkway atop ARoS Museum, Aarhus, Denmark, opened in 2011. Harpa Reykjavik Concert Hall and Conference Centre, 2005–11, for which Eliasson created the facades in collaboration with Henning Larsen Architects, won the Mies van der Rohe Award 2013. *Ice Watch* brought melting icebergs from Greenland to Copenhagen in 2014; to Paris on the occasion of the COP21 Climate Conference in 2015; and to London during COP24, in Katowice, in 2018.

Other projects include *Umschreibung* 2004, an 'endless staircase' for KPMG, Munich; *Eye see you* 2006, a light sculpture conceived for Louis Vuitton stores worldwide; *Your mobile expectations* 2007, an Art Car Project commissioned by BMW, from which grew a number of studio experiments and symposia; and Fjordenhus, a building for Kirk Kapital in Vejle, Denmark, the first building designed entirely by Eliasson and architect Sebastian Behmann with Studio Olafur Eliasson, completed in June 2018.

Eliasson is a frequent contributor to public conferences and panels. These include a TED talk in 2009; a series of lectures at the Alle School of Fine Arts and Design, Addis Ababa University in 2012; a panel discussion with the Dalai Lama at the Mind & Life conference in 2016; and a conversation with geologist Minik Rosing as part of The Arctic Imagination Project at the New York Public Library in 2017.

As a professor at the Berlin University of the Arts, Eliasson led the Institut für Raumexperimente (Institute for Spatial Experiments; 2009–14), a five-year experimental programme in arts education located in the same building as his studio.

In 2012 Eliasson and engineer Frederik Ottesen founded the social business Little Sun. This global project provides clean, affordable energy to communities without access to electricity, encourages sustainable development through sales of Little Sun solar-powered lamps and chargers, and raises global awareness of the need for equal access to energy and light.

Eliasson and Sebastian Behmann founded Studio Other Spaces, an international office for art and architecture, in Berlin in 2014. As an architectural counterpart to Studio Olafur Eliasson in the same building, Studio Other Spaces focuses on interdisciplinary and experimental building projects and works in public space.

Eliasson lives and works in Copenhagen and Berlin.

Websites
littlesun.com
olafureliasson.net
raumexperimente.net
soe.tv
studiootherspaces.net

EXHIBITED WORKS

Unless stated otherwise, measurements are given in centimetres, height before width and depth.

WINDOW PROJECTION 1990

Spotlight, gobo, tripod
Dimensions variable
Courtesy the artist; neugerriemschneider, Berlin; Tanya Bonakdar Gallery, New York / Los Angeles

A modified spotlight casts what appears to be the shadow of a window frame on the wall. This is an early example of Eliasson's use of light and shadow to shift viewers' perceptions of a space.

I GREW UP IN SOLITUDE AND SILENCE 1991

Candle, glass mirror
25 x 49.8 x 49.8
Edition 3 of 3
Courtesy the artist; neugerriemschneider, Berlin; Tanya Bonakdar Gallery, New York / Los Angeles

A candle situated at the centre of a circular mirror slowly burns down. Seen together with its reflection, the candle appears to traverse the mirror's surface and extend into the virtual space, flames burning at both ends.

WANNABE 1991

Spotlight
Dimensions variable
Courtesy the artist; neugerriemschneider, Berlin; Tanya Bonakdar Gallery, New York / Los Angeles

A spotlight hangs from the ceiling, shining a bright circle of light onto the floor. Visitors can stand in the spotlight, making themselves briefly into an object of attention.

UNTITLED 1993

Convex mirror, plaster rosette
Diameter 40, depth 5
Edition 2 of 10
Courtesy the artist; neugerriemschneider, Berlin; Tanya Bonakdar Gallery, New York / Los Angeles

A convex mirror within a circular rosette seems to gaze out at the viewer from the gallery wall.

BEAUTY 1993

Spotlight, water, nozzles, wood, hose, pump
Dimensions variable
Edition 1 of 3
Museum of Contemporary Art, Los Angeles. Purchased with funds provided by the Acquisition and Collection Committee, 2002.14

Nozzles arranged in a row spray a curtain of fine mist from the ceiling of a darkened space into the bright beam of a spotlight. From certain perspectives, a rainbow can be seen in the falling water; it shifts in intensity or disappears as the viewer approaches or moves away.

MOSS WALL 1994

Reindeer moss, wood, wire
Dimensions variable
Courtesy the artist; neugerriemschneider, Berlin; Tanya Bonakdar Gallery, New York / Los Angeles

Reindeer moss (*Cladonia rangiferina*), a lichen native to countries in the northern latitudes including Iceland, is woven into a wire mesh and mounted on the wall of a gallery. As the lichen dries, it shrinks and fades; when the installation is watered, the moss expands, changes colour again, and fills the space with its fragrance.

NO NIGHTS IN SUMMER, NO DAYS IN WINTER 1994

Steel, propane
Diameter 68
Courtesy the artist; neugerriemschneider, Berlin; Tanya Bonakdar Gallery, New York / Los Angeles

A metal ring studded by gas nozzles around its circumference is hung at eye level in a darkened room. When filled with propane and lit, small flame jets emit heat, light and a constant hiss. The title refers to the phenomenon that occurs in regions north of the Arctic Circle in which the sun does not rise or set for months at a time.

WAVEMACHINES 1995

Acrylic, transparent plastic sheet, water, ink (yellow), motors, transformer
25 x 900 x 212
Kunstmuseum Basel, purchase 2012, Inv. G 2012.18

Four long, shallow basins are each fitted with a small motor and filled with yellow water. The motors produce tiny waves in the water at different intervals, generating an ongoing series of ephemeral patterns.

SUNEY 1995

Transparent plastic sheet (yellow)
Dimensions variable
Kunstmuseum Basel, purchase 2012

A transparent yellow plastic barrier divides the gallery space in two, preventing visitors from crossing the room, which has two entrances. When visitors stand on one side and look through the yellow plastic, the space on the other side appears saturated with yellow light.

EINE BESCHREIBUNG EINER REFLEXION, ODER ABER EINE ANGENEHME ÜBUNG ZU DEREN EIGENSCHAFTEN 1995

(A description of a reflection, or a pleasant exercise on its qualities)
Spotlight, mirrors, projection screen, motor, tripod
Dimensions variable
Boros Collection, Berlin

A spotlight shines onto a circular mirror that directs the light onto a second, rotating mirror with an undulating surface. This mirror completes a full revolution every thirty seconds, reflecting, as it revolves, an irregular patch of light onto the reverse side of a circular projection screen.

VENTILATOR 1997

Fan, wire, cable
Dimensions variable
Edition 1 of 3
The Museum of Modern Art, New York. Gift of Gwen and Peter Norton in honor of the appointment of Klaus Biesenbach as director of MoMA PS1, 44.2011

An electric fan, suspended from the ceiling by its own cord, swings erratically and irregularly through space just above viewers' heads, propelled by the air it displaces.

ROOM FOR ONE COLOUR 1997

Monofrequency lamps
Dimensions variable
Courtesy the artist; neugerriemschneider, Berlin; Tanya Bonakdar Gallery, New York / Los Angeles

Lamps mounted to the ceiling of a white room emit a single wavelength of yellow light, reducing viewers' colour perception to yellow and black. In reaction to the yellow environment, viewers momentarily perceive a bluish afterimage on leaving the space.

REGENFENSTER 1999

(Rain window)
Metal, water, sprinkler, nozzles
Dimensions variable
Private collection, Berlin

A pipe, installed on the exterior of the museum above a window, is perforated with hundreds of tiny holes, each fitted with a nozzle. Water flows through the pipe and drips down onto the windows, giving the impression that it is raining outside.

THE GLACIER SERIES 1999

42 C-prints
Each: 34 x 50
Edition 4 of 6
Solomon R. Guggenheim Museum, New York. Purchased with funds contributed by the Photography Committee, 2000, 2000.69

In this series, massive glaciers are seen from above, at a distance from which one can appreciate their magnitude. The incremental movement of glaciers is a phenomenon understood by virtue of scientific knowledge; it cannot be seen with the naked eye.

THE RIVER-RAFT SERIES 2000

42 C-prints
Each: 31.5 x 41.5
Edition 2 of 6
Städtische Galerie im Lenbachhaus und Kunstbau München, KiCo Collection, Munich

These photographs, part of Eliasson's ongoing project to photographically map Iceland, are the result of his attempt to document the Markarfljót river while floating down it on a small rubber raft. The framing of the individual images was largely determined by the river itself, as the raft bounced unpredictably along the current.

THE STRUCTURAL EVOLUTION PROJECT 2001

Zometool construction sets
Dimensions variable
Hamburger Kunsthalle. Permanent loan Stiftung Hamburger Kunstsammlungen

This piece requires the participation of visitors, who collaboratively create a continuously evolving three-dimensional structure using Zometool construction sets. The Zometool system was invented by Steve and Holly Baer and inspired by the work of Buckminster Fuller.

YOUR SPIRAL VIEW 2002

Stainless-steel mirror, steel
320 x 320 x 800
Boros Collection, Berlin

This free-standing tunnel is constructed from steel plates that form two sets of spirals, coiling in opposite directions. Upon entering the work, visitors find themselves within a kaleidoscope in which the space they have just left and the space up ahead are mingled in reflected fragments.

Olafur Eliasson in collaboration with Einar Thorsteinn

MODEL ROOM 2003

Wood table with steel legs, mixed media models, maquettes, prototypes
Dimensions variable
Moderna Museet, Stockholm. Purchase 2015 funded by The Anna-Stina Malmborg and Gunnar Höglund Foundation

This selection of maquettes, prototypes and geometrical studies – many of which were preparatory studies for artworks – is a record of Eliasson's collaboration with Icelandic artist, mathematician, and architect Einar Thorsteinn (1942–2015), which began in 1996. *Model Room* evolved over time as new models were made, but this iteration was defined when the work was acquired by Moderna Museet in 2015.

THE CUBIC STRUCTURAL EVOLUTION PROJECT 2004

White Lego bricks (various sizes), wood
Dimensions variable
Queensland Art Gallery Foundation Grant
Collection: Queensland Art Gallery | Gallery of Modern Art
Acc.2005.109a. Purchase 2005

Heaps of white Lego bricks are spread out over a large table at which visitors are invited to build their vision of a future city. The models made by each person are modified and elaborated by subsequent visitors throughout the course of the exhibition.

MELTING ICE ON GUNNAR'S LAND 2008

12 C-prints
AP for an edition of 6
Each: 24 x 35.5
Courtesy the artist; neugerriemschneider, Berlin; Tanya Bonakdar Gallery, New York / Los Angeles

These twelve photographs document a chunk of ice as it melted away on land owned by Gunnar Örn Gunnarsson, a family friend of Eliasson's, in Iceland. The lighting conditions and the weather change in the background of the images as the ice disappears.

DIN BLINDE PASSAGER 2010

(Your blind passenger)
Fluorescent lamps, monofrequency lamps (yellow), fog machines, air circulation system, wood, aluminium, steel, fabric, plastic sheet
Dimensions variable
Courtesy the artist; neugerriemschneider, Berlin; Tanya Bonakdar Gallery, New York / Los Angeles

Upon entering this long, narrow corridor, visitors are temporarily blinded by brightly illuminated fog that requires them to rely on other senses to orient themselves. As they progress through the corridor, they move through zones of different hues. 'Blind passenger' is the Danish expression for a stowaway.

YOUR UNCERTAIN SHADOW (COLOUR) 2010

HMI lamps (green, orange, blue, magenta), glass, aluminium, transformers
Dimensions variable
Thyssen-Bornemisza Art Contemporary Collection, Vienna

Different coloured spotlights, positioned side-by-side on the floor, project light on a white wall where the colours blend to produce white light. When visitors walk into the space before the spotlights, their shadows appear on the wall as clusters of colourful silhouettes that amplify every movement and reveal the apparently white light's component colours.

COLD WIND SPHERE 2012

Stainless steel, coloured glass (dark blue, blue and light grey), mirror, colour-effect filter glass (blue), bulb
Diameter 170
Gift of the Clarence Westbury Foundation, 2013. Centre Pompidou, Musée national d'art moderne, Centre de création industrielle, Paris

Three spheres are layered one within another. In the centre of the sphere is a light bulb that casts shadows and reflections into the surrounding room in the shades of the blue glass pieces that sit between the layers, the grey outer layer, and the colours created by their superimposition.

BIG BANG FOUNTAIN 2014

Water, strobe light, pump, nozzle, stainless steel, wood, foam, plastic, control unit, dye
165 x 160 x 160
Courtesy the artist; neugerriemschneider, Berlin; Tanya Bonakdar Gallery, New York / Los Angeles

A strobe light illuminates a pulsing fountain of water, appearing to freeze its bursts into an ever-changing sequence of unique and unpredictable sculptural forms, each of which lasts for only an instant.

STARDUST PARTICLE 2014

Stainless steel, translucent mirror-filter glass, wire, motor, spotlight
Diameter 170
Tate. Presented by the artist in honour of Sir Nicholas Serota 2018

Two irregular polyhedra are embedded within one another to yield a single form made of partially reflective, translucent filter glass and thin stainless-steel struts. This hanging artwork changes appearance as the panes of partially reflective filter glass catch the light and reflect the surroundings.

THE SEEING SPACE 2015

Glass
Diameter 64
Courtesy the artist; neugerriemschneider, Berlin; Tanya Bonakdar Gallery, New York / Los Angeles

A large glass sphere, set into the wall, serves as an optical device that offers visitors distorted, inverted views of the activity in the room on the other side.

FOG COUCH 2018

Textile (wool, nylon), foam
Fourteen modules of various sizes
A collaboration with Kvadrat, courtesy the artist

This long sofa comprises modular segments of different dimensions; their shapes determined by the relationship between their elliptical backs and rectangular bases. Each is upholstered in a unique fabric that suggests the rippling sand left behind by a receding tide, designed by Eliasson in collaboration with the Danish textile firm Kvadrat.

GLACIAL CURRENTS (BLACK, GREEN) 2018

Watercolour, Indian ink, and pencil on paper
152.5 x 152.5 x 8
Courtesy the artist; neugerriemschneider, Berlin; Tanya Bonakdar Gallery, New York / Los Angeles

GLACIAL CURRENTS (YELLOW, SIENNA) 2018

Watercolour, Indian ink, and pencil on paper
152.5 x 152.5 x 8
Collection of Eleanor & Francis Shen

These watercolours were produced using chunks of ancient glacial ice that were fished from the sea off the coast of Greenland. The ice was placed atop thin washes of colour on a sheet of thick paper. As the ice gradually melted, the resulting water displaced the pigment, producing organic swells and fades of colour.

IN REAL LIFE 2019

Aluminium, colour-effect filter glass (green, yellow, orange, red, pink, cyan), LED light
Diameter 208
Courtesy the artist; neugerriemschneider, Berlin; Tanya Bonakdar Gallery, New York / Los Angeles

A large sphere composed of aligned, curling ridges is formed by individually folded modules of anodised aluminium held together by tense metal cables. The modules support panes of coloured glass; a lamp at the centre of the sphere shines out to project a colourful pattern of light and shadow onto the surroundings.

COLOUR EXPERIMENT NO.80 2019
COLOUR EXPERIMENT NO.81 2019

Oil paint on canvas
Each: diameter 125
Courtesy the artist; neugerriemschneider, Berlin; Tanya Bonakdar Gallery, New York / Los Angeles

A number of works in Eliasson's ongoing *Colour experiment* series analyse the colour palettes of specific painters. The colours in these two experiments were derived from two paintings by Caspar David Friedrich (1774–1840): *Der Mönch am Meer* (The Monk by the Sea) 1808–10, and *Der einsame Baum* (The Lonesome Tree) 1822. Each painting was abstracted into the range of colours it contains, which were then distributed proportionately around each circular canvas to form an alternative colour wheel.

WATERFALL 2019

Scaffolding, water, wood, plastic sheet, aluminium, pump, hose
Height 11 metres, diameter 12 metres
Courtesy the artist; neugerriemschneider, Berlin; Tanya Bonakdar Gallery, New York / Los Angeles

A tall, narrow waterfall cascades into a large basin of water. The visible infrastructure of the waterfall calls attention to the constructed nature of both the work itself and the surrounding architecture of Tate Modern and London's Southwark area, while the tumbling water highlights the presence of larger natural forces that play upon this built environment: the strength and direction of the wind; the conditions of the light at a particular moment.

ADRIFT COMPASS 2019

Driftwood, magnets, paint (blue, black, yellow, white)
38 x 134 x 24
Courtesy the artist; neugerriemschneider, Berlin; Tanya Bonakdar Gallery, New York / Los Angeles

A weathered piece of driftwood, harvested from the Icelandic coast, hangs from the ceiling. One end of the log has been planed down to a sharp angle, and the exposed wood painted. A magnetic rod suspended from the driftwood orients it along the north-south axis, like the needle of a compass.

GLACIAL SPHERICAL FLARE 2019

Silvered coloured glass (beige, white), silvered coloured glacier-rock-flour glass (various greens), gold ruby glass (pink), aluminium
180 x 180 x 3.5
Courtesy the artist; neugerriemschneider, Berlin; Tanya Bonakdar Gallery, New York / Los Angeles

The composition of circles and ellipses in this work is based on lens flare – rings and circles of light that appear in a camera's lens when it is pointed towards the sun or another bright light source. Panes of glass of different shapes in a range of colours work together to produce the appearance of a group of overlapping transparent forms.

YOUR PLANETARY WINDOW 2019

Glass mirrors, aluminium, steel
255 x 80 x 115
Courtesy the artist; neugerriemschneider, Berlin; Tanya Bonakdar Gallery, New York / Los Angeles

A row of tapering shafts is set into a wall; each is lined with reflective glass to produce a set of kaleidoscopes through which visitors can see the environment outside. The shape of each kaleidoscope causes the illusion of a different three-dimensional form to appear within; fragmented reflections of the surroundings continually shift in response to the movements of the viewer.

HOW DO WE LIVE TOGETHER? 2019

Stainless steel, paint (black), foil mirror
Dimensions variable, arc: 476 x 680 x 680
Courtesy the artist; neugerriemschneider, Berlin; Tanya Bonakdar Gallery, New York / Los Angeles

A semicircular arc mounted to a mirror on the ceiling visually combines with its reflection to create the illusion of a giant ring that traverses the mirror's surface, uniting the actual space of the gallery with the virtual space that appears in the mirror.

THE PRESENCE OF ABSENCE PAVILION 2019

Bronze
200 x 100 x 100
Courtesy the artist; neugerriemschneider, Berlin; Tanya Bonakdar Gallery, New York / Los Angeles

The space around a block of glacial ice was cast in bronze, producing a void that captures the shape of the vanished ice. The ice was harvested from the Nuup Kangerlua fjord off the coast of Greenland: the Greenland ice sheet loses tens of thousands of similar blocks each minute as a result of global warming.

Works installed in the Terrace Bar

SHORE COMPASS (06:00, YELLOW DISK) 2018
SHORE COMPASS (07:00, YELLOW) 2018
SHORE COMPASS (09:00, GREEN) 2018
SHORE COMPASS (11:00, YELLOW) 2018
SHORE COMPASS (19:00, GREEN YELLOW ORANGE) 2018
SHORE COMPASS (21:00, RED ORANGE) 2018

Mixed media
Various dimensions
Courtesy the artist; i8 gallery, Reykjavik

Over the years, Eliasson has explored countless variations on the compass. The *Shore compass* series combines materials gathered from remote beaches throughout Iceland with objects at hand in the studio. A magnet attached to each cluster of materials transforms it into a compass that aligns itself with the north–south axis.

OE QUASI LIGHT 2019

Recycled aluminium, recycled plastic, LEDs
Diameter 90

Eliasson's lamp for Louis Poulsen is composed of two contrasting shapes: a rigid outer frame and a soft, layered interior, both derived from Platonic solids. Light directed towards the lamp's core is reflected out onto the surroundings; the lamp's complex geometric shape invites movement and sustained attention.

Pre-exhibition installations

YOUR DOUBLE-LIGHTHOUSE PROJECTION 2002

Stainless steel, wood, fluorescent lights, colour filter foils (red, green, blue), projection foils (white, black), control unit
3.63 x 11.54 x 6.3 metres
Tate. Presented by Tate Members 2004

Your double-lighthouse projection comprises two circular rooms of different sizes. The larger space incorporates red, blue and green fluorescent tubes encased in a translucent wall whose colour gradually shifts through all the hues of the spectrum; the adjacent room, lit simply with white light, provides viewers with the opportunity to refresh their visual faculties. Exhibited at Tate Modern, 17 December 2018 – 3 February 2019.

Olafur Eliasson and Minik Rosing

ICE WATCH 2014

Blocks of glacial ice
Dimensions variable
Courtesy Olafur Eliasson and Minik Rosing

Installed at Tate Modern and Bloomberg European headquarters, 11 December 2018 – 2 January 2019. The installation was made possible by the generous support of Bloomberg Philanthropies.

ARTIST'S ACKNOWLEDGEMENTS

I would first of all like to thank Mark Godfrey and Emma Lewis from Tate Modern for their trust and co-thinking in creating this ambitious exhibition, as well as Achim Borchardt-Hume and Frances Morris for inviting me back to this museum, which has meant so much to my artistic trajectory. Thanks are also due to the various teams at Tate Modern – from development, marketing, press, visitor experience and interpretation and public programming to installation and art handling – for making this exhibition a reality.

In close dialogue with the team at Tate, Caroline Eggel of the studio's exhibition department has been deeply invested in the curation of the show, working with Daniel Mock, who planned and oversaw the execution of the exhibition design together with Dayoung Shin. The development of the Expanded Studio's mindmap was in the hands of Martin Enoch and Elizabeth McTernan, with Patricia Bondesson Kavanagh bridging the dialogue across teams. I would also like to thank the studio's production department, led by Myriam Thomas, and the installation team: Christian Uchtmann, Jöran Imholze, Anders Hellsten Nissen, Bendix Carabetta, Matt Willard and Andrew Amondson, as well as the studio's external collaborators Frank Meier, Sacha Hamacher, Oliver Reif, and Herwig Bretis. The realisation of the show would not have been possible without the financial supervision of Anja Gerstmann.

Thanks go also to Anna Engberg-Pedersen for anchoring all communications, including the exhibition catalogue. Camilla Kragelund coordinated our engagement with the press; María del Pilar García Ayensa realised exhibition identity photography with Kathryn Politis, who also developed the show's merchandise. I would like to thank Christina Werner, who, together with Lauren Maurer and Christine Bopp from the Studio Olafur Eliasson Kitchen, developed the collaboration with the Tate Terrace Bar, led by Hamish Anderson of Tate Catering and with chef Jon Atashroo. Many thanks to Sophie Erlund who worked on the public programme and to Vanja Žanko for her thoughtful assistance throughout the entire planning process.

I am deeply grateful to all the conversation partners featured in this catalogue for generously sharing their time and expertise with me. It was a supreme pleasure talking with all of them. I am also grateful to Patsy McCartan for making these conversations happen and Miranda Robbins and Vajra Spook for their editorial work, which gave these dialogues their written form. Thanks also to Michael Jensen for his thoughtful design and to Nicola Bion, Emma O'Neill and Bill Jones from Tate Publishing for bringing their skills and dedication to realising this catalogue together with Kristina Köper and the editorial team at the studio.

An undertaking as large and involved as this requires the skills of my entire team. It is important to me to express my deepfelt thanks to my studio as a whole: Saeed Aboud, Benjamin Albrecht, Andrew Amondson, Hlynur Snær Andrason, Stefano Arrighi, Nathan Baker, Jonathon Beattie, Soetje Marie Beermann, Sebastian Behmann, Zarina Belousova, Aleksandra Bielas, Florian Bielefeldt, Marie Bartz, Thomas Blumtritt-Hanisch, Marco Antonio Bocardo Fuentes, Patricia Bondesson Kavanagh, Ornruja Fame Boonyasit, Christine Bopp, Karl Bosch, Sylvain Brugier, Ruben Bygvraa, Bendix Carabetta, Catriona Collins, Karo Castro-Wunsch, Kate Chen, Michelle Chen, Odey Curbelo, Heide Deigert, Wolfgang Devine, Taylor Dover, Jesper Dyrehauge, Caroline Eggel, Victoria Eliasdóttir, Tegan Emerson, Anna Engberg-Pedersen, Emilie Høegh Engbirk, Martin Enoch, Sophie Erlund, Leonie Fischer, Guillaume Fournier, Laura Freiling, María del Pilar García Ayensa, Geoffrey Garrison, Timothy Gasbarro, Matthias Gerber, Anja Gerstmann, Celina Gonzalez Sueyro, Elisabeth Greinecker, Jessica Groome, Franziska Harnisch, Frank Haugwitz, Dorothea Hendrichs, Friedrich Herz, Petter Hoff, Phil Höhn, Florian Hollunder, Erik Huber, Jörg Hugo, Jöran Imholze, Brita Jaichner, Holger Jenal, Biljana Joksimović-Große, Philipp Käfer, Roger Kaiser, Olga Kalina, Britta Kampe, Judith Karla, Marcus Knupp, Kristina Köper, Vera Kox, Kimberly Kraczon, Camilla Kragelund, Anna Kreutzträger, Inga Krieger, Jakob Kukula, Susanne Kunkel, David de Larrea Remiro, Camilla Storgaard Larsen, Ilja Leda, Sharron Ping-Jen Lee, Luca Longagnani, Lars Lubnau, Julia Lutz, Margaret Lutz, Riccardo Mariano, Lauren Maurer, Patsy McCartan, Elizabeth McTernan, Jan Mennicke, Andreas Meyer, Niël Meyer, Daniel Mock, Minh-Tu Nguyen, Anders Hellsten Nissen, Jasper Nöllner, Reinhard Ostendorf, Kerstin Palermo, Marc Pätzold, Jan Plater-Zyberk, Róża Plater-Zyberk, Kathryn Politis, Matteo Rapini, Phillip C. Reiner, Petra Rickhof, Sharman Riegger, Bettina Roeder, Andreas Roscher, Fabian Schäfer, Dominic Schneider, Dayoung Shin, Salome Sommer, Vajra Spook, Alcuin Stevenson, Hannah Rose Stewart, Ramona Taterra, Caspar Teichgräber, Myriam Thomas, Stefanie Toch, Montse Torredà Martí, Christian Uchtmann, Patricia Vraber, Kajana Wagner, Michael Waldrep, Jill Wambach, Rabea Welte, Christina Werner, Matt Willard, Brigitta Witt, Nora Wulff, Vanja Žanko, Alexander Zerning and Ariana Zilliacus.

My Little Sun project, launched in 2012 at Tate Modern, is featured in the exhibition as well. Thank you to the entire team at Little Sun. And a special thank-you to Nicholas Serota, who invited us to launch Little Sun at Tate modern in 2012.

I would also like to express my gratitude to my gallerists – Tanya Bonakdar, Tim Neuger, Burkhard Riemschneider – for their unwavering support over the years.

Olafur Eliasson: In real life features many works that have found homes in public institutions and collections. Special thanks are due therefore to the many institutions and individuals who have shown confidence and trust in me over the years, and who have made the works available to this exhibition on loan.

And, finally, I'd like to express my loving thanks to my family.

Olafur Eliasson

CREDITS

Copyright

All artworks by Olafur Eliasson
© Olafur Eliasson 2019

Photo credits

Martin Argyroglo 170–1
Flemming Brusgaard 58–9
The Davis Enterprise 142 bottom right
Olafur Eliasson 15, 38, 39, 89
Joel Chester Fildes 37
Charlie Forgham-Bailey 11, 143 bottom, 172 top, 173–5
Thilo Frank / Studio Olafur Eliasson 23, 27, 125–7
María del Pilar García Ayensa / Studio Olafur Eliasson outside and inside front and back cover, 1, 32, 128–31, 162 bottom right, 163 top, 221–2, 223 top and centre, 240
Mark Godfrey 202 top
Eva Gommes 142 centre
BERTRAND GUAY/AFP/Getty Images 34
© IOM Ethiopia / Alemayehu Seifeselassie 143 top
Marcus Keibel 73
Little Sun 142 bottom left
Ari Magg 24
Noshe 18
Ole Hein Pedersen 26
Mark Sherwood, QAGOMA 25
Studio Olafur Eliasson 163 bottom, 223 bottom,
Anders Sune Berg 2, 35, 40–1, 46–9, 54–7, 63–7, 73–5, 80–3, 103–9, 138–41, 149–53, 159, 182–5, 191–3, 201, 202 bottom, 203, 210–15, 224–5
Justin Sutcliffe 172 bottom
© Tate, 2019 / Joe Humphrys 115–17; / Marcus Leith and Andrew Dunkley 21; / Seraphina Neville and Matt Greenwood 94–7
Markus Tretter 16–17
Michael Tsegaye 28
UNFCCC 142 top
Joshua White 33
Helmut Wieben 12
Sandro E.E. Zanzinger 162 centre, 162 bottom left
Jens Ziehe 90–3, 118–19, 137, 152–3, 176–7, 194–5, 204–5
Damir Žižić 31, 160–1, 162 top

INDEX

Page numbers in *italic* type refer to illustrations.

SUPPORTING TATE

Tate relies on a large number of supporters – individuals, foundations, companies and public sector sources – to enable it to deliver its programme of activities, both on and off its gallery sites. This support is essential in order for Tate to acquire works of art for the Collection, run education, outreach and exhibition programmes, care for the Collection in storage and enable art to be displayed, both digitally and physically, inside and outside Tate. Please contact us at:

DEVELOPMENT OFFICE
Tate
Millbank
London SW1P 4RG

Tel: +44 (0)20 7887 4900
Fax: +44 (0)20 7887 8098

TATE AMERICAS FOUNDATION
520 West 27 Street Unit 404
New York, NY 10001
USA

Tel: 001 212 643 2818
Fax: 001 212 643 1001

Donations, no matter the size, are gratefully received, either to support particular areas of interest, or to contribute to general activity costs.

TATE TRUSTEES

(As of November 2018)
John Akomfrah, CBE
Lionel Barber (Chairman)
John Booth
Dexter Dalwood
Tim Davie, CBE
Jayne-Anne Gadhia, CBE
Dame Moya Greene, DBE
Michael Lynton
Dame Seona Reid, DBE
Roland Rudd
James Timpson, OBE
Jane Wilson
Stephen Witherford

TATE FOUNDATION TRUSTEES AND HONORARY MEMBERS

Dr Maria Balshaw, CBE*
Abigail Baratta
Joseph P Baratta II*
Victoria Barnsley, OBE
John Botts, CBE*
Mrs James Brice
The Lord Browne of Madingley, FRS, FREng
Susan Burns
Christina Chandris
Melanie Clore
Sir Howard Davies
Dame Vivien Duffield, DBE
George Economou
Edward Eisler*
Maryam Eisler
Mala Gaonkar*
Sasan Ghandehari
Noam Gottesman
Oliver Haarmann
Peter Kellner
Catherine Lagrange
The Hon Mrs Rita McAulay
Ronald McAulay
Scott Mead*
Mandy Moross
Elisabeth Murdoch
Lord Myners of Truro, CBE
Marilyn Ofer
Simon Palley*
Franck Petitgas (Chairman)*
John Porter
Sir John Ritblat
Lady Ritblat
Emmanuel Roman*
Dame Theresa Sackler, DBE
The Rt Hon Sir Timothy Sainsbury
Sir Anthony Salz*
Peter Simon
Jon Snow
Lord Stevenson of Coddenham, CBE*
Mercedes Stoutzker
John Studzinski, CBE
Ian Taylor
Lance Uggla*
Viktor Vekselberg
Sir David Verey, CBE
Anita Zabludowicz, OBE

* Executive Trustee

TATE AMERICAS FOUNDATION TRUSTEES

Paul Britton
Estrellita Brodsky
Tiqui Atencio Demirdjian*
Jeanne Donovan Fisher
Glenn Fuhrman
Pamela Joyner (Chair)
Gregory R Miller*
Bob Rennie
Jay Rivlin
Erica Roberts*
Komal Shah
Jay Smith
John Studzinski, CBE
Marjorie Susman
Juan Carlos Verme
Christen Wilson*

*Ex-officio

TATE MODERN DONORS TO THE FOUNDING CAPITAL CAMPAIGN

29th May 1961 Charitable Trust
Alan Cristea Gallery
AMP
The Annenberg Foundation
Arts Council England
The Asprey Family Charitable Foundation
Lord and Lady Attenborough
The Baring Foundation
Ron Beller and Jennifer Moses
Alex and Angela Bernstein
David and Janice Blackburn
Mr and Mrs Anthony Bloom
BNP Paribas
Mr and Mrs Pontus Bonnier
Lauren and Mark Booth
Mr and Mrs John Botts
Frances and John Bowes
Ivor Braka
Mr and Mrs James Brice
The British Land Company plc
Donald L Bryant Jr Family
Melva Bucksbaum
Cazenove & Co
CGU plc
Clifford Chance
The Clore Duffield Foundation
Edwin C Cohen
The John S Cohen Foundation
Ronald and Sharon Cohen
Sadie Coles
Carole and Neville Conrad
Giles and Sonia Coode-Adams
Douglas Cramer
Thomas Dane
Michel and Hélène David-Weill
Julia W Dayton
Gilbert de Botton
Pauline Denyer-Smith and Paul Smith
Sir Harry and Lady Djanogly
The Drapers' Company
Energis Communications
English Heritage
English Partnerships
The Eranda Foundation
Esmée Fairbairn Charitable Trust
Donald and Doris Fisher
Richard B and Jeanne Donovan Fisher
The Fishmongers' Company
Freshfields Bruckhaus Deringer
Friends of the Tate Gallery
Bob and Kate Gavron
Giancarlo Giammetti
Alan Gibbs
Mr and Mrs Edward Gilhuly
GKR
GLG Partners
Helyn and Ralph Goldenberg
Goldman Sachs
The Horace W Goldsmith Foundation
The Worshipful Company of Goldsmiths
Lydia and Manfred Gorvy
Noam and Geraldine Gottesman
Pehr and Christina Gyllenhammar
Mimi and Peter Haas
The Worshipful Company of Haberdashers
Hanover Acceptances Limited
The Headley Trust
Mr and Mrs André Hoffmann
Anthony and Evelyn Jacobs
Jay Jopling
Mr and Mrs Karpidas
Howard and Lynda Karshan
Peter and Maria Kellner
Madeleine Kleinwort
Brian and Lesley Knox
Pamela and C Richard Kramlich
Mr and Mrs Henry R Kravis
Irene and Hyman Kreitman
The Kresge Foundation
Catherine and Pierre Lagrange
The Lauder Foundation – Leonard and Evelyn Lauder Fund
Lazard Brothers & Co., Limited
Leathersellers' Company Charitable Fund
Edward and Agnès Lee
Lehman Brothers
Lex Service Plc
Ruth and Stuart Lipton
Anders and Ulla Ljungh
The Frank Lloyd Family Trusts
London & Cambridge Properties Limited
London Electricity plc, EDF Group
Mr and Mrs George Loudon
Mayer, Brown, Rowe & Maw
Viviane and James Mayor
Ronald and Rita McAulay
The Mercers' Company
The Meyer Foundation
The Millennium Commission
Anthony and Deirdre Montagu
The Monument Trust
Mori Building, Ltd
Mr and Mrs M D Moross
Guy and Marion Naggar
Peter and Eileen Norton, The Peter Norton Family Foundation
Maja Oeri and Hans Bodenmann
Sir Peter and Lady Osborne
William A Palmer
Mr Frederik Paulsen
Pearson plc
The Pet Shop Boys
The Nyda and Oliver Prenn Foundation
Prudential plc
Railtrack plc
The Rayne Foundation
Reuters
Sir John and Lady Ritblat
Rolls-Royce plc
The Roman Family
Lord and Lady Rothschild
The Dr Mortimer and Theresa Sackler Foundation
J Sainsbury plc
Ruth and Stephan Schmidheiny
Schroders
Mr and Mrs Charles Schwab
David and Sophie Shalit
Belle Shenkman Estate
William Sieghart
Peter Simon
Mr and Mrs Sven Skarendahl
London Borough of Southwark
The Foundation for Sports and the Arts
Mr and Mrs Nicholas Stanley
The Starr Foundation
The Jack Steinberg Charitable Trust
Charlotte Stevenson
Hugh and Catherine Stevenson
John Studzinski
David and Linda Supino
The Government of Switzerland
Carter and Mary Thacher
Insinger Townsley
UBS
UBS Warburg
David and Emma Verey
Dinah Verey
The Vintners' Company
Clodagh and Leslie Waddington
Robert and Felicity Waley-Cohen
Wasserstein, Perella & Co., Inc.
Gordon D Watson
The Weston Family
Mr and Mrs Stephen Wilberding
Michael S Wilson
Poju and Anita Zabludowicz

and those who wish to remain anonymous

DONORS TO THE TATE MODERN PROJECT

Artist Rooms Foundation
Abigail and Joseph Baratta
Blavatnik Family Foundation
Lauren and Mark Booth
The Deborah Loeb Brice Foundation
The Lord Browne of Madingley, FRS, FREng
John and Michael Chandris, and Christina Chandris
James Chanos
Pierre Chen, Yageo Foundation, Taiwan
Paul Cooke
The Roger De Haan Charitable Trust
Ago Demirdjian and Tiqui Atencio Demirdjian
Department for Digital, Culture, Media and Sport
George Economou
Stefan Edlis and Gael Neeson
English Partnerships
Mrs Donald B. Fisher
Jeanne Donovan Fisher
Mala Gaonkar
The Ghandehari Foundation
Thomas Gibson in memory of Anthea Gibson
Lydia and Manfred Gorvy
The Granville-Grossman Bequest
The Hayden Family Foundation
Peter and Maria Kellner
Madeleine Kleinwort
Catherine Lagrange
Pierre Lagrange
London Development Agency
LUMA Foundation
Allison and Howard W. Lutnick
Donald B. Marron
Scott and Suling Mead
Sami and Hala Mnaymneh
Anthony and Deirdre Montagu
Mori Building Co Ltd
Elisabeth Murdoch
Eyal Ofer Family Foundation
Maureen Paley
Simon and Midge Palley
Stephen and Yana Peel
Daniel and Elizabeth Peltz
Catherine Petitgas
Franck Petitgas
The Roman Family
The Dr Mortimer and Theresa Sackler Foundation
The Sackler Trust
Lily Safra
Stephan Schmidheiny Family / Daros Collection
Helen and Charles Schwab
London Borough of Southwark
John J Studzinski, CBE
Tate Americas Foundation
Tate Members
Julie-Anne Uggla
Lance Uggla
Viktor Vekselberg
Nina and Graham Williams
Manuela and Iwan Wirth
The Wolfson Foundation

and those who wish to remain anonymous

TATE MODERN BENEFACTORS AND MAJOR DONORS

We would like to acknowledge and thank the following benefactors who have supported Tate Modern prior to November 2018.

Abrishamchi Foundation
Acquavella Galleries, Inc.
Alan Cristea Gallery
Raad Zeid Al-Hussein
Alison Jacques Gallery
Dilyara Allakhverdova
Art Fund
Art Mentor Foundation Lucerne
Arts Council England
Arts and Humanities Research Council
The Worshipful Company of Arts Scholars and The Company of Arts Scholars Charitable Trust
Charles Asprey
Austrian Federal Chancellery
Mr. Petr Aven
Axel Vervoordt Gallery
Miroslaw Balka, in honour of Sir Nicholas Serota
Lionel Barber
The Estate of Peter and Caroline Barker-Mill
Wilhelmina Barns-Graham Trust through the Art Fund
Beckett-Fonden
The Andre Bernheim Charitable Trust
Bloomberg Philanthropies

The Charlotte Bonham-Carter Charitable Trust
Pontus Bonnier
John Botts
Estate of Louise Bourgeois
Dr Luther Brady
The Estate of Dr Marcella Louis Brenner
British Association for American Studies
Laurel and Paul Britton
Estrellita Brodsky
Rory and Elizabeth Brooks Foundation
Beatrice Bulgari | In Between Art Film
Susan and John Burns
John Bute
The Estate of Lady Caro
The Estate of Anne Christopherson
The Clore Duffield Foundation
Clore Wyndham
The Clothworkers' Foundation
Denise Coates Foundation
Edwin Cohen and Dillon Cohen
Sadie Coles
Corinne Bellow Charity
Cowles Charitable Trust
Alan Cristea
Danish Arts Foundation
Danish Ministry for Culture and The Embassy of Denmark, London
Dimitris Daskalopoulos
Jeremy Deller, in honour of Sir Nicholas Serota
Tiqui Atencio Demirdjian and Ago Demirdjian
Department for Business, Innovation and Skills
Department for Digital, Culture, Media and Sport
The Destina Foundation
Anne Dias Griffin
Joe and Marie Donnelly
The Ekard Collection
Maryam and Edward Eisler
John Ellerman Foundation
European Union
Monir Shahroudy Farmanfarmaian
Faurschou Foundation
Jeanne Donovan Fisher
Fondation Walter & Nicole LeBlanc
Ford Foundation
The Estate of Lucian Freud
Froehlich Foundation, Stuttgart
Gagosian
Adrian Ghenie
Mr Giancarlo Giammetti
Thomas Gibson Fine Art Advisory Services
Nan Goldin, in honour of Sir Nicholas Serota
Sir Nicholas and Lady Goodison
Lydia and Manfred Gorvy
The Granville-Grossman Bequest
The Hakuta Family
Guy Halamish
Maggi Hambling, in honour of Maria Balshaw
Paul Hamlyn Foundation
Susan Hayden
The Drue Heinz Charitable Trust
Barbara Hepworth Estate
Roger J Hiorns
The Estate of Howard Hodgkin
Trustees of Lord Howard of Henderskelfe's Will Trust
The Estate of Mr John Hoyland
Ministry of Foreign Affairs and Trade of Hungary
Huo Family Foundation (UK) Limited
The Estate of Albert and Beatrice Irvin
Italian Cultural Institute
Tim Jefferies, in honour of Sir Nicholas Serota
Amrita Jhaveri
Pamela J. Joyner and Alfred J. Giuffrida
J. Patrick Kennedy and Patricia A. Kennedy
David Kordansky Gallery
Kurimanzutto Gallery
David and Amanda Leathers
Legacy Trust UK
Lin Lougheed
Henry Luce Foundation
Andrew Lugg
LUMA Foundation
Peder Lund
The Late Marion MacCallum Archibald
Caro MacDonald, in honour of the women of Zimbabwe
Mace Foundation
The Estate of Sir Edwin Manton
Marian Goodman Gallery
Matthew Marks Gallery
The Estate of Kenneth McGowan
Steve McQueen
The Mead Family Foundation
The Paul Mellon Centre for Studies in British Art
The Andrew W. Mellon Foundation
Naomi Milgrom Foundation
Lisa Milroy, in honour of Sir Nicholas Serota
Montana
Henry Moore Foundation
Mottahedan Family
The Estate of Jenifer Ann Murray
National Heritage Memorial Fund
The National Lottery Community Fund
The National Lottery Heritage Fund
The National Trust
New Carlsberg Foundation
Novatek
Batia and Idan Ofer
The Stanley Picker Trust
The Pivovarov Family
Emilio Prini
Qatar Museums Authority
Chandru Ramchandani
Carla Rapoport
The Robert Rauschenberg Foundation
Andrea Rosen
The Estate of Eugene and Penelope Rosenberg
Edward Ruscha
Sean Ryerson
Keith and Katherine Sachs
The Estate of Simon Sainsbury
The Estate of Khadija Saye
Gregor Schneider
Jake and Hélène Marie Shafran
Komal Shah
Leo Shih
Jon Shirley
Lord Stevenson of Coddenham, CBE
Norman and Norah Stone
Surgo Donor Advised Fund
Swiss Arts Council Pro Helvetia
Swiss Cultural Fund UK
Beth Swofford
Tate 1897 Circle
Tate Africa Acquisitions Committee
Tate Americas Foundation
Tate Asia-Pacific Acquisitions Committee
Tate European Collection Circle
Tate International Council
Tate Latin American Acquisitions Committee
Tate Members
Tate Middle East and North Africa Acquisitions Committee
Tate North American Acquisitions Committee
Tate Patrons
Tate Photography Acquisitions Committee
Tate Russia and Eastern Europe Acquisitions Committee
Tate South Asia Acquisitions Committee
Terra Foundation for American Art
The Estate of Mr Nicholas Themans
Tim Van Laere Gallery
The Estate of Mary Fedden and Julian Trevelyan
Trustees of the Chantrey Bequest
Luc Tuymans
Dr Suzanne Ullmann
Francis Upritchard
US Embassy
V-A-C Foundation
Mercedes Vilardell
Marie-Louise von Motesiczky Charitable Trust
Mark Wallinger
Hannah Wilke Collection & Archive
The Lord Leonard and Lady Estelle Wolfson Foundation
Erwin Wurm
YOUNG-HAE CHANG HEAVY INDUSTRIES
The Estate of Mr Anthony Zambra
David Zwirner

and those who wish to remain anonymous

PLATINUM PATRONS

Eric Abraham
Ghazwa Mayassi Abu-Suud
Maria Adonyeva
Mr Shane Akeroyd
Basil Alkazzi
Bobby Arora
Celia and Edward Atkin, CBE
Lars Bane
Alex Beard
Beecroft Charitable Trust
Jacques Boissonnas
Natalia Bondarenko
John Booth
Rory and Elizabeth Brooks
The Lord Browne of Madingley, FRS, FREng
Karen Cawthorn Argenio
Victoria Chu
Mr Stephane Custot
Pascale Decaux
Sophie Diedrichs-Cox
Valentina Drouin
Ashiya Dudhia
Mr David Fitzsimons
Edwin Fox Foundation
Stephen Friedman
Mrs Lisa Garrison
Hugh Gibson
Mr Florian Gutzwiller
Alexis and Anne-Marie Habib
Andrew Harcourt
David Herro
Misha and Theresa Horne
Mr and Mrs Yan Huo
Mr Phillip Hylander
Ms Natascha Jakobs
Mrs Gabrielle Jungels-Winkler
Maria and Peter Kellner
Anna Korshun
Lali Marganiya
Luigi Mazzoleni and Jose Graci
Scott and Suling Mead (Chair)
Pierre Tollis and Alexandra Mollof
Mr Donald Moore
Mary Moore
Afsaneh Moshiri
Anthony and Jacqueline Orsatelli
Hussam Otaibi
Simon and Midge Palley
Jan-Christoph Peters
Mr and Mrs Paul Phillips
Mr Gilberto and Mrs Daniela Pozzi
Frances Reynolds
Sybil Robson Orr
Jake and Hélène Marie Shafran
Andrée Shore
Maria and Malek Sukkar
Annie Vartivarian
Miss Cheyenne Westphal
Michael and Jane Wilson
Lady Wolfson of Marylebone
Chizuko Yashiro
Brian T K Yim
Poju Zabludowicz and Anita Zabludowicz, OBE
Meng Zhou

and those who wish to remain anonymous

GOLD PATRONS

Ms Mila Askarova
Francesca Bellini Joseph
Guya Bertoni
Shoshana Bloch
Elena Bowes
Louise and Charlie Bracken
Liza Cawthorn
Angela Choon
Beth and Michele Colocci
Harry G David
Ms Miel de Botton
Mr Frank Destribats
Mrs Maryam Eisler
Michael Herzog
Fiona Mactaggart
Alison Myners
Mr Francis Outred
Mariela Pissioti
Professor Richard Portes, CBE, FBA
Mathew Prichard
Garance Primat
Valerie Rademacher
Jordana Reuben
Almine Ruiz-Picasso
Franz Schwarz
Ralph Segreti
Carol Sellars
Mr and Mrs Stanley S Tollman
Manuela and Iwan Wirth

and those who wish to remain anonymous

SILVER PATRONS

Geoffrey and Julian Agnew Charitable Trust
Sharis Alexandrian
Ryan Allen and Caleb Kramer
Gregor Alpers
Mrs Malgosia Alterman
Dina Amin
The Anson Charitable Trust
Toby and Kate Anstruther
Mr and Mrs Zeev Aram
Hannah Armstrong
Shalni Arora
Mrs Charlotte Artus
Aspect Charitable Trust
Tracy Barakat
Peter Barham
Mrs Jane Barker
Oliver Barker
Mr Edward Barlow
Victoria Barnsley, OBE
Hazel Barratt
Jim Bartos
Dr Amelie Beier
Ms Anne Berthoud
Madeleine Bessborough
Janice Blackburn
David Blood and Beth Bisso
Bruno Boesch
Harry and Fabiana Bond
Mr Brian Boylan
Viscountess Bridgeman
Mr Dan Brooke
Ben and Louisa Brown
Beverley Buckingham
Michael Burrell
Mrs Marlene Burston
Piers Butler
Mrs Aisha Cahn
Sarah Caplin
Timothy and Elizabeth Capon
Mr Francis Carnwath and Ms Caroline Wiseman
Countess Castle Stewart
Roger Cazalet
Lord and Lady Charles Cecil
Dr Peter Chocian
Cynthia Clarry
Frank Cohen
Mrs Jane Collins
Dr Judith Collins
Terrence Collis
Mr and Mrs Oliver Colman
Mayte Comin
Carole and Neville Conrad
Giles and Sonia Coode-Adams
Cynthia Corbett
Mark and Cathy Corbett
Pilar Corrias
Tommaso Corvi-Mora
Mr and Mrs Bertrand Coste
Kathleen Crook and James Penturn
James Curtis
Richard Cyzer
Fiona Davies
Sir Howard Davies
Sir Roger and Lady De Haan
Elisabeth De Kergorlay
Giles de la Mare
Mr Damon and The Hon Mrs de Laszlo
Alexander de Mont
Anne Chantal Defay Sheridan
Jackie Donnelly Russell
Joan Edlis
Lord and Lady Egremont
Margaret Erbe
John Erle-Drax
Dr Nigel Evans
Stuart and Margaret Evans
Eykyn Maclean LLC
Mrs Heather Farrar
David Fawkes
Mrs Margy Fenwick
Laurie Fitch
The Sylvie Fleming Collection
Lt Commander Paul Fletcher
Katherine Francey Stables
Mr and Mrs Laurent Ganem
Mala Gaonkar
Lynn Gaunt
Elena Geuna
Mr Mark Glatman
Ms Emily Goldner and Mr Michael Humphries
Emma Goltz
Aphrodite Gonou
Kate Gordon
Dimitri Goulandris
Penelope Govett
Svitlana Granovska
Jennifer Greenberg
Judith and Richard Greer
Martyn Gregory
Richard and Odile Grogan
Carol Grose
Professor John Gruzelier
Mrs Helene Guerin-Llamas
Jill Hackel Zarzycki
Arthur Hanna
Mark Harris
Michael and Morven Heller
Christian Hernandez and Michelle Crowe Hernandez
Paul Higgins
Muriel Hoffner
James Holland-Hibbert
Lady Hollick, OBE
Holtermann Fine Art
Jeff Horne
John Huntingford
Helen Janecek
Sarah Jennings
Mr Haydn John
Mr Michael Johnson
Mike Jones
Jay Jopling
Mrs Brenda Josephs

Tracey Josephs
Mr Joseph Kaempfer
Andrew Kalman
Ghislaine Kane
Dr Martin Kenig
Mr David Ker
Mr and Mrs Simon Keswick
Mrs Mae Khouri
David Killick
Mr and Mrs James Kirkman
Brian and Lesley Knox
David P Korn
Kowitz Trust
Mr and Mrs Herbert Kretzmer
Linda Lakhdhir
Simon Lee
Tiina Lee
Leonard Lewis
Sophia and Mark Lewisohn
Yuandao Liu
Mr Gilbert Lloyd
Mrs Elizabeth Louis
Mark and Liza Loveday
Jeff Lowe
Alison Loyd
Mrs Ailsa Macalister
Kate MacGarry
Sir John Mactaggart
Audrey Mandela
Marsh Christian Trust
Daniele Mattogno
Ms Fiona Mellish
Mrs R W P Mellish
Professor Rob Melville
Dr Helen Metcalf
Dr Basil Ross Middleton
Victoria Miro
Jan Mol
Mrs Bona Montagu
Mrs William Morrison
Louise Nathanson
Ms Deborah Norton
Julian Opie
Pilar Ordovás
Desmond Page
Maureen Paley
Michael Palin
Mrs Kathrine Palmer
Mathieu Paris
Mrs Véronique Parke
Olga Pavlova
Frans Pettinga
Trevor Pickett
Frederique Pierre-Pierre
John Pluthero
Graham Powell
Susan Prevezer, QC
Mr and Mrs Ryan Prince
Ivetta Rabinovich
Patricia Ranken
Mrs Phyllis Rapp
Lady Ritblat
David Rocklin
Frankie Rossi
Mr David V Rouch
Mr James Roundell
Mr Charles Roxburgh
Mr Alex Sainsbury and Ms Elinor Jansz
Mr Richard Christo Salmon
Mr Richard Saltoun
Cherrill and Ian Scheer
Sylvia Scheuer
Mrs Cara Schulze
Hakon Runer and Ulrike Schwarz-Runer
Melissa Sesana
Ellen Shapiro
The Hon Richard Sharp
Neville Shulman, CBE
Ms Julia Simmonds
Simon C Dickinson Ltd
David Solo
Louise Spence
Mr Nicos Steratzias
Marie-Claude Stobart
Mrs Patricia Swannell
Mr James Swartz
The Lady Juliet Tadgell
Tot Taylor
Isadora Tharin
Elaine Thomas
Anthony Thornton
Marita Thurnauer
Ian Tollett
Victoria Tollman O'Hana
Karen Townshend
Andrew Tseng
Melissa Ulfane
Mrs Jolana Vainio and Dr Petri Vainio
Celine Valligny
Mrs Cecilia Versteegh
Gisela von Sanden
Andreas Vourecas-Petalas
Audrey Wallrock
Linda Waterhouse
Offer Waterman
Mrs Sian West
Professor Sarah Whatmore
Victoria Wilks
Mr David Wood
Mr Douglas Woolf
Sharon Zhu

and those who wish to remain anonymous

YOUNG PATRONS

10 Hanover
Yasmine Abou Adal
Nadine Adams
Letizia Afentakis Cramer
Maria Lorena Aisaguer
Estelle Akeroyd Hunt
Katrina Aleksa
Miss Noor Al-Rahim
HRH Princess Alia Al-Senussi
Lucy Attwood
Miss Olivia Aubry
Flavie Audi
Charles and Tetyana Banner
Federica Baretta
Lucy Barry
Mr Richard Bazzaz
Katrina Beechey
Sophie Beeftink
Penny Johanna Beer
Dr Maya Beyhan
Dorothee Boissonnas
Kit Brennan
Kate Bryan
Verena Butt d'Espous
Alexandre Carel
David Carpenter
Lauren Carpenter
Sean Carpenter
Marie-Louise Chaldecott
Alexandra and Kabir Chhatwani
Yoojin Choi
Aidan Christofferson
Bianca Chu
Julia Clemente
Thamara Corm
Tara Wilson Craig
Sophie Da Gama Campos
Henry Danowski
Grantland D'Avino
Mr Joshua Davis
Countess Charlotte de la Rochefoucauld
Giacomo De Notariis
Agnes de Royere
Raphaele Deghaye
Indira Dyussebayeva
Alexandra Economou
Eleanor A Edelman
Yasmina El Muslemany
Mr Will Elliott
Danae Filioti
Kate Finefrock
Dr L Foley
Jane and Richard Found
Sylvain Fresia
Laurie Frey
Brian Fu
Magdalena Gabriel
Mr Andreas Gegner
Rajasekhar Ghanta
Elissa Goldstone
Mr Taymour Grahne
Beth Greenacre
Miles Greenberg
Alex Haidas
Ayano Hattori
Ari Helgason
Alexis Hervieu-Causse
Simona Houldsworth
Kyu Hwang
Kamel Jaber
Karim Jalbout
Aled Jones
Miss Meruyert Kaliyeva
Mrs Vasilisa Kameneva
Zoe Karafylakis Sperling
Tamila Kerimova
Imogen Kerr
Zena Aliya Khan
Marika Kielland
Ms Chloe Kinsman
Maria Korolevskaya
Daria Kravchenko
Zoe Kuipers
Dominic Lamotte
Nicholas M Lamotte
Ms Aliki-Marcadia Lampropoulos
Patricia Lara
Nadja Laub
Madame Henriette Poppy Lefort
John Lellouche
Alexander Lewis
Ines Leynaud
Melissa Lilley
Claire Livingstone
Tessa Lord
Mr J Lueddeckens
Lucy MacLeod
Yusuf Macun
Stephanie Magistretti
Frederic Maillard
Ms Sonia Mak
Dr Christina Makris
Mr Jean-David Malat
Kamiar Maleki
Daria Manganelli
Ignacio Marinho
Zain Masud
Magnus Mathisen
Charles-Henri McDermott
Fiona McGovern
Mary McNicholas
Shahid Miah
Miss Nina Moaddel
Mr Fernando Moncho Lobo
John-Christian Moquette
Jacopo Moretti
Vanita Nathwani
Olga Nikolskaya
Ikenna Obiekwe
Aurore Ogden (Co-Chair, Young Patrons Ambassador Group)
Reine and Boris Okuliar
Berkay Oncel
Chloe O'Sullivan
Periklis Panagopoulos
Alexander V Petalas (Co-Chair, Young Patrons Ambassador Group)
Victor Petitgas
Robert Phillips
Mr Mark Piolet
Christopher Pullen
Chelsea Purvis
Ms Catherine Quin
Mr Eugenio Re Rebaudengo
Georgina Rees
Sydney Rogers
Nour Saleh
Sophie Samuelson
Paola Saracino Fendi
Count Indoo Sella Di Monteluce
Robert Sheffield
Ms Marie-Anya Shriro
Amar Singh
Evgenia Slyusarenko
David Smeralda
Jana Soin
Dominic Stolerman
Daniel Story
Melisa Tapan
Nayrouz Tatanaki
Vassan Thavaraja
Mr Leo Thetiot
Soren S K Tholstrup
Omer Tiroche
Simon Tovey
Mr M Travers
Mr Giancarlo Trinca
Mr Philippos Tsangrides
Ms Navann Ty
Mr Lawrence Van Hagen
Steffan Vaughan Griffiths
Damian Vesey
Alina Voronova
Luning Wang
Yu-Ge Wang
Alexandra Werner
Ewa Wilczynski
Anna Wilkie
Elizabeth Wilks
Kim Williams
Alexandra Wood
Edward Woodcock
Tyler Woolcott
Vanessa Wurm
Ms Eirian Yem
HRH Princess Eugenie of York
Nadia Zayan
Evgeny Zborovsky
Marcelo Osvaldo Zimmler

and those who wish to remain anonymous

INTERNATIONAL COUNCIL MEMBERS

Mr Segun Agbaje
Staffan Ahrenberg, Editions Cahiers d'Art
Mr Geoff Ainsworth, AM
Mr Ricard Akagawa
Michael J. Audain
The Ampersand Foundation / Jack Kirkland
Mrs Maria Baibakova and Mr Adrien Faure
Anne H Bass
Nicolas Berggruen
Pontus Bonnier
Paloma Botín O'Shea
William Bowness, AO
Ivor Braka
The Deborah Loeb Brice Foundation
Andrew Cameron, AM
Nicolas and Celia Cattelain
Mrs Christina Chandris
Richard Chang (Vice Chair)
Pierre Chen, Yageo Foundation, Taiwan
Mr and Mrs Attilio Codognato
Sir Ronald Cohen and Lady Cohen
Mr Dimitris Daskalopoulos
Mr and Mrs Michel David-Weill
Ms Miel de Botton
Suzanne Deal Booth
Tiqui Atencio Demirdjian and Ago Demirdjian
Joseph and Marie Donnelly
Mrs Olga Dreesmann
Füsun and Faruk Eczacibasi
Stefan Edlis and Gael Neeson
Fares and Tania Fares
Mrs Doris Fisher
Mrs Wendy Fisher
Amanda and Glenn Fuhrman
Mrs Belma Gaudio and The Butters Foundation
Candida and Zak Gertler
Mrs Yassmin Ghandehari
Alan Gibbs
Lydia and Manfred Gorvy
Mr Laurence Graff
Mr Xavier Guerrand-Hermès
Mimi and Peter Haas Fund
Margrit and Paul Hahnloser
Andy and Christine Hall
Mrs Susan Hayden
Ms Ydessa Hendeles
Marlene Hess and James D. Zirin
Ms Maja Hoffmann
Vicky Hughes
Ishikawa Foundation
Sangita Jindal
Dakis and Lietta Joannou
Sir Elton John and Mr David Furnish
HRH Princess Firyal of Jordan
Ms Monica Kalpakian
Mr Chang-Il Kim
C Richard and Pamela Kramlich
Mrs Grazyna Kulczyk
Andreas and Ulrike Kurtz
Catherine Lagrange
Mr Pierre Lagrange
The Lauder Foundation – Leonard and Judy Lauder Fund
Agnès and Edward Lee
Seo Hyun Lee
Jacqueline and Marc Leland
Ms Joyce Liu
Panos and Sandra Marinopoulos
Mr and Mrs Donald B Marron
Angela Westwater and David Meitus
Viktoria Mikhelson
Naomi Milgrom, AO
Mr Donald Moore
Simon and Catriona Mordant
Mrs Yoshiko Mori
Dr Mark Nelson
Mr and Mrs Takeo Obayashi
Mr and Mrs Eyal Ofer
Andrea and José Olympio Pereira
Hideyuki Osawa
Midge and Simon Palley
Irene Panagopoulos
Young-Ju Park
Yana and Stephen Peel
Daniel and Elizabeth Peltz
Catherine Petitgas (Chair)
Sydney Picasso
Jean Pigozzi
Lekha Poddar
Miss Dee Poon
Ms Miuccia Prada and Mr Patrizio Bertelli
Laura Rapp and Jay Smith
Maya and Ramzy Rasamny
Patrizia Sandretto Re Rebaudengo and Agostino Re Rebaudengo
Rennie Foundation
Frances Reynolds
Michael Ringier
Ms Hanneli M Rupert
Dame Theresa Sackler, DBE
Mrs Lily Safra
Muriel and Freddy Salem
Rajeeb and Nadia Samdani
Alejandro Santo Domingo
Dasha Shenkman, OBE
Dr Gene Sherman, AM
Jon and Kimberly Shirley
Uli and Rita Sigg
Norah and Norman Stone
Julia Stoschek
John J Studzinski, CBE
Maria and Malek Sukkar
Mr Christen Sveaas
Ms Lorraine Tarabay
Warly Tomei
Mrs Ninetta Vafeia
Paulo A W Vieira
Mercedes Vilardell
Robert and Felicity Waley-Cohen
Diana Widmaier Picasso
Christen and Derek Wilson
Mrs Sylvie Winckler
The Hon Dame Janet Wolfson de Botton, DBE
Dr Terry Wu

Poju Zabludowicz and Anita Zabludowicz, OBE
Michael Zilkha

and those who wish to remain anonymous

AFRICA ACQUISITIONS COMMITTEE
Kathy Ackerman Robins
The African Arts Trust
Adnan Bashir
Priti Chandaria Shah
Mrs Kavita Chellaram
Harry G David
Mr and Mrs Michel David-Weill
Robert and Renee Drake
Mrs Wendy Fisher
Diane B. Frankel
Andrea Kerzner
Samallie Kiyingi
Alexander Klimt
Othman Lazraq
Matthias and Gervanne Leridon
Caro Macdonald
Dale Mathias
Ms Ndidi Okpaluba
Mr Hussam Otaibi
Pascale Revert Wheeler
Emile Stipp
Pulane Tshabalala Kingston
Liese Van Der Watt and Stephan Pretorius
Josef Vascovitz and Lisa Goodman
Mercedes Vilardell (Chair)
Alexa Waley-Cohen
Peter Warwick
Marwan G Zakhem

and those who wish to remain anonymous

ASIA-PACIFIC ACQUISITIONS COMMITTEE
Matthias Arndt
Bonnie and R Derek Bandeen
Mr and Mrs John Carrafiell
Adrian Cheng
Jonathan Cheung
Lawrence Chu
Marcel Crespo
Mr Yan d'Auriol
Dani Duclos
Mrs Yassmin Ghandehari
Philippa Hornby
Shareen Khattar Harrison
Mr Chang-Il Kim
Mr Jung Wan Kim
Ms Yung Hee Kim
Ms Ellie Lai
Alan Lau (Co-Chair)
Woong-Yeul Lee
Jasmine Li
Mr William Lim
Lin Qi
Ms Dina Liu
Alan and Yenn Lo
Ms Kai-Yin Lo
Lu Xun
Lynn Ou
Mr John Porter
The Red Mansion Foundation
Dr Gene Sherman, AM (Co-Chair)
Leo Shih
Arif Suherman
Chikako Tatsuuma
Dr Andreas Teoh
Rudy Tseng
Yang Bin
Jenny Yeh
Fernando Zobel de Ayala

and those who wish to remain anonymous

LATIN AMERICAN ACQUISITIONS COMMITTEE
Monica and Robert Aguirre
José Antonio Alcantara
Tiqui Atencio Demirdjian (Co-Chair)
Francesca Bellini
Celia Birbragher
Estrellita B. and Daniel Brodsky
Simone Coscarelli Parma
HSH the Prince Pierre d'Arenberg
Renata Dias de Moraes
Marta Regina Fernandez Holman
Katherine Francey
Barbara Hemmerle Gollust
Julian Iragorri
Aimee Labarrere de Servitje
José Luis Lorenzo
Felipe and Denise Nahas Mattar
Susan McDonald
Gabriela Mendoza
Veronica Nutting
Victoria and Isaac Oberfeld
Silvia Paz Illobre
Countess Nicole Brachetti Peretti
Catherine Petitgas
Claudio Federico Porcel
Mr Thibault Poutrel
Frances Reynolds
Erica Roberts (Co-Chair)
Alin Ryan Lobo
Catalina Saieh Guzmán
Teresa Sapey
Lilly Scarpetta
Camila Sol de Pool
Teresita Soriano Zucker
Juan Carlos Verme

and those who wish to remain anonymous

MIDDLE EAST AND NORTH AFRICA ACQUISITIONS COMMITTEE
Ahmad and Sirine Abu Ghazaleh
HRH Princess Alia Al-Senussi
Abdelmonem Bin Eisa Alserkal
Mehves Ariburnu
Marwan T Assaf
Perihan Bassatne
Family Boghossian
Ms Isabelle de la Bruyère
Füsun Eczacibasi
Maryam Eisler (Co-Chair)
Shirley Elghanian
Delfina Entrecanales, CBE
Noor Fares
Hossein and Dalia Fateh
Negin Fattahi-Dasmal
Raghida Ghandour Al Rahim
Mareva Grabowski
Aysegül Karadeniz
Mr Elie Khouri
Maha and Kasim Kutay
David Maupin
Tansa Mermerci Eksioglu
Falak Naqvi
Dina Nasser-Khadivi
Mr Moshe Peterburg
Ramzy and Maya Rasamny (Co-Chair)
Thomas Rom
Mrs Karen Ruimy
Maria and Malek Sukkar
Faisal Tamer
Berna Tuglular
Sebnem Unlu
Mahdi Yahya
Mr Zahid and Ms Binladin
Roxane Zand

and those who wish to remain anonymous

NORTH AMERICAN ACQUISITIONS COMMITTEE
Alireza Abrishamchi
Jacqueline Appel and Alexander Malmaeus
Abigail Baratta
Dorothy Berwin and Dominique Levy
Dillon Cohen
Michael Corman and Kevin Fink
James E Diner
Mala Gaonkar
Jill Garcia
Shari Glazer
Amy Gold
Nina and Dan Gross
Pamela J Joyner
Patricia Kaneb Kelly
Nancy Kaneb Soule
Elisabeth and Panos Karpidas
Christian Keesee
Naznin and Mahmood Khimji
Miyoung Lee
Marjorie and Michael Levine
James Lindon
Sheryl and Eric Maas
Kathleen Madden and Paul Frantz
Rebecca Marks
Nancy McCain
Jeff Menashe
Stavros Merjos
Gregory R Miller (Co-Chair)
Rachelli Mishori and Leon Koffler
Sami Mnaymneh
Shabin and Nadir Mohamed
Jenny Mullen
Amy and John Phelan
Laura Rapp and Jay Smith
Carolin Scharpff-Striebich
Komal Shah
Francis and Eleanor Shen
Dasha Shenkman, OBE
Kimberly and Jon Shirley
Beth Swofford
Juan Carlos Verme
Charlotte Wagner
Christen Wilson (Co-Chair)
Derek Wilson

and those who wish to remain anonymous

PHOTOGRAPHY ACQUISITIONS COMMITTEE
Ryan Allen and Caleb Kramer
The Ampersand Foundation / Jack Kirkland
Nicholas Barker
Cynthia Lewis Beck
Carolin Becker
Pierre Brahm
Mrs William Shaw Broeksmit
Elizabeth (Co-Chair) and Rory Brooks
Mr and Mrs Michel David-Weill
Anthony Diamandakis
Mr Hyung-Teh Do
David Fitzsimons
Lisa Garrison
Emily Goldner and Mike Humphries
Ann Hekmat
Alexandra Hess
Mr Scott Mead
Sebastien Montabonel
Mr Donald Moore
Saadi Soudavar
Nicholas Stanley
Maria and Malek Sukkar
Francois Trausch, in memory of Caroline Trausch
Annie Vartivarian
Michael and Jane Wilson

and those who wish to remain anonymous

RUSSIA AND EASTERN EUROPE ACQUISITIONS COMMITTEE
Dmitry Aksenov
Dilyara Allakhverdova (Co-Chair)
David Birnbaum
Maria Bukhtoyarova
Francise Hsin-Wen Chang
Marian Gazdik
Patrick Hessel
Vilius Kavaliauskas and Rita Kavaliauskiene
Carl Kostyál
Mrs Grazyna Kulczyk
Peter Kulloi (Co-Chair)
Enikő Leányvári and Gábor Illés
Iveta Manasherova
Eduard Maták
Luba Michailova
Maarja Oviir-Neivelt
Florin Pogonaru
Petr Pudil
Neil K Rector
Valeria Rodnyansky
Robert Runták
Ovidiu Şandor
Zsolt Somlói
Elena Sudakova
Miroslav Trnka
Jo Vickery
Veronika Zonabend
Mr Jānis Zuzāns

and those who wish to remain anonymous

SOUTH ASIA ACQUISITIONS COMMITTEE
Shohidul Ahad-Choudhury
Mrs Sheetal Ansal
Krishna Bhupal
Dr Arani and Mrs Shumita Bose
Krishna Choudhary
Akshay Chudasama
Jai Danani
Shalini Amerasinghe Ganendra
Zahida Habib
Tarini Jindal
Deepanjana Klein
Simran Kotak and Vir Kotak
Ms Aarti Lohia
Yamini Mehta
Mr Yogesh Mehta
Mohammad N. Miraly
Shalini Misra
Mr Rahul Munjal and Mrs Pooja Munjal
Mrs Chandrika Pathak
Puja and Uday Patnaik
Lekha Poddar (Co-Chair)
Smita Prabhakar
Nadia Samdani
Rajeeb Samdani (Co-Chair)
Mrs Tarana Sawhney
Osman Khalid Waheed
Manuela and Iwan Wirth

and those who wish to remain anonymous

THE 1897 CIRCLE
Marilyn Bild
James Birch
David and Deborah Botten
Geoffrey Bradbury
Charles Brett
Sylvia Carter
Eloise and Francis Charlton
Mr and Mrs Cronk
Alex Davids
Jonathan Davis
Professor Martyn Davis
Sean Dissington
Ronnie Duncan
Joan Edlis
V Fabian
Lt Cdr Paul Fletcher
Mr and Mrs R.N. and M.C. Fry
Tom Glynn
Richard S. Hamilton
L.A. Hynes
John Janssen
Dr Martin Kenig
Isa Levy
Theodore Matoff
Jean Medlycott
Miss Sue Novell and Mr Graham Smith
Martin Owen
Simon Reynolds
Dr Claudia Rosanowski
Ann M Smith
Deborah Stern
Jennifer Toynbee-Holmes
Estate of Paule Vézelay
D. Von Bethmann Hollweg
Audrey Wallrock
Prof. Brian Whitton
Kay and Dyson Wilkes
Simon Casimir Wilson
Andrew Woodd
Mr Zilberberg

and those who wish to remain anonymous

EUROPEAN COLLECTION CIRCLE
The Ampersand Foundation / Jack Kirkland
Jacques Boissonnas
Karen Cawthorn Argenio
Lonti Ebers
Trustees of the Gaudio Family Foundation (UK) Limited
Agnès and Edward Lee (Chair)
Narmina Marandi
Danny Rimer

and those who wish to remain anonymous

TATE MODERN CORPORATE SUPPORTERS
Bank of America Merrill Lynch
Bloomberg LP
BMW
C C Land Holidings Ltd.
Christie's
Deutsche Bank AG
EY
Hyundai Card
Hyundai Motor
Laurent Perrier
LetterOne
Qantas
Red Hat Inc.
Uniqlo

and those who wish to remain anonymous

TATE MODERN CORPORATE MEMBERS
Ashurst LLP
Bank of America Merrill Lynch
BCS Consulting
Brooks Macdonald
Clifford Chance LLP
Deutsche Bank AG
Dezeen
EY
Finsbury
F-Secure Corporation
Haklyut & Company Ltd
HSBC
Imperial College Healthcare Charity
JATO Dynamics
LexisNexis
Linklaters
Morgan Stanley
Rothschild & Co
Tishman Speyer
Wedgewood Britain

and those who wish to remain anonymous

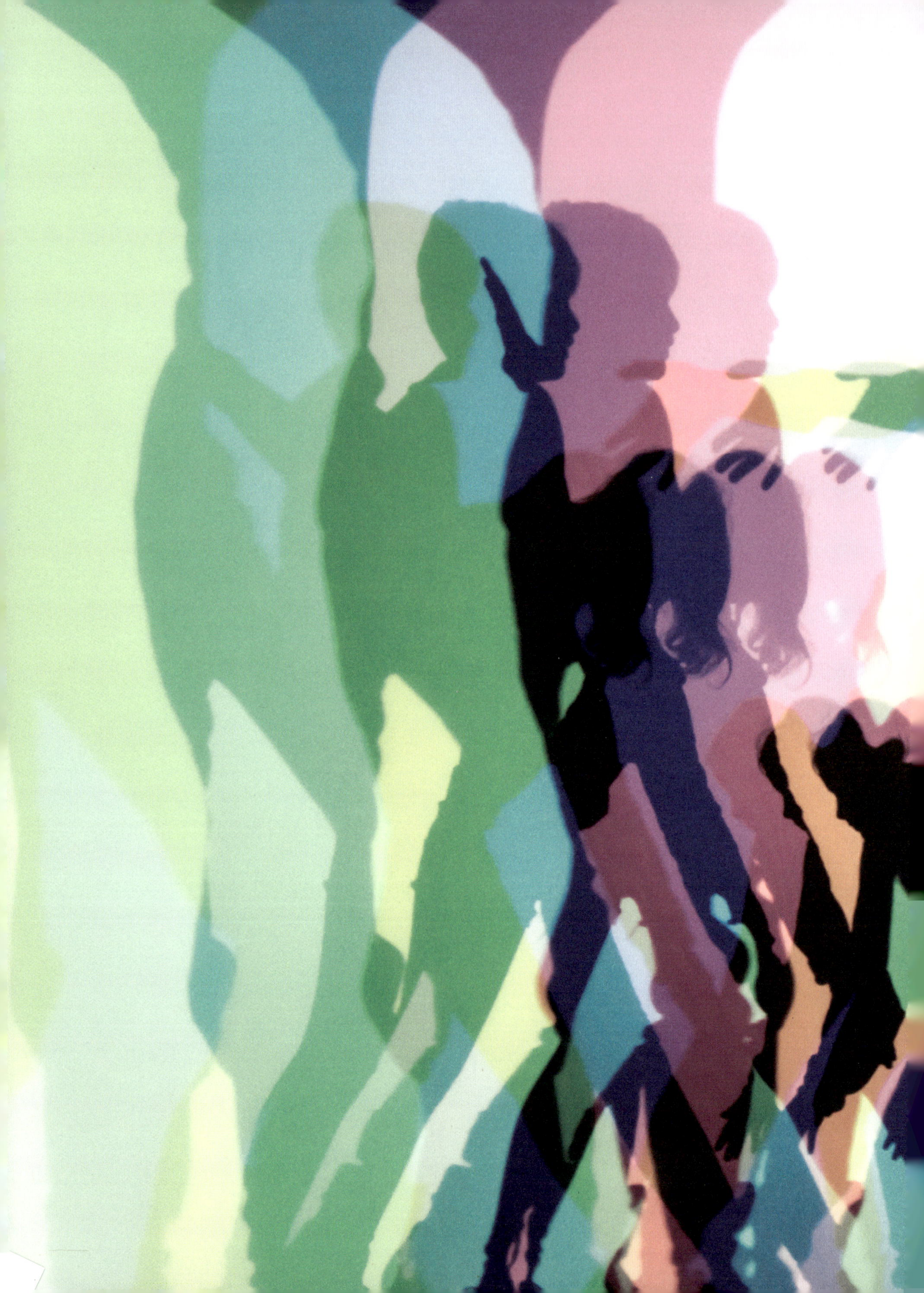